ASIA/PACIFIC

as

SPACE

of

CULTURAL PRODUCTION

a boundary 2 book

ASIA/PACIFIC

as

SPACE

of

CULTURAL PRODUCTION

Coedited by **Rob Wilson** *and* **Arif Dirlik**

Duke University Press

Durham and London 1995

Except for essays by William A. Callahan and Steve Olive, "Chemical Weapons
Discourse in the 'South Pacific,'" Chris Bongie, "The Last Frontier: Memories of the
Postcolonial Future in Keri Hulme's *the bone people*," Katharyne Mitchell, "The Hong
Kong Immigrant and the Urban Landscape: Shaping the Transnational Cosmopolitan in
the Era of Pacific Rim Capital," Epeli Hau'ofa, "Our Sea of Islands," and Haunani-Kay
Trask, "Hawai'i," the text of this book was originally published as volume 21, number 1
and volume 22, number 1 of *boundary 2: an international journal of literature and
culture*. "Memory" and "Turning It Over" by Lawson Fusao Inada, "From the Politics of
Identity to an Alternative Cultural Politics: On Taiwan Primordial Inhabitants' A-systemic
Movement" by Chiu Yen Liang (Fred), "Hawai'i" by Haunani-Kay Trask, and "Da
Mainland to Me" by Joseph P. Balaz are reprinted with permission of the authors and
publishers.

Library of Congress Cataloging-in-Publication Data
Asia/Pacific as space of cultural production / coedited by Rob Wilson and Arif Dirlik.
p.   cm.
"A Boundary 2 book."
Includes bibliographical references and index.
ISBN 0-8223-1643-9 (pbk.) ISBN 0-8223-1629-3
1. Asia—Civilization.   2. Pacific Area—Civilization.   3. Multiculturalism—Asia.
4. Multiculturalism—Pacific Area.   5. Asia—Literatures—History and criticism.
6. Pacific Area—Literatures—History and criticism.   7. Asia—Foreign public opinion.
8. Pacific Area—Foreign public opinion.   I. Wilson, Rob, 1947–   . II. Dirlik, Arif.
DS12.A69   1995
950—dc20   95-4775
                                                                                 CIP

Contents

Introduction:

Asia/Pacific as Space of Cultural Production

Rob Wilson and Arif Dirlik

You know, if we had more poeple like you around, the Pacific would develop so rapidly you wouldn't see it.
—Epeli Hau'ofa, "The Glorious Pacific Way"

Isn't there in the East, notably in Oceania, a kind of rhizomatic model that contrasts in every respect with the Western model of the tree?
—Gilles Deleuze and Félix Guattari, "Rhizome"

While some historians have compared "the Asia-Pacific region" to the hegemonic construction of a Pascalian sublime whose "circumference is everywhere and center nowhere," others no less enchanted by the de-territorializing power of oceanic vastness have projected the hypothesis as a contemporary displacement of Voltaire's God: If such a region did not exist, it would have to be invented by policy planners and social scientists along the East-West axis to figure forth an integrated source of bound-less markets, wondrous raw materials, and ever-expanding investments. However inchoate this cognitive mapping of political location and cultural identity, the Asia-Pacific region comprises, at this point of hyper-capitalist fluidity, a *terra incognita* of staggering complexity, discrepant hybridity, and nomadic flux that fascinates and, more strategically, *undoes* arboreal formations of the post–Cold War geopolitical imaginary: whose "Asia-Pacific" are we talking about, whose interests are being served, and when and how did this discourse of knowledge and power historically emerge? The conjunctions of local culture and global economy spreading across this region both as subcontracted networking and as micropolitical identity have given the "space of cultural production" new palpability as location of postmodern resistances.

As we enter a space-time reconfiguration that *Newsweek* consecrated in February of 1988 and that PBS tele-documented in 1992 as "the Pacific Century," and as we concede with former Ambassador to Japan, Michael Mansfield, that since the late 1970s, U.S. trade across the Pacific has surpassed that with Europe and superintends the teleology of any American future,[1] it has been convincingly argued that the invention, circulation, and maintenance of this geographically vast and culturally heteroglossic region—what can be traced as "the Asia-Pacific idea"—was dominantly a Euro-American formation.[2] From the era of Captain Cook and Melville, if not earlier through Magellan and Rousseau, Western centers of global power and the dynamics of the world market from Canton to London to Madrid have shaped and integrated the peripheries and multiple cultures and polities of the region to serve Euro-American interests in the name of God, imperial glory, catapulting profit, and national (/transnational) management. Yet, this global hegemony and plot of economic integration, we want to substantiate, has been breaking down from multiple directions even

1. See Michael Mansfield, "Prospects for a Pacific Community," in *Building a Pacific Community: The Addresses and Papers of the Pacific Community Lecture Series*, Paul F. Hooper, ed. (Honolulu: University of Hawaii Press/East-West Center, 1982), 86. This "Pacific Century" construction of rising co-prosperity across the region and into the next century is challenged as an ideological structure of late-capitalist teleology in R. A. Palat, "The Making and Unmaking of Pacific-Asia," in *Pacific-Asia and the Future of the World-System*, R. A. Palat, ed. (Westport, Conn.: Greenwood Press, 1993), 3–20.

2. "Entering the Pacific from the west or the east, the Portuguese, the Spaniards, the Dutch, the Russians, and the English, as well as their colonists in the Americas, all contributed in turn to the creation of a regional structure, in which Asian and Pacific societies provided the building blocks and the globalized interests of Euro-American powers furnished the principles of organization" (see the analysis of this contradictory structure in Arif Dirlik, "The Asia-Pacific Idea: Reality and Representation in the Invention of a Regional Structure," *Journal of World History* 3 [1992]: 66).

as the transnational rhetoric of Ronald Reagan would prophesy, in the late-capitalist market euphoria of 1984, that "the Pacific is where the future of the world lies."[3]

No longer can such a teleology of Euro-American progress/modernity drone on, at least not with the same theoretical arrogance, anthropological innocence, or economic presumption. The rise of Tokyo, Hong Kong, Seoul, Taipei, and Singapore as resurgent powers on the Pacific Rim, as well as the breakdown of the Cold War master narrative of bipolar superpowers that once legitimated the American military presence across the Pacific, has resulted in an ongoing de-centering of power beyond the hegemonic control and cartographic sublimations of the U.S. State Department and the military sway of the U.S. Pacific Command (CINCPAC). Given the post-communist reconfigurations of the European Economic Community (EEC), the North American Free Trade Agreement (NAFTA), and the Association of Southeast Asian Nations (ASEAN), and the instability of any geopolitical imaginary at this time, it remains incumbent upon postmodern knowledge-workers to trace the dynamics of the contemporary Asia/Pacific region as the force, flux, and possibility of a transcultural future. The local Pacific as space of cultural production is more than a vacant cipher or ex-primitive dumping ground to be simulated, militarized, and customized into transnational cyberspace.

Transnational corporations are already tracing these global-local interfaces, to be sure. When Toyota Motor Corporation president, Tatsuro Toyoda, recently theorized the downturn of automobile sales in the Japanese domestic market, he looked forward to expanding overseas markets, especially throughout the expanding co-prosperity reaches of the Asia-Pacific. Toyoda envisaged a future in which production facilities would be located "at the center of large overseas markets, such as North America, Europe, Southeast Asia, and Oceania," with new automobiles of local customization (such as recreational vehicles and compact trucks) being ex-

---

3. President Reagan's vision of a transnationally integrated Asia-Pacific region in which "the vast Pacific has become smaller, but the future of those who live around it is larger than ever before" is quoted in Simon Winchester, *Pacific Rising: The Emergence of a New World Culture* (New York: Prentice Hall, 1991), 24. The rapacity of global capitalism to incorporate and dis-authenticate Pacific cultures and identities, via soft-sell dynamics of transnational tourism, is tracked in Dean MacCannell, *Empty Meeting Grounds: The Tourist Papers* (London and New York: Routledge, 1992), see especially "Cannibalism Today," 17–73.

ported to developing markets in neighboring countries as well as back across Oceania to Japan.[4] In other words, the disparate cultures and non-synchronous polities of Oceania, the ASEAN countries, and the Pacific Rim continent of North America would comprise the bulk of this transnational New World Order, if not service this so-called *borderless* region, in which offshore transnational corporations flexibly scan the Asia-Pacific horizon for the lowest wages (as does Nike footwear from its design headquarters in Beaverton, Oregon) from South Korea to Taiwan, from China to Indonesia and Thailand.

Still, the Pacific Rim powers' very promotion and circulation of such an Asia-Pacific community as an integrated economic region from China to Alaska and from Chile to New Zealand has meant that the so-called Pacific Basin countries contained in the region are habitually excluded from mapping and contesting these megatrend visions of "economic cooperation" and "cultural exchange" that bear down upon their heteroglossic well-being and threaten their local survival as distinct cultures and alternative histories. Ratu Kamisese K. T. Mara, confronting sublimated plans for "Building a Pacific Community" on some idealized basis of economic cooperation and cultural exchange that had been going on in economic think tanks since the mid-1960s, uncannily disrupted the Pacific Rim pipe dreams emanating from Tokyo and Washington, if not Canberra and Sydney, by suggesting, in 1980, that

> there is a Pacific community already, and that it has already been there—or should I say "here"?—for at least two and a half thousand years. Not only was it a community, but it was an organized and specialized community. There were specialists (I hesitate to brand them as experts) in religion, housebuilding, agriculture, navigation, the arts, etc.[5]

As the prime minister of Fiji recognizes with local awe and global terror, *there* soon becomes *here* given the instantaneous telecommunication of place into space, capital flight, tourist simulations of Pacific ex-primitive au-

4. Takeshi Sato, "Toyota Looking to Overseas Markets," *The Hawaii Hochi* 81 (30 Oct. 1992): 1. Also see the *Far Eastern Economic Review*, "Nike Roars: All American, Made in Asia," 5 Nov. 1992, on the "economic Darwinism" adopted by Nike across Asia; and Walden Bello, *People and Power in the Pacific: The Struggle for the Post–Cold War Order* (London: Pluto Press, 1992), 37–49, on local resistance to hegemonic mappings.
5. Ratu Kamisese K. T. Mara, "Building a Pacific Community," in *Building a Pacific Community*, 41.

.thenticity at hyperspaces such as the Polynesian Cultural Center on Oahu, and the consequent dislocations of local knowledge and ethnic community in this New World Disorder. As the Fijian prime minister warns, given these contexts of internal struggle and the global marketing of place and culture, the promise is always there for a new, soft, more supple form of Orientalist knowledge and transnational control rephrased as a postmodern co-prosperity sphere. Although the Cold War has surely ended and American hegemony over the Pacific lake is threatened on all sides, the Pacific Islanders, whose home has been the site of the destructive U.S. nuclear weapons testing in the Marshall Islands and the French struggle for technological grandeur in Polynesia, now fear they will become hosts for the dismantling of these same Cold War nuclear weapons. The potential for catastrophic accident and environmental contamination across Oceania remains great and demands coalitional resistance on diverse fronts.

At state-funded sites of Western knowledge/power such as the East-West Center in Honolulu, Pacific Community Seminars at Canberra, and the Pacific Rim Studies institutes that have sprung up across the state of California in the boom phase of the 1980s, the move toward mapping "megatrends in the Asia-Pacific" as a locus of economic surge and trans-Pacific promise often entails ignoring the cultural micropolitics of the region as a source of dynamic opposition and local difference worthy of international recognition. It becomes possible for John Naisbitt and Patricia Aburdene to prophesy "The Rise of the Pacific Rim" in *Megatrends 200* as the pivotal site for the furious globalization of informations, cultures, and technologies on the model of a transnational, Japan-oriented America ("The Pacific Rim is emerging like a dynamic young America but on a much grander scale," to recall Naisbitt's hegemonizing trope of transnational Americanization) without once factoring in even one Pacific Basin country or island culture as a political-economic player or, for that matter, without even mentioning the state of Hawaii as a space caught between the Pacific Rim geo-imaginary hallucinations of Los Angeles and Tokyo.[6]

The futurology of Pacific Rim Discourse that would take semiotic and

6. John Naisbitt and Patricia Aburdene, *Megatrends 2000: Ten New Directions for the 1990s* (New York: Avon, 1990), 184–227. In the Adamically transnationalized gaze of President Clinton, the Asia-Pacific region still beckons as American challenge and transnational promise: "Our [American] trade relations with the Pacific Rim are critically important to the United States, our Asian partners, and the global economy" (quoted in Don Oberdorfer, *Clinton and Asia: Issues for the New Administration* [New York: The Asia Society, 1993], 3).

conceptual possession of the entire region depends upon *repressing* those Pacific Basin others who have not yet subscribed to the "world economy" as a post–zero-sum game. Ideology and opposition at the level of everyday culture still matter. In Pacific Rim visions of Asia-Pacific integration, as in the articulation of Confucian spirituality to microchip technologies, the motions of Asian and Pacific peoples that have produced networks endowing the region with social reality and cultural texture are downplayed in favor of solidifying capital and commodity flows and military-political relationships that would restructure the Asia-Pacific into a coherent region of economic exchange. A cyborg capable of Buddha-nature can better serve as icon of this economistic "Pacific Rising," as the oceanic sublime of *Moby-Dick* implodes into the dematerialized matrix of cyberspace spanning from Los Angeles to Tokyo to Mars.

Whatever the heteroglossic reach and hypertext-thick sway of postmodern theorizing, these cultures and politics of difference within the Asia/Pacific region are all but equally ignored as sources of innovation and production. Uncanny knowledges of culture, politics, and economics are kept segregated and isolated across the Asia/Pacific region even as a complex new micropolitics of location and memory begins to flourish and interact. "Let resistance write its own geography," Chris Connery trenchantly warns in his analysis of Pacific Rim Discourse as a transnational American construct emanating from the boom-cycle geopolitics of the 1980s as well as from a residual Cold War imaginary. The Trukese poet-scholar Theophil Saret Reuney offers one such counter-mapping of the Pacific sublime with his culture's key navigational poem, "The Pulling of Olap's Canoe," the first time such an indigenous mapping of Truk has been translated and explained in hegemonic English. The global situation is now one in which we must begin to historicize, question, and *undo* those conceptual categories, maps, imaginary geographies, master narratives, self-evident discourses, and configurations of Western knowledge/power that threaten even the most counter-hegemonic and oppositional projects of national identity and cultural location in Taiwan, Hawaii, New Zealand, Australia, Truk, and South Korea.

To stake our discursive claim: The all-but-reified "Asia-Pacific" formulated by market planners and military strategists is inadequate to describe or explain the fluid and multiple "Asia/Pacific" of social migration and transcultural innovation. The slash would signify linkage yet difference. This counter-hegemonic "space of cultural production" shall be exemplified and affirmed throughout this Asia/Pacific collection within geopolitical contexts of transnational capital and localizations that form our shared horizon.

• • • •

The title of this collection of works in theory and cultural production remains ambiguous, at the outset, and would point to two perspectives around which it is organized: First, these essays and cultural works begin to draw forth and illuminate the hegemonic Euro-American production of "the Asia-Pacific." By this we mean not just the construction of the Pacific as libidinous fantasy ("Blue Hawaii" as site of erotic excess and tourist rejuvenation for advance-industrialized California, or "Japan" as locus of the Zen *zaibatsu*) but the invention and mapping of the Asia/Pacific as a geographic, economic, political, and military entity threatened by outside domination and semiotic control. The fantasy invention in other modes of Western knowledge/power are not unrelated to earlier mappings and journeys across "the Happy Isles of Oceania," as shall be seen. Tropologies of the Pacific have not only dynamized Euro-American activity since the time of Cook and Melville, as M. Consuelo León W. traces, but have also served to disguise, distance, and distort the concrete realities of the region, still, as a non-Western black hole capable of being ignored, mall-ified, or used as a nuclear dumping site as at Johnston Atoll (Hawaiians still call it Kalama Island) even now. The reduction of the historical Pacific to a fantasmatic "South Pacific" backdrop for military purposes has proved helpful to the pacific instrumentalization of the Pacific by the United States, France, Canada, and other Western powers as military testing sites. Pacific anthropology, as Jeff Tobin argues, can uncritically play a part in ratifying the knowledges of the liberal state and in destabilizing the claims of interior Pacific cultures to articulate themselves as political agents forging a sovereign state and alternative cultural/national identity in Hawaii, as in *Aotearoa* (New Zealand).

Second, this gathering of essays should also help to circulate, within theories of transcultural flux, transnational ethnicity and postmodern border-thinking, emerging counter-hegemonic practices and flows that would remain staunchly "local" in orientation and resistant in political design. Complexly articulated to the dynamics of modernity, as John Fielder shows in his trenchant study of urban Aboriginality in Australia, culture can serve as one of the primary means of identification through which diverse inhabitants (largely Asian and Pacific in makeup) of this multiplex region have sought to resist ingestion into a global fantasy by an assertion of historical experiences and local enclaves of resistance, survival, and colonial critique. To describe myriad practices of the Asia/Pacific as "local," within contexts of transnational capital that would bypass, warp, or integrate them, is not to trivialize or parochialize them but to underscore their historicity and their strategic necessity at this time. Heteroglossic spatiality, as in Hawaii, can threaten the hegemonic modernity of the nation-state.

It is by means of such concrete cultural practices and intermediate perceptions of what "the Pacific" has been, is, or still could be that a landscape and language of postcolonial survival can be measured against the homogenization of that same region into an economic zone worthy of transnational manipulation. This semiotic and economic redemption takes place in "centers," as the urban geographers Edward Soja and David Harvey contend, or as transnational spectacles such as *Neuromancer* furiously enact, located in Los Angeles, Tokyo, and postnational regions of financial cyberspace that remain, like any transnational sublime, "located everywhere and regulated nowhere" (as was said of the deregulated hyper-capital circulating at the now defunct Bank of Credit and Commerce International, or BCCI).

If this global/local interface comprises a complex and hybrid two-way dialectic, *the global deforms and molests the local* in ways that need to be accounted for and challenged west of Los Angeles and east of Tokyo in unmapped, ignored, forgotten, or hyper-toured pockets of transnational capital. The "space of cultural production" we posit, therefore, refers at once to regional enclaves and to local spaces as contradictory locations inserted, and insurgent, within the world-system as cultural formations of the Asia/Pacific. The multicultural and indigenous literatures of *Bamboo Ridge* that have emerged since 1975 in Hawaii, for example, can be seen, in theory and as practice, to propose a regionally and ethnically inflected ground, however illusory, for claims of cultural resistance. These Pacific dynamics need to be linked not only to gaining canonical space in the *Heath Anthology of American Literature*, as it were, but also to articulating dynamics of decolonization; linguistic and cultural survival, as in the urgent struggle for Hawaiian nationalism ("Ea") conducted via diet, hula, poems, songs, chants, lawsuits, outraged polemics, ecology, and an antinuclear politics and place-bound identity rooted relentlessly in body, place, and the spiritual polity of culture.[7] Given the late capitalist hegemony over space-time

7. See Rob Wilson, "Blue Hawaii: Bamboo Ridge as 'Critical Regionalism,' " in Arif Dirlik, ed., *What Is in a Rim?: Critical Perspectives on the Pacific Region Idea* (Boulder, Colo.:

by globally flexible post-Fordist modes and the often merciless re-creation and destruction of landscape, community, and culture by simulacrous technologies, the aesthetics of place and reassertion of local culture are very much back on the postmodern agenda.[8]

"Local" links to the Asia/Pacific decolonization literatures of Albert Wendt, Patricia Grace, Keri Hulme, Subramani, Tsushima Yuko, Joseph Balaz, Haunani-Kay Trask, Kenzaburo Oe, and Michael Ondaatje have worked to help imagine community and to coalesce regional resistance. These projects still need to be circulated within the circles of postmodern theory that *boundary 2* represents and helps, actively through special issues such as this, to link up, interact with, and to inform. While certain tropes and master narratives of Asia-Pacific discourse may be viewed as strictly Euro-American inventions, it is also clear that rapid shifts in the reconfiguration of the late-capitalist world-system have qualified the power of the original (or emergent) forces of difference within the region. Power relations of the Pacific are no longer just products of Euro-American/Asian confrontation, to be sure, but involve social relations of an intra-Asia/Pacific nature. Japan's relationship to the North Pacific is the most immediate instance and the most polemicized in Hawaii, for example, with the "takeover of Waikiki" by Japanese and other transnational interests. Western tropicality dissolves in the waters and rooted peoples of Oceania.

Some fifty years after Pearl Harbor and Hiroshima deformed the indigenous Pacific into a technoscape on the nuclear grid of the Cold War binary-machine and the transnational security-state, we still need to question whether these relationships are simply a further expression of the original "invention" of Asia-Pacific by Tokyo/Washington, D.C. (perpetuated through the spectacular image media of the capitalist world-system as in Ridley Scott's *Blade Runner* or *Black Rain*), or whether they are expressive, against all odds, of emerging departures in which local con-

---

Westview, 1993); Stephen H. Sumida, "Sense of Place, History, and the Concept of the 'Local' in Hawaii's Asian/Pacific Literatures," in *Reading the Literatures of Asian America*, Shirley Geok-lin Lim and Amy Ling, eds. (Philadelphia: Temple University Press, 1992), 215–37; Haunani-Kay Trask, "Kupaʻa ʻAina: Native Nationalism in Hawaiʻi," in *Politics and Public Policy in Hawaiʻi*, ed. Zachary A. Smith and Richard C. Pratt (Albany: State University of New York Press, 1992), 243–60; and Haunani-Kay Trask, *From a Native Daughter: Colonialism and Sovereignty in Hawaii* (Monroe, Maine: Common Courage Press, 1993). On Trask's cultural nationalism, see Jeffrey Tobin's essay in this collection.
8. See David Harvey, *The Condition of Postmodernity: An Enquiry into the Origins of Cultural Change* (Oxford: Blackwell, 1989), 303.

cerns and situated practices will become paramount. Dialogical and cross-cultural analysis of "America's Hiroshima" and "Hiroshima's America" by Peter Schwenger and John Whittier Treat makes intertextually apparent, even at this late date, that this traumatic Pacific event and postmodern turning point at Hiroshima has not yet been represented across cultural or across national imaginaries in ways that would allow for a *demilitarized* future to emerge in the region. The exchange of Pacific knowledge remains asymmetrical even in this post–Cold War era of fragmentation, postcolonial hybridity, and flux. The ecology of the Asia/Pacific region demands more than hypertextual self-indulgence or projects troping the tropics into occidental master narratives and postcolonial language games.

Amalgamated via British and American power dynamics over the course of the last two centuries, World English has become "the major hegemon language" of the transnational capitalist class and of transnational political practices across the global system.[9] Serving as the main medium of interethnic and intraregional linkages and communication across the region, this English, paradoxically enough, can now function as a tool to cut across region and nation-state to challenge ruses of neocolonial domination. "We must get the [postcolonial] context right first," as the Maori novelist Witi Ihimaera warned in articulating this new Pacific as a space of ongoing cultural production: "Nowhere in the Pacific is the indigenous language the first language. The first language in the Pacific is English. That's the reality of the situation in the Pacific."[10]

Yet, this hybrid, warped, nonstandard, localized English, in Subramani's wide-ranging argument, has been diversely enlisted into the formation of an insurgent regional consciousness and now proves "the language of the new literature [of Oceania] and also the 'Pacific Way.'"[11] This commitment to critical regionalism informs pan-Pacific aspirations to oceanic integration as enacted, in this volume for example, by the cross-cultural mixtures of Indian memory and Fijian future in Subramani's own "Childhood as a Fiction" or in Albert Wendt's hybrid poem dedicated to Kenzaburō Ōe as a Samoan-Hawaiian mentor, not to mention in novels of mythic displace-

9. Leslie Sklair, *Sociology of the Global System* (Baltimore: Johns Hopkins University Press, 1991), 26.

10. *Interviews with Writers of the Post-Colonial World*, Feroza Jussawalla and Reed Way Dasenbrock, eds. (Jackson, Miss.: University of Mississippi Press, 1992), 233.

11. Subramani, *South Pacific Literature: From Myth to Fabulation* (Suva, Fiji: University of the South Pacific Press, 1992), 28–29.

ment, such as Wendt's *Pouliuli* or Patricia Grace's *Potiki* or Epeli Hau'ofa's outrageously hybrid *Tales of the Tikongs*.

Our critical contention is that the complex networks and maps of knowledge/power disseminated across this contemporary Asia/Pacific region need not belong exclusively to the circulations of hegemonic power, whether they emanate from Tokyo, Washington, London, Hong Kong, or Vancouver. The repressed claims of the "comfort women," kidnapped and coerced into sexual service by the Japanese military in World War II, have resurfaced and networked across the region—as in the ongoing Pacific denuclearization movement. "Like a volcanic eruption, this issue," as Alice Chai has claimed, "is a by-product of the Asia-Pacific feminist movement." [12] This kind of ascription of cultural unity to the Asia/Pacific region, as a strategic coalition linking diverse spaces and times, can be a strategy for doing transnational battle and de-sublimating the historically repressed and ethnically silenced subjects of the nation-state.

Finally, does the very idea of an Asia/Pacific region point to a future (multicultural, de-centered, regionally entrenched) different from the past because of the role societies in the region will play in these new dynamics, or will these societies perpetuate hegemonic relationships, since they themselves are shaped by the capitalist world-system? To put it bluntly, do social and cultural differences finally make any difference in the transnational formation of postmodern markets whose aim is to generate the same fantasies, localize the same products, and infiltrate a mythic banality of social progress and shared prosperity, even if the agent of domination and fascination (as Leo Ching documents) is not America but postmodern Japan? How can we continue to discuss these transcultural complications of global/local relations and national identities "in a world where Japan, South Korea, Hong Kong, Taiwan, Singapore, or Indonesia simply don't exist, certainly not as *forces* in emergent structure of world power"?, as Meaghan Morris challenged the Eurocentric and trans-Atlantic speculations of post-Birmingham "cultural studies." [13] The acceleration of translation/transplantation on both

12. Quoted in Teya Maman, "Film Says Japanese Must Acknowledge Its War Legacies," *Ka Leo O Hawaiʻi* 87 (17 Nov. 1992), 1. On regional tactics that would resist the crisis-level intrusion of the West into the contemporary Pacific as nuclear power superstate and that would challenge transnational practices such as the deforestation of Papua New Guinea and Malaysia, see *Women's Voices on the Pacific: The International Pacific Policy Congress*, ed. Lenora Foerstel (Washington, D.C.: Maisonneuve, 1991).
13. See Meaghan Morris's Australian-based speculations on global positionality/mar-

sides of the Pacific may be not only shrinking space and de-centering time but also exacerbating regional and cultural contradictions.

We aim, then, through the hard-hitting forays of this collection, to address a new regional conceptualization that, whether or not it is real, expresses ideologically the drive to reorganize the economies, societies, politics, and cultures of the Asia-Pacific Basin and Rim. We would help inaugurate a more critical orientation toward area studies that transcends individual countries/islands/states and that ties in with world-system analysis in noncategorical ways. The fluid, furious, and dislocational "transnationalization" of public space and local culture that is under way in all areas of life, from material to cultural production, would appear to be fundamental to the changes we observe and call forth responses in critical thinking (or rethinking) of the Asia-Pacific region as cultural-political location. Local culture—that is to say, as produced from the ground and body of this place, this time, as this new "space-time"—is simulated and molested by the workings of multinational capital. Here, as symptom and as tool of postmodern knowledge, cultural theory can play its timely, if at times overreaching, part. The role of culture and postmodern knowledge, given these powerful dynamics of "global interactive space,"[14] need not be reactive and belated but, on the contrary, formative of alternative subjectivities and of heteroglossic communities, and informed, as well, with coalitional energies and movements to shape a counter-hegemonic future.

There remain many hard, impious, Gramscian kind of questions that need to be asked of global hegemony/counter-hegemony in the Asia/Pacific region from interconnected disciplines of "cultural production": In one of the first transdisciplinary and transregional collections of its kind, we draw upon a range of scholars and writers from literature, history, technology studies, sociology, geography, political science, and ethnography to interrogate, document, if not to help reinvent the region from diverse grounds and hybrid contexts. Such is the space Miriam Fuchs, among others, would posit (through the complexly temporized Maori fiction of Patricia Grace) as the "postcolonial" condition confronting global-local identity

---

ginality of Pacific Rim cultures in "'On the Beach,'" in *Cultural Studies*, ed. Lawrence Grossberg, Cary Nelson, and Paula Treichler (New York: Routledge, 1992), 476.

14. David Harvey, *The Condition of Postmodernity*, 314. This globalization of local space and transnationalization of national identity informs Pacific Rim literature from the outset, as in Philip K. Dick's proto-cyberpunk *The Man in the High Castle* (New York: Putnam, 1962), with its U.S. West Coast ruled by Japanese with a taste for Cold War Americana.

and cross-cultural exchange. Refusing occidental narratives of economic warfare and transgressing disciplinary tactics of the end-of-ideology liberal state, a new knowledge of the undertheorized Asia/Pacific region will begin to emerge from untimely spaces and discounted global positions.

As a postmodern assemblage taken from disparate languages, genres, contexts, and disciplines, this issue would juxtapose materials from knowledges and locations that would represent and manage this area from afar via Euro-American and Japanese hegemonic mappings and markets. We would also marshal cultural materials (from scholars, poets, and activists) that worry and enact the multiplex cultural production that has been going on from within the Asia/Pacific region at least since 1975. Without waxing nostalgic for any master-code or discourse-of-discourses, local literature (as in the tourist gaze "747 Poem" of Terese Svoboda or Joseph P. Balaz's pidgin geography of Hawaii as "da mainland to me") is used not just as supplement but as invention, as counter-text, as enclave of counter-production as in the originary days of *boundary 2*, under William V. Spanos, when literature proved energizing to the larger theoretical project: to construct counter-logics and counter-hegemonies from within the imperial Moby Dick of a beast.

Problematics that emerge in this special issue include the following: (1) the spread of consumer culture throughout the region via the economic and cultural dynamics of Japan and the United States; (2) Aboriginal struggles to reclaim land, legal rights, and cultural rehabilitation (in Hawaii, in Australia, in Taiwan); (3) the rhetorical and disciplinary construction of the Pacific by insiders (such as Wendt, Reuney, and Inada) and outsiders (such as Thomas Jefferson, James Michener, and George Kennan); (4) the use of nationalism and indigenous traditions as alternatives to construct social identity; (5) genealogies of the modern uses and postmodern images of the Pacific (as "Basin" and as "Rim"), especially as these knowledges were implemented to serve military and industrial interests of the aging nation-states and emerging transnational conglomerations; (6) the local as space of global resistance and cultural contention to transnational projects such as the Asia-Pacific Economic Conference (APEC) with its megatrend rhetoric of co-presence and co-prosperity.

The Asia/Pacific region enacts the reconfigured space of nation-state deterritorialization, reinvention, struggle, and flight as power leaks out of the Cold War binary-machine: "To continue the use of geographical terms: imagine that between *the East and the West* a certain segmentarity is introduced, opposed in a binary-machine, arranged in the State apparatuses, overcoded by an abstract machine as the sketch of a World Order."[15] As power leaks from cognitive maps and binary-machines of the nation-state and begins to undo prior East/West linkages of region to globe, Cold War knowledge proves inadequate to contain or represent the micropolitics of the minor and multiple, and "it is then from North to South [that] the destabilization takes place,"[16] or so we can hope.

15. Gilles Deleuze and Claire Parnet, "Many Politics," in *Dialogues*, trans. Hugh Tomlinson and Barbara Habberjam (New York: Columbia University Press, 1987), 131.
16. Deleuze and Parnet, "Many Politics," 131. The glibly economistic habit by which Latin America is reified as impoverished "South" and thus excluded from contemporary Pacific Rim Discourse, even though Chile has the longest coastline of any country in the Pacific, and Easter Island (Rapa Nui) remains Spanish, is outlined in Francisco Orrego Vicuña, "The Pacific Islands in a Latin American Perspective: Towards a Special Relationship?" in Hooper, *Building a Pacific Community*, 94–118. For an Atlanticist critique of "regional coherence" in the Asia/Pacific, see Gerald Segal, *Rethinking the Pacific* (Oxford: Oxford University Press, 1990); on gender and class inequities across and within the Pacific, see the essays in Dirlik, *What Is in a Rim?*

Mappings

Foundations of the
American Image of the Pacific

M. Consuelo León W.

In recent decades, specialists and scholars have agreed that the study of perceptions and popular images can offer new insights into the history of international affairs.[1] In this sense, the images held by Americans about the Pacific Ocean can explain much about American policies over the past two centuries.[2]

The author wishes to thank Jason K. Moore for his editorial assistance.

1. See the interesting perspectives of Jerald Combs, *American Diplomatic History: Two Centuries of Changing Interpretations* (Berkeley and Los Angeles, Calif.: University of California Press, 1983); Paul A. Varg, *Missionaries, Chinese, and Diplomats: The American Protestant Missionary Movement in China, 1890–1952* (Princeton, N.J.: Princeton University Press, 1958), who emphasizes the existence of parallel images and their impact in the American foreign policy; and Akira Iriye, *Across the Pacific: An Inner History of American–East Asian Relations* (New York: Harcourt, Brace and World, Inc., 1967).

2. Many historians have emphasized that American interest in the Pacific actually began only in 1840 with the California gold rush, but there is evidence that suggests that citizen and governmental interests were "as old as the Republic itself," or even older. See Kenneth J. Bertrand, "Geographical Exploration by the United States," in Herman R. Friis, ed., *The Pacific Basin: A History of Its Geographical Exploration* (New York: American Geographical Society, 1967).

The consolidation of the Pacific image in American minds has been a long process, the beginnings of which may be traced to the information about Asia that reached Europe in the thirteenth century. The process continued with the subconscious accumulation of knowledge transferred to Americans through British culture. By the 1820s, the Pacific image was crystalized through the efforts of traders, explorers, and politicians. This essay will attempt to substantiate the fact that in early nineteenth-century America's image of the Pacific, the area was neither a copy nor a continuation of its British heritage. Rather, this early image resulted from a progressive perception built on America's unique geography, on European tradition, and on its own economic and intellectual history.

The Literary Background

The American perception of the Pacific Rim was shaped in large part by accounts of travelers' experiences, published in different countries over several centuries. These books became popular during the late eighteenth and early nineteenth centuries.[3]

The accounts that European missionaries sent to the Mongolian court in the early thirteenth century and Marco Polo's voyage to the Orient in 1271 were cornerstones of the American image of the Pacific region and perpetuated an idea of a paradise "[that was] very rich in gold and [that] produce[d] all kinds of jewels."[4] Also influential were the accurate descriptions of Jesuit missionaries in China, Japan, and California sent to Europe in the sixteenth and seventeenth centuries.

Richard Ruggles says that Englishmen lacked curiosity about any region of the world "beyond those in which they [had] immediate contact"[5];

3. If a book is mentioned by historians or translated into English, and reedited several times, I have deemed it significant in image formation. Using this criteria, and considering the high American literacy rate during the first decades of its republican life, one may infer the popular images of the Pacific. See Lee Soltow and Steve Edwards, *The Rise of Literacy and the Common School in the United States: A Socioeconomic Analysis to 1870* (Chicago: University of Chicago Press, 1981), 17.

4. For example, the missions led by the Franciscan Giovanni Carpini in 1245, Camaldulian Fra Mauro, and Giovanni of Montecorvino (1305–1306). See Hisroshi Nakamura, *East Asia in Old Maps* (Tokyo: The Center for East Asian Cultural Studies, 1963), 9. The influence of Polo is undeniable: more than one hundred editions of his books in different languages have been published. See Henry H. Hart, *Venetian Adventurer: Marco Polo* (St. Louis: Taylor Printing Co., 1921), 27, 260–62; Nakamura, *East Asia in Old Maps*, 25.

5. Richard Ruggles, "Geographical Exploration by the British," in Friis, *The Pacific Basin*, 222.

however, in the sixteenth century, attempts to establish control in the Pacific revealed a British perception of the Pacific as an area for settlement and commerce.[6]

John Dee, Richard Eden, and the Hakluyts developed and popularized knowledge in England about the Pacific, and their enthusiasm, in turn, created a climate of opinion that encouraged further voyages and colonization. These geographers helped Drake plan his expedition that proclaimed English sovereignty over New Albion.[7] William Dampier's books, published in the last years of the seventeenth century, were also considered "spectacular literary successes." His influence can be noted in the publication and translation of several treatises of Pacific geography and in the creation of a national plan for the occupation of the South Seas.[8]

The 1743 publication of George Anson's *Voyage Round the World* and his capture of the legendary galleon of Manila, a historical objective of English navigators of the Pacific Ocean, perpetuated the myth of Pacific richness. In the late eighteenth century, the search for the geographical *chimeres*, such as Terra Australis and the Northwest Passage to China, led the British government to endorse a series of voyages to the Pacific, the most famous of which was led by James Cook. According to Sinclair Hitchings, Cook's voyages "stirred intense popular interest."[9] Through his account, the friendly Pacific paradise, full of beautiful, accessible women and economic possibilities, became well known in Europe and Anglo-America.[10] The establishment of a colony in Australia and the migration of missionaries to some island groups were the result of the consolidation of the British image of the Pacific.

In 1783, John Ledyard, an American who sailed in Cook's third expedition, published *The Journal of Captain Cook's Last Voyage to the Pacific Ocean in the Quest of a North West Passage*, which was "very popular at the time."[11] Ledyard emphasized the possibilities of fur trade between China

6. Roger Barlow and Roger Thorne believed that British destiny was in the mythical Terra Australis Incognita, and Humphrey Gilbert proposed to plant a colony on the Pacific Coast near Sierra Nevada. See Friis, *The Pacific Basin*, 223, 238.

7. Friis, *The Pacific Basin*, 227.

8. Dampier's *A New Voyage Round the World* (1697), *Voyages and Discoveries* (1699), and *Voyage to New Holland* developed popular feelings toward the area. See Friis, *The Pacific Basin*, 236, 237.

9. James Kenneth Munford, *John Ledyard's Journal of Captain Cook's Last Voyage* (Corvallis: Oregon State University Press, 1963), xvii.

10. Hugh Cobbe, ed., *Cook's Voyage and Peoples of the Pacific* (London: British Museum Publishers Limited, 1979), 34.

11. Despite the interest of the British admiralty in keeping certain nautical knowledge

and the Northwest Coast of America, and he would later convince Thomas Jefferson of the importance of the West Coast to the United States.[12]

During the early nineteenth century, Europeans and Americans were fond of reading about exotic adventures. The London edition of La Perouse's *Voyage Round the World* (1798) explained the importance of the American Northwest Coast for Louis XVI's court and would come to have a profound impact on Jefferson's behavior later.[13]

Among the best-known books in America were George Vancouver's *A Voyage of Discovery to the North Pacific Ocean* (1793), which contributed to the geographical knowledge of the Columbia River Basin and its vicinity, and Alexander Humboldt's *Political Essay of the Kingdom of the New Spain*, published in New York in 1811, which had an enormous impact on Jefferson and on the American intellectual community. Also popular were the detailed accounts of the British Northwest Company man, Alexander MacKenzie, whose *Voyage from Montreal through the Continent of North America to the Frozen and Pacific Ocean in 1789 and 1793* was published in 1801, and the New Englander Robert Shaler's *Journal of Voyage between China and the North West Coast of America in the Year 1804*, which popularized the possibilities of American trans-Pacific commerce.[14]

Books used for teaching purposes within the United States established another category of literature that had permanent repercussions for Americans. For example, Reverend Jedidiah Morse's children's texts, *Geography Made Easy* (1784) and *Elements of Geography* (1895), greatly influenced the young generations' perceptions of the West and the Pacific seacoast.[15]

---

out of the public domain, other crewmen of Cook's expedition published their diaries. John Rickman published his *Journal* in 1781, and it was later reprinted in Philadelphia. The reference to the popularity and profit that Ledyard's book produced is quoted from personal correspondence with the editor of Ledyard's journal (quoted in *John Ledyard's Journal*, 10 Dec. 1821, xxxv).

12. Jefferson, according to his personal correspondence, read and sent the book to his friends (Munford, *John Ledyard's Journal*, xxxviii).

13. For the French's taking possession of the northern Pacific Coast, see Donald Jackson, *Thomas Jefferson and the Stony Mountains* (Urbana: University of Illinois Press, 1981), 51.

14. William A. Williams, *Shaping the American Diplomacy* (Chicago: Rand McNally and Company, 1972), 160.

15. Carl I. Wheat, *Mapping the Trans-Mississippi West* (San Francisco: The Institute of Historical Cartography, 1957), 85.

The Cartographical Background

The analysis of published maps divulges not only the development of geographical knowledge and international rivalries among the powers but also the beliefs and assumptions of their mapmakers and owners. At the same time, maps influenced subsequent explorations, war, and commerce.[16]

America's cartographical background is primarily the product of Western cartographical knowledge accumulated over the centuries. Examples of the fifteenth-century contributions are Francesco Berlingheri's 1482 *Geographia*, one of the earliest printed Ptolomaic maps of the world, and the celebrated *Nüremberg Chronicle*, in which appear the images of non-Europeans as they were perceived at the time.

During the sixteenth century, the great voyages of discovery hastened the development of cartography. Gerardus Mercatus, and his forty-seven editions of *Atlas Sive Cosmographicae Meditiones de Fabrica Mundi*, had a formidable impact on his contemporaries and future generations, as did Ortelius, whose 1586 *Typis Orbis Terrarum* and 1590 *Maris Pacifici* were good barometers of late sixteenth-century cartographical knowledge.[17] The Pacific remained full of maritime monsters and demonstrated a mythical Southern Continent, but it had no exact dimensions.[18] The 1587 Hakluyt map and the 1596 Balgrave map showed the early British concern and knowledge for the Pacific at that time.[19]

Despite some specialists' suggestions that the seventeenth century was a period of great geographical development, the Pacific, as a region, did not receive much attention. Some areas, such as Japan, however, were mapped thoroughly by Jesuit cartographers. In the next century, the search for new markets produced accurate maps of specific parts of China, but the graphic image of Japan remained static. Because of Japan's isolationism, cartographers merely copied and reproduced earlier images.[20] The image

16. Specialists' opinions and the map publications in popular books were the criteria utilized to select the fifty maps that may have contributed to the American image of the Pacific.
17. See those maps in Rodney W. Shirley, *The Mapping of the World: Early Printed World Maps, 1472–1700* (London: The Holland Press, 1983).
18. See Shirley, *The Mapping of the World* and *The Map Collectors' Circle* 36 (London: Durrant House, 1967).
19. See Richard Hakluyt's "New World" in Wheat, *Mapping the Trans-Mississippi West*, and John Balgrave's map in Shirley, *The Mapping of the World*.
20. Compare, for example, 1692 Coronelli (Venice) and 1740 J. G. Scheuchzer (Amsterdam), in *The Map Collectors' Circle* 36 (London: Durrant House, 1967).

of parts of the Pacific Basin was inaccurate and incomplete at the end of the eighteenth century, even though the ocean had been sailed by Cook a decade earlier.[21]

Cartographic images of the Pacific prepared by the same country, and even by the same family of cartographers, did not necessarily become more accurate over time. Such is the case of the De L'Isle family, whose *Hemisphere* of 1724 was more accurate than those produced forty or fifty years later.[22]

British cartography of the Pacific Ocean, especially that of Faden-Jefferys and Arrowsmith, showed an increasing British concern for the Pacific and Australia, then named New Holland.[23] The Arrowsmith family, through its connections with commercial companies, greatly collaborated in the description of the Pacific Basin.[24]

By 1791, S. Whittemore Boggs argues, American geographical knowledge of the Pacific was "fragmentary,"[25] but there was a deep interest in the area.[26] America's firsthand knowledge of the Pacific increased with the fur trade with China and, especially after 1792, with the activities of whalers and sandalwood traders across the ocean.[27]

The American perception of the Pacific was also documented in charts, plans, and maps published in America around 1800. Assuming that quantity and subject matter denote the preference of Americans, of the 915 published maps, forty-one were of Asia (especially China), and twenty were of South America's Pacific shore. There were forty-three maps of the world, of which ten depicted Cook's voyages, and nine were of the latest

21. See 1798 Giovanni Cassini "Nouva Olanda," in *The Map Collectors' Circle* 64 (London: Durrant House, 1970).

22. Compare the American West Coast in the 1724 and 1760 De L'Isle "Western Hemisphere" maps in *The Map Collectors' Circle* 33 (London: Durrant House, 1967).

23. Ruggles, "Geographical Exploration by the British," 152, 251. See William Faden-Jefferys's map in *The Map Collectors's Circle* 66 (London: Durrant House, 1970).

24. See Arrowsmith's most popular maps, including his "Pacific Ocean," in *The Map Collectors' Circle* 68 and 69 (London: Durrant House, 1971) and in E. W. Gilbert, *The Exploration of Western America, 1800–1850: An Historical Geography* (New York: Cooper Square Publishers, 1966), 1.

25. S. Whittemore Boggs, "American Contributions to Geographical Knowledge of the Central Pacific," in *The Geographical Review* 28 (1938): 180.

26. Kenneth Bertrand, "Geographical Exploration by the United States" in Friis, *The Pacific Basin*, 256.

27. See Friis, *The Pacific Basin*, 260–62, and J. N. Reynolds, *Pacific and Indian Ocean, the South Sea Surveying, and Exploration Expedition* (New York, 1841), quoted in Boggs, "American Contributions," 186.

discoveries in the South Pacific. The Pacific region held geopolitical interest for Americans, and the increasing number of maps of the area drawn in the last two decades of the eighteenth century substantiates this.[28]

The American domestic reproduction and elaboration of maps increased in the early nineteenth century. In 1802, Nathaniel Bowitch published his famous *The New American Practical Navigator*, but sailing the Pacific Ocean still continued to be difficult because of numerous geographical features not mentioned in the nautical maps.[29] The American government was committed to obtaining geographical knowledge about the access to the ocean through the American continent and about the Pacific Ocean itself. A good example of such governmental commitments are the 1818 Rector and Roberdeau's "Sketches," which show how quickly the results of the Lewis and Clark expedition were transferred to mapmaking and contributed to the American idea of the Pacific shore.[30] In his 1825 Address to the Congress, President John Quincy Adams recommended sending a scientific expedition to map the Pacific. The congressional and popular support for his initiative was obtained, in great part, because of Jeremiah N. Reynolds, who traveled extensively throughout the nation demanding that official expeditions be sent to the Pacific and to the Antarctic.[31]

In the early nineteenth century, the United States had a certain image of the Pacific area based on literary and cartographical backgrounds. This image was neither completely accurate nor balanced. Asia attracted attention, especially China and Japan, because of its perceived wealth. Latin America obtained limited attention, while the islands, especially those of the South Pacific, were considered idyllic paradises.[32] This image would crystallize because of both the international situation and the interests of the ruling elites.

28. James C. Wheat and Christian F. Burn, *Maps and Charts Published in America before 1800: A Bibliography* (New Haven: Yale University Press, 1969), vii.
29. Friis, *The Pacific Basin*, 263.
30. William Rector was an American surveyor and Roberdau was a military topographical engineer. See their work, "Sketches of the Western Part of the Continent of North America between Latitudes 35 and 52 [degrees] North," in Gilbert, *The Exploration of Western America*, 194.
31. Jeremiah N. Reynolds, *A Report . . . in Relation to Islands, Reefs, and Shoals in the Pacific Ocean* (New York, 24 Sept. 1828, 23d Cong., 2d sess., House Doc., 105, 1835), 3, quoted in Boggs, "American Contributions," 185, and Friis, *The Pacific Basin*, 263.
32. See Figure 1, illustrating the American perception of the Pacific region in the early nineteenth century.

Figure 1. American Perception of the Pacific Region, Early Nineteenth Century.

International Affairs

The international rivalries among European powers certainly influenced the American image of the Pacific. Moreover, America had inherited from the English its interest in trade, some of its sailors,[33] and the belief in the necessity of controlling the seas. In 1783, John Ledyard, a former member of Cook's expedition, was the first person to attempt to persuade American merchants to finance trading ventures between the Northwest Coast and China.[34] Robert Morris, Robert Gray, and John Kenrick were pioneers of trans-Pacific commerce, and between 1794 and 1814, ninety American ships arrived at the Northwest Pacific Coast, while only a dozen of British origin did so.[35]

---

33. David Syrett, *Shipping and the American War, 1775–1783* (London: Atholone Press, 1970), vii, ix, 243. See also Irwin Unger, *These United States: The Questions of Our Past* (Englewood Cliffs, N.J.: Prentice Hall, 1989), 179.

34. Munford, *John Ledyard's Journal*, xiv.

35. Unger, *These United States*, 144. A. Jon Kimerling and Philip L. Jackson, *Atlas of the Pacific Northwest*, 7th ed. (Corvallis, Oreg.: Oregon State University Press, 1985), 11.

After the Nootka Sound Controversy,[36] an agreement established British navigational rights and also allowed settlements on the Northwest Coast in places not already occupied by either power. Later, the United States and Spain signed an important treaty in 1819 that revealed the strength of the Pacific image in American decision-makers' minds. In accordance with that agreement, America obtained a title to transcontinental domain. Secretary of State Adams recognized, "The acknowledgment of a definite line of boundary to the South Seas forms a great epoch in our history."[37]

In the 1800s, America grew concerned that France might regain control of Louisiana as the first step to reestablishing the French Empire in America.[38] When President Jefferson received the information that Napoleon sought to sell the Louisiana territory in 1803, he seized the opportunity to consolidate America's rights to the West and to the Pacific Coast.[39] With the Louisiana Purchase and the Lewis-Clark expedition, Jefferson commenced a new era that continued to build the American image of the Pacific. In the period from 1803 to 1819, the Pacific Coast gained recognition as an integral part of American territory. The popularization of these sentiments would occur in the 1840s with the California gold rush and the rise of San Francisco as the most important port of the West Coast.

The Russians' expedition to Northeast Asia in 1785, their victories against Napoleonic armies, and their expansion and settlement along the Northwest Coast concerned both the British and the Americans. In 1821, an imperial *ukase* declared the North Pacific from the Bering Straits to the 51st parallel closed to trade and navigation by vessels of any power other than Russia. The American response was clear with the 1823 Monroe Doctrine, and the Russians did not challenge this.

British interest in the West was sustained by two national economic

36. After Cook's voyages, some English traders came to the Northwest Coast, and Robert Meares started a settlement at Nootka Sound, which was, at that time, Spanish territory. See Gilbert, *The Exploration of Western America*, 2, and Foster Dulles, *America in the Pacific: A Century of Expansion* (Boston and New York: Houghton Mifflin Co., 1938), 13.
37. Quoted in Dulles, *America in the Pacific*, 27; see also Philip Coolidge Brooks, "The Pacific Coast's First International Boundary Delineation," *Pacific Historical Review* 1 (1932): 62.
38. Ronald Smith, "Napoleon and Louisiana: Failure of the Proposed Expedition to Occupy and Defend Louisiana, 1801–1803," *Louisiana History* 12, no. 1 (1971): 22. See also Dulles, *America in the Pacific*, 27.
39. Louis Houck, *The First American Frontier: The Boundaries of the Louisiana Purchase* (St. Louis: L. S. Taylor Printing Co., 1901), 39.

institutions—the Hudson Bay and Northwest Companies—who were engaged in a fierce struggle for the control of Northwest trade. During the
War of 1812, English Canadians succeeded in dominating the area, and,
with the capture and later purchase of Fort Astoria, the British Northwest
Company was "in virtual control of the whole Rocky Mountains as far south
as it chose to go." According to William Goetzmann, however, they were
"merely fur traders" and were not yet looking for a place to settle permanently.[40] Trade and international rivalries exposed the real value America
placed on the Northwest Coast and the trans-Pacific commerce, and they
undoubtedly encouraged pursuit of American hegemony in the area.

Thomas Jefferson and His Policies

By the time of Thomas Jefferson's 1801 presidential inauguration,
the American idea of the Pacific was nearing crystallization. America simply
needed leaders who could understand the feelings Americans had about
the Pacific and who would encourage the integration of the Pacific into
daily life through well-defined policies. Jefferson, whose vast geographical
knowledge was augmented by political pragmatism,[41] fostered a metamor-
phosis of the American perception of the Pacific from a rich, but vague,
notion to one that demanded concrete governmental policies that protected
American interests.

During his stay in Paris as ambassador, Jefferson met John Ledyard,
who informed him of the possibilities of the trans-Pacific fur trade. Jefferson bought "a pretty full collection of English, French, and Spanish authors,
on the subject of Louisiana," and these books would later become useful
to him.[42] Charles Sanford appropriately asserts that Jefferson's libraries
were important because of their "influence upon Jefferson's thought and
life and, through him, upon American history."[43] A listing of his collection
of works on American geography and exploration occupies 197 pages in

40. William H. Goetzmann, *Exploration and Empire* (New York: W. W. Norton and Co.,
1966), 80.
41. George Thomas Surface, "Thomas Jefferson: A Pioneer Student of American Geography," *Bulletin of the Geographical Society* 12 (1909): 744; Lally Weymouth, *Thomas
Jefferson: The Man, His World, His Influence* (New York: G. P. Putnam's Sons, 1973), 111.
42. Jefferson's letter to William Dunbar on 31 Mar. 1804, quoted in Francis W. Hirst, *Life
and Letters of Thomas Jefferson* (New York: The MacMillan Press, 1926), 396.
43. Charles Sanford, *Thomas Jefferson and His Library* (Hamden: Archom Books,
1977), 49.

Millicent Sowerby's Annotated Catalog, an accurate barometer of the president's interest therein. Some of these books would help him prepare memorandums for Congress and provide him with historical arguments for later international controversies.[44]

According to Merril Peterson, Jefferson's ideas about the Pacific Coast were formed "about the time of the American revolution."[45] Therefore, it is not surprising that he sponsored the 1793 Andre Michaux transcontinental expedition to the Pacific Ocean, and when the presidency was his, he personally prepared another transcontinental expedition. He selected Meriwether Lewis, his personal secretary, to be chief of the exploration, and William Clark of the United States Army to be the second-in-command, and he carefully studied all the maps available to him, even the most recent by Soutard, MacKay, and Evans.[46]

Jefferson obtained money from Congress to, in the Spanish ambassador's words, "discover the way by which the Americans may someday extend their population and their interest up the coast of the South Sea."[47] In 1804, when Lewis and Clark left St. Louis, they were traversing American territory because the Purchase of Louisiana had become a reality. They were also the vanguard for thousands of settlers who, in the mid-nineteenth century, would create an American empire stretching to the Pacific.

After his presidential years, Jefferson continued to be concerned about the West and the Pacific. In 1811, he encouraged John Astor, the New York fur magnate, to send expeditions to the mouth of the Columbia River with the purpose of establishing a permanent American outpost in the Northwest and developing the trans-Pacific fur trade with Canton.[48]

When Jefferson left the presidency, the image of the Pacific had been completely consolidated in American minds. This consolidation, however, was not the product of a single man or president. There were several important groups or circles of interest aiding the formation of the Pacific

44. Louis Helpenin, Daniel Coxe, Le Page du Pratz, Cook, and Mackenzie were, for example, some of the authors consulted for the 1804 memorandum and for Lewis and Clark's instructions.
45. Merril D. Peterson, *The Portable Thomas Jefferson* (New York: Penguin Books, 1975).
46. Jefferson had numerous maps in his own collection, including, among others, Arrowsmith's, Vancouver's, De L'Isle's, D'Anville's, and Moll's. See Weymouth, *Thomas Jefferson*, 115.
47. Letter to the Spanish foreign minister on 2 Dec. 1802, quoted in Weymouth, *Thomas Jefferson*, 114.
48. Goetzmann, *Exploration and Empire*, 34.

image, and all were connected in various ways to Jefferson. The American Philosophical Society was an elite group that possessed enormous political power and was formed by "whatever the American World had of distinction in philosophy and science."[49] Jefferson's relationship with the Society grew closer when he was elected president of the United States. He, as a member of the Society, prepared the expedition of 1783,[50] and other Society members instructed Lewis and Clark at Jefferson's request.[51] After the Louisiana Purchase, Jefferson wrote a memorandum on its boundaries, a subject of extreme international sensitivity, and sent copies to his colleagues for their information.[52]

Another group that influenced the consolidation of the Pacific image in American minds included travelers, whalers, and traders, all of whom, long before others, saw the richness of the Pacific. Among these were John Ledyard, the Bostonian traders who impressed the home port citizens with the rich cargo from China, and John Astor, who, according to John Terrel, intended "to take the Northwest for himself" and beat the British commercial companies.[53] Whaling activities increased in the nineteenth century, and they were also important. There were 119 American whaleships sailing the Pacific about 1819, and a few years later, Honolulu became the center for Pacific whaling.[54] Whalers and traders considered the Pacific Basin a commercial arena, and their interests inspired the political elites' decision-making.

The political circle was important in the consolidation of the Pacific idea in American minds. This elite was formed by the so-called Virginia dynasty, which ruled the country in the last years of the eighteenth century and first decades of the nineteenth century. Members James Monroe,

49. Jefferson's letter to the secretary of the Society on 28 Jan. 1797. See Jackson, *Thomas Jefferson*, 85.

50. Jackson, *Thomas Jefferson*, 43.

51. Jefferson wrote to Benjamin Barton, Winstar, Patterson, Dr. B. Rush, and the surveyor Andrew Elliot. See Jackson, *Thomas Jefferson*, 135.

52. Jefferson's *Chronological Series of Facts Relative to Louisiana* was not to be published until a century later, and it remains in the Society library in Philadelphia. See Jackson, *Thomas Jefferson*, 115.

53. His companies were the American Fur Company and Pacific Fur Company founded in 1808 and 1810, respectively. His partners were Alexander McKay, Donald McKenzie, Duncan McDougal, David Stuart, Wilson Price Hunt, Ramsay Crooks, Robert McClelland, and Joseph Miller. John U. Terrel, *The Six Turning Major Changes in the American West, 1800–1834* (Glendale, Calif.: The Arthur H. Clark Co., 1968), 88.

54. Bertrand, "Geographical Exploration by the United States," 262.

John Quincy Adams, James Madison, Secretary Gallatin, and naval officer J. B. Prevost generally shared Jefferson's perspectives and understood the importance of the American presence and trade in the Pacific.

By 1820, American residents had an image of the Pacific Ocean and its shores that had resulted from innumerable perceptions and beliefs based on everything from maps to hearsay. The formation of this particular image took generations to develop, and it was formed through a process of conceptualization in which cartography and literature played important roles. Americans grew aware of the wealth this region offered by witnessing the commerce and international rivalry that occurred on and around the Pacific. The United States, as a new nation, understood that, regardless of its relationship to Europe, the Pacific Ocean would be the more decisive element in defining its future.

Pacific Rim Discourse:
The U.S. Global Imaginary in the
Late Cold War Years

Christopher L. Connery

. . . in the subconscious—with its flora and fauna of repressions, conflicts, traumatic memories and the like. Travelling further, we reach a kind of far West, inhabited by Jungian archetypes and the raw materials of human mythology. Beyond this region lies a broad Pacific. Wafted across it on the wings of mescaline . . . we reach what might be called the Antipodes of the mind.
—Aldous Huxley, *The Doors of Perception*

Thus this mysterious divine Pacific zones the whole world's bulk around it; makes all coasts one bay to it; seems the tide-beating heart of earth.
—Herman Melville, *Moby Dick*

It is no longer continents that have become agglomerated but the totality of the planet that is diminished. . . . The continental translation

I would like to thank those who commented on this essay on the several occasions when I presented it publicly. Special thanks to Jim Clifford, Tak Fujitani, Harry Harootunian, Ted Juters, Kristin Ross, Mary Scott, and Marilyn Young for the extra time they took.

that, curiously enough, we find both in the geophysician Wegener [Gondwanaland], with the drift of land masses, and in Mackinder, with the geopolitical amalgam of lands, has given way to a worldwide phenomena of terrestrial and technological contraction that today makes us penetrate into an artificial topological universe: the direct encounter of every surface on the globe.
—Paul Virilio, *Speed and Politics*

In the outer-space photograph most popular in this country, North America and South America are poised on the far right of the globe. The Earth is largely a cloud-laced ocean; the land a near irrelevancy: Melville's totalizing Pacific. Even without photographs, we have lived in the era of a cartographic Real for several centuries. "Imagined communities" and other geopolitical desires have always been read against a conjurable totality that gives the beyond to a border. Maps are ideology. Think of Fredric Jameson's synthesis of Kevin Lynch and Louis Althusser, where Lynch's "cognitive mapping" is read as Althusser's definition of Ideology itself: "the Imaginary representation of the subject's relationship to his or her Real conditions of existence."[1] Jameson's piece "Cognitive Mapping" is a call for a Utopian aesthetic—a cognitive mapping performed in the individual sphere *against and beyond* the dominant totality of capital. This essay is on the psycho-geography of capital itself—the prescriptive cognitive mapping performed by capital's institutions in the service of the global imaginary—which is at once the imaginary of the totality and the prescribed Real against which any individual imaginary is constructed.

My argument, simply, is that the idea of the Pacific Rim came into being in the mid-1970s, that it was dominant in the U.S. geo-imaginary until the end of the 1980s, and that this dominance was determined by the particular stage of late capitalism marked by that period and by the economic and political situation of the United States in the late Cold War years.[2] Pacific Rim Discourse is an imagining of U.S. multinational capitalism in an era when the "socialist" bloc still existed, and it is the socialist bloc that is the

1. Fredric Jameson, "Cognitive Mapping," in *Marxism and the Interpretation of Culture*, ed. Cary Nelson and Lawrence Grossberg (Urbana and Chicago: University of Illinois Press, 1988), 353.
2. To my knowledge, Arif Dirlik is the first scholar to call attention to both the ideological character and the specific U.S. character of "the Asia-Pacific" idea. See Arif Dirlik, "The Asia-Pacific Idea: Reality and Representation in the Invention of a Regional Structure," *Journal of World History* 3 (Spring 1992): 55–79.

principle discursive and strategic Other. Pacific Rim Discourse, though, is a *non*-othering discourse. Unlike Orientalism, which Edward W. Said delineates genealogically as a discursive formation centered on a fundamental othering—an othering further grounded in the specific histories of colonialism and imperialism—Pacific Rim Discourse presumes a kind of metonymic equivalence. Its world is an interpenetrating complex of interrelationships with no center: neither the center of a hegemonic power nor the imagined fulcrum of a "balance of power."

The Pacific Rim is a well-used term that, since the late 1970s, has come to signify something to most Americans. It is almost exclusively an American usage; in East Asia, the Pacific island nations, Australia, and New Zealand, its use is clearly U.S.-derived. By 1973 or 1974, it appears to mean the United States and East Asia. The most extensive geographical definition of the term has been: peninsular and island Southeast Asia; China; Northeast Asia, including the Soviet Pacific region; Australia; New Zealand; Papua New Guinea; the islands of the South Pacific; and the Pacific Coast of South, Central, and North America. For practical discursive purposes, the Pacific Rim consists of the United States, Canada, Mexico (tenuously, though—Mexico is often left out), Japan, China, the Four Tigers—also known as the Little Dragons or the East Asian NICs[3]—Taiwan, Hong Kong, South Korea, and Singapore—and the up-and-coming, or minor-league, players: Malaysia, Thailand, Indonesia, and the Philippines.[4] The psychic center of the Pacific Rim is the United States-Japan relationship. China has played an important role in the mythic construction of the Pacific Rim as telos.

The origin of the term is geological, referring to the rim of volcanic and tectonic activity around the Pacific Ocean—the Bering Strait, Japan, China, Southeast Asia, and the Pacific Coasts of North and South America. In the 1960s, the term, or the related *Pacific Basin*, comes to be used

3. NIC stands for Newly Industrialized Country. Although I prefer Bruce Cumings's acronym BAIR, for Bureaucratic-Authoritarian Industrializing Regimes, NIC is the choice of Pacific Rim Discourse.

4. Alexander Besher, *The Pacific Rim Almanac* (New York: HarperPerennial, 1990), xix. This is one of the single best sources for gauging the content and the tone of the Pacific Rim as "trend." The cover states: "A complete resource guide to the new center of the economic world. Covering all the facts, statistics, trends, products, and technologies of the entire Asia Pacific Region." For the identity of the Pacific Rim, see also Arif Dirlik, "The Asia-Pacific Idea," and Peter Gourevitch, "The Pacific Rim: Current Debates," *The Annals of the Academy of Political and Social Science* 505 (1989): 8–23.

primarily in a national security context, as in the document by Mike Mansfield on the U.S. Senate Committee on Foreign Relations' study mission to
the Western Pacific, *The Rim of Asia* (1967). The Vietnam War kept alive
the national security context in which the Pacific Rim was discussed: Vietnam was a domino threatening the rest of Southeast Asia; Japan's security
would be threatened by a Communist Asian mainland; Soviet interests in
the Pacific were ominous. The end of the Vietnam War gave the lie to the
domino theory, and although an anxiety over Soviet intentions in the Pacific
continued to be voiced throughout the Reagan administration, it was always
abstract; there was never any clear articulation of what those intentions
might have been.

Many factors came together in the mid-seventies that both diminished the national security context and established the fundamental ground
for Pacific Rim Discourse, among them: (1) the United States-China rapprochement; (2) the end of the Vietnam War; (3) the indisputable economic
strength of Japan, with the attendant realization that Japan was no longer
an admirable latecomer to modernization but an economic giant—a First
World country; and (4) the worldwide economic downturn of the mid-1970s.
It was an age when U.S. hegemony was questioned, or doubted, as never
before in the postwar era.[5]

Pacific Rim Discourse has multiple genealogies and is better understood in the context of several discursive trajectories. I will treat primarily
Orientalism, modernization theory, left-liberal humanist internationalism,
and Cold War discourse. Pacific Rim Discourse was a tentative move into
the anxious mythology of a putative new era, an era during which that fundamental characterization of the hegemon's view of its other—Orientalism—
loses some of its utility. Although one encounters many Orientalist tropes,
such as Japan bashing and more benign forms of essentializing in representations of East Asia during the Pacific Rim Discourse years, certain
key structural factors have changed. Orientalism presumes an othering that
is articulated in terms of categorical asymmetry: the Western hegemonic

---

5. Functionalist discussions of hegemony and "hegemonic stability" became quite common in political science and political economy beginning in the early to mid-1970s. For
histories and critiques of the hegemony debates, see Arthur A. Stein, "The Hegemon's
Dilemma: Great Britain, the United States, and the International Economic Order," *International Organization* 38 (Spring 1984): 355–86; Bruce Russet, "The Mysterious Case of
Vanishing Hegemony," *International Organization* 39 (Spring 1985): 207–31; and Susan
Strange, "The Persistent Myth of Lost Hegemony," *International Organization* 41 (Autumn
1987): 551–74.

national or imperial power counterpoised to its colony, dependency, frontier, or to an "Asiatic" empire or tribal confederation. When these sub- or extranational categories disappear (for the most part), however, the world knows only one category: the nation-state. At this horizon of the nation-state, the transnational imaginary can only become more abstract, more mythological, less analyzable in the strictly hegemonic terms on which Orientalism depends. There is, also, in this era, the more concrete perception that capitalism has worked its transformative miracles in one land of the Other—East Asia, particularly Japan. While Cold Warriors had wanted a strong, economically vibrant Japan, they had imagined Japan as a strictly *regional* hegemon. Japan as global power necessitated a reimagining of global categories.

Economic exploitation and Said's othering coincided in the imperial age, when an ideology of Western cultural or racial superiority overshadowed any theorizing of capitalism's teleological promise. The undeveloped world was undeveloped because of local factors. Modernization theory shifted the othering to a more purely temporal plane, in keeping with its capitalist universalist teleology. It could speak of "latecomers,"[6] whereby the Western present was the East Asian future. Just as modernization theory obliterated the spatial, the new realities of multinational capitalism in the Carter and Reagan years erased modernization theory's temporality. Japan and the East Asian NICs were no longer the West's past. In the eighties, if Japan was anywhere in time, it was in the future, with Taiwan, Singapore, Hong Kong, and South Korea at the very least in some version of the present. The Rim was a perfect image for a centeredness with no central power.

In his treatment of Louis Massignon, author of that oracular phrase "Nous sommes tous les Sémites," Said gives a crumb of respect to the humanist universalism that allowed such a line to be possible. Of course, this kind of internationalism is an affordable luxury to an imperial power. As E. H. Carr has noted, internationalism is the British credo in times of British hegemony, the French credo in times of French hegemony, and the U.S. credo in times of U.S. hegemony.[7] Tom Ferguson and Bruce Cumings, among others, identified an internationalist capitalist interest group who

6. For example, Marion J. Levy, Jr., *Modernization: Latecomers and Survivors* (New York: Basic Books, 1972).
7. E. H. Carr, *The Twenty Years' Crisis: 1919–1939; An Introduction to the Study of International Relations* (New York: Harper and Row, 1964), 108.

gained ascendancy in the Roosevelt presidency and from whom came the principal architects of Cold War policy.[8] There was also a group of scholars and critics during the Roosevelt years whose internationalism was more liberal-idealist. Like Massignon, the Asia scholars associated with the Institute for Pacific Relations and the journal *Amerasia* represent a tradition that is fundamentally *pre*–Cold War, antifascist left-wing humanist. As E. H. Norman wrote in 1937, in the first issue of *Amerasia*,

> We are united in the belief that citizens of the United States as members of a democracy have an inalienable right to know all the pertinent and efficient causative factors involved in our Pacific and Asiatic commitments and relations, that they may actively and critically follow the methods employed by our government in carrying out its policy in that region. We are also united in striving to attain the ultimate objective of promoting among all peoples inhabiting the periphery of the Pacific Ocean a harmony of relationships which transcends the merely legalistic concepts of justice with its emphasis on property over human rights or upon specious national honor or sovereignty over the economic welfare and the spiritual needs of the 700 million people who live on the islands or in the countries bordering the Pacific.[9]

In 1947, the poet Charles Olson published *Call Me Ishmael*. He reads the whaleship as the first American factory, and the American pursuit of the sperm whale into the Pacific (American whalers were the first to hunt the sperm) as prefiguring the United States as Pacific hegemon, a process Olson saw coming into fruition during World War II. For Olson, the Pacific was deliverance from the tyranny of Judeo-Christian humanism: "The Pacific is the end of the UNKNOWN which Homer's and Dante's Ulysses opened men's eyes to. END of individual's responsibility only to himself. Ahab is full stop."[10] Olson reworked the book while serving during the war at the Office of War Information, in its early years a bastion of liberal

8. Thomas Ferguson, "From Normalcy to New Deal: Industrial Structure, Party Competition, and American Public Policy in the Great Depression," *International Organization* 38 (Winter 1984): 41–94; Bruce Cumings, *The Origins of the Korean War*, 2 vols. (Princeton: Princeton University Press, 1990), 2: 3–121.

9. Quoted in John W. Dower, ed., *Origins of the Modern Japanese State: Selected Writings of E. H. Norman* (New York: Pantheon, 1975), 38–39.

10. Charles Olson, *Call Me Ishmael* (New York: Reynal and Hitchcock, 1947), 119.

antifascist idealism that was a direct descendant of the federally supported writers' projects of the New Deal.[11] Olson quit the OWI in 1944, when he became convinced of its growing rightward turn. The right-wing U.S. China lobby had triumphed in its efforts to turn U.S. policy against Mao Tse-tung and the Chinese Communist Party (CCP), specifically by the cancellation of Henry Wallace's planned visit with Mao in 1944.[12] The Cold War was beginning to emerge from World War II.

For Olson and like-minded antifascists, the wrong turn made by the United States became more clear with the dumping of Henry Wallace in favor of Harry Truman for vice-president and the gradual ascent of anti-communism over antifascism. Norman, the Institute for Pacific Relations, and *Amerasia* would later fall victim to Cold War hysteria in the United States, and the shadow of McCarthyism and anticommunism would color East Asian Studies in the United States into the 1960s. The utopian universalism articulated during *Amerasia*'s historical moment would never be revived. Pacific Rim Discourse is in no way a revival of that humanism, nor is it the opportunistic internationalism that is the luxury of a dominant power. It is an economically determined discourse that functions as the mythology of multinational capitalism within a national sphere. The United States, Japan, the East Asian NICs, and the second tier of developing Pacific nations (Thailand, Malaysia, Indonesia, coastal China) are linked in a Rim that is an imagining of transnational capital, a co-prosperity sphere. Japan and the NICs represent capital's transformative promise—their recent history is capital's teleology. China is the certain future. The discourse of equality and connectedness reflects, in part, a reaction to East Asian "success": When Japan is number one, the only way not to be number two is to transcend the nation.

A nation-state is a most particular mixing of the abstract and the material; in all articulations of nationhood, there is an abstraction—an idealism—that conflicts with the physical boundaries of any given nation-state. The United States, conceiving itself more than most nation-states in terms of lack, of externality (manifest destiny, the frontier, the new frontier, etc.),

11. Allan M. Winkler, *The Politics of Propaganda: The Office of War Information, 1942–1945* (New Haven: Yale University Press, 1978), 21. Tom Clark, *Charles Olson: The Allegory of a Poet's Life* (New York: Norton, 1991), 84–107.

12. Tom Clark, *Charles Olson*, 85. Wallace's name is probably better known in Northwest China than it is in the United States today. A pear-shaped melon he brought into China as a gift on this visit became widely cultivated in the Lanzhou area, where it is known in China today as a "Wallace-melon" (Chinese: *Walasi-gua*).

has been prone to the worst excesses of the violence of abstractionism. This impulse has been forcefully documented in Robert Drinnon's *Facing West: The Metaphysics of Indian-Hating and Empire-Building* (the title is an allusion to Melville, who named Ahab's ship after the first Indian tribe to fall victim to colonial American genocide). Drinnon's book (1980) ends with the Vietnam War, on the eve of Pacific Rim Discourse. Although, as I have argued, Pacific Rim Discourse as non-othering discourse can be described as post-Orientalist, there are important links to the metaphysics of the Cold War.

America's territorial ideology—its land-renouncing abstraction—has always been matched in policy by actions of absolute horror. The Cold War carried geopolitical abstraction to new limits, accompanied always by those weapons that could render the planet truly abstract. In *The Origins of the Korean War*, Bruce Cumings has given a convincing political economy of modern American foreign policy that is a welcome corrective to the status quo in the field of international relations.[13] He sees the particular Cold War ideologies of internationalism and containment theorized and practiced by Acheson, Kennan, Forrestal, Dulles, Rusk, Nitze, Harriman, among others, as having root in their own careers on Wall Street and in other institutions of U.S. finance capital that stood to benefit from an international economy free of trade barriers, anchored by strong regional economic powers. The Cold War geo-imaginary was similarly shaped by the psychic structures of the most developed stage of international capitalism.

For the Cold Warriors, the principle structural impediment to the international open market was inwardness. Nazi Germany had made Europe an inner-directed, self-supplied system. In the perverse logic of Cold War capitalism, communism was read not as class-based internationalism but as a Soviet expansionist replay of European totalitarianism. Acheson and Kennan's project was to counter the threat of a Soviet-dominated Eurasian continent turned away from the "free" world. William Pietz has convincingly shown the discursive continuities between Orientalism and Cold War discourse.[14] With the Soviet bloc constructed as the West's strategically significant Other, and with one defining characteristic of that Otherness being an Oriental closedness, the analytical project of the Cold Warrior becomes

13. For a trenchant critique of the ideology of the field, see Bruce Andrews, "The Domestic Content of International Desire," *International Organization* 38 (Spring 1984): 321–27.
14. William Pietz, "The Post-Colonialism of Cold War Discourse," *Social Text* 19/20 (Fall 1988): 55–75.

more purely psychological, more prone to metaphor and re-situations. So, in Cold War strategy, and in the field of international relations, we commonly encounter such bizarre formulations as the nation that "behaves," diplomacy as game theory, and "national interests." As Anders Stephanson characterized George Kennan's analytical project:

> Two discernible projects are therefore involved in understanding the other side. The first is the overarching task of determining the "real" position of the opponent, a task that can be carried out only within one's own given terms of truth. The second is the subordinate problem of understanding how the other party *thinks* he or she thinks and acts.[15]

This kind of essentializing psychologism combined with the strategic character of nuclear warfare to de-spatialize the globe. George Kennan was probably the last of the spatialists, articulating a geographically specific Western civilization as the strategic center for U.S. policy. Western Europe was the focus of his doctrine of containment, because "the older cultural centers of Europe are the meteorological centers in which much of the climate of international life is produced and from which it proceeds."[16] Another example of early Cold War spatiality was the notion of regional hegemony. Southeast Asia, viewed immediately after World War II as a market and raw materials source to alleviate Western Europe's dollar drain, is subsequently incarnated as Japan's potential hinterland, source of *its* markets and raw materials. NSC 68, authored primarily by Paul Nitze, and the principal justification for U.S. military intervention worldwide, internationalized the containment strategy. In giving every region in the world equal symbolic value, it made a world consisting *only* of abstract, symbolic values. Thus, Dean Acheson could completely deny the local character of the Korean War[17] and thereby strengthen the course that led to Vietnam. Military strategy in Korea and Vietnam followed neatly from this abstractionism: Nearly every town in Korea was leveled by U.S. bombing; Vietnam was first home to "strategic hamlets" and later the target of more aerial bombardment than the totals of all previous wars.

The binarism of Cold War thinking obliterated "local conditions"

---

15. Anders Stephanson, *Kennan and the Art of Foreign Policy* (Cambridge: Harvard University Press, 1989), 4.
16. Quoted in Stephanson, *Kennan and the Art of Foreign Policy*, 157.
17. Cumings, *The Origins of the Korean War*, 2:628.

everywhere, Europe and the United States included. But capitalist universalism, the ideology that constructed the open world market as "natural," could never structurally abide the binary world inscribed by the *realpolitik* of containment. Cumings traces the evolution of the Korean war strategy from one of containment to the failed strategy of "rollback." Actually, an implied rollback was present in early containment thinking. Kennan thought that merely by slowing Communist momentum, Eastern European and Soviet communism would fall on their own when simply faced with the superiority of Western capitalism.[18] By the mid-1970s, the founding years of Pacific Rim Discourse, several developments fundamentally changed the Cold War binary equation: (1) the "loss" of Vietnam is utterly without geopolitical consequence; (2) Nixon and Kissinger's opening to China give the lie both to Communist solidarity and to the Asian domino theory; (3) it is clear that Japan's prosperity is not due to a position as regional hegemon but to its North American and Western European trade; (4) the failed revolution in Portugal and the definitive defeat of the Italian Communist Party (PCI) in Italy finally make it clear that communism will not expand into putatively vulnerable "Southern Europe" (itself an ideological construction of the geo-imaginary); (5) Western bloc détente with the Soviet Union and Eastern Europe seems to constitute an implicit renunciation of rollback tendencies.

By the mid-1970s, the Cold War binarism remains, but with less grip on the United States's geo-imaginary. Kennan's European-centered Western civilization, to be defended against Soviet barbarism, had been an easy and natural equation. Since the space of the Other can be occupied only by one category, however, the later emergence of a powerful Asian capitalist power can be accommodated only in the "us" of Western capitalism, which has the somewhat paradoxical effect of rendering moot Western capital's geographic specificity. As the Cold War drags on, particularly after its last "hot" outbreak in Vietnam, it becomes a bad old story. Europe becomes metonymically aligned with the static confrontationalism of U.S.-Soviet hostility and thus consigned to an anti-teleology from which the Pacific Rim is a deliverance. Reagan's "evil empire" is really a nostalgic, albeit macabre, blip on the discursive screen, serving mainly as an excuse to maintain a high-powered domestic military economy and to wage limited techno-war on the Third World.

The Cold War had codified that geopolitical abstractionism that made

18. Melvyn P. Leffler, *A Preponderance of Power: National Security, the Truman Administration, and the Cold War* (Stanford: Stanford University Press, 1992), 150–51.

possible the post-binary abstractionism of Pacific Rim Discourse. Indeed, the late Cold War's anti-teleology required a new spatial mythology for U.S. international capital. The idea of the Pacific Rim had a further advantage: It centered on an ocean. Water is capital's element. The idea of an ocean-centered westward movement of history, beginning with the Mediterranean, passing on to the Atlantic, and culminating in the Pacific, was common-place in the late nineteenth-century United States. And as an extension of *America*, the Pacific would be at its essence a *non*colonial space where a pure capital would be free to operate. This mythology was behind President McKinley's secretary of state John Hay's Open Door policy for China and served in general to de-imperialize U.S. expansionist moves into the Pacific. The bourgeois idealization of sea power and ocean-borne commerce has been central to the mythology of capital, which has struggled to free itself from the earth just as the bourgeoisie struggled to free itself from tilling the soil. Movable capital is liquid capital, and without movement, capital is a mere Oriental hoard.

Indeed, as John Hay's remarks suggest, a truly *world* history happens only on and around oceans. John Hay's mentor was William Seward, secretary of state in the 1860s, who "understood that the primary objective of expansion would no longer be territorial, once the economy had been more industrialized. He considered that commercial expansion would now be the key to making America 'the master of the world.' " [19] The debate over Seward's policies and their consequences, the most immediate conse-quence being the United States's imperial ventures in the Pacific in the late nineteenth century, would last in modified form until the bipartisan triumph of internationalism in the Cold War years.

American isolationism has always found its greatest support in the interior. A history of the rise of the United States as an international power could be written as its escape from the predial bonds of its continentality. George Kennan wrote often of the Soviet national character as being deter-mined less by Marxism than by its vast open plains—its terrestriality. Here, he echoes Hegel, whose *Lectures on the Philosophy of World History* like-wise divides the world into land and sea. For Hegel, terrestrial man can be content with simple fulfillment of needs. He who takes to the seas, however, does so for profit.[20] Kennan feared the insular tendencies that periodically

19. Gareth Stedman Jones, "The History of U.S. Imperialism," in *Ideology in Social Science*, ed. Robin Blackburn (New York: Pantheon, 1972), 222.
20. G. W. F. Hegel, *Lectures on the Philosophy of World History, Introduction: Reason*

surfaced in the United States almost as much as the landlocked tyrannical illiberality spawned on the Russian steppe.[21] Containment is containment of the awesome landedness of the Eurasian continent. We can read the Cold War on one level, as Orwell did in *1984* with the names of his world powers, as Ocean versus Land.

The Pacific, as Melville, Seward, Hay, and Olson had intuited, was the Last Ocean. Late nineteenth-century expansionist Whitelaw Reid called it "the American Lake," a sentiment that could still be echoed in 1949 by Douglas MacArthur, who called it an "Anglo-Saxon lake."[22] John F. Kennedy would specifically invoke the Pacific as part of his "New Frontier" in his acceptance speech at the 1960 Democratic Convention in Los Angeles. With the economic ascent of Japan and the East Asian NICs, however, the Pacific's multinational character was undeniable. The Pacific was no longer an American lake, and the 1973–1974 recession had rendered somewhat precarious any capitalist power's entry into a new frontier of prosperity. And from this precariousness: The Rim. Consider the word *rim*: A rim unites—it unites across oceans, across ethnic and racial divides. It presumes a unity, a centeredness with no center, a totality, an unbrokenness. A rim is thin. It is stable but precarious. One can fall off a rim. A rim is a horizon: the horizon of capital, of history, of space and time. It is a topology for the "suppression of distance" said to be characteristic of our times.

Third World countries are off the Rim. In the Cold War, Kennan had criticized all U.S. involvement in the Third World, including the Vietnam War and the rapprochement with China, as unnecessary attention to irrelevant localisms. He feared a diversion of U.S. attention away from its more pressing commitment to Europe.[23] This is symptomatic of the anachronistic character of all Cold War thinking. By the mid-1970s, Western Civilization was simply no longer a geographically meaningful construction. The opening to China—and all that it promised—was one significant mythological foundation for the new global imagination.

---

in History, ed. Johannes Hoffmeister and trans. H. B. Nisbet (Cambridge: Cambridge University Press, 1974), 156–61.

21. Stephanson, *Kennan and the Art of Foreign Policy*, 203–4.

22. John W. Dower, "Occupied Japan and the American Lake, 1945–1950," in *America's Asia: Dissenting Essays on Asian-American Relations*, Edward Friedman and Mark Selden, eds. (New York: Pantheon, 1971), 170–71.

23. Stephanson, *Kennan and the Art of Foreign Policy*, 264. This is also the conclusion in Leffler, *A Preponderance of Power*, which has been reviewed as the most authoritative new history of Truman's Cold War.

The opening to China coincided with the winding down of the Vietnam War and also with some significant developments in the capitalist economy. The 1974 oil-shock recession was a dramatic demonstration of the interdependency and the volatility of the international economy. The 1974 recession inaugurated into the Western economies a rising level of structural unemployment, with an attendant weakness in the position of labor. Just as the solidarity of labor eroded, so did markets for industrial goods differentiate and fragment. Among manufacturers' responses to this general uncertainty were flexibility in working methods (particularly distribution, subcontracting, and inventory practices) and in labor markets. The labor force was segmented into a permanent skilled core and an unskilled part-time, casual, and largely female periphery.

I use the spatial terms *core* and *periphery* ironically, for in the post-1974 world, they have limited applicability as global geographic terms. Cores and peripheries coexist in the former cores and peripheries. The United States has primary and tertiary manufacturing zones, as well as the kinds of export processing zones one finds in Sri Lanka.[24] And the direction in the sub-tier of the Pacific Rim NICs, particularly Indonesia, Thailand, and the Philippines, seems to be not toward the generally equitable income distribution of Japan and the Four Tigers but toward a developed, urban core (Jakarta or Bangkok) with impoverished peripheries (Borneo or Northeast Thailand). Pacific Rim Discourse arises, in part, out of the impossibility of imagining a core in the old, concentric terms. The meaningless of core and periphery at the global level is one indication of the need for a new spatial imaginary. The difficulty of the economic imaginary is illustrated in the mid-seventies' phenomenon of the economic oxymoron, "stagflation" and "global Keynsianism" being two memorable examples.

The imaginative crisis was evident in 1977 at the beginning of the Carter presidency with his famous malaise speech, which illustrated for all the diminishment of the United States as a totalizing concept. Yet, Carter's first tactic in an economic downturn was inflationary, the most nation-bound of economic solutions. The increasing turn toward militarism in the late Carter presidency prefigured the global logic of Reaganism. The means of debt payment during the Reagan era would be more in keeping with Pacific Rim Discourse: paying with money borrowed from abroad. As Reagan's presidency progressed, Japan and the NICs were more and more the

24. As Mike Davis illustrates in Los Angeles. See Mike Davis, *City of Quartz: Excavating the Future in Los Angeles* (New York: Verso, 1990).

source of those funds. As we all now know, the Reagan recovery was a reverse New Deal. Big growth was exclusionary and benefited the poor very little. Appeals to national concerns, as in the rhetoric of the New Deal or the Great Society, were replaced by an extra-national trust in the market. Reaganism thus contributed in a distinct way to the conceptual deflation of the nation in the U.S. global imaginary. The United States could signify itself as a nation only militarily, hence the "evil empire" and adventurism in Grenada, Lebanon, Panama, et cetera. The lack of a comprehensible fit, however, between militarism and any articulable global politics or economics, rendered this signification system unworkable at the level of mythology. Hence the turn to the Pacific Rim.

The year 1974 also witnessed the election of Jerry Brown as governor of California. California figures very heavily in Pacific Rim Discourse in all of its stages. As I have mentioned before, the Pacific Rim is teleology, and its teleological character has been shaped in part by a residual American frontierism. The original frontier—the rush to the coast—is itself a dimension of the fear of land I mentioned earlier. What is the frontier, however, when it is no longer spatial? John F. Kennedy's evocation of the new frontier had located it not only spatially but temporally—as newness, promise. The idea of California fits into this in important ways. California was the cultural capital of the American late 1960s, and Jerry Brown's election was a confirmation of California's "unique character." Brown liked to talk of California as if it were an independent country ("the seventh largest economy in the world," he often said), as a place that faced both ways: back toward the East, and West, across the Pacific.

Over the course of the late seventies and eighties, California would be constructed ideologically as a multicultural, new world semi-nation, as the primary designated recipient of Japanese, Taiwanese, and South Korean capital. Los Angeles, of course, played a central role in this. *LA 2000: A City for the Future*, a report commissioned and financed by a corporate-dominated, mayorally appointed committee, painted a radiant picture of LA as capital of the twenty-first century, serving as a financial conduit to the Pacific trade, flush with Asian capital influx and enlivened by the "new immigrants," largely from Asia (read: "good" immigrants who have money and work hard). Los Angeles and California: interpenetrated and liking it.

This teleology, in which even a concrete space such as California is articulated more temporally than spatially, is also reflected in popular futurology. Its most conspicuous exponent has been Alvin Toffler, in his trilogy, appearing with a decennial regularity that in itself emphasizes its temporality, consisting of *Future Shock* (1970), *The Third Wave* (1980), and *Powershift* (1990). To quote Toffler:

> *Future Shock*—which we defined as the disorientation and stress brought on by trying to cope with too many changes in too short a time—argued that the acceleration of history carries consequences of its own, independent of the actual directions of change.

> *The Third Wave* . . . [described] the latest revolutionary changes in technology and society . . . placed them in historical perspective and sketched the future they might bring.

> *Powershift* . . . focuses on the crucially changed role of knowledge in relationship to power.[25]

Most of the Pacific Rim Discourse is, as one might expect, in *The Third Wave*, which, as Toffler has on many occasions been proud to point out, was a best-seller in China and a favorite of Deng Xiaoping and Zhao Ziyang. There is nothing exceptional or unpredictable in *The Third Wave*'s particular instancing of the new global imaginary. It is typical Pacific Rim Discourse, full of "new trade patterns," "new alliances," "new interpenetrations," et cetera. The phenomenon described and/or created in *Future Shock*, though, is more formative of the character of the discourse. The new anxiety of the seventies and eighties, of which Toffler is a prophet, differs from the anxiety during the height of the Cold War, which naturally focused on a drastically uncertain future. Future shock is not really an anxiety about the future but about the present. What does the world look like? What's going on right now? How can we produce faster? How can we turn products around faster? It is the anxiety of pure speed as the spatial that is continually transcended and refashioned.

The Pacific Rim, being the new, the future, the space of temporality, and not coincidentally arising in the "information age," is constructed around an anxiety over knowledge, an anxiety created in part by the unexamined and undertheorized positing of knowledge as the new commodity. The American of the late Cold War years is exhorted to *learn*: learn Japanese; learn how they did it; learn where Taiwan is; learn from the experts. In 1975, one of the foundational years of Pacific Rim Discourse, the Harvard sociologist Ezra Vogel published one of the discourse's foundational texts, *Japan as Number One*, subtitled *Lessons for America*.

25. Alvin Toffler, *Powershift: Knowledge, Wealth, and Violence at the Edge of the 21st Century* (New York: Bantam, 1990), xix–xx.

John Dower very effectively documents the ideological and historical nature of the hegemony of modernization theory in discourse on Japan in the 1960s, which derived from the broader interests of American capital, as well as from the specific goals of suppressing radical analyses of Japan and Japanese-American relations.[26] Japan, the successful latecomer, was not only to be living proof of capital's teleological promise but was to serve the specific function of example to the rest of Asia and counterexample to China.[27] By 1971, however, John Hall could say that "the heavy emphasis on modernization is clearly over," predicting inaccurately that the academic future would be the study of "tension models and confrontation situations."[28] Ezra Vogel's important book represented a different direction—the direction of Pacific Rim Discourse. Vogel's basic thesis is that Japan "modernized" by picking the best of what the world had to offer in administrative, fiscal, and productive technologies, and grafted these onto "Japanese" values, such as commitment to education, group organization, common goal-ism, and long-term planning-ism. The historicity of these "Japanese" values is, of course, unexamined in Pacific Rim Discourse. What is formative in Vogel's book, however, is the notion that in learning from Japan, the United States is really learning from a purified version of itself.

Much follows from this Vogelian moment. Social sciences once more fulfill their prescriptive promise, especially in "management science." By the end of the 1970s, the new management science became the most important cutting-edge component in American business schools. This reflects, of course, the explosive growth in the management-dependent service and information economy. It also reflects, however, the anxiety over productivity that characterizes the late seventies and eighties, despite a fundamentally expanding economy. Although management can rely, to a great extent, on workers' fear generated by the creation of a permanent high unemployment rate, fear itself is no solution to the productivity problem. Reconciling fear and the need for productivity increase is what is behind the new management. And the United States *can* learn from Japan. William Ouchi's *Theory Z: How American Business Can Meet the Japanese Challenge* (1981) is the most popular representative of a yearly increasing body of work on Japanese management following Vogel's exhortation.

26. See his introduction to *Origins of the Modern Japanese State*.
27. The nation as "counter-example" was a potent ideological construction in the late sixties and seventies. For example, Mexico would serve, during the Kennedy and Johnson administrations, as the Latin American counter-example to Cuba. It was for this reason that the United States lobbied so hard to have the 1968 Olympics in Mexico City.
28. Quoted in Dower, *Origins of the Modern Japanese State*, 65.

In the urge to learn from Japan, Confucianism gets created as a national characteristic capable of explaining the success of Japan and the NICs. It is a very Protestant (in the Weberian sense) Confucianism,[29] however, embodying a strong work ethic that respects hierarchies and education. The explanatory power of Confucian essentialism was even bought by some Asian countries on the Rim. Confucius was revived in China, and, starting in the late 1970s, the Singaporean Ministry of Education began to carry out a restructuring of secondary and higher education to include a more coherent Confucian curriculum (with the aid of Western scholars of Confucianism, such as A. C. Graham, Yu Ying-shih, and Tu Wei-ming!). Learning from the group-oriented "team management" style of the Japanese corporation has been articulated in very concrete ways in the United States, most notably in U.S.-Japanese joint ventures as that between Toyota and General Motors in the NUMMI plant in Fremont, California. What "team management" is to the purveyors of Pacific Rim Discourse, however, is experienced as "management by stress" by workers, as Mike Parker and Jane Slaughter have so forcefully documented in their 1988 study of Fremont's NUMMI plant, *Choosing Sides: Unions and the Team Concept.* Anxiety and stress have a newly dominant role in the daily experience of post-1974 economic life. Pacific Rim Discourse produces and offers a solution for that anxiety.

One measure of the success of the various "learn from Japan" programs, and the generalized perception in the United States of the interdependency of the U.S. and Japanese economies, can be gauged in a *New York Times*-CBS poll, which found that in 1985, a central year of Pacific Rim Discourse, only 8 percent of Americans characterized their feelings toward Japan as "generally unfriendly." This figure rose to 19 percent in July of 1989 and 25 percent in February of 1990,[30] reflecting the protectionist, isolationist impulses that arise at what I describe as the endpoint of Pacific Rim Discourse. The antiprotectionist character of Pacific Rim Discourse is strong up until the beginning of its demise in 1989–1990, recalling the ascendancy of antiprotectionism in the internationalism of the Roose-

29. Related to the Confucian-Protestant equation, Harry Harootunian, in an unpublished paper entitled "America's Japan and Japan's Japan," has pointed out the connection between Robert Bellah's *Tokugawa Religion* and his later coauthored book about community in the United States—*Habits of the Heart.*
30. These statistics are quoted in Charles Burress, "The Dark Heart of Japan Bashing," in *This World*, magazine supplement to the Sunday *San Francisco Examiner and Chronicle*, 18 Mar. 1990, 7.

velt years. Any American articulation of an internationalist discourse will, of course, be antiprotectionist. There are important differences, however, between Kennan's antiprotectionism and that characteristic of Pacific Rim Discourse.

At an address to a conference on the Pacific Rim in Laguna Niguel, California, in 1985, Reagan's secretary of state, George Schultz, said, "We are all members of the community of nations surrounding the Pacific. The Pacific has become the twentieth century's economic fountain of youth."[31] Schultz's anti-protectionism vis-à-vis Japan, at the very twilight of the Cold War (Gorbachev became premier in March 1985), represents a significant shift from Kennan's anxiety over American isolationism with regard to Western Europe. For Kennan, free trade was the legacy of the liberal enlightenment and was of a piece with Enlightenment notions of democracy and civil society. Kennan feared that without a strong identification with the values of Western Civilization, which he located geographically in Western Europe, U.S. anti-Soviet resolve could weaken and the United States itself could face internal decay. In Schultz's formulation, in Pacific Rim Discourse, civilization is conflated with the de-spatialized, purely temporal character of capital itself. The discontinuity between Cold War discourse and Pacific Rim Discourse could not be expressed more strongly.

In what follows, I will examine Pacific Rim Discourse in select locations, both institutional and generic, concluding with some speculation on the end of the discourse. It is natural that, given the coincidence of Pacific Rim Discourse and the information age, with its attendant anxieties over knowledge, Pacific Rim Discourse would be prominently staged in the U.S. academy. An article in the *Chronicle of Higher Education* on 17 May 1989 documented the proliferation of programs in Pacific Rim or Pacific Basin studies in American universities over the course of the 1980s. This has been a national phenomenon, but it is disproportionately present on the West Coast, particularly in California. The Pacific Rim Task Force was formed by the California state legislature in 1985, and it made numerous policy recommendations and reports to the legislature in 1986 and 1987. In 1986, the California state legislature passed ACR (Assembly Concurrent Resolution) 82, which mandated public institutions of higher education in California to assess ways of "meeting the needs of the state in furthering [California's] economic position and leadership within the Pacific Rim," to "carry out its responsibilities to immigrants of Pacific Rim countries," and to assess the

---

31. Publicity brochure, Center for Pacific Rim Studies, University of San Francisco.

need for Pacific Rim specialists, scholarly exchanges, and exchange programs, and for a Center for Pacific Rim Studies.[32] UCLA had opened its Center for Pacific Rim Studies (an interdisciplinary nondegree-granting research and teaching center) in 1985. UC San Diego won the University of California system's prize: the Graduate School of International Relations and Pacific Studies (IRPS). Several private colleges and universities in California, among them the University of San Francisco and Dominican College, have also established institutes of Pacific Rim studies. The 1987 report of the Pacific Rim Commission of California State Universities was entitled *The Future of the Pacific Rim Is Now*.

The publicity literature of nearly all of these institutions reveals the articulation of Pacific Rim studies as a business discourse. They are centered around the social sciences or on business/management curricula. All have significant degrees of multinational corporate funding. Those that offer graduate degrees, such as IRPS at UC San Diego, emphasize in their placement literature the new and special knowledge that their graduates possess to enable them to work in Pacific Rim institutions or locales. These institutions represent the next stage of evolution of the increasingly unfashionable "area studies" programs. "Area studies," in the United States, were tied ideologically and financially to U.S. defense strategy. It is only natural that as the Pacific Rim achieved discursive prominence in the waning years of the Cold War, business and economics would become its main foci in the academy.

The academically fashionable character of Pacific Rim studies, and the attendant amount of money going into it, has occasioned a significant amount of academic retooling, particularly among social scientists originally working on Latin America or Africa. East Asia is the right way to develop— its success is also the path to professional success for scholars working in development-related fields. Gary Gereffi is a sociologist at Duke University, whose earlier work was on Latin America but who, in 1990, with Donald Wyman, published *Manufacturing Miracles: Paths of Industrialization in Latin America and East Asia*. Gereffi noted in 1989 that "it is virtually impossible to find a conference on Latin American development that does not incorporate comparative research on East Asia."[33]

32. California Postsecondary Education Commission, Report 87-25, *Institutional Reports on Pacific Rim Programs*, Sacramento, Calif., 1987: 1.
33. Ellen K. Coughlin, "Confronting the 'Asian Century': Scholars Turn Westward to the Pacific Rim," *The Chronicle of Higher Education*, 35, no. 36 (17 May 1989), A10.

The discourses of newness and knowledge anxiety fueled a spate of special series and articles in newspapers and news magazines throughout the 1980s, with numerous cover stories in *Time, Newsweek, Fortune, Forbes*, and other publications. In 1985, the editors of *Time* magazine organized "Time Newstour '85," a month-long tour of East Asia by journalists and three dozen major corporate heads. In 1986, the *Los Angeles Times* inaugurated a weekly Pacific Rim supplement (which was discontinued by 1990).

The historical romance was an important source of the American imagining and essentializing of Asia. The founding text here, of course, is *Shogun*, James Clavell's best-seller, published in 1975. The tremendously popular television mini-series based on Clavell's book was first aired in 1980. *Shogun* romanticized the first Western contact with the then "new" Japan, a Japan that was hyperaestheticized, cultured, strong, and pure. Its hero triumphs and humanizes himself by "turning Japanese," underscoring Vogel's lesson, which was published in the same year as Clavell's book. There have been many *Shogun* spin-offs, mostly set in China.

Slightly more highbrow is a subgenre of novel I call the Japanese *Wanderjahre*. In these novels, young American men go to Japan for a year or two and either find themselves or muse on the confusion of life reflected in the odd juxtapositions that surround them (such as Coke machines in Buddhist temples). Jay McInerney's *Ransom* (1985) is typical of the subgenre in which the hero learns some aspect of traditional Japanese culture (karate, in this case) and thereby grows up and gains the centeredness and strength with which to combat American dissipation.[34] Brad Leithauser's *Equal Distance* (1985) is a mixture of the modern American family romance with the Hemingwayesque expatriate novel.[35] The debt to *The Sun Also Rises* is obvious, down to the triangular configuration of young angst-ridden male, cynical older expatriate male, and expatriate female love interest. Hemingway's earthy significations of the European "real" are replaced by the facilely essentialist cultural juxtapositions that provide the background to all work in this genre.

---

34. Another example of this subgenre is John David Morley's *Pictures from the Water Trade: Adventures of a Westerner in Japan* (Boston: Atlantic Monthly Press, 1985). In this case, the Western hero is initiated into the modern Japanese demimonde of bars and sex, and learns about life through his Japanese love affair.

35. See also, in this vein, John Burnham Schwartz, *Bicycle Days* (New York: Summit Books, 1989).

The use of the Japanese setting for what are otherwise fairly typical *bildungsroman* serves in part to naturalize the locationality of Japan. Although there is a certain amount of evocation of Japanese traditional customs, what is generally most exoticized in these novels are the very juxtapositions of "East" and "West" referred to above. The Coke machines are, in the paradoxical workings of Pacific Rim Discourse, more exotic than the Buddha images. *Equal Distance* also offers a cynical 1980s reading of the internationalist humanism of E. H. Norman and the Institute for Pacific Relations. The novel's protagonist is on leave from Harvard Law School, nominally serving, during a year in Japan, as research assistant to a Japanese professor of international law. The professor's fervent desire for a genuine international law based on moral principle is read as Japanese quirkiness, like those Coke machines in the temples.

During the fifteen years following the United States-China rapprochement, it seemed that nearly every American who spent more than two months in China wrote a book about it, thus The China Journal. These China journals took two main forms: accounts by journalists who had been posted in China after the "opening," [36] and more personal accounts written by Americans who had gone to China to teach or work. [37] A major subtext informing all of these writings was the Cultural Revolution. During the Cultural Revolution, China had been "closed." Now that China was "open," it was the newest land of the new. No U.S. writing about any other foreign country during this period approaches the volume of writing about China. Why the interest? The journalists' accounts pictured a repressive government and, depending on the particular journalist, a social structure embodying various degrees of repression. Nevertheless, there were important cases

36. A representative sample includes Fox Butterfield, *China: Alive in the Bitter Sea* (New York: Times Books, 1982); David Bonavia, *The Chinese* (New York: Lippincott and Crowell, 1980); John Fraser, *The Chinese: Portrait of a People* (New York: Summit Books, 1982); and all of the China-related writings of *New Yorker* writer Orville Schell.

37. This is a much longer list. Some randomly selected titles include: Lois Fisher-Ruge, *A Peking Diary: A Personal Account of Modern China* (New York: St. Martin's Press, 1979); Vera Schwarcz, *Long Road Home: A China Journal* (New Haven: Yale University Press, 1984); Richard Terrill, *Saturday Night in Baoding* (Fayetteville: University of Arkansas Press, 1990); Peter Brigg, *Shanghai Year: A Westerner's Life in the New China* (San Bernardino: Borgo, 1987); Mark Salzman, *Iron and Silk* (New York: Random House, 1986); Rosemary Mahoney, *The Early Arrival of Dreams: A Year in China* (New York: Fawcett Columbine, 1990); Bill Holm (with an introduction by Harrison Salisbury), *Coming Home Crazy: An Alphabet of China Essays* (Minneapolis: Milkweed Editions, 1990).

of individual heroism and massive evidence of the people's fundamental humanity and understandability.

Pictorially and representationally throughout most of the twentieth century, China had been the location of the human mass, the crowd—that surfeit of humanity which is, by its nature, inhuman. The China journals re-humanize. The "year in China" genre, often in diary form, is relentless in its depictions of the minutiae of the authors' daily lives: eating, shopping, traveling, teaching, and socializing. Daily life signifies humanity, and I locate these writings within Pacific Rim Discourse in that their familiarization of Chinese daily life serves to extend the discursive space of a generalized humanity to the world's most populous country and formerly most massively designated Other. There is also, however, in these writings, a note of nostalgia for a vanished sense of American daily life. China is somehow more "real," because the stakes of interpersonal relations are higher. Although the universalism that is demonstrated in Americans' ability to live in China, to understand China, and to make Chinese friends has in it some of the leftist humanist universalism we noted in Massignon and in *Amerasia*, it is recuperated discursively to new ends.

The role of film in the construction of the post–World War II global imaginary cannot be overstated. Just as Hollywood studios scripted the rhythms and motions of wartime daily life for American matinee-goers, so did the deluge of Hollywood films that hit Western Europe after V-E Day function as an advance guard for the Marshall Plan. European hearts and minds were won over from a recrudescent communism, or they at least softened toward international capitalism, by the big screen American visions of cleanliness, abundance, and speed. The facility with objects deployed so regularly in postwar Hollywood films—cigarette lighters, cocktail accessories, cars, clothes, et cetera—stimulated a commodity cathexis, a new kinetics of commodified culture, that helped consumption to proceed at its needed rapid pace. And while the United States played on Western European screens, a particular vision of Europe began to return to the United States. In the 1950s, and extending into the pre-Vietnam 1960s, as the United States became more and more accustomed to itself as the predominant global power, big Hollywood technicolor productions set in Europe began to appear with greater frequency, with stars such as Cary Grant, James Stewart, David Niven, Audrey Hepburn, and Doris Day. I refer to films such as *An American in Paris* (1951), *Roman Holiday* (1953), *To Catch a Thief* (1955), *Paris Blues* (1961), *Charade* (1963), and *The Two of Us* (1966). The European location shots give the films the look of the

most expensive travelogues ever made, full of long tracking shots and overheads of iconically European sites (the Roman forum, Notre Dame, the
Trevi Fountain, Mont Blanc . . .) from cranes and helicopters. The cinema-
scopic arrogance of these shots accords with the new American hubris, the
new post–Marshall Plan, Europe-directed internationalism. Europe is not
an exotic, as Asia continues to be represented in films during these years,
but a luxurious and hoary realm of material and historical excess, newly
consumable thanks to U.S. pluck and technical know-how. The colorful and
luxuriant foreign locale becomes, through this European origin, an important marketing device in American film and television (in television, note
the series "I Spy"), generally, and a significant reflection of American global
hegemony.

There were far fewer of these films after the beginning of the Vietnam War. Europe began to lose its signifying power, and the pattern of the
foreign locale seems to be more generalized, less overtly emblematic of
the U.S. position in the globe, and more purely visually exotic. There is no
definitive pattern of Pacific Rim films in the United States. Their numbers do
not match the number of films with European locales during the formative
era of American cinematic internationalism. The vocabulary of the Pacific
Rim location[38] can be traced, though, in two somewhat related films, one
produced at the beginning and one near the end of the period of Pacific Rim
Discourse: *The Yakuza* (1975, Sidney Pollack directs, Paul Schrader writes,
Robert Mitchum and Takakura Ken star) and *Black Rain* (1989, Ridley Scott
directs, Michael Douglas and Takakura Ken star).

In *The Yakuza*, the enemies are bad *yakuza* and bad American
gangster-capitalists who are in cahoots. (Difficult as it may be to imagine
now, the anticorporate message was fairly common in American films of the
late sixties and seventies). The heroes are Takakura's character, a retired,
honorable *yakuza*, and Mitchum's character, a World War II occupation
hand returning to the Japan he loves and to the women he has left behind.
Mitchum, in a spirit somewhat reminiscent of *Shogun*, grapples a lot with *on*
and *giri*, "traditional" Japanese values which he acquires and with which he
triumphs over evil. In *Black Rain*, the heroes are police (Takakura's character is a Japanese detective; Douglas's character is a New York detective
tracking a killer in Japan) and the villains are *yakuza*.[39] But the *most* evil

---

38. I except Vietnam War films, which are part of a different discursive trajectory.
39. Andy Garcia plays Douglas's fellow policeman, a happy, carefree, culturally sensitive,
virilely heterosexual American. In order for the Fiedleresque homoerotic miscegenation
subtext to proceed, he, of course, must meet an early death.

villain is a new breed of *yakuza*—young, immoral, and referred to in the film by older *yakuza* as being more like an American criminal. Takakura's character, through his association with Douglas's character, learns to be less stiff, less bound by the rules, to "go for it." Douglas's character, through his association with Takakura's, is purified. He was a corrupt cop in New York; now no more. The formula for success for Americans is, then, the "natural" American spirit purged of moral laxity. For Japanese, it is "Japanese" honor and humanity purged of bureaucratic inhibition and psychological rigidity. Americans need to work harder and to be less selfish; Japanese need to open up their closed psychic markets.

The visuals of the two films are also revealing. *The Yakuza* consists mainly of interior shots, which are either hypermodern office shots or hyper-aestheticized "traditional Japanese" residential interiors. The look of *Black Rain*, as in all of Ridley Scott's films, is one of its stars. It is very pointedly set in Osaka, with many shots establishing the hypercommercialized glitz and grit that is a Ridley Scott trademark. The film opens with an aerial shot of a smog-drenched sunrise as the camera pans down over an industrial district punctuated with smokestacks. One climactic scene is in an Osaka steel mill, which appears as an eerie mixture of Japanese automation and dark, American industrial heartland grit. The final scene—the big gun-down—is extra-cinematically emblematic of the nearing American economic decline that would be one of the end-markers of Pacific Rim Discourse. The earlier Osaka scenes were very expensive to shoot, and the finale, set on a *yakuza* country estate, had to be filmed on a very un-Japanese-looking Sonoma County vineyard. This locational dissonance was probably not noticed by most American viewers, partly because of the very Japanese-looking farmhouse constructed in the vineyard. I have been told that the owners of the vineyard were planning to convert the farmhouse into a restaurant.

Postnationalism or transnationalism has, of course, always been central to science fiction in books, comic books, and in films, and it is thus a natural location for Pacific Rim discursive moves. Philip K. Dick's *The Man in the High Castle* (1962), set largely in Japanese-occupied San Francisco (the Japanese and the Germans won World War II), is eerily prescient. Dick's fiction has had a strong influence on the newer sub-genre of cyberpunk, which posits a hyper–information age, postnational neural network of computers and artificial intelligence, and a withering of all boundaries—whether between nation and nation or between humans and machines. A Japanese-American linguistic and cultural mix and a trans-national, de-centered corporate authority structure inform such novels as William Gibson's trilogy and Bruce Sterling's *Islands in the Net* (1988), as well as new comic book titles, such as *Hard Boiled*, *Big Numbers*, and *Give Me Liberty*. The ocean gives way to "the net." Ridley Scott's film *Blade Runner* (1982), based on Dick's novel *Do Androids Dream of Electric Sheep* (1968), was very influential in providing the visual imaginary of this postcatastrophic, Asian-Californian demimonde mix,[40] and the visuals of *Blade Runner* have influenced all of the futuristically noir comic book series mentioned above.

Related to the cyberpunk trans-Pacific imaginary is the *anime* subculture in the United States, which consists largely of fan networks that report on and exchange Japanese *manga* and film—animation and live action—that are generally set in a dystopic future and involve violent clashes between humans and robots. *Akira*, an anticorporate apocalypse that had a limited commercial release in the United States, and *Gunhed*, a cheaply made multinational cloning of *The Terminator* and *Alien*, which exists in live-action and animated versions and which circulates primarily on bootlegged tapes in the *anime* subculture (there is at least one electronic bulletin board devoted to *anime*), are two examples of this. The *anime* subculture values the once-disparaged computer-generated artificiality of much Japanese animation, seeing in its animation technique—fewer variations between frames combined with wildly distorted mise-en-scène—a version of hacker-accessible high aesthetics suited to its members' garage-punk nihilism. The cyberpunk and *anime* enactments of the trans-Pacific postnation are largely dystopic—the alienated underside to the dominant character of Pacific Rim Discourse I have described thus far.

The End of Pacific Rim Discourse

Toward the end of the 1980s, several factors signal a weakening of the hold of Pacific Rim Discourse on the U.S. global imaginary. The failed movement in Tiananmen Square and the attendant sense that China might not, after all, be on the Rim taints one of the region's most tantalizing promises. More important was the end of the Cold War—in Berlin, Prague, Bucharest, and Moscow. The Pacific Rim as a localized, sheltered space, sheltered from the U.S.-USSR confrontation, loses some of its necessity.

40. The "director's cut" of *Blade Runner* was even stronger on the atmospheric visuals, and less centered on the film-noir ruminations of its central character, played by Harrison Ford. The Japanese cultural mix of *Blade Runner*, however, is original to Scott's film and is not a feature of Dick's novel.

The recent economic downturn in the United States, and the outbreak of Japan bashing that has accompanied it, undoubtedly has also contributed to the weakening of capital's global myth-engine.

A significant quantity of recent "Japan bashing"[41] signals a retreat from Pacific Rim Discourse internationalism. In two prominent examples, James Fallows's article "Containing Japan" (*Atlantic Monthly*, May 1989) and Clyde Prestowitz's book *Trading Places: How We Allowed Japan to Take the Lead* (1988), Japan is criticized precisely for being too Japanese, for subscribing too rigidly to its myth of uniqueness and, for Fallows, for having insufficiently developed universalist principles. Both of these writers show the desire to localize universality, which is the standard American nativist incarnation of bourgeois Enlightenment thought.

These critiques of a failed internationalism are matched by the post–Pacific Rim and by the post-1989 free marketeers who have abandoned even the wide confines of the Pacific. This is seen in Besher's use of the term "global rim,"[42] or in "management guru" Ken'ichi Omae's notion of the Interlinked Economy, which he elaborates in his recent book, *The Borderless World* (1990):

> An isle is emerging that is bigger than a continent—the Interlinked Economy of the Triad (the United States, Europe, and Japan), joined by aggressive economies such as Taiwan, Hong Kong, and Singapore. . . . It is becoming so powerful that it has swallowed most consumers and corporations, made traditional national borders almost disappear, and pushed bureaucrats, politicians, and the military toward the status of declining industries.[43]

Pacific Rim Discourse does not simply end. A recent conference of "Pacific Rim" business and trade representatives in San Francisco (September 1992) included several speeches suggesting that the Pacific Rim's fall from fashion in the wake of Europe's transformation might have been premature, in view of Europe's current difficulties. Yet, the functional lives of global imaginaries seem to be getting shorter and shorter—witness the early death of the New World Order or the two-week life span of Bill Clinton's New

41. On Japan bashing, see Masao Miyoshi, "Bashers and Bashing in the World," in Masao Miyoshi, *Off Center: Power and Cultural Relations between Japan and the United States* (Cambridge: Harvard University Press, 1991), 62–96.

42. Besher, *Pacific Rim Almanac*, xxi–xxii.

43. Ken'ichi Omae, *The Borderless World* (New York: HarperBusiness, 1990), x–xi.

Covenant. The American power structure's current imaginative vacuum—the bankrupting of American mythological image production capacity—is unparalleled in U.S. history.

Pacific Rim Discourse will have residual life in many of those areas where pure newness is the currency, such as in academic conference organizing and management seminars. Pacific Rim Discourse—perhaps the most obvious articulation of Paul Virilio's notion of the disappearance of space and time as tangible dimensions of social life—will resist the attempt to historicize it. Its mutation into "the global rim" is characteristic of its reach. But a failure to historicize it, and a failure to question its conceptual categories, can allow it to threaten even the most counter-hegemonic and oppositional projects. The current rewriting of Atlantic history, as in the work of Marcus Rediker and Paul Gilroy, is a valuable re-creation of a working-class Atlantic, or an Atlantic of the African Diaspora, that contests the Atlantic of Western imperialism. But perhaps there is a danger in working within the dominant conceptual category of the ocean, given that it is capital's favored myth-element. We should likewise be wary of constructing an oppositional Pacific Rim, seeing in its "dynamism" a new challenge to U.S. and European hegemony. Such challenges might, indeed, be taking place, across national boundaries and in the Pacific region. But let resistance write its own geography. We should always bear in mind how, why, and by whom the idea of the Pacific Rim was created. Here, in the early 1990s, when all transformations disappoint and nothing seems to really end, the need to historicize remains as great as ever.

Chemical Weapons Discourse
in the "South Pacific"

William A. Callahan and Steve Olive

Cultural production is a source of empowerment. The information age provides many channels for resistance to oppression. Indeed, faxes were instrumental in spreading the word about the massacre at Tiananmen Square within China, and videos were instrumental in getting word out into the provinces and to the world of the 1992 Bangkok massacre.

Yet, the way the media was managed by the United States Army during the Gulf War shows how cultural production in the information age is a double-edged sword. It is a tool that anyone can deploy: television sets and printing presses themselves have no politics. As the Thai Army argues about its responsibility for the hundreds of missing people: Where is the video to prove it? Blood on the streets does not matter as much as blood on celluloid.

We would like to thank Michael J. Shapiro, Geoff White, Rob Wilson, Arif Dirlik, and Hayden Burgess for their comments on various drafts of this essay—not to mention the comments from the three anonymous reviewers who rejected it for another publication. Carl Young's work in compiling documents and articles on Johnston Atoll has also been of immeasurable help.

The purpose of this essay, then, is to examine how the United States Army exerts its power not just with guns but also through the use of cultural signs as a different sort of weapon. The signs and representations in the army's discursive arsenal are used to suppress and control—in a word, manage—resistant voices to ensure that the army's mission is accomplished.

Rather than simply moralizing that the United States Army is good or bad, we argue that a close cultural analysis of the United States Army's representations is useful to show how bureaucratic workings of its deadly programs manage "the public," and thus "public opinion." This essay shows how the army frames policy statements in such a way as to guide the discourse to questions that will legitimate its actions and, perhaps more importantly, to guide the discourse away from questions that might serve to problematize its policies.

To illustrate the intimate relation of knowledge and power in this process, we will discuss the plan the United States Army developed to transport chemical weapons from Europe to Kalama Island[1] for incineration and disposal at the Johnston Atoll Chemical Agent Disposal System (JACADS) facility despite protests from a number of local, national, and international groups. JACADS is an important example, because it shows how cultural analysis and public policy analysis can aid each other: to understand the public policy of "chemical demilitarization," it is important to understand the discourse of the "South Pacific."

Though JACADS is certainly an example of the secretive nature of the United States Army, we should be clear that this essay is not concerned with conspiracy theories and secret information, or with the (private) motives of individual leaders or officers. Rather, it aims to show how the army manages resistance to its policies through the discourse of its *public* representations. In other words, we did not have to dig through documents released through the Freedom of Information Act. We are on the army's mailing list.

Just because we use the army's materials, however, does not mean that we are limited to their "propaganda." There are many meanings contesting each other in these seemingly straightforward "public information"

---

1. Even the naming of this patch of land in the Pacific is political. Hawaiians call it Kalama Island, while the United States government calls it Johnston Atoll.

documents. In shaping this "discursive event," the army concentrated on the "Why" questions, arguing that chemical weapons disposal is part of a narrative of disarmament, and on certain "How" questions, assuring the public through a narrative of technical expertise that the process is scientific and thus safe for affected populations.

This tactic was demonstrated most clearly when Colonel Moss, the commander of the facility on Kalama Island, slipped into "Why" questions when the "How" questions of public safety were asked too loudly. His response was, "Wouldn't the world be a better place without these chemical weapons?"

In this essay, we follow Hawaiian activist Hayden Burgess's response to this question: "Yes, but why are you destroying weapons made in America and deployed in Europe in the Pacific?" Indeed, we cannot let the thrill of disarmament blind us as to how it is carried out and who bears the costs, especially when this "disarmament" is actually an upgrading for a "new generation" of chemical weapons.[2]

The narrative of safety can be politicized by temporarily shifting the military's line of inquiry from "What (JACADS is)" and "Why (it needs to be done)" to issues surrounding the question words "Who (is making the decisions)," "Where," and "When (will these decisions be carried out)." While "What" and "Why" questions are more metaphysical and tend to naturalize the procedure, the "Who," "Where," and "When" queries can raise some of the many environmental and human rights questions that have been repressed in the chemical weapons disposal discourse as the army has ordered it.

All of these political questions are wrapped up in the issue of "How" the discourse was produced. In short, we focus on *the technology of the "chemical weapons disposal" discourse*, rather than on *the technology of the JACADS incinerators*, as the army does.

---

2. The arsenal of unitary chemical weapons is being destroyed to make the way for an expanded arsenal of binary chemical weapons. "By 1987 the Pentagon, with congressional approval, was producing a new generation of ecologically safe chemical weapons, the binaries. These two-part warheads could not produce poison gas unless their two chemical components mixed. . . . In exchange, the Pentagon agreed to destroy all the old unitary gas weapons." See Hesh Kestin, "They May Not Be Weapons at All," *Forbes*, 18 Sept. 1989, 45.

Geography and Representations

Geography is central in both the positioning of JACADS (in the "empty" Pacific) and the (Pacific Islanders') resistance to it. Yet, is it a physical geography or a symbolic geography that is at issue? The answer to this question is "yes," and to see how the symbolic and physical geographies are intertwined, we need to go to *South Pacific*, if not to the South Pacific itself.

The film *South Pacific* is an entertaining example of the production and management of signs to create representations and thus to direct meaning within the Pacific context.[3] This film, which was produced in Hollywood and is one of the few links for the (mainland) American audience with the "Pacific Islands," is thus both a product and a producer of the myth of the "South Pacific."

The film is also helpful in explaining how the United States Army and recent presidents form their policies: considering his World War II military service record as a pilot in the Pacific War theater, George Bush could very well have been a character in *South Pacific*. Jimmy Carter blurred the physical and symbolic even more when he sent James A. Michener, author of *Tales of the South Pacific*, on which the film is based, as well as the Com-SoPac historical officer for the Pacific War,[4] to be the U.S. representative at Vanuatu's independence declaration on 30 July 1980.

So how was the "South Pacific" produced in this film? Though the title of the film tells us it is about "the Pacific," the story is more about Americans and Europeans (like the most recent Pacific narrative centered around Kalama). The setting in the Pacific is mostly for the scenery. And when the Natives *do* appear in this film, which is billed as a representation of the "South Pacific," they are not (clearly) Pacific Islanders. The sacred island of Bali-h'ai has Tonganese/Tonkinese[5] living on it, yet the scenes

3. Joshua Logan, director, and Buddy Adler, producer, South Pacific Enterprises, Inc., 1958.

4. James A. Michener, *Tales of the South Pacific* (New York: Macmillan Company, 1947). In 1942, Michener was ordered "to start compiling a history of the Navy . . . in these waters" (James A. Michener, *The World Is My Home: A Memoir* [New York: Random House, 1992], 52).

5. The management of races is fascinating in both the film and the book. There is a blurring of the Asia and the Pacific that follows history: the French brought laborers from Indochina to work on their Pacific plantations. Bloody Mary looks like a Tongan, yet her daughter Liat is clearly Tonkinese. (And the actress playing Liat is herself a blurring of Asia and Europe in both parentage and name: France Nuyen.)

contain a scattered mixture of romanticized representations from all over the Pacific and Asia.[6] In short, the film is an admixture of various "exotic" cultures that serves to build a myth of the "Paradise of the South Pacific," even though the film was shot in the North Pacific space of the Hawaiian island of Kaua'i, not to mention the Hollywood sets.

George Bush reproduces this romanticized representation in the closing remarks of the "United States-Pacific Island Nations Summit," which was held in October 1990 to address the Pacific Island leaders' concerns about JACADS:[7]

> The Pacific Islands have a special place in the minds and hearts of the American people. And on my own visits, starting almost fifty years ago, I've witnessed the natural charm of the Island peoples and the natural beauty of the Islands. Their reputation is well deserved.[8]

The natural charms and beauties are blatantly constructed in *South Pacific* through an obvious manipulation of colors as signs. Film producer Buddy Adler states in an amazing promotional brochure for the film, "We hope we have captured the magic of the 'South Pacific.'" Just after this natural description, however, Adler tells us of the technical marvels of this magic of color: "Cinematographer Leon Shamroy introduced revolutionary ideas to create the imaginative moodlighting which subtly accentuates the romance of a moment or a melody's enchantment."[9] The Pacific itself is not charming or romantic enough, for red and blue filters are used not so "subtly" to manage the color to evoke the passion of the paradise of Bali-h'ai. Yellow,[10] orange, and pink are deployed for the toast of two lovers on "Some Enchanted Evening." The whole sequence of scenes for "Bali-h'ai" is shrouded in a soft focus of color once this paradise is reached. This management of color is hard to read at first; with the significant power of

6. Though Vanuatu is in Melanesia, the film credits list a group of actors under the heading "the Polynesians."

7. Actually, it is more accurate to say that Bush came to Hawai'i in October 1990 to campaign for the Republican candidate for Senate in a very close election race. The "United States-Pacific Island Nations Summit" was in many ways an afterthought; Bush did not come to Hawai'i until it was campaign season.

8. George Bush, "Text of Remarks by the President at the Conclusion of the United States-Pacific Island Nations Summit" (East-West Center, 27 Oct. 1990, Mimeographed), 1.

9. "South Pacific" (South Pacific Enterprises, Inc., 1958, promotional brochure).

10. This yellow coloring reminded one observer at a seminar of mustard gas, one of the first chemical weapons.

the signs of music and song, one is swept away like breezes through the mists of dried ice. The shock of signification comes when the "coloration" is removed and the characters are back to "normal."

Indeed, there are so many shifts in color that it is difficult to gauge what is "real"—are the nights really so royal blue in the "South Pacific"?—but actually, Michener's insistent statements aside,[11] none of it is "real." The story is a complex of representations, it is a multilayered myth far removed from any nameable time or place. The film itself is hard to pin down; indeed, it comes at the end of a chain of representations. It is based on a Broadway play, originally produced by Richard Rogers, Oscar Hammerstein II, Leland Hayward, and Joshua Logan, which in turn is based on James A. Michener's World War II stories from *Tales of the South Pacific*.

No one can locate this elusive Bali-hʻai on a map. Many have speculated about Bali-hʻai's location and origin.[12] Michener was stationed in Vanuatu (then the New Hebrides) on Espíritu Santo, yet there is no island in the location that he charts for us. A geographer of the Pacific, Charles Johnston (no relation to the Charles Johnston after whom Kalama was renamed) speculates that Bali-haʻi might have some relation to the Indonesian island of Bali. He notes that because of its beaches, coral, and surf, Bali was an elite tourist destination in the Pacific before World War II.[13]

Yet, today, the symbolic/physical geography has shifted. During World War II, another geographical entity, "Southeast Asia," was created as a war theater to include islands such as Bali. The Pacific now starts in the snowcapped mountains of New Guinea. Indeed, "Bali-hʻai" and the "South Pacific" are unstable concepts. Michener has recently revealed that the name *Bali-haʻi* is taken from "one of the most miserable Melanesian villages" located on Mono Island in the Solomon Islands.[14] And although this instability adds to the power of the mystery and the magic, the image still needs to be managed: "Bali-haʻi" is an empty sign that needs to be filled up with meaning. In short, *South Pacific* is not a simple reflection of a place; the film was directed to produce a new space.

11. In both the book and the promotional brochure for the film, Michener insists that the stories are REAL, "compos[ing] a report of what life was actually like on a Pacific backwater" (from the promotional brochure). And remember, Michener was the "historical officer" of the United States Navy.

12. Even its spelling varies from Michener's book—*Bali-hʻai*—to the film brochure's rendering of *Bali Haʻi*.

13. Interviews at the Geography Department, University of Hawaiʻi, January 1991.

14. Michener, *The World is My Home*, 184.

To some extent, this representation is directed by the powerful relationship between the military and the "South Pacific": for example, Michener was writing not a history of the Pacific but a "history of the [United States] Navy . . . in these waters."[15] And in the opening sequence of the film, the following statement is superimposed on a "tropical beach scene" with swaying palms at sunset:

> The Producers thank the Department of Defense, the Navy Department, the United States Pacific Fleet, and the Fleet Marine of the Pacific for their assistance in bringing this motion picture to the screen.

"South Pacific," then, is an example of the construction of meaning through a management of signs. It is not a place in relation to the physical geography of the equator (South) and a large body of water (Pacific), so much as in the symbolic space of power relations. The "South Pacific" is not a place but a discourse.

In what follows, we will examine the army's more sophisticated positioning of topics such as technology and disarmament to justify the construction of the JACADS facility as part of its latest cultural production of the "South Pacific": the North Pacific island called, in Hawaiian, Kalama.

Chemical Weapons Settings

During World Wars I and II, lethal and highly toxic chemical weapons were manufactured in the United States by the army. Most of these weapons were stored at military bases in the United States, while the rest were shipped to Europe and Okinawa. In 1970, the Okinawans and the Japanese demanded that the weapons on Okinawa be removed, thus they then were shipped to Kalama Island.

Because these rockets are now obsolete and have begun to leak, the United States Congress mandated that all nerve gas rockets stored within the United States be destroyed by 1995. An Environmental Impact Statement (EIS) was written by the army, which argued that the best method for disposing of the nerve gas rockets would be to incinerate them on-site at Johnston Atoll and on the other eight army bases where the rockets are currently stored, because transporting these weapons would be "too risky."

Despite a great deal of public protest, the EIS was adopted in 1988,

15. Michener, *The World is My Home*, 52.

and incinerators were scheduled to be built at the eight storage sites on the continental United States and at Kalama. The incinerator at Kalama was completed and started chemical weapons disposal on 30 June 1990. It was then scheduled to be tested for eighteen months to ensure safety of the technology before other incinerators on the mainland United States could begin construction.

In February 1990, however, there was a new development. European chemical weapons were added to the list of Pacific-based rockets to be destroyed at JACADS. The army thus submitted a draft supplemental to the 1988 EIS that would allow it to meet President Bush and Chancellor Helmut Kohl's commitment to transport nerve gas weapons out of Germany to Kalama by the end of 1990.

This shift in plans—from destroying chemical weapons on-site to shipping them halfway around the world to Kalama—aroused much public opposition. The EIS process mandates a public hearing and a period of time for the public to write comments pertaining to the EIS before it becomes final. Therefore, on 20 March 1990, a public hearing was held, and the deadline for public comments was set for 26 March 1990.[16]

This meeting brought together the United States Army's arsenal of technical and cultural artifacts. A close reading of the process of public policy through the military's use of public hearings, glossy brochures, and EIS documents demonstrates the production of "public opinion" through the "South Pacific." Cultural theory can help to analyze the symbolic workings of the military—the symbolic workings that have very physical effects on the North Pacific as well as the "South Pacific."

Legitimization: Safety

The main topic of the cultural productions of "chemical demilitarization" is safety, and we will analyze how safety is deployed before examining

---

16. All of the sophisticated cultural/technical arguments aside, this hearing is an example of the abuse of the public review process. According to U.S. law, the army was required to hold a public hearing and allow public comment on the EIS before it was accepted.

The army attempted to limit the impact of this public hearing by (1) releasing the draft copy of the EIS only a short time before the public hearing; (2) limiting the distribution of the EIS; and (3) allowing only six days for the public to submit written comments after the public hearing. Clearly, the army was trying to exclude other arguments by limiting the time frame in which the public could review the intensely technical document. Is this an example of the army's commitment to full information?

the army's program on other, more overtly political fronts. The army utilizes a complex network of signs to focus on the strong points of its plan to incinerate the weapons, while at the same time drawing attention away from the weak points of the plan.

These diverse sets of representations have a unifying theme: they serve to naturalize the army's statements, shifting them from arguments for possible options to just reports of the "facts" of their policies. "Naturalize" here refers to the process whereby a discourse hides its own process of production and thus limits the critique.

In its public representations, the army appeals to the naturalizing power of photographs and the discourse of science. Although they seem beyond manipulation, photographs are orchestrated productions of light, and the practice of natural science contains value decisions, such as which questions should be asked and which ones should not. Using Roland Barthes's terms, one could say that the army utilizes these naturalizing signs to re-present the myth of disarmament and safety: "Myth consists in turning culture into nature or, at least, the social, the cultural, the ideological, the historical into the 'natural.' "[17] Photography and science both efface questions of how, where, and when their discourses are produced, focusing on what the picture is and why science studies chemical weapons. Umberto Eco's definition of semiotics, then, seems frighteningly appropriate here with the army's management of "public opinion": "Semiotics is in principle the discipline studying everything which can be used in order to lie."[18]

One of the artifacts in this network is an informational brochure, entitled "The United States Chemical Stockpile Disposal Program," which was distributed at the public hearing on 20 March 1990.[19] In many ways, this brochure parallels the promotional brochure for *South Pacific* mentioned above in its framing of the discourse in a positive way.

The informational brochure, produced by the military to sell its public policy, provides an intriguing entrance into the analysis of the United States Army's discourse of chemical weapons disposal, which utilizes technical reports, public performances, as well as popular culture[20] and advertising.

17. Roland Barthes, *Image/Music/Text* (New York: Hill and Wang, 1977), 165.

18. Umberto Eco, *A Theory of Semiotics* (Bloomington: Indiana University Press, 1976), 7.

19. United States Army, "The United States Chemical Stockpile Disposal Program" (Program Manager for Chemical Demilitarization, Office of the Chief of Public Affairs, Aberdeen Proving Ground, Maryland, 1990).

20. There is a gift shop on Johnston Atoll that sells things such as postcards and commemorative calendars to celebrate the military in the Pacific and the history of JACADS.

The promotional brochure, which was produced by the Program Manager for Chemical Demilitarization, serves as an exemplary case of the management of signs for legitimization through the rhetoric of "the natural." It functions much like the advertising of the promotional brochure for *South Pacific* and its technical marvels that produced natural charms.

The army's ten page, full-color glossy publication is packed with signs: a written text laid out around figures, maps, and photographs, with a patriotic eagle always in the upper right-hand corner. (The SANE and Greenpeace informational xeroxes, which were available on a different table at the hearing, literally paled in comparison to the army's slick brochure.) Yet, as in other military representations, important things are missing from this sophisticated cultural/technical production. Indeed, there are no page numbers, thus making it unac-count-able and hard to quote.

This complex brochure tells many stories, and it is useful to temporarily divide the narrative of chemical weapons disposal into the visual and verbal-written texts to see how they interrelate. In many ways, the two texts *are* separate and free-floating: there are few captions to tie the verbal and visual texts together. More to the point, the two sets of texts often work against each other. While the written text is committed to—as one subheading tells us—RAISING THE LEVEL OF KNOWLEDGE, the visual discourse, with its pretty pictures, serves to raise the level of distraction in our increasingly postliterate society.

It is very easy to just flip through this attractive brochure looking only at pictures and pausing on boldfaced headings, such as HISTORY OF OUR COMMITMENT, FOCUS ON SAFETY, and PROTECTING THE PUBLIC AND THE ENVIRONMENT. The visual signs draw one's attention away from the "information."

For example, the above-mentioned section entitled RAISING THE LEVEL OF KNOWLEDGE, which reportedly "provides information on the characteristics and effects of the two primary categories of chemical agents designated for destruction" (page seven), has three visuals: (1) a photograph of a white man instructing a white woman in a park-like setting, (2) a photograph of a pristine lake, and (3) a figure representing molecular struc-tures. Yet, what is the purpose of these visuals? Rather than "keeping the public informed" (page seven), the visuals actually have little to do with the "characteristics and effects" of chemical weapons. They certainly do not show the effect that chemical weapons have on people and the environment; rather, they tend to naturalize the argument by (1) appealing to pleasant scenes of nature and education, while (2) adding the scientific legitimation of a chemical diagram. The diagram is meaningless, however, in these same scientific terms, because it is unlabeled.

Photography and Progress

These seemingly disjointed pictures, charts, and graphs are woven into a particular narrative. The visuals of the brochure are part of an argument of (scientific and social) PROGRESS trying to explain (away) the horrors of chemical weapons in an upbeat fashion. Progress here is a linear movement from the "bad past" (the Dark Ages) upward to a rational solution of the problems and thus a better life (the Enlightenment).

For example, on what would be pages five and six, the chemical weapons disposal program is related to the narrative of progress in a representation of a step-by-step process that moves like an arrow diagonally upward from the lower left to the upper right to join PUBLIC SAFETY (page five) with MOVING TOWARD OUR GOAL (page six). The box that is the last step says "Process complete" and "Goal achieved" before the recurrent eagle flies away from the upper right-hand corner of the brochure.

The discourse of progress is also conveyed through the technical means of photography. The historical narrative of progress and moral betterment through technical means is even more powerfully produced through the juxtaposition of color and black-and-white photography in the promotional brochure: as in *South Pacific* and its promotional brochure, bright colors are for good times.

This tactic is most apparent on the cover of the brochure, where a black-and-white photo of artillery shells stored aboveground in a wooded area is positioned behind a color photo of a different wooded area with no weapons. The story that the photographs tell seems again to have little to do with the brochure title, "The United States Chemical Weapons Disposal Program," which is written above them. There is no mention that the shells in the black-and-white photo are the ones that contain the nerve gas. Actually, the nerve gas canisters are currently being stored underground or in sealed igloos. The army's brochure, however, legitimizes the disposal program by making it appear as if the rockets in the black-and-white photo will just magically disappear, and the forest will return to full color.

Unfortunately, the events have shown that this colorized disappearing act is another of the army's performances of the "magic of the South Pacific": European weapons disappear into the Pacific, while Pacific Islanders have to deal with the problems and the chemical by-products of "chemical demilitarization." "Demilitarization," then, is actually quite an accurate description of chemical weapons disposal. The chemicals do not disappear, they are not completely destroyed. They are honorably discharged into carcinogenic civilian chemicals.[21]

This myth of an immaculate process of progress is repeated throughout the visual text of the brochure: the only other black-and-white photo is over the first section, HISTORY OF OUR COMMITMENT; it again represents the past in the trope of enlightened progress. All the other photographs and figures in the brochure are in color and are generally pleasing to the eye.

Science and Safety

As we have seen with the photographic rhetoric, the discourse legitimizes the chemical weapon disposal program by using signs that show the positive impacts of the program, while at the same time ignoring negative consequences. The discourse achieves this goal by concentrating on the "Why" and "How" questions—the depoliticized questions of technology, which naturalize the discourse through "natural science" and scenes of "natural beauty." This section addresses how the rhetoric of expertise and the rhetoric of science are used in the brochure, in the Environmental Impact Statements, and in public hearings to naturalize the army's projects.

Logic and probability theory are man-made sign systems that link knowledge to language.[22] The JACADS discourse often utilizes the "objective and neutral" logic of science and probability theory to present the program. Yet, these scientific discourses, methods, and technical jargon are used only when these sign systems are advantageous to the army's project.

---

21. Part of the resolution adopted on 10 December 1990 by the Hawaii Medical Association reads, "Many scientific studies have shown that the incineration of hazardous wastes with state-of-the-art technology release, in the form of gaseous emissions, residual ash, and effluents of pollution control devices, uncombusted chemicals, heavy metals, and newly formed chemical products of incomplete combustion including polychlorinated dioxins and polychlorinated furans."

The EPA's only response to questions of dioxins and furans is, "We do not expect the significant formation of such products" ("Johnston Atoll: Questions and Answers," U.S. Environmental Protection Agency, Region IX, 75 Hawthorne Street, San Francisco 94105, no. 1 [Dec. 1990], 2).

22. Michel Foucault, The Order of Things: An Archeology of the Human Sciences (New York: Random House, Pantheon Books, 1970).

The brochure legitimizes the project through the discourse of expertise by stating, "The disposal process has been endorsed and is overseen by the prestigious National Academy of Sciences" (page two) and that the army has "more than sixteen years of extensive testing and experience in employing environmentally sound methods for disposing of chemical agents" (page 5). These statements are misleading, however. Incineration of these types of chemical weapons has never been done before nor proven to be completely safe. Therefore, what is the meaning of a "prestigious" organization fully endorsing an unproven technology and the army's claim of "years of experience" when this kind of technology has never been safely used before? These statements are even more confusing when one recognizes that the army's history of chemical disposal on Kalama itself is hardly noteworthy: part of the island is off-limits to personnel because of a spillage of Agent Orange in the early 1970s; and after it became operational, JACADS released traces of nerve gas on 8 December 1990.[23]

To overcome its own history, the army uses technical jargon to legitimate the project and lead the public to believe that the disposal system is safe. The orderly and rational phrases "normal operations" and "standard operating procedures" are often pronounced at public hearings and written in the EIS to allay public concerns. Just what *are* "normal operations" and "standard operating procedures," and what happens when something unexpected occurs?[24]

In brochures and public hearings, the army also uses the phrase "state-of-the-art" technologies. But, again, what does this phrase mean? It means only that the chosen technology is the best one available of its kind, which does not necessarily mean that the technology is safe. As the *Marshall Islands Journal*, the Hawaii Medical Association, and people attending the 1990 public hearing all comment, state-of-the-art incinerator technologies may not be safe enough in dealing with lethal chemical weapons.[25]

What about disposal techniques other than incineration? How do they rate in terms of safety? This is a question that cannot be asked within the army's vocabulary. Though Dr. Wayne Landis, formerly head of the environmental toxicology at Aberdeen Proving Grounds, criticized the army

23. Jim Borg, "Johnston Incinerator Leaks Trace of Nerve Gas," *Honolulu Advertiser*, A3.
24. For example, the Johnston Atoll 1991 calendar lists two serious hurricanes that struck the island in the 1980s.
25. *Marshall Islands Journal* 16, no. 38 (1985):4; Resolution of the Hawaii Medical Association (10 Dec. 1990); and Public Hearing (20 Mar. 1990).

for its unreasonable "failure to consider alternative disposal methods,"[26] once the incineration project was chosen, it automatically became state-of-the-art. Since there was no adequate technology available for chemical weapons disposal, this "state-of-the-art" naming is tautological—any other detoxification process chosen would likewise have been "state-of-the-art" due to the funding for research and development. With this management of the discourse, media such as the *Honolulu Advertiser* can state in their editorials that disposal at Kalama is "the best, if not the only, near-term alternative," instead of thinking of long-term responsibilities or asking for whom it is best.[27]

How were such questions managed? The military presented its case at a public hearing in downtown Honolulu on 20 March 1990 with the discursive weapons of "science and expertise," which were loaded with state-of-the-art cultural ammunition. The simple placement of the microphone, the logistics of the room, and other proto-discursive moves show how the discourse of "public opinion" was managed by the army.

The meeting and its outcome were orchestrated with the authority of science in mind. Uniformed army officers in charge of managing the EIS sat at the front table raised above the "public." Their presentations were anchored in technological discourse, using a highly specialized military language for this public meeting. They used large olive drab overheads to outline their objectives.

Though the meeting was billed as a "public hearing," the physical setting for the meeting was arranged in a way that decreased the significance of the large crowd that gathered there. The podium with the microphone for the "public voice" was placed so that the "public" would face the committee, not the audience.

The moderator, a woman with a southern United States accent, often mispronounced non-European names, drawing smiles from the brass at the front of the table. As a result, the army, with its use of language, served to delegitimize the local speakers by mispronouncing their names. When people *did* get a chance to speak, the conversation was limited. The overheads narrowed the discussion to areas that the army was comfortable in discussing.

Still, even within the confines of this technical discourse, many disturbing problems with the EIS were raised. Even with the short period—six

26. "The Battle for Johnston Atoll," *Pacific Islands Monthly*, Sept. 1990, 7.
27. *Honolulu Advertiser* (13 Aug. 1990), A8.

days—for comment, many agreed that the EIS was an incomplete document, with some even going so far as to characterize the EIS as "shoddy." The army excluded some important environmental impact data from the 1990 EIS: there is no discussion of the endangered species located around Kalama that could be threatened by a release of nerve gas into the ocean environment.[28] There is no mention in the 1990 EIS of who is liable for the cleanup and compensation for damaged parties should an accident occur involving these weapons.[29] The information paper handed out at the public hearing stated, "The United States is responsible for all security and emergency response functions." Yet, can the U.S. government guarantee to pay for the cleanup and compensation should a major accident occur?

Lastly, there is the question of JACADS and international law. Ocean dumping and incineration are already outlawed by the London Convention on the Prevention of Marine Pollution by Dumping Wastes and Other Matter of 1972.[30] Incineration at Kalama could be seen as ocean incineration, especially since most of Kalama's land surface is man-made—bulldozed-over living reefs, that is.[31]

Yet, the army's cultural-technical arsenal managed the discourse to overwhelm these crucial scientific, policy, and legal concerns.

Silences and Safety

The confusing noise of technical discourse disguises the silences where the "natural" logic breaks down into the political issues of time, place, and actor: who, where, and when. The army states that full information has been disclosed regarding the chemical weapons disposal program and that it is committed to "raising the level of knowledge" of the public.

The army, however, in its control of the discourse, enforces a divi-

28. Alfred Picardi, Greenpeace review of Johnston Atoll Chemical Agent Disposal System (JACADS) 1988 Final Draft Supplemental Environmental Impact Statement (Greenpeace International, Washington, D.C., 1989).

29. Ian Anderson, "Destruction of Chemical Arms Comes Under Fire," *New Scientist*, 4 Aug. 1990.

30. See "Convention on the Dumping of Wastes at Sea," *Journal of World Trade Law* 7 (1973):485, and Ursula Wasserman, "Attempts at Control Over Toxic Waste," *Journal of World Trade Law* 15 (1981):410.

31. Testimony of Jon M. Van Dyke, Professor of Law, William S. Richardson School of Law, and Director of the University of Hawai'i Institute for Peace, Public Hearing (20 Mar. 1990).

sion of knowledge that authorizes the narrow range of questions that can be asked about the disposal of the chemical weapons. Hence, not only are the technical arguments that might make one doubt the safety of JACADS managed through the discourse but, perhaps more importantly, this technical discourse evades the more political issues that would question the location, timing, and personnel of the project. At an "information meeting" on 20 August 1990,[32] a common response to public query was, "Sorry, that's outside the area we are prepared to address today," or "We can't comment on matters under litigation." These were silences uttered with a smile.

The army also exercises a strategy of divide and contain through knowledge. Rather than writing one document to address the disposal of German-based chemical weapons on Kalama, the army had three separate documents addressing (1) transportation within Germany, (2) ocean transport (The Global Commons Report), and (3) the unloading and incineration of nerve gas at Kalama (the 1990 supplemental EIS).

By separating these functions into separate documents, the discourse managed the project plan in such a way to make it difficult for resistance groups to protest the whole program. The army did not speak about the accumulated risks of the entire disposal program from Europe to Kalama and thus discouraged a connection between the resistance groups in Hawai'i and those in the rest of the world.

For example, at the public hearing in March 1990, the army wanted to hear comments only on the Johnston Atoll EIS and not on the other documents. The other two documents were unavailable at the public hearing and are difficult, if not impossible, for the general public to obtain for "national security" reasons.[33] The army would not reveal the authors of these reports nor let people know how they could obtain a copy of them. Though the army is obligated to solicit comments only from U.S. citizens regarding the Johnston Atoll EIS, it is unclear who can make comments on the other two documents.

Hence, the army separated resistance groups from each other to limit the impact of each one. It was difficult for the people in Europe who objected to transportation to join forces with the people of the Pacific who

32. The meeting was to address the extension of the permit allowing the storage of chemical weapons under the Resource Conservation and Recovery Act (RCRA).
33. Department of the Army, Final Second Supplemental Environmental Impact Statement for the Storage and Ultimate Disposal of the European Chemical Munitions Stockpile (Program Manager for Chemical Demilitarization, Aberdeen Proving Ground, Maryland), 1990.

protested the JACADS disposal—since the Global Commons Report for the ocean shipment of chemical weapons was secret, there was no opportunity for protest at all. The Pacific Island Nations, which would perhaps be most affected by the JACADS program, had no legal way to voice their concerns regarding the Global Commons Report, the 1990 EIS for Kalama, or transportation in Europe. They would receive the risks, without having representation in the decision-making process.

Another rhetorical tactic pervades the "scientific discourse" of the EIS. The army reversed the "logic" used in a previous decision regarding the disposal of the chemical weapons; therefore, it had to manage the interpretation of its reverse in logic. In the 1988 EIS, the army stated that the best method was to incinerate the weapons on-site where they were currently being stored, because transportation of the weapons was too risky. The undersecretary of the Department of the Army, James Ambrose, spoke out strongly against the transportation of the weapons at the public hearings held on the U.S. mainland at the other eight storage sites. Major Phil Soucy said, "We feel destroying it [the nerve gas] where it is, is the safest way possible to get rid of it. It is much better than moving it all over the planet."[34] But today, the army has done just that—moved the weapons all over the planet—without any change in state-of-the-art technology, stated reason, or even recognition that it had said otherwise at another time and place.

The 1988 EIS states that the incinerator built at Kalama would be used to destroy only the weapons already stored there. The 1990 EIS states that the incinerator will also be used to destroy the European stockpile, and then it will be shut down. What will be the next EIS mandate for incineration at Kalama? Does the army have more materials it wants to incinerate there? These are some of the questions that the "public" asked, but the army refused to answer.

Actually, the army cannot answer them. It cannot guarantee that more weapons will not be shipped to Kalama, because that is a political decision that can be—and has been—made and unmade. In his summit with Pacific Island leaders, President Bush did not say that no more chemical munitions or hazardous wastes will be burned on Kalama; he said, "We have no plans."[35] And as Pacific Islanders have seen, plans change.

The way the army presents it, there are no other options than Kalama. The Aberdeen Proving Grounds in Maryland, which is scheduled to have

34. The Bureau of National Affairs, *Environmental Reporter* 18 (1988):37.
35. Bush, "Concluding Remarks," 2.

an incinerator built soon, is much closer to Germany than Kalama. Yet, the 1990 Supplemental EIS states that this was not a viable option because the nerve gas would have to pass through the Chesapeake Bay, which is an "environmentally sensitive area."[36] What the army did not say is that the Chesapeake Bay is more polluted than Kalama. Kalama is a national wild-life refuge and a bird sanctuary. It is surrounded by a coral reef and is likely to be much more "environmentally sensitive" than the Chesapeake Bay—just look at the fish and coral in the army's Johnston Atoll 1991 calendar.

The army's promotional brochure, the media, and Hollywood movies are helpful in explaining this double standard. When listing the chemical weapons disposal sites, the brochure lists only the continental U.S. facilities by name in the text and on a map. Kalama is mentioned only as being a test facility in the remote Pacific: "A full-scale facility will first be operated at the isolated Johnston Atoll in the Pacific" (page five). When the chemical weapons shipment out of Germany started in July 1990, Tom Brokaw, anchor for NBC news, disclosed the name of the village—Klausen—in Germany but said that the weapons were being shipped "to an island in the Pacific." Klausen has a name, it has citizens, it can be photographed. Kalama is empty and nameless—it is restricted to JACADS personnel.

This nameless empty notion of the Pacific has a history with the U.S. military. Recall that according to the U.S. government, Kalama was nameless and had to be (re)named with a proper Anglo-American appellation in 1858: Johnston Atoll. According to the U.S. military, the Pacific is not just an empty ocean, but even the islands seem empty and nameless until the soldiers add value. Indeed, Kalama has value only when it is full of waste: first the United States was interested in its guano, now there is JACADS.

In the promotional brochure for *South Pacific*, James Michener provides a telling mix of the images of the Pacific and the military. When he names "his island" in the "Pacific backwater," it is not the native name, or even a European imperialist name, but the United States Navy's appellation "CASU-10"—which makes perfect sense, since he was hired not to write the history of the Pacific but to write the history of the United States Navy in the Pacific. And in the opening lines of the film *South Pacific*, what is the response when Joe Cable asks the pilot, "What are those islands over

36. Alfred Picardi, Greenpeace Review of Johnston Atoll Chemical Agent Disposal System (JACADS) 1988 Final Draft Supplemental Environmental Impact Statement (Greenpeace International, Washington, D.C.), 1989.

there?" The answer he gets is not a name or a place but simply the relevant military signifier: "Japanese."

Indeed, this is not a problem of just the military but an issue that pervades discussions of the Pacific. *American Lake: Nuclear Peril in the Pacific* is a remarkable book that carefully analyzes the terrifying plans for nuclear war in the Pacific. Yet, the authors also talk little about the Pacific itself. Though highly critical of U.S. military policy in the Pacific, they basically adopt the discourse of the "South Pacific" as something that is flown over to more important things. The discussion revolves around the Pacific Rim, largely bypassing the islands in the Pacific Basin, to discuss Korea, Southeast Asia, and Australia/New Zealand.

Even though the antinuclear movements in Vanuatu, Belau, and even Hawai'i are mentioned, these exemplary movements are mentioned only in passing—sometimes as just otherwise nameless "island states."[37] It is worth noting that Michener's "South Pacific" is Vanuatu, and the film was shot in Hawai'i—two centers of antinuclear activity. These are ignored, however, since the Pacific is still someone else's lake.

Thus, Kalama Island and the surrounding Pacific Ocean are represented by American media—both military and civilian—as being empty and nameless. The Pacific is then deemed remote enough to swallow up the First World's toxic garbage. It is deemed "responsible," because Kalama and the other islands are far enough away from "American shores" to be insignificant.

Chemical Reactions in the Pacific

The U.S. government uses this rhetoric of responsibilities against the interests of the Pacific, saying that the United States was responsible for the weapons and was obligated to take them out of Germany. Thus, it is time to shift the questions of safety to questions of responsibility and democracy: responsible to whom, and just who is responding? In *South Pacific*, the only islanders of interest are "exotic" women and children—who are probably Asian. So who is deciding where to dispose of European chemical weapons, and who is affected in the new "South Pacific"?

The army evades the political aspect of the "Where" and "Who"

37. Peter Hayes, Lyuba Zarsky, and Walden Bello, *American Lake: Nuclear Power in the Pacific* (New York: Penguin, 1986), see especially 10, 404, and 420.

questions. The decision to incinerate in the Pacific was made in Bonn and Washington, D.C.: a North Atlantic problem was solved by sending it to the "South Pacific."

Indeed, the political show of "chemical demilitarization" is much like the song and dance in *South Pacific*. Bush sang to Kohl much like (the American) Nellie sings of her problems with (the European) Emile in the film. This song of Euro-American relations is "born on the opposite sides of the sea." Which sea, however? Nellie sings her song by the shore of the Pacific, not the Atlantic, just as George Bush and the army sang in the Pacific about current problems in the Atlantic alliance without Pacific voices in the policy-making process.

Bush, the army, and the State Department merely reported what was being done to Pacific Islanders. At the 1990 annual South Pacific Commission Meeting, Australia aided the United States Army and even used some of its tactics against the Island leaders: "An Australian foreign affairs cable spell[ed] out tactics, agreed upon with the Americans, to 'manage' the debate."[38] One of these tactics was for Australia to withhold scientific reports until the last moment, so that informed criticism would be difficult—just as in the EIS process in Honolulu.

The song and dance of chemical weapons disposal thus eroded other political processes by excluding the Pacific region's leaders. And when the criticism from Pacific Island leaders continued, the U.S. government demonstrated that it wants only agreement with its policies: on 11 September 1990, the State Department stated that it was "insulted" by Pacific Island leaders' persistent protests after "information sessions."

Concerned citizens in Honolulu also questioned the JACADS program, which activists saw as another example of a white patriarchal organization dumping its wastes into the Pacific, far away from white populations. The group wondered why the army was willing to heed to the German's request to take the nerve gas out of their country and transport it into the fishing areas and marine environment of Pacific Islanders. The Pacific Islanders did not build or support the construction of these weapons, and they were not protected by the weapons stored in Europe. "Why do the Germans have more influence than Pacific Islanders—in the Pacific?" many protestors asked.

While this may seem a rhetorical question in Washington or Bonn,

38. Karen Mangnall, "A Tale of Two Hotels," *Pacific Islands Monthly*, Sept. 1990, 11.

in Honolulu it was a question of survival. In the public meeting of March 1990, some of the Hawaiian nationalists tried to utilize the power/knowledge dynamic by switching language as a means of resistance. Naming is a method of exercising power, so resistance groups referred to the island by its Hawaiian name—Kalama—rather than its Anglo-American name—Johnston. Some speakers used the Hawaiian language at times to express their concerns, which disrupted the army's dominant, jargon-filled discourse. The spokesperson for the Hawaiian nation ended her testimony by pleading with the army to "please listen to our pleas."[39] This was after she shifted the podium so that she could speak to the audience, not just to the army brass.

This use of language and positioning served to help highlight the racial nature of the program and thus to consolidate Hawaiian resistance, but it was ignored by the army. The army's response to these speakers was no response—another silence. The army was not capable of addressing the argument on these terms; therefore, it simply ignored these speakers or swept them away as General Buss did in August 1990 by thanking Marsha Joiner for her "eloquence."

In many ways, it was a "privilege" to even air these concerns. The public hearings were held only in Honolulu, Hawai'i, excluding any input by the peoples of the Pacific. Pacific Islanders, perhaps remembering Bikini nuclear testing, have unanimously opposed the JACADS project. The army's response to this reportedly was: "There's no good reason to hold hearings in Micronesia. There will be no impacts. Even if you're right next to it downwind there's going to be no problem."[40]

The South Pacific Commission thought otherwise, drawing its conclusions in terms of a "science of marine environments" as opposed to the army's "science of the continents": "Unfortunately, islands are not totally isolated from the rest of the biosphere. The oceanic and atmospheric systems surround them and link them with the rest of the world."[41] And as one doctor put it, "It is a real worry that Pacific Islanders, including we

---

39. Testimony of Marsha Joiner, 20 Mar. 1990.
40. *Marshall Islands Journal* 16, no. 30 (20 Sept. 1985):16.
41. *South Pacific Commission Environmental Newsletter*, no. 3 (Feb. 1980), 11. Or as Jean-Marie Tjibaud of the New Caledonian Government Council put it in 1982, "The great ocean that surrounds us carries the seeds of life. We must ensure that they don't become the seeds of death" (Hayes et al., *American Lake*, 393).

in Hawaii . . . may be vulnerable to contamination via our fish and other migratory creatures." [42]

The army's response, once again, was no response. The EIS was again accepted and the JACADS program rolled on.

Conclusion: Policy Proposals

Even with the army's elaborate deployment of its cultural arsenal of "science and silences" to overwrite the "illogical" decisions that were made on very political grounds, certain things are clear: the United States Army manufactured chemical weapons, and it is now responsible for the destruction of this stockpile. Rather than limiting ongoing critique of JACADS to the issues of public policy, however, and thus limiting the response to a lamentation of the army's production of what Hayden Burgess accurately describes as "a public policy process gone haywire," [43] it would be useful to examine the army's responsibility—to make it respond better to affected people.

As this essay has argued, a critique of army policy involves confronting not just the discourse of "chemical demilitarization" but also the discourse of the "South Pacific." With the information age, public policy analysis is not complete without a cultural analysis of the context that frames the JACADS project and thus produces the disputes. Cultural theory, then, is useful in the task of forming a public policy that will not reproduce these relations of power and waste. Cultural theory is vital when the goal is not just to shift the microphone at public meetings but to reorganize the production of the discourse—both technical and cultural.

The army should not have such exclusive control over the environmental impact assessment process. The disposal program must be produced and reviewed by a more diverse group of organizations—local, national, and international—with specific action taken to include Pacific Islanders.

A possible solution would be to prepare an EIS that covers all phases of the project, so that a full range of alternatives can be developed and considered by the army, U.S. citizens, nongovernmental organizations, inter-

42. Testimony of Steven Moser, M.D., EPA Public Hearing, 11 Dec. 1990, Honolulu, Hawai'i, 3.
43. See Mary Adamski, "Johnston Island Gas-burning Foes Fear Contamination via Food Chain," *Star Bulletin*, 12 Dec. 1990, 3.

national organizations, and other countries. The EIS should be written by an autonomous organization that solicits input from a variety of reputable sources and should be reviewed by all nations who would be affected by the decision. This solution would be very time-consuming and expensive; however, it would lead to a safer and more equitable outcome, and set an example of thinking of environmental problems in global terms as well as serving to rewrite the "South Pacific." This solution would shift the knowledge/power relationship, whereby the army would, as Trihn T. Mihn-ha writes, "commit [it]self to understanding and by understanding, choosing to share [its] power,"[44] thus changing some of the actors in the "South Pacific," as well as the songs they sing.

44. Trihn T. Mihn-ha, *Woman Native Other* (Bloomington: Indiana University Press, 1989), 86.

Shrinking the Pacific

Lawson Fusao Inada

The problem, as I see it, is *water*.
Not that there's too much or too little of it—

because there's always been exactly, precisely,
just enough water to go around
and around and up and down the world,
again and again and again and again and again—

but *where* it is has bearing on my existence.
Now, this is simply my own personal perspective,
but just this once, on my own initiative,
permit me to conduct a little experiment:

I'll hold the world in my hands
and, slowly, slowly, easily, appropriately,
proceed to squeeze some land together,
proceed to make some water move elsewhere,
and, there, without inconveniencing anybody,

I've gone and done it: Shrunk the Pacific.

Notice that everything still lines up
accordingly:

> Sydney with Santiago,
> Manila with Acapulco,
> Canton with Mazatlán
> (with Taipei/Honolulu
> conveniently between),
> and then there's Tokyo
> offshore San Francisco.

Pretty neat, eh? All these proximities
and possibilities to deal with, enjoy . . .
Like, it's no big deal for me to simply
drive over to the coast now, overlooking
the Pacific Inlet, hop a ferry, a plane,
or maybe even take the gleaming bridge,
and bop into and around Hokkaido for lunch.

Maybe stay the night, or come back to Oregon,
which, by now, is full of Hokkaido tourists.
Neighbors, actually—it's hard to tell which.

Ah, yes—tired of those West Coast places?
Let's go to Japan! Let's go to Asia!
Or, let's just sit here, overlooking
the Inlet at all those mountains and lights!

The Atlantic, of course, is just *gigantic*—
but, oh, well, that's their problem to deal with.
In the meantime—where am I? Hungry, again.

Memory

Lawson Fusao Inada

Memory is an old Mexican woman
sweeping her yard with a broom.
She has grown even smaller now,
residing at that vanishing point
decades after one dies,
but at some times, given
the right conditions—
an ordinary dream, or practically
anything in particular—
she absolutely looms,
assuming the stature
she had in the neighborhood.

This was the Great Valley,
and we had swept in
to do the grooming.
We were on the move, tending
what was essentially

someone else's garden.
Memory's yard was all that
in miniature, in microcosm:
rivers for irrigation,
certain plants, certain trees
ascertained by season.
Without formal acknowledgment,
she was most certainly
the head of a community, American.

Memory had been there forever.
We settled in around her;
we brought the electricity
of blues and baptized gospel,
ancient adaptations of icons,
spices, teas, fireworks, trestles,
newly acquired techniques
of conflict and healing, common
concepts of collective survival . . .

Memory was there all the while.
Her house, her shed, her skin,
were all the same—weathered—
and she didn't do anything, especially,
except hum as she moved;
Memory, in essence, was unmemorable.

Yet, ask any of us who have long since left,
who have all but forgotten that adulterated place
paved over and parceled out by the powers that be,
and what we remember, without even choosing to,
is an old woman humming, sweeping, smoothing her yard:
    Memory.

Turning It Over

Lawson Fusao Inada

According to Nilak,
it's a custom,
a tradition,
a way of being

to reach
down and turn
over a piece
of driftwood—

"just to
give it some
relief."
See:

                                                     sun

                                    head
                                    neck

```
                 arm       arm
           hand      body      hand
                 leg       leg

      driftwood     foot     foot
```

ocean ice/shoreline snow/ice/rocks/sand/permafrost   tundra/continent

Now, keeping
with that
concept,

consider
this poem
driftwood:

Turn it over!

Our Sea of Islands

Epeli Hau'ofa

This essay raises some issues of great importance to our region, and offers a view of Oceania that is new and optimistic. What I say here is likely to disturb a number of men and women who have dedicated their lives to Oceania and for whom I hold the greatest respect and affection, and will always.

In our region there are two levels of operation that are pertinent to the purposes of this essay. The first is that of national governments and regional and international diplomacy, in which the present and future of the Pacific islands states and territories are planned and decided. Discussions here are the preserve of politicians, bureaucrats, statutory body officials, diplomats and the military, and representatives of the financial and busi-

"Our Sea of Islands" originally appeared in the book *A New Oceania: Rediscovering Our Sea of Islands*, published by the School of Social and Economic Development of the University of the South Pacific, in association with Beake House, 1993. Reprinted with permission of the publisher.

I would like to thank Marshall Sahlins for convincing me in the end that not all is lost and that the world of Oceania is quite bright despite appearances. This essay is based on lectures delivered at the University of Hawai'i at Hilo, and the East West Center, Honolulu, March/April, 1993. Vijay Naidu and Eric Waddell read a draft of this paper and made very helpful comments. I am profoundly grateful to them for their support.

ness communities, often in conjunction with donor and international lending organizations, and advised by academic and consultancy experts. Much that passes at this level concerns aid, concessions, trade, investment, defense and security, matters that have taken the Pacific further and further into dependency on powerful nations.

The other level is that of ordinary people, peasants and proletarians, who, because of the poor flow of benefits from the top, skepticism about stated policies and the like, tend to plan and make decisions about their lives independently, sometimes with surprising and dramatic results that go unnoticed or ignored at the top. Moreover, academic and consultancy experts tend to overlook or misinterpret grassroots activities because these do not fit in with prevailing views about the nature of society and its development. Thus views of the Pacific from the level of macroeconomics and macropolitics often differ markedly from those from the level of ordinary people. The vision of Oceania presented in this essay is based on my observations of behavior at the grassroots.

Having clarified my vantage point, I make a statement of the obvious, that is, that views held by those in dominant positions about their subordinates could have significant consequences on people's self-image and on the ways that they cope with their situations. Such views, which are often derogatory and belittling, are integral to most relationships of dominance and subordination, wherein superiors behave in ways or say things that are accepted by their inferiors who, in turn, behave in ways that serve to perpetuate the relationships.

As far as concerns Oceania, derogatory and belittling views of indigenous cultures are traceable to the early years of interactions with Europeans. The wholesale condemnation by Christian missionaries of Oceanic cultures as savage, lascivious, and barbaric has had a lasting effect on people's views of their histories and traditions. In a number of Pacific societies people still divide their history into two parts: the era of darkness associated with savagery and barbarism; and the era of light and civilization, ushered in by Christianity.

In Papua New Guinea, European males were addressed and referred to as "masters," and workers as "boys." Even indigenous policemen were called "police boys." This use of language helped to reinforce the colonially established social stratification along ethnic divisions. A direct result of colonial practices and denigration of Melanesian peoples and cultures as even more primitive and barbaric than those of Polynesia can be seen in the attempts during the immediate postcolonial years by articulate Melanesians to rehabilitate their cultural identity by cleansing it of its colonial taint and denigration. Leaders like Walter Lini of Vanuatu and Bernard Narokobi of Papua New Guinea spent much of their energy extolling the virtues of Melanesian values as equal to if not better than those of their erstwhile colonizers.

Europeans did not invent belittlement. In many societies it was part and parcel of indigenous cultures. In the aristocratic societies of Polynesia, parallel relationships of dominance and subordination with their paraphernalia of appropriate attitudes and behavior were the order of the day. In Tonga, the term for commoners is *me'a vale*, the "ignorant ones," which is a survival from an era when the aristocracy controlled all important knowledge in the society. Keeping the ordinary folk in the dark and calling them ignorant made it easier to control and subordinate them.

I would like, however, to focus on a currently prevailing notion about islanders and their physical surroundings that, if not countered with opposite and more constructive views, could inflict lasting damage on people's image of themselves, and on their ability to act with relative autonomy in their endeavor to survive reasonably well within an international system in which they have found themselves. It is a belittling view that has been unwittingly propagated mostly by social scientists who have sincere concern for the welfare of Pacific peoples.

According to this view, the small island states and territories of the Pacific, that is, all of Polynesia and Micronesia, are much too small, too poorly endowed with resources, and too isolated from the centers of economic growth for their inhabitants ever to be able to rise above their present condition of dependence on the largesse of wealthy nations.

Initially, I agreed wholeheartedly with this perspective, and I participated actively in its propagation. It seemed to be based on irrefutable evidence, on the reality of our existence. Events of the 1970s and 1980s confirmed the correctness of this view. The hoped-for era of autonomy following political independence did not materialize. Our national leaders were in the vanguard of a rush to secure financial aid from every quarter; our economies were stagnating or declining; our environments were deteriorating or were threatened and we could do little about it; our own people were evacuating themselves to greener pastures elsewhere. Whatever remained of our resources, including our Exclusive Economic Zones, was being hawked for the highest bid. Some of our islands had become, in the words of one social scientist, "MIRAB Societies," that is, pitiful microstates condemned forever to depend on migration, remittance, aid, and bureaucracy, and not on any real economic productivity. Even the better resource-endowed Melanesian countries were mired in dependency, indebtedness, and seemingly endless social fragmentation and political instability. What hope was there for us?

This bleak view of our existence was so relentlessly pushed that I began to be concerned about its implications. I tried to find a way out but could not. Then two years ago I began noticing the reactions of my students when I described and explained our situation of dependence. Their faces crumbled visibly, they asked for solutions, I could offer none. I was so bound to the notion of "smallness" that even if we improved our approaches to production for example, the absolute size of our islands would still impose such severe limitations that we would be defeated in the end.

But the faces of my students continued to haunt me mercilessly. I began asking questions of myself. What kind of teaching is it to stand in front of young people from your own region, people you claim as your own, who have come to the university with high hopes for the future, and to tell them that their countries are hopeless? Is this not what neocolonialism is all about? To make people believe that they have no choice but to depend?

Soon the realization dawned on me. I was actively participating in our own belittlement, in propagating a view of hopelessness. I decided to do something about it, but I thought that since any new perspective must confront some of the sharpest and most respected minds in the region, it must be well researched and thought out if it was to be taken seriously. It was a daunting task indeed. I hesitated.

Then came invitations for me to speak at Kona and Hilo on the Big Island of Hawai'i at the end of March 1993. The lecture at Kona, to a meeting of the Association of Social Anthropologists in Oceania, was written before I left Suva. The speech at the University of Hawai'i at Hilo was forming in my mind and was to be written when I got to Hawai'i. I had decided to try out my new perspective although it had not been properly researched. I could hold back no more. The drive from Kona to Hilo was my "road to Damascus." I saw such scenes of grandeur as I had not seen before: the eerie blackness of regions covered by recent volcanic eruptions; the remote majesty of Maunaloa, long and smooth, the world's largest volcano; the awesome craters of Kilauea threatening to erupt at any moment; and the lava flow on the coast not far away. Under the aegis of Pele, and before my very eyes, the Big Island was growing, rising from the depths of a mighty sea. The world of Oceania is not small; it is huge and growing bigger every day.

The idea that the countries of Polynesia[1] and Micronesia are too

1. For geographic and cultural reasons I include Fiji in Polynesia. Fiji, however, is much bigger and better endowed with natural resources than all tropical Polynesian states.

small, too poor, and too isolated to develop any meaningful degree of autonomy, is an economistic and geographic deterministic view of a very narrow kind, that overlooks culture history, and the contemporary process of what may be called "world enlargement" carried out by tens of thousands of ordinary Pacific islanders right across the ocean from east to west and north to south, under the very noses of academic and consultancy experts, regional and international development agencies, bureaucratic planners and their advisers, and customs and immigration officials, making nonsense of all national and economic boundaries, borders that have been defined only recently, crisscrossing an ocean that had been boundless for ages before Captain Cook's apotheosis.

If this very narrow, deterministic perspective is not questioned and checked, it could contribute importantly to an eventual consignment of groups of human beings to a perpetual state of wardship wherein they and their surrounding lands and seas will be at the mercy of the manipulators of the global economy and World Orders of one kind or another. Belittlement in whatever guise, if internalized for long, and transmitted across generations, could lead to moral paralysis and hence to apathy and the kind of fatalism that we can see among our fellow human beings who have been herded and confined to reservations. People in some of our islands are in danger of being confined to mental reservations, if not already to physical ones. I am thinking here of people in the Marshall Islands, who have been victims of the U.S. atomic and missile tests.

Do people in most of Oceania live in tiny confined spaces? The answer is "yes" if one believes in what certain social scientists are saying. But the idea of smallness is relative; it depends on what is included and excluded in any calculation of size. Thus, when those who hail from continents, or islands adjacent to continents—and the vast majority of human beings live in these regions—when they see a Polynesian or Micronesian island they naturally pronounce it small or tiny. Their calculation is based entirely on the extent of the land surfaces that they see.

But if we look at the myths, legends and oral traditions, and the cosmologies of the peoples of Oceania, it will become evident that they did not conceive of their world in such microscopic proportions. Their universe comprised not only land surfaces, but the surrounding ocean as far as they could traverse and exploit it, the underworld with its fire-controlling and earth-shaking denizens, and the heavens above with their hierarchies of powerful gods and named stars and constellations that people could count on to guide their ways across the seas. Their world was anything but tiny. They thought big and recounted their deeds in epic proportions. One legendary Oceanic athlete was so powerful that during a competition he threw his javelin with such force that it pierced the horizon and disappeared until that night, when it was seen streaking across the skyline like a meteor. Every now and then it reappears to remind people of the mighty deed. And as far as I'm concerned it is still out there, near Jupiter or somewhere. That was the first rocket ever sent into space. Islanders today still relish exaggerating things out of all proportions. Smallness is a state of mind.

There is a gulf of difference between viewing the Pacific as "islands in a far sea" and as "a sea of islands."[2] The first emphasizes dry surfaces in a vast ocean far from the centers of power. When you focus this way you stress the smallness and remoteness of the islands. The second is a more holistic perspective in which things are seen in the totality of their relationships. I return to this point later. It was continental men, namely Europeans, on entering the Pacific after crossing huge expanses of ocean, who introduced the view of "islands in a far sea." From this perspective the islands are tiny, isolated dots in a vast ocean. Later on it was continental men, Europeans and Americans, who drew imaginary lines across the sea, making the colonial boundaries that, for the first time, confined ocean peoples to tiny spaces. These are the boundaries that today define the island states and territories of the Pacific. I have just used the term "ocean peoples" because our ancestors, who had lived in the Pacific for over 2000 years, viewed their world as a "sea of islands," rather than "islands in the sea." This may be seen in a common categorization of people as exemplified in Tonga by the inhabitants of the main, capital island, who used to refer to their compatriots from the rest of the archipelago, not so much as "people from outer islands" as social scientists would say, but as *kakai mei tahi* or just *tahi*, "people from the sea." This characterization reveals the underlying assumption that the sea is home to such people.

The difference between the two perspectives is reflected in the two terms used for our region: Pacific Islands and Oceania. The first term, "Pacific Islands," is the prevailing one used everywhere; it connotes small areas of land surfaces sitting atop submerged reefs or seamounts. Hardly any anglophone economist, consultancy expert, government planner, or development banker in the region uses the term "Oceania," perhaps because it sounds grand and somewhat romantic, and may connote something so vast that it would compel them to a drastic review of their perspectives and

2. I owe much to Eric Waddell (pers. comm.) for these terms.

policies. The French and other Europeans use the term "Oceania" to an extent that English speakers, apart from the much maligned anthropologists and a few other sea-struck scholars, have not. It may not be coincidental that Australia, New Zealand, and the U.S., anglophone all, have far greater interests in the Pacific and how it is to be perceived than have the distant European nations.

"Oceania" connotes a sea of islands with their inhabitants. The world of our ancestors was a large sea full of places to explore, to make their homes in, to breed generations of seafarers like themselves. People raised in this environment were at home with the sea. They played in it as soon as they could walk steadily, they worked in it, they fought on it. They developed great skills for navigating their waters, and the spirit to traverse even the few large gaps that separated their island groups.

Theirs was a large world in which peoples and cultures moved and mingled unhindered by boundaries of the kind erected much later by imperial powers. From one island to another they sailed to trade and to marry, thereby expanding social networks for greater flow of wealth. They travelled to visit relatives in a wide variety of natural and cultural surroundings, to quench their thirst for adventure, and even to fight and dominate.

Fiji, Samoa, Tonga, Niue, Rotuma, Tokelau, Tuvalu, Futuna, and Uvea formed a large exchange community in which wealth and people with their skills and arts circulated endlessly. From this community people ventured to the north and west, into Kiribati, the Solomon Islands, Vanuatu, and New Caledonia, which formed an outer arc of less intensive exchange. Evidence of this is provided by existing settlements within Melanesia of descendants of these seafarers. (And it would have to be blind landlubbers who would say that settlements like these, as well as those in New Zealand and Hawai'i were made through accidental voyages by people who got blown off course presumably while they were out fishing with their wives, children, pigs and dogs, and food-plant seedlings, during a hurricane.) Cook Islands and French Polynesia formed a community similar to that of their cousins to the west; hardy spirits from this community ventured southward and founded settlements in Aotearoa, while others went in the opposite direction to discover and inhabit the islands of Hawai'i. And up north of the equator one may mention the community that was centered on Yap.

Melanesia is supposedly the most fragmented world of all: tiny communities isolated by terrain and at least one thousand languages. The truth is that large regions of Melanesia were integrated by trading and cultural exchange systems that were even more complex than those of Polynesia and Micronesia. Lingua francas and the fact that most Melanesians were and are multilingual make utter nonsense of the notion that they were and still are babblers of Babel. It was in the interest of imperialism, and it is in the interest of neocolonialism, to promote this blatant misconception of Melanesia.[3]

Evidence of the conglomerations of islands with their economies and cultures is readily available in the oral traditions of the islands concerned, and in blood ties that are retained today. The highest chiefs of Fiji, Samoa, and Tonga, for example, still maintain kin connections that were forged centuries before Europeans entered the Pacific, in the days when boundaries were not imaginary lines in the ocean, but rather points of entry that were constantly negotiated and even contested. The sea was open to anyone who could navigate his way through.

It would be remiss of me not to mention that this was the kind of world that bred men and women with skills and courage that took them into the unknown, to discover and populate all the habitable islands east of the 180th meridian. The great fame that they have earned posthumously may have been romanticized, but it is solidly based on real feats that could have been performed only by those born in and raised with an open sea as their home.

Nineteenth-century imperialism erected boundaries that led to the contraction of Oceania, transforming a once boundless world into the Pacific islands states and territories that we know today. People were confined to their tiny spaces, isolated from each other. No longer could they travel freely to do what they had done for centuries. They were cut off from their relatives abroad, from their far-flung sources of wealth and cultural enrichment. This is the historical basis of the view that our countries are small, poor, and isolated. It is true only in so far as people are still fenced in and quarantined.

This assumption, however, is no longer tenable as far as the countries of central and western Polynesia are concerned, and may be untenable also of Micronesia. The rapid expansion of the world economy since the post–World War II years may indeed have intensified Third World dependency, as has been noted from certain vantage points at high level aca-

---

3. I use the terms Melanesia, Polynesia, and Micronesia because they are already part of the cultural consciousness of the peoples of Oceania. Before the nineteenth century there was only a vast sea in which people mingled in ways that today's European-imposed threefold division has not been able to eradicate: the "boundaries" are permeable. This important issue is, however, beyond the purview of this essay.

demia, but it also had a liberating effect on the lives of ordinary people in Oceania, as it did in the Caribbean islands. The new economic reality made nonsense of artificial boundaries, enabling the people to shake off their confinement and they have since moved, by the tens of thousands, doing what their ancestors had done before them: enlarging their world as they go, but on a scale not possible before. Everywhere they go, to Australia, New Zealand, Hawai'i, mainland U.S., Canada and even Europe, they strike roots in new resource areas, securing employment and overseas family property, expanding kinship networks through which they circulate themselves, their relatives, their material goods, and their stories all across their ocean, and the ocean is theirs because it has always been their home. Social scientists may write of Oceania as a Spanish Lake, a British Lake, an American Lake, and even a Japanese Lake. But we all know that only those who make the ocean their home and love it, can really claim it theirs. Conquerors come, conquerors go, the ocean remains, mother only to her children. This mother has a big heart though; she adopts anyone who loves her.

The resources of Samoans, Cook Islanders, Niueans, Tokelauans, Tuvaluans, I-Kiribatis, Fijians, Indo-Fijians, and Tongans, are no longer confined to their national boundaries; they are located wherever these people are living permanently or otherwise. This is as it was before the age of Western imperialism. One can see this any day at seaports and airports throughout the central Pacific where consignments of goods from homes-abroad are unloaded, as those of the homelands are loaded. Construction materials, agricultural machinery, motor vehicles, other heavy goods, and myriad other things are sent from relatives abroad, while handcrafts, tropical fruits and rootcrops, dried marine creatures, kava and other delectables are dispatched from the homelands. Although this flow of goods is generally not included in official statistics, yet so much of the welfare of ordinary people of Oceania depends on an informal movement along ancient routes drawn in bloodlines invisible to the enforcers of the laws of confinement and regulated mobility.

It should be clear now that the world of Oceania is neither tiny nor deficient in resources. It was so only as a condition of colonial confinement that lasted less than a hundred of a history of thousands of years. Human nature demands space for free movement, and the larger the space the better it is for people. Islanders have broken out of their confinement, are moving around and away from their homelands, not so much because their countries are poor, but because they had been unnaturally confined and severed from much of their traditional sources of wealth, and because it is in their blood to be mobile. They are once again enlarging their world, establishing new resource bases and expanded networks for circulation. Alliances are already being forged by an increasing number of islanders with the *tangata whenua* of Aotearoa and will inevitably be forged with the native Hawaiians. It is not inconceivable that if Polynesians ever get together, their two largest homelands will be reclaimed in one form or another. They have already made their presence felt in these homelands, and have stamped indelible imprints on the cultural landscapes.

We cannot see the processes outlined above clearly if we confine our attention to things within national boundaries, and to the events at the upper levels of political economies and regional and international diplomacy. Only when we focus our attention also on what ordinary people are actually doing rather than on what they should be doing, can we see the broader picture of reality.

The world of Oceania may no longer include the heavens and the underworld; but it certainly encompasses the great cities of Australia, New Zealand, the U.S., and Canada. And it is within this expanded world that the extent of the people's resources must be measured.

In general, the living standards of Oceania are higher than those of most Third World societies. To attribute this merely to aid and remittance, which latter is misconstrued deliberately or otherwise as a form of dependence on rich countries' economies, is an unfortunate misreading of contemporary reality. Ordinary Pacific people depend for their daily existence much, much more on themselves and their kinfolk wherever they may be, than on anyone's largesse, which they believe is largely pocketed by the elite classes. The funds and goods homes-abroad people send their homeland relatives belong to no one but themselves. They earn every cent through hard physical toil in their new locations that need and pay for their labor. They also participate in the manufacture of many of the goods they send home; they keep the streets and buildings of Auckland clean, and its transportation system running smoothly; they keep the suburbs of the west coast U.S. trimmed, neat, green, and beautiful; and they have contributed much, much more than has been acknowledged.

On the other hand islanders in their homelands are not the parasites on their relatives abroad that misinterpreters of "remittance" would have us believe. Economists do not take account of the social centrality of the ancient practice of reciprocity, the core of all Oceanic cultures. They overlook the fact that for everything homelands relatives receive they reciprocate with goods they themselves produce, and they maintain ancestral roots and lands for everyone, homes with warmed hearths for travellers to return to at the end of the day, or to re-strengthen their bonds, their souls and their identities before they move on again. This is not dependence but interdependence, which is purportedly the essence of the global system. To say that it is something else and less is not only erroneous, it denies people their dignity.

What I have said so far should already have provided sufficient response to the assertion that the islands are isolated. They are clearly not. Through developments in high technology, communications and transportation systems are a vast improvement on what they were twenty years ago. These may be very costly by any standard, but they are available and used. And telecommunications companies are making fortunes out of lengthy conversations between breathless relatives thousands of miles apart.

But the islands are not only connected with regions of the Pacific Rim. Within Oceania itself people are once again circulating in increasing numbers and frequency. Regional organizations—inter-governmental, educational, religious, sporting, and cultural—are responsible for much of this mobility. The University of the South Pacific, with its highly mobile staff and student bodies comprising men, women and youth from the twelve island countries that own it, and from outside the South Pacific, is an excellent example. Increasingly the older movers and shakers of the islands are being replaced by younger ones; and when they meet each other in Suva, Honiara, Apia, Vila, or any other capital city of the South Pacific, they meet as friends, as people who went through the same place of learning, who worked and played and prayed together.

The importance of our ocean for the stability of the global environment, for meeting a significant proportion of the world's protein requirements, for the production of certain marine resources in waters that are relatively clear of pollution, for the global reserves of mineral resources, among others, has been increasingly recognized, and puts paid to the notion that Oceania is the hole in the doughnut. Together with our Exclusive Economic Zones, the areas of the earth's surface that most of our countries occupy can no longer be called small. In this regard, Kiribati, the Federated States of Micronesia, and French Polynesia, for example, are among the largest countries in the world. The emergence of organizations such as SPACHEE, SPREP, Forum Fisheries and SOPAC; of movements for a nuclear-free Pacific, the prevention of toxic waste disposal, and the ban on the wall-of-death fishing methods, with linkages to similar organizations and movements elsewhere; and the establishment at the University of the South Pacific of the Marine Science and Ocean Resources Management programs, with linkages to fisheries and ocean resources agencies throughout the South Pacific and beyond; indicate that we could play a pivotal role in the protection and sustainable development of our ocean. There are no more suitable people on earth to be guardians of the world's largest ocean than those for whom it has been home for generations. Although this is a different issue from what I have focused on for most of this paper, it is relevant to the concern with a far better future for us than has been prescribed and predicted. Our role in the protection and development of our ocean is no mean task; it is no less than a major contribution to the well-being of humankind. As it could give us a sense of doing something very worthwhile and noble, we should seize the moment with dispatch.

The perpetrators of the smallness view of Oceania have pointed out quite correctly the need for each island state or territory to enter into appropriate forms of specialized production for the world market, to improve their management and marketing techniques and so forth. But they have so focused on bounded national economies at the macro-level that they have overlooked or understated the significance of the other processes that I have just outlined, and have thereby swept aside the whole universe of Oceanic mores, and just about all our potentials for autonomy. The explanation seems clear: one way or another, they or nearly all of them are involved directly or indirectly in the fields of aided development and Pacific Rim geopolitics, for the purposes of which it is necessary to portray our huge world in tiny, needy bits. To acknowledge the larger reality would be to undermine the prevailing view, and to frustrate certain agendas and goals of powerful interests. They are therefore participants, as I was, in the belittlement of Oceania, and in the perpetuation of the neo-colonial relationships of dependency that have been and are being played out in the rarefied circles of national politicians, bureaucrats, diplomats, and assorted experts and academics, whilst far beneath them there exists that other order, of ordinary people who are busily and independently redefining their world in accordance with their perceptions of their own interests, and of where the future lies for their children and their children's children. Those who maintain that the people of Oceania live from day to day, not really caring for the long-term benefits, are unaware of the elementary truth known by most native islanders: that they plan for generations, for the continuity and improvement of their families and kin groups.

As I watched the Big Island of Hawai'i expanding into and rising from the depths, I saw in it the future for Oceania, our sea of islands. That future lies in the hands of our own people, and not of those who would prescribe for us, get us forever dependent and indebted because they could see no way out.

At the Honolulu Airport, while waiting for my flight back to Fiji, I met an old friend, a Tongan who is twice my size and lives in Berkeley, California. He is not an educated man. He works on people's yards, trimming hedges and trees, and laying driveways and footpaths. But every three months or so he flies to Fiji, buys eight to ten thousand dollars worth of kava, takes it on the plane flying him back to California, and sells it from his home. He has never heard of dependency, and if he were told of it, it would hold no real meaning for him. He told me in Honolulu that he was bringing a cooler full of T-shirts, some for the students at the university with whom he often stays when he comes to Suva, and the rest for his relatives in Tonga, where he goes for a week or so while his kava is gathered, pounded and bagged here. He would later fill the cooler with seafoods to take back home to California, where he has two sons he wants to put through college. On one of his trips he helped me renovate a house that I had just bought. We like him because he is a good story teller and is generous with his money and time. But mostly because he is one of us.

There are thousands like him, who are flying back and forth across national boundaries, the international dateline, and the equator, far above and completely undaunted by the deadly serious discourses below on the nature of the Pacific Century, the Asia/Pacific co-prosperity sphere, and the dispositions of the post–cold war Pacific Rim, cultivating their ever growing universe in their own ways, which is as it should be, for therein lies their independence. No one else would give it to them—or to us.

Oceania is vast, Oceania is expanding, Oceania is hospitable and generous, Oceania is humanity rising from the depths of brine and regions of fire deeper still, Oceania is us. We are the sea, we are the ocean, we must wake up to this ancient truth and together use it to overturn all hegemonic views that aim ultimately to confine us again, physically and psychologically, in the tiny spaces which we have resisted accepting as our sole appointed place, and from which we have recently liberated ourselves. We must not allow anyone to belittle us again, and take away our freedom.

Movements

Sacred Sites and the City:
Urban Aboriginality, Ambivalence,
and Modernity

John Fielder

1

If Australia is situated on the Asia-Pacific Rim, it is the eastern Australian states that best qualify for regional membership. Western Australia fits more squarely on the Indian Ocean Rim. Nevertheless, Australia as a whole is slowly renegotiating its place in the world and is developing stronger ties with Southeast Asian countries. Accompanying this process is a growing awareness that our Anglocentric allegiance has become essentially sentimental and symbolic. For the many Australians who seek to conserve an idealized English cultural heart—which functions as a form of hegemonic ethnicity against which "multicultural others" are defined, and marginalizes even the significant Celtic influence in this country—or for the many who assume their European origins are superior to those of non-Europeans, Asia is still frequently inscribed as culturally inferior and less "civilized." It is in this sense that there persists a popular perception that no capital is as foreign as Asian capital: European and American investment in Australia does not confront the same level of popular resistance as does Asian investment.

Within this context, Perth—the capital city of Western Australia—constructs itself as on the fringe of the fringe, the rim of the rim. Perth, one of the most isolated cities in the world, in terms of proximity to other large cities, is a somewhat anxious place that takes itself very seriously. It has sought to construct a modern image, a big-city facade. This construction trend over the past couple of decades has emerged at the cost of the old, "heritage" buildings—to such an extent that there is now a strong drive to preserve the few remaining structures considered as possessing historical value.

I make these sweeping generalizations to establish the context of a monumental conflict that has been hotly contested for about four years. The conflict revolves around a site known as the Old Swan Brewery to most Western Australians, but as Goonininup to Nyungahs.[1] I describe the conflict as "monumental" for two reasons: first, because this is the way the issue is perceived by many Nyungah people and Aboriginal organizations across Australia; and, second, because this conflict represents a re-contestation of one of the sites of early confrontation between Nyungahs and British exploration/settlement parties. The significance of this drawn-out conflict is attributable to the fact that this amounts to a land claim by urban Aborigines, a claim on a foundational site of colonization, a prime site of economic significance. On one side, there is the state government and developers seeking to refurbish an old building, and, on the other, Aborigines, unions, and environmentalists seeking to have the building demolished to restore the river foreshore to bushland/parkland. The Nyungahs' concern is to prevent further desecration of a crucial sacred site and, in this way, to reassert the viability of their culture against popularized assumptions about its total disintegration. This account of the conflict is a tendentious one, for, although Goonininup is one of the most well-documented sites in the Perth area, white heritage is yet again being given priority over black heritage.

In this essay, I examine how the logic of modernity connects to a

1. *Nyungah* is the broad term by which Aboriginal people in the southwestern area of Western Australia refer to themselves. There have been some differences among Nyungahs concerning the nature of the site's significance and who has authority to speak for the site. The government has strategically exploited these differences. Still, the vast majority of Nyungahs and Aboriginal organizations have supported the protest. One particular group, the Swan Valley Fringedwellers, camped "illegally" on their own land at Goonininup from 2 January 1989 until they were forcibly removed by the police on 9 October 1989. Reconstruction of the site has still not proceeded because of legal action and a daily picket line.

colonial or neocolonial logic to dismiss urban Aboriginal land claims. I also examine the ways in which Zygmunt Bauman's and Jon Stratton's conceptions of postmodernity open up possibilities for postcolonial tactics that undermine, or at least frustrate, the imperial impulse of modernity.[2] In particular, I explore Bauman's argument about the threat that ambivalence poses to the fantasy of movement toward ideal order, to systemic rationality. I would suggest that urban Aboriginality represents a flashpoint of ambivalence within the logic of modernity. Furthermore, this ambivalence is intensified by the anomalous position of "fringedwellers" within cultural pluralist policies founded on liberal-humanist principles.[3]

2

In an earlier article on the Goonininup dispute, I focused on the strategic mobilization of persistent stereotypes about Aboriginal people and the threat that fringedwellers pose to the order of things in Perth, Western Australia.[4] I drew on Mary Douglas's work on purity and pollution, and on Homi Bhabha's theorization of colonial discourse's fetishization of cultural purity and authority, to offer some explanations as to why Aboriginal people are represented as dirty and disorderly. In short, the fact that the fringedwellers protested so visibly on such a central site (a major road runs alongside the Swan River, linking the city of Perth with prestigious suburbs) meant that the Aborigines were read as "matter out of place," as a threat to "the system," even though many of these passersby supported the demolition of the Old Brewery for reasons other than anticolonial ones.

The problem with such an analysis—of urban Aboriginality as representing dirt and danger—is the tendency to universalize this reading in such a way as to gloss over specific social and historical complexities and contradictions. So, to place this previous reading of Goonininup in a broad historical context, I will outline the way in which Stratton explains different epistemic domains and will outline, as well, Bauman's account of the logic

2. Zygmunt Bauman, *Modernity and Ambivalence* (Ithaca, N.Y.: Cornell University Press, 1991); and Jon Stratton, *Writing Sites: A Genealogy of the Postmodern World* (Ann Arbor: University of Michigan Press, 1990). Subsequent references to Bauman and Stratton will be cited parenthetically as *MA* and *WS*, respectively.
3. I use the term *fringedweller* generally to signify urban Aboriginal people, who predominantly do live on the fringes of urban Australia—if not spatially, certainly socially.
4. John Fielder, "Purity and Pollution: Goonininup/The Old Swan Brewery," *Southern Review* 24, no. 1 (March 1991): 34–42.

of modernity and postmodernity. Stratton focuses on changes in economic formations and also on shifts in epistemes of representation. He draws no clear-cut boundaries between these different epistemes and identifies tendencies rather than distinct elements. This is especially important to remember when dealing with the more recent shift from modernity to post-modernity, for the transition is a recent one. And, because the transition is still very much in process, many modern tendencies prevail.

Stratton adds postmodernity to the epistemes identified by Foucault: the classical and modern. The classical episteme, which I will not deal with in this essay, assumes that

> perfect representation is possible, that knowledge can be identified with an absolute Truth; that language can provide a perfect representation of the world. The modern episteme signals the shift from the assumption of the attainability of absolute Truth to a recognition of the difficulty of acquiring knowledge, and the uncertainty of the knowledge acquired. Knowledge became preoccupied with generating the most perfect representation possible. There was an increased concern with method. (WS, 6)

Following on with this focus on truth, Stratton later contrasts the shift from modernity to postmodernity:

> In epistemes of representation truth is always "out there," it must be searched for, acquired with difficulty. For the modern episteme, as the project of science exemplifies, it was always possible to strive for truth, to attempt to make the perfect representation, but it required method, the institutionalization of reason. For the postmodern episteme truth is in its nature problematic. It always refers back on itself as that which is excluded lays claim to inclusion. Truth becomes a shifting element in an endless system of relays and sites. (WS, 225)

Interconnected to these epistemic shifts, Stratton outlines "the intimate link between the form of economic organization known as capitalism and representation" (WS, 23). He argues that the transition from the modern to the postmodern is accompanied by the transition from production capitalism to consumption capitalism:

> In consumption capitalism, consumption is valorized as the moment of the system's reproduction. Consumption 'sutures' the system, and in the process establishes its own presence. Consumption is articulated as productive; but to be so—to replace production—it must be

excessive to it. Representation articulates itself as presence through excess.[5]

Stratton goes on to suggest leisure as the site of excess, and this cues my discussion of the Old Swan Brewery redevelopment in terms of the drive for the tourist dollar.

One of the primary motives for the redevelopment of the site relates to its potential as another tourist "stop off" along the Swan River. This would complement the casino and the old tea rooms, and would also consolidate the plans for a radical redevelopment of the river foreshore in the central city region. The commercial potential for the site is unquestioned. But countless opinion polls clearly signal the fact that the majority of Western Australians oppose redevelopment. This is because of its position at the base of the Kings Park escarpment: Overlooking Perth, Kings Park functions as a white sacred site, and indeed the whole area is of special significance to Nyungahs. The government has maintained its pro-development stance on the grounds of the building's heritage value. To understand the government's persistence with this project, what must be taken into account is the economic boom of the mid-1980s—a boom, that has subsequently been revealed, in which entrepreneurs, bankers, and governments took unconscionable risks, a boom that saw many speculative property developers make huge profits, with little or no lasting "trickle-down." The height of this euphoria was symbolized by Perth hosting the America's Cup yacht-racing series (in Fremantle, part of the Perth metropolitan area). This is not simply to blame "the government," or "big business," for all of Perth was infected with unsustainable nationalist euphoria, and an optimism fueled by both economic good times and a sporting spectacle.

The relevance of these elements relate to the fact that Australia, like "everywhere" today, is attempting to sell itself to the world as a tourist playground. And so much of what Perth has to offer in this regard centers on sun, surf, and sand. The Swan River, as much as Perth's golden beaches, is part of this water-based gloss. Within this logic, the protestations of indigenous people and environmentalists are constructed as extremist and irrational rantings that are obstacles to development and that therefore threaten the possibility of economic recovery and employment growth. This all bears mentioning, because these corporate excesses have occurred under state

5. This particular quotation comes from Jon Stratton, "Crossing the Border: Tourism as Leisure," *Sport and Leisure: Trends in Australian Popular Culture*, ed. David Rowe and Geoff Lawrence (Sydney: Harcourt Brace Jovanovich, 1990), 259.

and federal Labor governments that have shifted to the Right and adopted the economic rationalist policies that have predominated globally over the past decade.

Within this logic, failing to exploit the economic potential of the Old Swan Brewery represents a waste of prime real estate. Condemning Goonininup to being a parkland reserve, however, poses an even greater strategic threat to this logic. The government made it clear early on in the dispute that acceding to the Nyungahs' request would set a precedence for numerous other sites of significance in the metropolitan area. If ever there was needed a clear expression of the government's regard for the protection of urban Aboriginal heritage, then such a statement says it all. Development must take precedence over the maintenance of what remains of Nyungah cultural heritage. To have the minister for Aboriginal Affairs utter such a remark demonstrates the appropriate force of the deployment of the term *neocolonial* in relation to the administration of Aboriginal affairs in Western Australia in particular, but throughout Australia in general.

3

This neocolonialism is evident in the negotiation of what constitutes a "sacred site," or "site of significance." Clearly, there are conflicting understandings of what is appropriate recognition of the site's significance to the Nyungahs. The state government wanted to acknowledge the site's significance without having to scrap its plans for redevelopment. But the government was going to have problems all along trying to respect the beliefs of Nyungah people and also to protect its own interests. The government's attempts to serve its own interests, however, involved exempting itself from its own Aboriginal Heritage Act so that plans for the site were not delayed.[6]

After effectively declaring itself above its own law, the government also mobilized the liberal discourse of negotiation. This discourse masks the crucial inequality in power relations that allows one party to set the grounds for such notions as negotiation and compromise: In effect, this sporting and fair-minded discourse means that the government's compromise causes them very little pain. This is illustrated by the sort of compromise they advocated: determining the precise track of the "Waugal" and fencing it off—constructing the car park around it.[7] This signals adherence to the logic

6. Martha Ansara, *Always Was, Always Will Be* (Sydney: Jequerity Pty Ltd., 1989), 30.
7. *Waugal* is the Nyungah name for the serpent that inhabits certain rivers, springs, and wetlands, and is comparable to the Rainbow Serpent story shared by many Aborigines throughout Australia.

of modernity as described by Stratton—the logic of scientific rationality, whereby, in the same way truth is strived for and perfect representation, too, "things" are as clearly as possible defined, delimited, delineated. Accordingly, space is carved up both physically and symbolically. Paul Carter suggests, in a similar way as does Michel de Certeau, that space is transformed into place by place-naming.[8] Borders are constructed so that these places can be managed, policed.

Needless to say, there is a huge difference between what can be described as "European" cultural space and that of "Aboriginal" cultural space. The colonial process commenced by assuming that the "natives" did not possess the land, did not map it, did not farm it in any way. These assumptions can be made when European logic is imposed on others as an absolute standard—when no alternative logic is allowed. The colonial process continues as this logic is imposed on the indigenous people as the only legitimate logic. So dispossession must always be understood in very broad terms, not simply in the act of taking land.

Dispossession need not be totally irreversible, however. The popular perception is that Nyungah culture, the culture of Aboriginal people in southwestern Australia, is a lost culture, a dead culture. Acts of resistance, such as the struggle to save Goonininup, can be understood as attempts to repossess cultural practices and places on Aboriginal people's terms. Indeed, this is the only way Nyungah people will ever achieve ethnogenesis, for the pastoral lobby and state governments have made it clear that land rights are out of the question in the southwest. Fencing off a small portion of land and limiting this as the dreaming track of the Waugal is not in the spirit of appropriate recognition of Nyungah cultural heritage. It signifies the fundamentally neocolonial logic of the state government, which refuses to listen to the strong Aboriginal call for land and self-determination. It signifies the government's denial of the fact that its management of Aboriginal people has been a failure.

4

Bauman argues that one of the central fantasies of modernity is that "problems" can be managed out of existence. It is in this sense that both he and Stratton regard postmodernity as a promising change. Bau-

8. See Paul Carter, *The Road to Botany Bay: An Essay in Spatial History* (London: Faber and Faber, 1987), xxiv. Also see Michel de Certeau, *The Practice of Everyday Life*, trans. S. F. Rendall (Los Angeles: University of California Press, 1984).

man's account of the transition from modernity to postmodernity focuses on similar epistemic elements to Stratton's. But, first, he makes this important distinction between modernity and modernism:

> "Modernity" [being] a historical period . . . achieved its maturity: (1) as a cultural project—with the growth of the Enlightenment; (2) as a socially accomplished form of life—with the growth of industrial (capitalist, and later also communist) society. . . . [Modernism] is an intellectual (philosophical, literary, artistic) trend . . . which in retrospect can be seen (by analogy with the Enlightenment) as a "project" of postmodernity or a prodromal stage of the postmodern condition. In modernism, modernity turned its gaze upon itself and attempted to attain the clear-sightedness and self-awareness which would eventually disclose its impossibility, thus paving the way to the postmodern reassessment. (*MA*, 4 n. 1)

In this last sentence, Bauman alludes to the problematization of representation that Stratton asserts characterizes the postmodern episteme: "[The fact that] the claim to the possibility of the perfect representation of absolute Truth through the methodical use of reason elided the relation between truth and power. . . . The relation between truth and power has become apparent, and has become a site of contestation, in the postmodern episteme" (*WS*, 226). Both Stratton and Bauman, then, imply that postmodernity opens up possibilities for postcolonial resistance that exploits this fracture in the very foundations of Western culture's appeal to the transcendental truth that validates its ascendancy.

Goonininup is just one of many sites of conflict, and potential sites of conflict, at a juncture in which postcoloniality is challenging the neocolonial logic that still is a potent force within modernity-postmodernity. In order to identify the ways in which neocolonial strategies are deployed—whether consciously or unconsciously—under the guise of concern for indigenous peoples, it may be helpful to consider Bauman's account of the logic of modernity. Bauman provides this understanding of modernity:

> We can think of modernity as a time when order—of the world, of the human habitat, of the human self, and of the connection between all three—is reflected upon; a matter of thought, of concern, of a practice that is aware of itself, conscious of being a conscious practice and wary of the void it would leave were it to halt or merely relent. (*MA*, 5)

Modernity's drive for order must be maintained, for disorder always threatens to "cut loose." I use this metaphor purposefully, to suggest that modernity represents disorder as a wild beast, tied up and yet to be tamed. The rhetoric of taming the beast is still prevalent, because the authority and veracity of modernity is tied to this fantasy. It is this "supplementarity" that Bauman explores in his theorization of ambivalence. Drawing on Derrida, Bauman argues that dichotomization is an exercise of power, with the differentiating power hiding

> as a rule behind one of the members of the opposition. The second member is but the other of the first, the opposite (degraded, suppressed, exiled) side of the first and its creation. . . . Both sides depend on each other, but the dependence is not symmetrical. The second side depends on the first for its contrived and enforced isolation. The first depends on the second for its self-assertion. (*MA*, 14)

In other words, the system and order, which modernity has established as naturalized and normative, produces its difference against the beastly other of disorder and chaos.

So, within the logic of modernity, "primitive" Aboriginality—the tribal, the traditional—represents disorder. Thus, the concomitant colonial manifestation of modernity sought to manage this otherness, hoping for it either to die off or to be assimilated. But the postcolonial "Aboriginal problem" that ensued challenges the very foundations of modernity, and this is best exemplified by the position of urban Aborigines. At this stage, I will simply describe these Aborigines as fringedwellers, not only because this represents their social and spatial status in Australia but also because many Aborigines have appropriated this term in recognition of the anomalous position they inhabit within white Australia.

The subversive potential of fringedwellers can also be understood in terms of Derrida's theorization of "undecidables." Bauman points out that Derrida deploys a number of terms that resist being understood within the master opposition of "inside" and "outside": "Undecidables brutally expose the artifice, the fragility, the sham of the most vital of separations. They bring the outside into the inside, and poison the comfort of order with the suspicion of chaos" (*MA*, 56). Undecidables threaten the very grounds of the opposition. The fact that Aboriginality has not been assimilated into a compliant and servile bourgeois subject informs persistent unofficial racism that attributes this to the irredeemable primitive nature of Aborigines. Such common knowledge about the nature of Aboriginality masks the particularity of historical forces that have contributed to Aborigines' fringe-dwelling status. This is not to construct Aborigines simply as helpless and passive victims of white colonial rule but to acknowledge, more importantly, the fickleness and failures of white attempts to manage the indigenous peoples of Australia.

Identification of the mismanagement of Aborigines not only demonstrates that the "Aboriginal problem" is essentially a white problem—or more specifically a problem of the whole colonial enterprise—it also indicates the ambivalence of modernity-coloniality. Bauman argues that, with the rise of modernity, order and chaos emerged as the "*modern* twins" (*MA*, 4, Bauman's emphasis—as are all subsequent emphases in his quotations). He suggests that the modern era involves a "particularly bitter and relentless war against ambivalence," with an acute "awareness that the reduction of ambivalence is a problem of the discovery and application of proper *technology*: a *managerial* problem" (*MA*, 3). He summarizes his position by suggesting that "we can say that existence is modern in as far as it is effected and sustained by *design, manipulation, management, engineering*" (*MA*, 7).

5

The state's attempts to manage Aboriginal people have been destructively ambivalent, particularly with respect to "half-caste" children. As it became increasingly clear that the "Aboriginal problem" was not going to resolve itself "naturally," with the remaining population dying off on reserves, alternative strategies were put in place. Barry Morris, in *Domesticating Resistance*, asserts that

> the reserves, or "soothing pillows for a dying race," had been created on the understanding that Aborigines were incapable of transcending their own biological limitations. The dominant society's appropriation of Aboriginality was an abstraction which culturally and biologically froze it into a particular historical moment. The ideological representations of Aborigines had basically denied them a historical trajectory.[9]

But Morris points out that, within the reserves, Aborigines were at least allowed to farm and maintain relative independence, preserving most cul-

9. Barry Morris, *Domesticating Resistance: The Dhan Gadi Aborigines and the Australian State* (New York: Berg, 1989), 98.

tural practices. In the early part of the twentieth century, the policy commenced of systematically removing children from their Aboriginal environment and, more generally, with instituting what Morris calls "bureaucratic custodianship." Under these policies, governments [10]—recognizing that environmental factors were the key element in the retention of cultural practices—implemented strategies that bred dependency: "They were expected to exercise no control over the direction of their lives and . . . there was no provision for them to be consulted or permitted to influence decisions made on their behalf." [11]

Fickle colonial management has produced a destructive form of ambivalence among Aboriginal people. As Albert Memmi points out, ambivalence is unavoidable for the colonized because they are forced to deal with social and political practices that are imposed upon them.[12] The more "successful" the process of colonialism, the greater the resistance required to maintain cultural practices that in some shape or form constitute indigenous cultural heritage. Effective resistance depends greatly on the belief that the practices a culture is seeking to preserve are desirable and have some currency among the people who identify themselves racially or culturally by them. In this sense, oppositional political tactics generally involve the masking of ambivalence in an effort to eradicate negative stereotypes by replacing them with positive ones.

For the colonizers, ambivalence does not represent the crippling cultural crisis it does for the colonized—even if it is considered a persistent problem or weakness. This is because the dominant culture enshrines certain practices and values that are naturalized and generally understood as beyond question. And, certainly, in political antagonisms/battles, positions are constructed in such a way as to mask and deny ambivalence or doubt. One possible postcolonial tactic could involve a process whereby the dominant group—the privileged group in the power relations of political negotiation—is encouraged or forced to acknowledge its ambivalence and thereby allows a form of negotiation that Homi Bhabha argues for in his article "The Commitment to Theory." [13] Recognizing that this verges on

10. I refer to "governments" because federation occurred in Australia in 1901, but Aborigines continued to be completely within the state governments' jurisdiction for many years after.

11. Morris, Domesticating Resistance, 111.

12. Albert Memmi, The Colonizer and the Colonized (New York: Orion Press, 1965), 87–89.

13. Homi Bhabha, "The Commitment to Theory," New Formations 5 (Summer 1988): 5–23.

idealism, tactics need to be developed to force the institutional powers' hands by using what leverage liberal legal and political practices allow. In other words, a fundamental recognition of the hegemonic colonial impetus of modernity necessitates radical forms of resistance—even if the limitations of such frequently utopian posturing is evident. Such resistance may not be, at the everyday level, spectacular; in fact, for Aboriginal cultures in Australia, resistance has been most effective when kept outside of the gaze of the colonizer.[14]

Radical resistance is necessary not only when explicit forms of colonial domination are in place; radical resistance is necessary when neocolonial policies—under the guise of an enlightened, liberal, and caring ethos—continue to disallow Aboriginal people control over their own affairs. In *Domesticating Resistance*, Morris demonstrates how such liberal policies within the cultural pluralist program function as "welfare colonialism" and develop "relations of dependency between indigenous minorities and welfare departments."[15] Morris outlines the problem with this particular technology of power:

> The cultural pluralist program attempts to resolve the anomaly the original inhabitants pose for the modern state, but without acknowledging their sovereign status. The present solution to the Aboriginal "problem" is sought through the recognition of cultural differences rather than the specificities of colonial dispossession and domination. This stress on cultural distinctiveness is not arbitrary, but grows out of the "legal fiction" on which the constitutional sovereignty of the nation-state is based. When the constitutional basis of pluralist policies is separated from its political rhetoric, "self-determination" reflects more the expansion of the welfare system into Aboriginal affairs than a recognition of indigenous rights.[16]

Morris goes on to discuss the struggle over the politics of identity,

> whereby a subjugated group is turned into an object of knowledge. With respect to cultural pluralism, in the production of knowledge

14. Barry Morris, in *Domesticating Resistance*, describes how Aborigines developed sophisticated tactics of silence and secrecy to escape the gaze of whites (145).
15. *Domesticating Resistance*, 203. "Cultural pluralism" is a federal policy that evolved from the earlier policy of multiculturalism introduced in the 1970s. There is a distinct pattern throughout Australia of state government resistance to the federal government's liberal policies, and this is one of the primary reasons national land rights legislation has never been enacted.
16. Morris, *Domesticating Resistance*, 202.

about the past of minority groups, the state becomes the possessor and producer of the collective representations of transgenerational knowledge. In effect, minority groups lose the right to speak for themselves as the production of their past, their history, is invested in experts and authorities and mediated by institutions of the state system.[17]

Stephen Muecke identifies this process as permeating all forms of discourse—unofficial and official discourse, popular and institutional.[18] Aborigines are primarily talked about. And, within the web of cultural pluralism, when Aboriginal people speak publicly, their enunciation is framed by white institutions. Blacks who speak outside of these institutional frameworks are represented as extremist, disruptive, and politically self-interested.

Possession of institutional power is required to shift the social and political frame in such a way as to demonstrate that it is, in fact, Aboriginal people's interests that have been, and continue to be, compromised by neocolonial policies. Fringedwellers—urban Aborigines predominantly consisting of underclass blacks—lack access to the resources that enable such empowerment. The fringedwellers who occupied the Goonininup site for more than nine months protested successfully because they connected with other sympathetic groups. Indeed, it has been the solidarity of several key trade unions that has prevented reconstruction of the Old Swan Brewery for the past three years.[19] The fringedwellers who occupied the site exploited their underclass position in neocolonial power relations: They had little to lose in the way of a "comfortable lifestyle," for the tentland conditions through the wet winter of 1989 were not much different to their basic living conditions further up the Swan River. Understanding these harsh circumstances checks the tendency to romanticize the carnivalesque impulses of the fringedwellers' resistance.

6

Bauman comes very close to proposing an idealized version of postmodernity as a kind of conscious revision of modernity: "Postmodernity is modernity coming to terms with its own impossibility; a self-monitoring

17. Morris, *Domesticating Resistance*, 203.
18. Stephen Muecke, "Available Discourses on Aborigines," in *Theoretical Strategies* (Sydney: Local Consumption Press, 1982), 98–111.
19. The Nyungahs also received support from certain lawyers, churches, and environmental groups.

modernity, one that consciously discards what it was once unconsciously doing" (MA, 272). This statement posits postmodern ambivalence as some redeeming reformation of modernity, a less certain, less hegemonic form of modernity. Although he does identify "healthy" postmodern revisions of modernity, however, I say he comes close to this idealization only because he emphasizes the fact that "postmodernity is a site of opportunity and a site of danger" (MA, 262). And the dangers are great, for, as Bauman puts it, "awareness of contingency does not 'empower' " (MA, 237). Further, "the unfinished business of modern social engineering may well erupt in a new outburst of savage misanthropy, assisted rather than impeded by the newly legalized postmodern self-centeredness and indifference" (MA, 260). To counter these dangers, Bauman argues that solidarity must displace tolerance; and I would add that postcoloniality must also partner postmodernity to achieve this displacement.[20]

The need for this political shift is exemplified by the neocolonial tendencies of the liberal policies that have presided over the continued dispossession of Aboriginal people. Bauman argues that modernity, "characterized as it has been from its inception by a radical intolerance of any form of life different from itself, . . . can conceive of such difference only as ignorance, superstition, or retardation" (MA, 224). Hence, working from within the logic of modernity, the state government, architects, and developers typically characterize those opposing such developments as the Old Swan Brewery in this thoroughly modern way. The Waugal is framed as some wildly primitive superstition: It is read in cynically realistic terms, as a "real" mythical creature. This is a strategic refusal to read the Waugal in terms of postmodernist, or even modernist, reading formations. Realist reading codes are simplistically mobilized—in the context of "serious" journalism and political debate—in a way that they generally would not be with regard to modern sacred sites at the heart of white cultural traditions, such as the church, the monarchy, war memorials, and the like. Such pervasive popularized readings disregard and devalue the cultural, institutional, and symbolic value the Waugal represents to Nyungahs.

The dominant disparaging reading of the "mythical Waugal" clearly demonstrates the imperial nature of Western rationality, where our logic renders all other logics as essentially illogical, irrational—not to be thought

20. By "postcoloniality," I refer not simply to some idea of colonialism as being something of the past (postcolonialism) but rather as signifying an ongoing social and political struggle for decolonization.

of as logic at all. This colonizing logic sets the grounds for debate. As I mentioned before, earlier in the dispute, when the state government was being so wonderfully tolerant, there was much talk of compromise. The parameters for negotiation, however, were established by the government. The government represented itself as so benevolently flexible by being open to modifying plans to lessen the impact of the redevelopment on the Waugal's dreaming track, but scrapping the redevelopment was out of the question. Under these terms the position of the fringedwellers was inevitably going to appear extremist, inflexible, defiantly nonnegotiable. And all this confirms stereotypes of the other's irrationality.

The limitations of the logic become apparent if the frame is shifted. If the grounds for debate encompass the inner-metropolitan area, then the nonnegotiable logic of neocolonial management of "Aboriginal affairs" is exposed. There is little or no evidence of compromise on the part of state urban planners that demonstrates a genuine respect for Nyungah culture, a respect that is manifested in even a token gesture. And, most definitely, there is no permanent allocation of land for Aboriginal use in the Perth area, or in the southwest of Western Australia, for that matter. The closest thing to such a symbolic recognition is a statue of the leader of one of the few recognized Nyungah resistant fighters, Yagan. The statue is out of sight and out of mind, toward the end of Herrison Island—an island in the Swan River that is cut in half by a major road connecting the city with the southeastern suburbs. This pattern is in accordance with the fact that, for many decades, Nyungahs were banished from the city—and they have been allowed back in only on white terms. Hence, Aboriginality is appropriated and celebrated as a cultural artifact, as a museum piece, as an idealized and spiritualized supplement for Australia's nationalist desire to fill our cultural lack.[21] In short, the idea of Aboriginality is fetishized while, materially, Aborigines continue to be colonized.

7

Bauman, like Morris, recognizes the insidious dimension of liberal notions such as tolerance and the policies that are anchored on such patronizing ideals:

21. Andrew Lattas, "Aborigines and Contemporary Australian Nationalism," in *Writing Australian Culture*, ed. Julie Marcus (Adelaide: University of Adelaide Press, 1989), 50–69.

> Tolerance as "mere tolerance" is moribund; it can survive only in the form of solidarity. . . . Survival in the world of contingency and diversity is possible only if each difference recognizes another difference as the necessary condition of the preservation of its own. Solidarity, unlike tolerance, its weaker version, means readiness to fight; and joining the battle for the sake of the other's difference, not one's own. Tolerance is ego-centered and contemplative; solidarity is socially oriented and militant. (*MA*, 256)

What Bauman seeks to uphold is a notion of postmodern tolerance that is not founded upon the condescending, benevolent, and idealist ideologies of liberal humanism. The reason Bauman holds such hope for postmodernity is because of its self-reflexivity:

> Like all other human conditions, postmodern tolerance and diversity has its dangers and its fears. Its survival is not guaranteed—not by God's design, universal reason, laws of history, or any other suprahuman force. In this respect, of course, the postmodern condition does not differ at all from all other conditions; it differs only by knowing about it, by its knowledge of living without guarantee, of being on its own. This makes it exceedingly anxiety-prone. And this also gives it a chance. (*MA*, 256–57)

Certainly, there is cause for some optimistic construction of solidarity as an opportunity for tolerance within postmodernity. It is exactly at this point, however, that the ambivalence of Bauman's own narrative must be emphasized.

At the very moment Bauman posits this opportunity for postmodern solidarity, he outlines the conditions that militate against its formation:

> It is only too easy for postmodern tolerance to degenerate into the selfishness of the rich and resourceful. . . . There seems to be a direct relation between exuberant and expanding freedom of the "competent consumer" and the remorseless shrinking of the world inhabited by the disqualified one. The postmodern society has split the world into the happy seduced and unhappy oppressed halves—with postmodern mentality celebrated by the first half of the division while adding to the misery of the second. (*MA*, 259)

This persistent fracture of the modern fantasy of prosperous progress for "all" helps explain why postmodernity itself is an ambivalent condition. Celebration of postmodernity, then, seems to function as a strategy of exuberant indulgence that allows people some insulation from the despairing ambivalence that seems to accompany self-reflexivity. Self-reflexivity requires a political dimension to save it from the privatized, solipsistic tendency of postmodern fragmentation. It is this privatization and commodification that, Bauman argues, has "rendered postmodern society so spectacularly immune to systemic critique and radical social dissent with revolutionary potential" (*MA*, 261).

8

The process of transition from modernity to postmodernity in the Australian context has not greatly improved Aboriginal people's material conditions. Nearly two decades of federal government policies promoting cultural pluralism have not dealt with the persistent call for land rights and self-determination by Aboriginal activists seeking to resist the fragmentation of postmodernity and the destructive effects this has had on the passing on of law and other cultural practices. Policies that have promoted cultural difference within the confines of individualistic ideologies have fostered tolerance and "attitudinal change" while allowing structural racism to continue, albeit less overtly. Cultural pluralist policies since the mid-seventies have given tolerance a slightly harder edge, by celebrating cultural difference on narrowly defined "cultural" grounds, but have failed to allow Aboriginal people to define and control their own difference. Meanwhile, Aboriginal people, as underclass, dispossessed people, have remained at the bottom of the heap. The grandest of modern plans to "solve the Aboriginal problem" have never materialized because it is white management that is essentially the problem.

Modernity's project persists in the neocolonial policies that work toward cultural integration by means other than overt assimilation. Aboriginal people have been given token self-determination, but any talk of a treaty or of sovereignty is off the political agenda—an agenda administered by white politicians dictated to by public opinion. What *is* on the agenda is "reconciliation." Reconciliation—aside from carrying Christian overtones—is a thoroughly liberal and modern concept; it is a process that takes place within the confines of already existing structures and policies administered by white government. Neocolonial forces prevail through the quest for modern order that, Bauman suggests, produces the very ambivalence that the enterprise of modernity seeks to abolish.

It is within this ambivalent space that fringedwellers celebrate their survival, their success in resisting total domestication. In a recent interview, Bhabha refers to "culture as a strategy of survival." [22] This conception was developed as a postcolonial critique of cultural conflict, "in which advanced European forms of technology and techne became part of the lives of third world peoples—those whose labor was actually producing such technologies." [23] He argues that the people, in this context,

> constituted their lives in a kind of agonistic struggle between indigenous practices and imposed forms, a negotiation that couldn't be reduced to the polarity between a preconstituted western tradition and an authentic native tradition. People were weaving their cultural existence in a much more strategic, interstitial, in-between kind of space. [24]

This point is particularly important in relation to the positionality of fringe-dwellers, for they are often denied cultural credibility because they do not comply with idealized constructions of cultural purity or Aboriginal authenticity. What Bhabha disallows is any utopian oppositionality in which some form of cultural or racial purity allows a transcendental position of truth or justification outside of the messiness of specific social and historical struggles.

Much of the "messiness" of the struggle to save Goonininup, and one of the reasons the Nyungahs have not received as much support as expected, [25] relates to the fact that their campaign has been spearheaded by fringedwellers. The particular group of fringedwellers involved has as their spokesperson Robert Bropho, a man commonly represented and popularly perceived as a troublemaker. Bropho does not fit the idealized image of tribal Aboriginality; Bropho speaks for the urban land "in here," not "out back." Worse still, he does not fit the image of the conciliatory negotiator; he has learned from experience that such an approach has gained little for urban blacks. This clearly intimidates whites generally but, specifically, most unsettles white leaders, who like to keep Aborigines "on side"—but also "in line."

22. Homi Bhabha, "The Postcolonial Critic: Homi Bhabha Interviewed by David Bennett and Terry Collits," *Arena* 96 (Spring 1991): 49.
23. Bhabha, "The Postcolonial Critic," 51.
24. Bhabha, "The Postcolonial Critic," 51.
25. In an excellent article on the Goonininup dispute, Stephen Mickler notes how it is easier for Australians to advocate postcolonial solidarity for conflicts "elsewhere" than it is to deal with the complex postcolonial politics "here." He offers this as a reason for the relatively low level of support. See "The Battle for Goonininup," *Arena* 96 (Spring 1991): 69–88.

Bropho represents a fringedweller who touches the raw nerve of ambivalence in those politicians who like to represent themselves as antiracist and sympathetic to the "Aboriginal cause." In so doing, he upsets their reasonable, liberal facade, and forces their hand so that the neocolonial logic of their policies becomes very clear to those who look beyond the rhetoric. It is in this sense that I refer to fringedwellers in terms of Derrida's undecidability; they elicit an ineradicable ambivalence that neocolonialism attempts to repress or deny. Finally, understood in terms of Bhabha's theorization of colonial discourse, the liberal rhetoric of "stamping out" racism itself comes very close to the compulsive reiteration of fetishistic stereotypes that derives from the disavowal and denial of difference: "If only fringedwellers could actually become good bourgeois subjects 'like us'; if only 'they' would comply with the order 'we' seek to establish."

What I have sought to do in this essay is identify the destructive ambivalence at the heart of the logic of coloniality and modernity; more precisely, I have attempted to identify an insidious manifestation of ambivalence in ostensibly benevolent and enlightened policies. Such ambivalence can be productively transformed only by changing the power relations, by establishing genuinely postcolonial policies whereby Aborigines manage their own affairs.

From the Politics of Identity to an Alternative Cultural Politics: On Taiwan Primordial Inhabitants' A-systemic Movement

Chiu Yen Liang (Fred)

Since the Kuomintang (KMT) was defeated by the Chinese Communist Party (CCP) on the Chinese mainland in 1949 and fled to Taiwan, it has ruled that island with an iron hand. A rule of martial law with a garrison command control system was imposed on the populace for the prevention of "Communist insurgence." It was only in July 1987, under the accumulated pressure of waves of protests and demonstrations, that this ruling regime was forced to lift martial law. As a face-saving device, officials claimed that the lifting of martial law was, in fact, a sign of Taiwan's socioeconomic and political development, and therefore a show of self-confidence. Nevertheless, it was clear that the Kuomintang's monopoly of thirty-eight years over power and social resources had been broken. This victory, however, was

The first five sections of this essay were adapted from an earlier paper I wrote entitled "Taiwan's Aborigines and Their Struggle towards Radical Democracy," prepared for the Ethnicity and Social Transformation Symposium, New Delhi, 3–5 Jan. 1988, which was organized by the Asian Regional Exchange for New Alternatives (ARENA) and LOKAYAN. The paper subsequently was published as a chapter in *Ethnicity: Identity, Conflict, and Crisis*, ed. Kumar David and Santasilan Kadirgamar (Hong Kong: ARENA Press, 1989).
    All translations from Chinese are mine.

one that belonged exclusively to the island's Han-Chinese majority and its bourgeoisie. It did not involve either the socially underprivileged or the Aborigines. For Taiwan's Aborigines, Kuomintang rule has meant a warping of their social existence; they have had to face what has been described as "a deadly crisis of genocide."[1] This genocide is evident in terms of various developments.

Demographic Trends

According to demographer Jen-ying Wang,[2] during the period 1906–1964, the population of Aborigines doubled from 113,163 to about 234,920. He says that around 1956, the rate of natural increase was over 3 percent, which signifies a "population explosion." If this trend were to have continued, the Aborigine population would have doubled every twenty-five years; in 1990, it would have touched 440,000. In 1988, however, the total Aborigine population, according to figures released by the government, was just slightly over 300,000. In other words, during the period 1964–1988, the Aborigine population grew at a rate of just 1 percent. What happened? Wang seeks to explain it in this way:

> In 1956–1964, the average natural growth rate in high-mountain tribes [Aborigines] approximated 30/1000. However, members who married with "plains-people" [Han-Chinese who lived in the coastal plains] and moved out from high-mountain tribe communities, which resulted in changed identity (lost the identity as mountain people), amount to 5/1000 per annum. Accordingly, the population increase rate was reduced to 24/1000 per annum.

"Married with plains people" really meant, in the majority of cases, that Aborigine girls had been purchased by Han military personnel—the resulting "changed identity" is, in fact, but one of social dislocation of Taiwan's Aborigines.

Thus, in 1900, the Aborigines constituted 3.7 percent of the total population in Taiwan.[3] Three-quarters of a century later, in 1977, they con-

1. *High Mountains Are Green* (the first magazine of the Taiwan Aborigines, available in Chinese only), 1 May 1983.
2. Jen-ying Wang, "Population Change of Formosa Aborigines," Institute of Ethnology, Academia Sinica, monograph no. 11 (available in Chinese only, abstract in English), 1967.
3. Sun Te-hsiung, "Population in Taiwan's Mountain Areas," in *Taiwan's Mountain Economy*, Taiwan Study Monographs, no. 81, Bank of Taiwan (available in Chinese only), 1966.

stituted only 1.77 percent of the total population.[4] This ratio has been decreasing steadily in the last ten years.

The Exodus to the Cities

In 1970, 42.5 percent of the 113,572 Aborigines were forced to join the exodus from their mountain homes.[5] In that year, three times as many Aborigines moved into the slums of big cities than the number in 1962. And only six years later, eight times the number in 1971 flooded the city slums all over the island. According to Taiwan Provincial Government statistics, in 1980, the male net emigration rate of the Aborigines reached 12.8 percent, and that of the female was even higher, at 21.4 percent, mostly between the ages of 15 and 35.

As much as 99 percent of the emigrating Aborigines were in laboring trades. Among those trades, according to unofficial estimates, 30,000 out of 100,000 female Aborigines aged 13–34 were involved in various forms of prostitution. At the same time, young Aborigine men constituted 80 percent of the crew on oceangoing fishing boats. This is one of the most hazardous occupations in Taiwan. Every year, an average of 250 people are killed in accidents, and another 250 are arrested and jailed by foreign governments for illegal fishing. In each case, more than 200 are Aborigines. In 1984, a big coal mining disaster killed 72 miners—38 were Aborigines. Among the 800 miners in the same pit, more than 500 were from the mountains. These figures are telling. They do not, however, reflect some of the most degrading conditions that the dislocated Aborigine faces. There are hundreds who live on the "garbage hills" in the suburbs; they have to pay "protection fees" to local bullies for securing the "right" to recycle the garbage.[6]

4. Lee Yi-yuan, "Mountain Tribes Adjustment to Modernization in the Cities," in *Taiwan Aborigines Societies and Cultures* (Taipei: Lien-jin Publishing Co., 1982) (available in Chinese only).

5. Hwang Yin-Kwei, "Postwar Economic Changes among the Taiwan Aborigines," in *Bulletin of the Institute of Ethnology, Academia Sinica*, special issue entitled "Symposium on Taiwan Aborigines: Retrospect and Prospect," no. 40 (Autumn 1975): 85–96 (available in Chinese only).

6. *Primordial Inhabitants: Battle Cry of the Oppressed*, pamphlet published by the Alliance of Taiwan Aborigines (available in Chinese only), 1987.

Crowding out the Aborigines

The exodus to the cities is attributed to the accelerating bankruptcy of the natural economy of the mountain areas. How did this happen in Taiwan, where two-thirds of the island consists of mountains with rich forests and vegetation? The fact is, the mountain area was never the real home of the Aborigines, historically or geographically, socially or politically.

The Aborigines on the islands of Taiwan and Lanyu belong to at least ten different linguistic or cultural groups (Figure 1), some of which were said to have come from southwestern China, and some of which were of Polynesian-Melanesian stock. According to historical evidence, they had lived on the island for over two thousand years. About three hundred years ago, the Han people, living in the southeastern coastal provinces of the Chinese mainland, initiated waves of migration to the western plains of the island. Gradually, the natural hunter-gatherer economy of the Aborigines was replaced by the Han immigrants' wet-rice cultivation. Those Aborigines who had not been, or would not be, assimilated were driven deeper and deeper into the forests of the Central Mountains. In 1896, when the island was ceded by the Ch'ing government to the Japanese, almost all of the as yet recognizable Aborigines had been dubbed "people of the mountains." In 1931, after the Aborigines' bitter armed resistance against Japanese atrocities, the Japanese colonial authority systematically destroyed all of their villages. They were forced to resettle in new locations under constant police surveillance, strict isolation, and movement control, as well as relentless "Japanization."

In 1945, after the Second World War, the Japanese handed Taiwan back to the Chinese, and the island fell under the control of the Kuomintang nationalist government. The Aborigines who made their living in the mountains were under a control as strict as, if not worse than, that during the Japanese occupation. What had changed was the rhetoric of suppression. The control of the mountain population's movements was cleverly disguised as a move to establish the huge area of the Central Mountains into a "mountain people reserve district." This district was under the direct control of the provincial Mountain Administration Unit and occupied an area of 15,815 square kilometers—44 percent of the total island.

In actual fact, the land given to the Aborigines to cultivate was only a very small fraction—about 5.5 percent of the island, and 12.2 percent of the so-called reserve district. According to the 1960 provincial government statistics, among 20,176 Aborigine households in the area, each

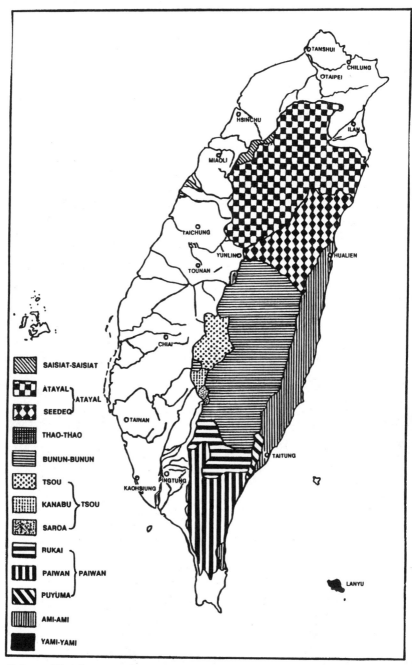

Taiwan: The Geographical Distribution of Aboriginal Peoples

Map courtesy of ARENA Press, Hong Kong. Reprinted with permission of the publisher.

household had an average of 0.59 hectares to cultivate. And less than 30 percent of this land, an average of 0.17 hectares, was irrigated. Besides the fact that the productivity of the soil in the area is 60 percent lower than that in the plains area, the sheer quantity of land that an Aborigine could work on amounted to only half of that available to the Han agriculturists in the plains.[7]

Of a substantial portion of the district supposedly reserved for the Aborigines, over 87 percent was declared a "state-owned forest." During the past decades, Kuomintang bureaucrats franchised Han merchants to lumber the forest, and rapid, unchecked deforestation has taken place. And yet, the Aborigines were frequently jailed for "stealing firewood" and for "illegal occupying of public land."

It is clear that what the "mountain peoples' reserve district" reserves are only the privileges and monopolies of the Kuomintang and its associates. By making the mountain area a special administrative unit, the area is isolated from society at large. In forty years, the Aborigines' culture and way of life have been destroyed in the name of "equalization and plainization." Their lifestyle has been equalized to that of the urban pauper. And they have been pushed into the ghettos of the plains. Chased by Han immigrants to the mountains three hundred years ago, they are once again driven away from the mountains, dispersed and scattered in the Han-dominated urban regions. They have lost their homes and, worse, their communities.

Controlled Flow

While there was a continuous stream of Aborigines from the mountain area to the plains seeking a livelihood, the mountain area remained an area of "controlled flow." Even today, after the lifting of martial law, nobody can go into the reserved district without applying for a special permit from the prefecture police unit unless he or she is a government officer of mountain affairs or a missionary who spreads beliefs in the mountain areas. Under the "mountain control scheme," even the Aborigines themselves were forced to apply for the special permit in order to go back to their homes or to get into the mountains once they had moved down to the plains. In a sense, the Kuomintang control of flow was a less "apartheid-like" apparatus compared with the Japanese one, for it controlled only population

7. Chiu Ya-fei, "On Taiwan's Minority Problems," in *Taiwan and the World Monthly*, 27 (Dec. 1985–Jan. 1986): 50 (available in Chinese only).

in-flow, not out-flow. Ironically, however, under the pretext of "ensuring the security in mountain areas and protecting mountain peoples' interests," the Aborigines were further isolated as a "closed population." What is worse, the push forces from within and the pull forces from without kept draining the most valuable human resources from the Aborigines' homeland. Needless to say, controlling population in-flow does not necessarily have the effect of deterring economic penetration, manipulation, or dominance from and by the plains-dwelling Han majority. On the contrary, it has actually facilitated all kinds of economic interference, and it has helped to conceal this from the public.

The money economy backed by administrative coercion destroyed the time-honored exchange system. The decaying ecology made the self-rejuvenating diet scheme and food chain collapse and forced cultivation to commercialize. The absence of transportation, warehousing, and a marketing infrastructure in the mountain areas resulted in the Aborigines being at the mercy of the Han merchants. Thus, in a few years, the self-supporting Aborigine agriculturist was turned into a contract farmer, and, in a few more years, this contract farmer was turned into a debt-laden peon. Government records showed an increasing number of cases in which Aborigines "voluntarily" applied to the government agencies to "forfeit" the land they were assigned to cultivate.

None of the other natural resources in the mountain areas was at the disposal of the Aborigines. Both the aboveground wealth—the forests—and the underground wealth—the mines—were "state-owned," and the government franchised these out for lumbering or mining to only Han-established economic interests. It was this dual process—governmental monopoly, on the one hand, and private appropriation, on the other—that not only siphoned out the mountains' resources and destroyed the natural economy but also forced the Aborigines into exile.

It is clear that what happened to the Aborigines in Taiwan was by no means an isolated phenomenon. Rather, it was part of an overall social transformation that swept over the whole island since the beginning of the Cold War. The Kuomintang authoritarian regime reinforced its alliance with international capitalist interests and made its presence felt in every aspect of peoples' lives; society as a whole was violently divided and segmented.

In the past four decades, the Kuomintang has solicited the backing of foreign powers and their commercial interests for its own survival. It adopted a policy that pushed the island to be incorporated in the network of the U.S.-dominated international division of labor. This policy, which tried to make economic dependency a partisan asset, has meant a very high social cost for the people of Taiwan.

If we say that Taiwan society as a whole experiènced a neocolonialistic appropriation at an international level, to the Aborigines this meant being subcolonized to the lowest social strata via a process of "internal colonization."

Out in the Open

Under the Kuomintang's sophisticated information control and censorship, the facts presented in the previous sections remained unknown to the majority of the people in Taiwan. Only very recently have certain events been brought out into the open, striking people with surprise.

On 1 May 1983, *High Mountains Are Green*, the first magazine of, and by, the Aborigines was published. The front cover of this issue states, "We have to say that Taiwan High Mountain Tribes are facing a deadly crisis of genocide." Hence, a social movement of the Aborigines for their own emancipation and salvation forced its way into an arena where several other struggles were in the nascent stage.

In 1984, there were two big mining disasters in which almost two hundred people were killed, half of them Aborigines. These two disasters not only helped heighten social consciousness on industrial safety but also alerted people of the socioeconomic predicament in which the Aborigines were trapped. By the end of 1984, the first Aborigines' organization, in English, the "Alliance of Taiwan Aborigines" (ATA), formally declared its existence. This organization coined the term "primordial inhabitants" for all of the ten existing Aborigine groups. This first major step taken by the Aborigines to show their self-awareness marked the beginning of their struggle for survival, not only as isolated individuals but as societies and cultures.

As Eric R. Wolf says, "The ability to bestow meanings—to 'name' things, acts, and ideas—is a source of power. Control of communication allows the managers of ideology to lay down the categories through which reality is to be perceived."[8] What is more, this naming, or categorization, "conversely, entails the ability to deny the existence of alternative cate-

8. Eric R. Wolf, *Europe and the People without History* (Berkeley and Los Angeles: University of California Press, 1988), 388.

gories, to assign them to the realm of disorder and chaos, to render them socially and symbolically invisible."[9] This is precisely the politics of "rectification." Predicated upon the notion that history is a business of "account-making"[10] and "performance,"[11] I would argue that the people who have had the longest and most intimate relations with the island of Taiwan—the Aborigines—are not without their own names and voices when speaking about, and for, themselves, but their voices have been overwhelmed, and their names have been stolen, co-opted under layers and layers of historical accounts in alien languages.

Among the ten existing tribes today in Taiwan, the Atayal, Bunun, Tsou, and Tau (Yami) peoples refer to themselves by these names, which actually mean "human being." The Tsarisan people, whose name means "people of the mountains," now call themselves the Rukai. Panapanaya (now Puyuma) is a name originally used by their neighbors to the north, the Ami; Puyuma means "guests." And Ami itself is a name used by the Panapanaya to mean "the northern(ers)."[12] The remaining three groups are the Thao, Saisiat, and the Paiwan; it is not known what their terms of self-address mean.

In historical and present-day practices, these names have been used in specific circumstances and in highly confined contexts to denote non-Han cultural populations in Taiwan. They are little known to the population at large, except to a small circle of "mountain area" administrators, missionaries, and scholars who have built their careers upon them and therefore cannot afford *not* to acknowledge their existence.

Throughout history, however, these peoples have been lumped together under different labels by different "others" in different circumstances. Aborigines in Han-centric Chinese historical accounts were most frequently called "Fan." Fan, as a category, encompasses whatever is excluded from

9. Wolf, *Europe and the People without History*, 388.

10. Bernard S. Cohn, "History as Account-making" (Unpublished paper presented in Professor Marshall Sahlins's seminar "History and Anthropology," University of Chicago, 1984).

11. Greg Dening, "Transformations that Present the Past: A Poetic for History" (Unpublished paper presented in Professor Marshall Sahlins's seminar "History and Anthropology," University of Chicago, 1984).

12. All terms used by the Aborigines on the island, whether as self-address or as reference to neighbors, are terms basically asserting the subject in reference to their human existence. This is quite different from the Han-centered formulations that make reference to others in terms of animals or ghosts.

what is deemed or claimed to be Han. This category has become so encompassing that in actual practice, it is virtually meaningless. Thus, prefixes had to be coined. Aborigines in the island were labeled "east-fan," "dirt-fan," "wild-fan," "raw-fan," "cooked-fan," "already-assimilated-fan," "not-yet-assimilated-fan," "transforming-fan," "mountain-fan," "plains-fan," et cetera.[13]

After 1945, fifty years of Japanese colonial rule ended. The postwar reformulation of the Aborigines by the Chinese under a new republican ide-ology was also transformed. The Han-centric administration began to label the Aborigines as "mountain tribes," "mountain tung-pao" (brethren of the mountains), or simply "mountain-pao."

Given this bureaucratic context in which Aborigines were labeled as ruled subjects, permutations of the ill-formulated "mountain-pao" became not only possible but, in a sense, necessary. Consequently, we have terms such as "mountain-area mountain-pao" and "plain-area mountain-pao" ap-pearing in provincial government bulletins and, later, in academic reports. The most recent permutation actually reflects the exodus of these people from their long-designated habitations to the city slums. So, nowadays, we hear of "city-dwelling mountain-pao." In addition, occupations were also used as designations. Some people venture to suggest that the most appro-priate categorizations today would be something such as "mountain-pao in the coal pits," "mountain-pao on the high seas," "mountain-pao hanging on the high-rise scaffold," and "mountain-pao of the whorehouse."[14]

Thus, the stage was set for the "real natives" to speak out for them-selves. On 15 February 1985, the first page of the first issue of *Primordial Inhabitant*, a bimonthly newsletter published by the ATA (established on 29 December 1984), published an article entitled "Primordial Inhabitant: Why We Chose This Name." The Aborigines chose this name because it is "pure," and it makes clear that it refers to the peoples who were the original masters of this island, and because it is a newly coined term that has not yet been contaminated.

In the years between its establishment and the lifting of martial law, the ATA has carried out a series of educational and social service tasks catering mainly to the dislocated urban slum Aborigines. Politically, they

13. Chiu Yen-Liang, "Some Observations on Social Discourse Regarding Taiwan's Pri-mordial Inhabitants" (Paper presented at the First International Symposium on Taiwan Studies, University of Chicago, 9 July 1985).
14. Chiu, "Some Observations."

protested the execution of Tang Yin-sun, a teenager who resisted the unbearable abuses of his Han employer and finally killed the employer's family in a fury; they demonstrated in the prostitute district of Taipei, protesting the institutionalized system of teenage prostitution—especially the buying and selling of Aborigine girls for prostitution; they also managed to force the Kuomintang ministry of education to agree to scrap the Han chauvinistic myth of Woo-fong from elementary school textbooks.

Judging from what had been said and what has been done, the leaders of this newly born social movement are of great maturity and creativity. They are by no means aiming at any "return" to any imagined "primordial states" or to their pristine cultural origins. They are faced squarely with the realities of today that threaten their survival, not only of individuals but of ten dying societies and their cultures.

"New Social Movements" in a Radical Democratic Perspective

The various actions of the Aborigines in the years 1983–1985 were made possible, and successful, by the extended support they received from the non-Aborigine and nonparty-affiliated (*Tan-Wai*) (黨 外) groups of progressives: feminists, environmentalists, antinuclear activists, labor organizations, liberation theologians, conservationists, writers, professors, and editors.

These people believed that the independent development of multiple social movements in Taiwan was proof that various important issues were at stake. As a result of the highly dispersed and fluid nature of these movements, their coalition under a leftist umbrella became not only possible but also necessary. A leftist logo or stamp, however, cannot be printed on such a coalition. These multiple struggles, whose interests converge at so many points, must be woven together. And from a radical democratic perspective, one would suggest that the Aborigines form the warp of this fabric. No sincere social movement in Taiwan could remain untouched by the Aborigine issue. For example:

• The Yami people's homeland, Lanyu, was used as a nuclear waste dump, and no action whatsoever has been taken by the authorities neither to resettle nor to compensate the Aborigines there. Is this not the concern of a left-oriented antinuclear movement as much as it is of the Yami?

• Thousands of teenage Aborigine girls are being either sold or pawned to brothels. Their plight is as significant to the Aborigines as it is to the left-oriented feminist movement.

• Is it possible to push for conservation without addressing the issue of the Aborigines' struggle for survival space and their basic land rights?

• Traditional fishermen in Taiwan are now at the mercy of large capitalist fishing enterprises. As a consequence, a majority of fishermen have become fishery workers with abysmal incomes and working conditions. Today, the Aborigines constitute the majority of these fishermen-serfs. Any social movement that aims to help the fisherman cannot but address the reasons for the disproportionately high number of Aborigines in this trade.

• The Kuomintang has controlled or manipulated peasant associations and sacrificed their interests for those of the commercial capitalists. A social movement committed to defend the peasants against exploitation and oppression must recognize the fact that such control and exploitation has been at its worst in the mountain areas.

• As in the fishing trade, the Aborigines are concentrated disproportionately in trades such as coal mining, ship dismantling, and high-rise construction work. These trades are hazardous, offer the least job security, and are the least unionized. Can the labor movement take off without using these trades as major battlegrounds?

To be sure, all of this is not to suggest that the Aborigines be made a nodal point of Taiwan's various social movements. One would, however, hope for a radical democratic articulation. It is in the context of a variety of social movements that the Aborigines can find their proper place. And more importantly, it is largely in relation to the Aborigines and their suffering that all non-Aborigine progressives can define and realize their cause. In this sense, to all Han progressives or leftists (or whichever titles they may identify with), we say: Without the emancipation of the 300,000 Aborigines, the emancipation of Taiwan is impossible.

The Squeeze of Primordial Inhabitants' Discourse during the Postmartial-law "Democratic Turn"

History not only twists, it bounces. The lifting of martial law, retrospectively speaking, signified not the enhancement of but the setback of social movements in general and of the primordial inhabitants' self-saving movement in particular. This ebbing of spontaneous societal resistances occurred while

1. political parties emerged instantly and mushroomed;

2. major political actors over-"politicized" their stance on the issue of independence/unification;

3. previously backseat politicians jumped en masse on the bandwagon of "electoral democracy" and exhausted all socially available resources and mobilizational capacities; and

4. existing social movements became objects of appropriation by contesting political interests in the fulfillment of short-term power gain. Movements were turned into either their proprietors' private property or, worse, were used as tokens, or were simply reduced to "physical acts."

Eight months before the lifting of martial law, a new political party forced its way into existence, calling itself the Democratic Progressive Party (DPP). This move shocked the Kuomintang and shook the island—it had defied a party that had ruled for forty years. The DPP was a hastily established party, whose only unifying element was the opposition to the existing political order. Forces that formed this coalition were of an extremely diverse nature in terms of their power base, ideological persuasions, political orientation, economic interests, as well as the stance taken with minorities and national problems.

Judging from the DPP's manifesto, various communiqués, and its actual performance in the past, it is clear that it was manned by middle-class intellectuals and politicians. On the one hand, their political goal was to defend the interests of large- and middle-sized businesses; on the other hand, they wanted to break the Kuomintang's monopoly. This is not to say they were opposed to monopoly as such. Were it to be shared or substituted—especially by a group of neo-power elite that might emerge from the battle in a more liberalized general election—the opposition to the monopoly of power might cease to exist. Criticisms and accusations of the DPP soon arose, as they were seen as a party whose politics were to substitute rather than transform, share rather than reform, the power structure. The DPP was compared with the Kuomintang and strong similarities were pointed out, from behavior patterns to institutional arrangements, political orientation, ruling mentality, and the philosophy of a two-party system together with all the relevant and irrelevant rhetoric.

Most significantly, the Aborigine issue was wholly absent from the political programs of the DPP. The Kuomintang, even during the period in which it controlled the central government in China, had never been confronted with the problems of minorities or "frontier nations." At that time, the control of many regions was merely nominal, especially with regard to the minority areas. After the "northern expedition," the five-stripe flag of "a republic of five nations" was replaced by a flag of "red earth with white sun and blue sky." Since that time, the notion that China was a multination state had been virtually unacknowledged—neither in the Kuomintang's ideology nor in its various versions of the constitution. The peoples of China became one single nation—the "Central Flower Nation"—a nation composed of people of varying degrees of Han-ness, graded (degraded) from the Han center to its periphery. The DPP shared this attitude. It made no mention of the multinational or multicultural reality of Taiwan's people.

One of the major issues among the DPP's rival cliques concerned the future political affiliations of Taiwan—whether to push for "independence" under *pax Americana* or to acquiesce in unification with the Chinese mainland in the future. There had also been talk of an independent "Taiwan nation." This notion of an independent Taiwan, however, recognized as "Taiwanese" only groups of Han immigrants from China (except, of course, the most recent group of Han military personnel and their families who fled recently to Taiwan together with the ruling Kuomintang). It was the offspring of Han immigrants to Taiwan from the Ch'ing dynasty, who spoke Southern Fukian (now called Taiwanese), who were to be the "Taiwanese" sui generis. The boundary between the Han and the ten non-Han Aboriginal groups was clearly marked—this was Han chauvinism in full swing and in its most manifest state.

While claiming itself representative of the interests of all people, the DPP neglected all social classes except itself—the bourgeoisie. Given this position, it is understandable that it would be blind to both the development of labor movements and the growth of the Aborigines' struggle in recent years.

In countering such a power constellation and its drive toward a U.S.-modeled bipartisan parliamentary scheme of interests/power-sharing, the *Tan-Wai* Left was forced to join with a nonaffiliated legislator, Y. S. Wong, who suddenly announced he was forming a third party, the Labour Party (LP). The strategy of the *Tan-Wei* Left was to overwhelm Wong with both manpower and political steadfastness. This group of people managed to staff the organizing secretariat of the nascent LP and drafted all the founding statements as well as the party platform.

In their "Declaration on the Founding of the Labour Party," a full paragraph is devoted to the "primordial inhabitant":

The primordial inhabitants were first deprived of their arable land by the Han immigrants, then deceived of their fruits of labour through various forms of exchange of unequal values. Since the 1960s, their society has further disintegrated. Their traditional societies and cultures of the mountain regions are being destroyed. And they have been transformed to man the most backward and rock-bottom segments in Taiwan's capitalist development. Furthermore, the very existence of their race is in danger. On the one hand, there is no way to eke out a living in a bankrupt mountain economy, on the other hand, it is difficult to find a decent job outside of their mountains. The thousands of young Aborigine girls working as prostitutes is evidence of their unbearable suffering. The Labour Party is of the opinion that the suffering of the primordial inhabitants is a burden on the Han people to assist the primordial inhabitants in their rejuvenation and independent development.

On 6 December 1987, the LP held its first congress and passed its manifesto. It was divided into twelve sections: politics, mainland policies, economics, education, social rights, culture, environment, women's rights, primordial inhabitants, labor, mid-/small-sized business, and agriculture and fishing. On the primordial inhabitants, they elaborated further on what had been said in the declaration: Concrete propositions were needed to recover primordial inhabitants' land rights, to establish autonomous districts, and to allow them to retain Aborigine status outside the mountain regions.

The LP party patchwork had been so hastily put together in a forced and expedient manner that the team of Wong, as the party chairman, and the party secretariat had to break up even before the first upcoming election. A lukewarm and lonely Wong, and his LP, were stuck with an unwelcome, most progressive platform. At the same time, the progressives, choked with frustrations and disillusions, were left without a party and without a meaningful political declaration to which they could again claim to subscribe.

Months later, some of these progressives regrouped under the banner of a "workers'" party (勞 動 黨). This time, it was the "new old Left" who were dominating. In the party's platform, there were only three short points concerning the primordial inhabitants.

While the party was obviously trying to rally the combined forces of various social movements for the advancement of all working peoples' rights and interests, it gave the working class center stage, a privileged nodal position. This approach is not without its problems. It could prove counterproductive in terms of opening up the maximum political space in which to rally all the possible social forces. The fear had been realized that the workers' party, while successfully avoiding the pitfalls of bourgeois democratic opportunism and statism, could very well find themselves trapped in "classism" and working-class essentialism instead. This, no doubt, hampered the formation of a united front of various new social movements.[15]

Under such circumstances, the issues concerning the primordial inhabitants and their discourse were conveniently squeezed out of the political agenda of both the opposition Right and the opposition Left. The primordial inhabitants themselves were left out in the cold again. Han-chauvinism was yet again reincarnated under the auspices of a "democratic turn."

Identity Politics in Its Many Guises

It wasn't surprising that both the liberal Right and progressive Left should have abandoned the primordial inhabitants once a "democratization" free ride was offered. Both groups took such a move as an irreversible passage, from particularism to universalism, from tradition to innovation, from belief to reason, and, therefore, from identity to democracy. In Touraine's words, they "both [were] led to exclude the idea of identity from their ideology."[16] In effect, both, especially the institutionalized Left, not only enshrined "CITIZEN" as the only possible social actor but constantly called on the state to dispense with local luminaries or collectives.[17] Under such a "high-modern" onslaught, the primordial inhabitants' social resistances were "forced" to withdraw back into the realm of identity politics, with all of its ambiguities and double-edged swords. I am ready to admit that such moves were meant to withdraw into the defense, or, if you wish, that such moves were a withdrawal to "an appeal to a nonsocial definition of the social actor."[18] In the concrete practice of our case, it actually referred to both a metasocial guarantor of social order as well as an infrasocial and natural force. In other words, the group identity valorization axes were once again shifted back to primordiality and focused on claims made around signs of ethnicity.[19] I, therefore, understand the discourse practices, in the form of

15. Stuart Hall, "Gramsci's Relevance for the Study of Race and Ethnicity," *Journal of Communication Inquiry* 10, no. 2 (Summer 1986): 5–27.

16. See Alain Touraine, *Return of the Actor: Social Theory in Postindustrial Society* (Minneapolis: University of Minnesota Press, 1988), 76. The following discussion is basically a discourse in response to his thesis of "the two faces of identity."

17. A discussion of the similarity between the liberal and the Left, as well as their historical consequences, can also be found in Immanuel Wallerstein, *Unthinking Social Science: The Limits of Nineteenth-century Paradigms* (Cambridge, Mass.: Polity Press, 1991).

18. Touraine, *Return of the Actor*, 75.

19. For further discussion on group identity valorization schemes and operations in Han-

social actions, as variations of an identical leitmotif; an identity politics in its many guises.

Since the space allowed for this essay does not warrant a detailed analysis, I will simply itemize the most publicized examples as follows:

• In March–May 1987, in protest against the destroying of seventeen ancestor tombs of the Bunun by Han developers, primordial inhabitants in central Taiwan with fifteen social groups, led by the ATA, went out on the streets of Taipei. A coffin placed on a truck headed the march, which ended at the presidents' palace when a protest letter was accepted by one officer.

• In June 1987, the protest was sounded and a petition was made by leaders of the ATA against the retaining of the "Mountains Control Scheme" for reasons of "public security." They exposed the fact that such a "revision" of "national security law" actually places the mountain areas and the Aborigines under even stricter control when martial law of the "whole island" had supposedly been lifted. They instead requested a genuine "Aborigine's reservation area" to be established (for self-rule).

• In September 1987, the press was dominated by primordial inhabitants' struggles waged against the official legend of Woo-fang (吳 鳳), who was said to render himself the victim of a headhunter in order to teach the "Fans" to stop killing. The temple, as well as the statue of Woo-fang, which personified a Han hegemonic project a la "whiteman's burden," became the main targets of protests. Demonstrations were also made to press the government to change the name of "Woo-fang Hsiang" (subcounty units, comprising several villages), whose residents were mainly primordial inhabitants. Symposiums were held in Taipei and attended by many nonprimordial inhabitants scholars, writers, and activists in denouncing the Great-Han chauvinism and its various practices.

• In October 1987, a movement of "restoring primordial inhabitants' proper names" echoed from various corners of the island. The primordial inhabitants wanted to readopt their names in their mother tongue, make them official, and at the same time give up their superimposed Han names. Stories emerged that the Han names were hastily "given" to the primordial inhabitants by Han petty clerks in an arbitrary and random manner some forty years ago, and that primordial inhabitants who met in the cities and fell

related settings, see Fred Y. L. Chiu, "Cultural Repertoires and Social Practices of Identity Valorization: Logics and Discursive Formations in Han-related Settings" (Paper presented at the International Conference on Cultural Criticism 1993—Public Sphere and Public Culture, Hong Kong, Dec. 1992–Jan. 1993).

in love—even married—discovered that they were close kin. The Taiwan primordial inhabitants also complained that they were the only "minorities" of the "Republic of China" who were forced to adopt Han names, and that the few hundred Mongolians and Tibetans who came to Taiwan with the KMT to serve as tokens for the regime to claim and imagine itself as representative of a Great China were not.

• In February 1988, three hundred young people from the smallest Aborigines group—the Yami, with a total of three thousand people—supported by fifty non-Aborigine social movement activists, launched a well-publicized antinuclear parade on their island of Lanyu. This was aimed at stopping the government from dumping nuclear waste in a yard next to their yam fields and their burial grounds. The young Yami leaders also managed to mobilize their tribal elderly, who not only participated in the parade but also performed a traditional ritual to curse and spell the "evil spirit" par excellence, the contemporary nuclear wastes.

• In August 1988, primordial inhabitants formed a coalition to promote and coordinate their land rights movements. They launched yet another parade in Taipei and pressed for their rights of space of survival.

• In October 1988, a memorial service and ceremony was made to Monanutao, who was killed by the Japanese in the famous battle of Wu-sheh (霧 社). The battle ended in an ethnic slaughter, with the Japanese using not only heavy artillery but poisonous gas. After that, the Japanese colonizers completely altered their "mountain policy," began to destroy natural settlements, and concentrated the Aborigines under heavy surveillance. In the ceremony, Monanutao's name was restored in his mother tongue. His Japanese name was abandoned, and he was made a hero of all primordial inhabitants in the island, regardless of their tribal affiliations.

• In November 1988, the name "Woo-fang Hsiang" was scrapped. The place was renamed "Ah-li mountain Hsiang." Ah-li is the name of the mountain region and, supposedly, a name derived from Aborigines' nomenclature. The ATA suggested that the Woo-fang Temple in the area be transformed into a memorial hall of "intertribal peaceful co-inhabitation."

Outreaching and Its Many Limits and Frustrations

Within a postmartial-law environment, in which political power was rapidly shifting and in which political alliances were rapidly forming and dissolving, the primordial inhabitants were not immediately aware that their struggle, as a social movement, was eroded, suppressed, and neglected by the politicking parties and their activities. On the contrary, they were impelled into engaging in political activities at large, and at all, levels—county, prefecture, provincial, national, even international—before it occurred to them to say no. Such an act of giving oneself to the unknown was not without consequences. Among the consequences, the discovering of the limits, as well as frustrations, embedded in various forms of outreaching could be considered positive ones. What follows is a summary of some of them:

Electoral Politics and Its Dilemmas

The election of different levels of parliamentarians—county, prefecture, provincial, and national—was practiced by the KMT ever since it exerted effective control of the island and declared martial law. These electoral displays were acts to claim that the "Republic of China" was a "Free China," a "Democratic China," and a China deserving international recognition in the form of a seat in the United Nations (and its Security Council) and in the form of military, as well as economic, aid from the United States. Over the years, however, unintended consequences developed from such a cosmetic practice, and the electoral process increasingly became a means for challenging KMT domination, a contestation for local power and a forum for genuine democratization. Nevertheless, the election of parliamentarians for the Aborigine and for the Aborigine areas was still under the firm grip of the KMT. It was not until the end of martial law that two young primordial inhabitants ran against the candidates of the KMT for the first time. The two men suffered humiliating defeats, but their supporters felt good about their act of challenging the KMT in a highly symbolic show of defiance. In the postmartial-law era, a few more people joined in the race, but only to suffer the same defeat. They were too poor to support their candidacy in a "golden-cow" politics. Their areas were too vast to cover and too difficult to reach. Their ethnic affiliation was too wide-ranging (ten tribes and ten different mother tongues), and the constraints they had to face were too grave—they had to apply for "mountain entry permits" even to go back to their own homes to campaign for their cause. What is ironic is that the Aborigines were so weak and small (in terms of block votes) that they were not even worth co-opting by the opposition. Except for candidates backed by the ATA, there was no candidate running for the Aborigines' seats who was supported by the DPP or other oppositional parties.

Understanding China and Its Disillusionment

After the KMT regime lifted the travel ban to the Chinese mainland, groups of Taiwan primordial inhabitants took advantage of the chance to "discover" their fellow "minorities" across the Taiwan Strait, and they tried to learn about their situation. What they first learned about were the miserable experiences during the Cultural Revolution years, endured by a handful of Taiwan Aborigines who fled to China from Taiwan after the February 28 Massacre carried out by the KMT in 1947. They also realized that there was a tremendous gap between the words and the deeds that the Communist Chinese Government imposed upon its "national minorities" in the past forty years. While they traveled, accompanied by party cadres and other escorts, they saw poverty behind the official facade and people who had been turned into either subjects or submissive vassals. What irritated them the most was the fact that the Chinese authorities called the Taiwan primordial inhabitants the "Taiwan High Mountain Tribe." In doing so, they not only denied the fact that there were at least nine separate linguistic groups, and, therefore, tribes, in Taiwan but also insisted that such issues could be recognized and rectified only after Taiwan had been successfully "reunited" with China. What came with the "Taiwan-mountain-tung-pao" from their remote China was the rubric and concept of a "national regional autonomy." Yet, the notion of autonomy had to be radically redefined and its contents thoroughly reconstructed under a totally different sky of a present-day Taiwan.

International Networking and Its Disappointments

A relaxed political control in Taiwan also made international networking possible for primordial inhabitants' activists. Nevertheless, it did not take long for the leaders of the "tribal peoples' struggle" on the island to realize that the greatest gain from it for their movement on the ground was, at best, something rather "symbolic." The famous Paiwan blind poet Monarneng went to North America and Hawaii, attending an international conference for endangered tribal peoples and cultures. What he found was just talk and more talk. His trip to Hokkaido, Japan, left him with a deep sense of loss as he realized that the Ainu in the North, as well as the untouchables in the inner cities, were in a worse situation than the Taiwan primordial inhabitants, for the very existence of these subaltern groups was not even acknowledged by the society at large. Furthermore, individuals within such groups not only did not identify themselves with fellow members but lacked any means—their own language, territory, way of life, or even a minimum of symbolic representations—to do so should they want to. Ahwoo, the Paiwan woman in charge of the Aborigines journal *Hunter Culture* (獵 人 文 化), flew to the Arctic Circle to meet with Eskimos and representatives from North American Native Americans. Day in and day out, the meeting turned into something like a competition for telling stories of misery and suffering and of an ongoing collective lamentation. Ahwoo's lecture on strategies of societal self-defenses finally offered hope for the future.

Panu went to Thailand, as the representative of the ATA, to attend a general assembly called by the Indigenous Peoples Forum. He became a member of the executive council and participated in the drafting of the Asia Indigenous Peoples Pact. The forum, and its Asia Indigenous Peoples Pact, had almost no influence on the social struggle of Taiwan's primordial inhabitants. No one, not even the primordial inhabitants themselves, know much about the event, not to mention the pact. Their goal of simply spreading the news, without breaking through the KMT and other political parties' tight grip on media control, was difficult to achieve.

Legislation Reform and Its Failures

Under the pressure of the ATA and other groups of Aborigines, two KMT legislators drafted a "basic law for primordial inhabitants" to be adopted by the Legislative Yuan. This failed. During the process of amending the constitution, public hearings were held with regard to the "rectification" of the name of Aborigines from "mountain-pao" to "primordial inhabitants." The interior ministry was fiercely against such an idea and argued that it would be "unfair" to other social groupings if such a name were adopted. Some so-called progressive scholars and, especially, anthropologists suddenly changed their "pro-Aborigines" stance and declared that there was no evidence that the Aborigines now in Taiwan were offspring of the earliest Homo sapiens on the island. They suggested calling the Aborigines "earlier residents." In May 1992, protests and demonstrations were launched against the "new constitution." On 26 May, the constitution was adopted, but the Aborigines on the island remained known as "mountain-pao."

The DPP, after all that had happened, finally adopted a "treatise on primordial inhabitants' rights" as their internal position paper. But such a token appeasement had come a little too late, and as too little.

Soul-searching amidst the Onslaughts of Multiple Systematization

Postmartial-law politics in Taiwan, in sum, have been a process in which contesting political powers compete for domination and hegemony.

To the primordial inhabitants' survival struggle, however, what was detrimental was that all of the competing powers were strengthening themselves through acts of expansion and appropriation. All previously existing or burgeoning social movements were either co-opted or suppressed. The sole criterion for such a flip-flop in attitude had been based on the judgment that the said "movement" could enhance immediate political gain—both in the name of public policy and in the language of the technocrats—through a "democratic" game of "quantitative authoritarianism" and via an "exchange" in the political market.

To put this in yet another perspective, what the political power, or power-to-be, did was to push through its systemic drives to strengthen its "political capital." This was true for both the advocates of "Taiwan independence" and the supporters of "China reunification." This is even more real than might be obvious, as the KMT was driving at reinstating a new "state," while the DPP strived for the making of a new "nation." Without any doubt, both the KMT and the DPP were motivated by the same things: a nineteenth-century, Western-modeled state-building, and nation-making to hegemonize yet another state-nation—or, if you will, the so-called nation-state, as myths have it.

Bombarded by multiple inroads of systematization, and after suffering numerous setbacks and disillusionments, the primordial inhabitants and their survival struggle can only begin to rethink and unthink the past as well as the future. Since the lifting of martial law and the sudden upsurge of social discourse on the "Taiwanese consciousness" and the "we-province/ other-province contradiction," the Aborigines of this island voiced their doubt about the relevancy of such a Great-Han versus Small-Han formulation of social privilege and dogmatization. They were also keenly aware of what the "mountain area development initiative," promoted by the provincial government, meant to their habitat for thousands of years. We heard the rather sophisticated discussion by Yifan Yeogan, the editor general of *Hunter Culture*, and his colleagues on the detrimental effects of market forces, as well as the need to remain special as societal groupings and to be deserving of specific rights—such as hunting and the access to traditional natural resources—for tribal/cultural reproduction. There were also sober reflections on the longtime, overpublicized "debate" on independence versus unification. In contrast, the focus has been carefully directed toward details of cosmetic changes as well as all their possible consequences. Finally, there was serious discussion on the relationship between the primordial inhabitants' social movement and the so-called parliamental/electoral politics. The soul-searching covered areas on the nature of the KMT—and possibly the DPP—state(s), the possibility/impossibility of self-defense, the self-production of civil society, as well as the limits and deceptive effects of party politics.

All the brainstorming gradually conveyed the forming of a strategy of "base enhancement" for cultural regermination. According to the primordial inhabitants' own slogan, as proposed by Taipang Sesale, editor general of *Aborigine Post* (原 報), struggle means "fighting on the land of the primordial inhabitants as bases" (原 鄉 戰 鬥) and "outreach from the tribal settlements with expedition" (部 落 出 擊).

The Coming-into-being of an A-systemic Positioning and a Strategy of Alternative Cultural Politics

The idea of cultural regermination and regeneration is not something imagined or invented by Taipang Sesale. It has been in effect for quite some time. Although the slogan adopted by Taipang Sesale sounded somewhat militaristic, it was strictly cultural, or for that matter, "hunteral." In a paper entitled "When Taiwan's Aborigines Write in Chinese," Daiwei Fu observed that, in the emerging literature in Chinese by the Aborigines, it is the city-dwelling Aborigines who hunt for words in a concrete forest in order to carve out a living space in a culture filled with *Bailong* writings.[20] Nevertheless, it is now the same hunters who had turned their faces toward their ancestors' forest, who sneaked back into it, to try to relearn the skill of dealing with nature and the living, in recuperating and re-creating their strayed self as well as the collective.

Beginning with the end of martial law, there was a practice of reclaiming the right to mother tongues in addition to the claims of land rights. There were quite a few mother-tongue teaching materials, published by the Aborigines themselves, and I am sure there will be more in the future. *Hunter Culture* made its first appearance in August 1990. Its staff established a Humanities and Cultural Center in October 1992. *Aboriginal Post* has entered its fifth year. Primordial inhabitants' art groups and dance

20. Daiwei Fu, "When Taiwan's Aborigines Write in Chinese" (Unpublished paper presented at the International Conference on Cultural Criticism 1993—Public Sphere and Public Culture, Hong Kong, Dec. 1992–Jan. 1993).

   Bailong, which means "bad people," according to Fu, is an Atayal rendition of "Han-people," a refraction of Hokien language spoken in Taiwan.

troupes, organized and administered by themselves, have visited various sites and ceremonies for intensive field studies. They have brought back a wealth of art and remade them as living manifestations embedded in an everyday practice context. Sakuliu Pavavalung, the self-taught stone carver, pot maker, stone-plat house architect, ethnobotanist, folklorist, has taught a whole new generation of practitioners of Aborigines' arts.

What has been uniquely significant is a quest to rehabilitate and to reinhabit ancient settlements that were abandoned for decades. In October 1991, more than twenty Bunnun elderlies set out on their journey back, for the first time, to their Dandar settlement, which the Japanese had forced them to abandon some fifty years ago.[21]

Sustained efforts were made in Pingtung to rebuild the Rukai's oldest settlement of Kochapogan. The reconstruction was led by Aovini, who had been working in Taipei until he was forty. His "success" in Han society, however, only prompted him to become more critical of that denatured, hypocritical practice of a life-style of hyperaccumulation. He gave up all he had and moved back to the mountain to recover a self-reliant way of life, to the self-generating society of new Kochapogan. His cause has gathered substantial momentum and support in the past few years. A few old stone-platted traditional houses have already been restored and are ready to be inhabited.

Of course, none of the above concrete cultural praxes was politically "innocent." On the contrary, firm convictions in cultural regermination have been responsible in sustaining and reproducing a similar tactic in diversified manifestations. The tactic is "depoliticizing," precisely in the quest for "cultural sovereignty"; it is self-gazing and self-fulfilling, precisely to firmly rebuild self-confidence; and it celebrates diversity and multiplicity of cultural expressions, precisely to countervail the dominant ideology of homogeneity and uniformity. The leaders of such a cultural movement believe that their efforts enrich us all by preserving local languages and everyday practices, precisely to rehabilitate our rapidly depleting cultural gene pools.

In a strategic sense, such praxes turn out to be the only genuine act of anti-hegemonic practice. They are precisely not to counter-hegemonize, not to substitute a systematization with yet another other-systematization. They are, if you will, the genuine alternative form of cultural politics, which I would call a hard-fought a-*systemic positioning.*

---

21. See the field report by Woo Chih Chin, entitled "Bunnon of Dandar Settlement Looking for Roots," *The Earth* 51 (June 1992): 112–29.

During the spring of 1993, I was asked to present my views on field practice for a workshop on oral history and alternative ethnographies organized for the primordial inhabitants. It was truly a lifelong memorable experience for a first-time pilgrim in Kochapogan. On the morning of the third, and final, day, we gathered in front of the transparent water pool for a farewell dialogue. By the end, Monarneng, the blind poet of the primordial inhabitants, told everyone:

> I had an icy cold shower under the waterfall this morning. While the water rushed down my face and my body, I felt I was reborn. I prayed immediately to our ancestors. I thanked them for washing away all my sorrows and cleaning away every single bit of my resentment. The voices echoing in the air told me clearly, so clearly, that we had to fight so hard, for the recovery of our identity is meant precisely to give it up once again, it is to set an example for all mankind to give it up. We are re-creating Kochapogen. Yes, what we are really re-creating is a fairer tomorrow for us all.

I don't have better words to end this essay. I have to stop here.

Pasts and Futures

Cultural Construction and Native Nationalism: Report from the Hawaiian Front

Jeffrey Tobin

"Cultural construction" is but one name for a discourse that goes by many names. There are differences between "cultural construction," "the construction of culture," "social construction," "discursive sociology," and "the politics of culture," to name just a few. But there are also fundamental similarities. All such discourses share a certain distance from "reality," which is, of course, always in quotation marks. The quotation marks indicate a discourse that is about discourse, in which nothing is natural but is naturalized, and nothing is present but is represented. This sort of scholarship is characterized by its step back—its step out of the hustle and bustle of everyday meaning into the stratified world where meanings are made. The emphasis is not on culture but on the context in which culture is produced.

Jean Jackson has called attention to a significant side effect of the

I wrote the first draft of this essay while I was a degree participant at the East-West Center's Institute of Culture and Communication. It was presented as a Pacific Island Seminar at the invitation of Terry Teaiwa. I owe much to Michael Graves for his generously critical readings and for his ongoing support. I am also indebted to Ibrahim Aoudé and Marta Savigliano for accompanying me through relevant readings.

cultural construction discourse. She observes that when anthropologists talk about "making culture," they frequently find that they are "making enemies."[1] She argues that phrases such as "making culture" have negative connotations, and, accordingly, the people being written about in such terms tend to take offense. She argues that anthropologists should be responsive to such concerns, and that "with a little creating and inventing of our own, we can come up with models and metaphors describing indigenous responses that are acceptable to them, at least to some of them some of the time."[2] According to Jackson, the issue is one of showing as much respect for the "construction of culture" as an earlier generation of anthropologists showed for "culture" per se.[3]

Jackson's analysis is acute, but her solution is too facile. According to her, the problem is not what anthropologists say, but how they say it. Thus, she suggests that anthropologists come up with less pejorative language to describe what we now call "making culture." It is true that the language of cultural construction is pejorative, but this pejorativeness is not incidental to the cultural construction discourse. Whether anthropologists talk about "making culture" or of something fancier, such as "the semiotics of peoplehood," Native nationalists are likely to be angry, because they rightly perceive the cultural construction discourse as a challenge to their own political projects. Contrary to Jackson's suggestion, no amount of prettying-up can diffuse this challenge. More respectful language may obscure the conflict, but the conflict between cultural constructionists and Native nationalists is not so easily resolved. Richard Handler has argued that this conflict is intrinsic in the cultural construction discourse. In critiquing old-fashioned anthropology, Handler observes that he is led to critique nationalism as well, for "the portrayal of social realities in terms of reified cultures, each imagined as neatly bounded and distinctive from all others, is

1. Jean Jackson, "Is There a Way to Talk about Making Culture without Making Enemies?" *Dialectical Anthropology* 14 (1989): 127–43.
2. Jackson, "Is There a Way to Talk," 129.
3. Jackson draws an analogy between culture and language, or, more specifically, between colonially constructed cultures and colonially constructed languages, that is, creoles. She suggests that anthropologists follow linguists in raising the status of colonial constructions. Linguists once looked down at creoles and pidgins, treating them as nonlanguages, much, Jackson argues, as anthropologists treat postcontact cultures. But linguists came to recognize that all languages—not just creoles—are constructed, and so they began to treat creoles with more respect. According to Jackson, anthropologists should likewise raise the status of colonially constructed cultures.

as central to nationalist rhetoric and ideology as it is to the traditional anthropological worldview."[4] Thus, it is not surprising for a critique of old-fashioned anthropology to lead to a critique of Native nationalism.

The conflict with Native nationalists puts cultural constructionists in an awkward position. George Marcus has observed that "the conventional attitude of empathy and admiring sympathy usually displayed by ethnographers . . . is difficult to reconcile with the full implications of an invention of culture approach that probes deception, demystification of 'tradition,' and cultural struggle."[5] Handler notices the same tension between ethnographic empathy and an emphasis on cultural construction. He argues that anthropologists should be critical, which means demystifying cultural reification, but he also recognizes that anthropologists should respect their subjects' subjectivity. A conflict arises because the demystification of nationalist discourse would seem to undermine the nationalist's subjectivity; the cultural construction discourse is, at least implicitly, a critique of Native nationalism. Handler thus notes an opposition between the demands that anthropology be critical and that it be respectful.

Handler decides that "a destructive analysis of shared premises is more important than a dialogue with those who share them."[6] According to him, anthropology must, first of all, be critical, and this does not preclude being critical of nationalist subjects. Ethnographers must be prepared to confront mystifications, even if, in doing so, they contradict their subjects. But, fortuitously, Handler finds that destructive analysis does not necessarily destroy the respect that anthropologists traditionally grant to the subjects of anthropological inquiry. On the contrary, he hopes that "a destructive analysis of our shared presuppositions can become the anthropologist's contribution to a dialogue that respects natives by challenging rather than romanticizing them."[7] That is, anthropologists might show more respect for their subjects by offering them sincere criticism than by offering them ingenuous respect.

Roger Keesing has come to a very similar conclusion. Like Handler,

---

4. Richard Handler, "On Dialogue and Destructive Analysis: Problems in Narrating Nationalism and Ethnicity," *Journal of Anthropological Research* 41 (1985): 171–82. See also Richard Handler, *Nationalism and the Politics of Culture in Quebec* (Madison: University of Wisconsin Press, 1988), 15.
5. George Marcus, "Review of *Children of the Land* by Jocelyn Linnekin," *Pacific Studies* 10 (1986): 133.
6. Handler, "On Dialogue and Destructive Analysis," 181.
7. Handler, "On Dialogue and Destructive Analysis," 181.

Keesing recognizes that the cultural construction discourse is a challenge to Native nationalisms. But he argues that

> specialists on the Pacific do not best serve the interests of a less hegemonic scholarship or best support the political struggles of decolonizing and internally colonized Pacific peoples by suspending their critical judgement or maintaining silence—whether out of liberal guilt or political commitment—regarding mythic pasts evoked in cultural nationalist rhetoric. Our constructions of the real pasts are not sacrosanct, but they are important elements in a continuing dialogue and dialectic.[8]

Keesing, like Handler, suggests that openly confronting nationalists is more respectful than indulging their fantasies about culture, and that a dialogue can be maintained that includes a destructive analysis of indigenous myths.

My intention is to examine these claims, to look at the dialogue between cultural constructionists and Native nationalists. What does this new anthropology contribute to the "dialogue that respects natives by challenging rather than romanticizing them"? How does cultural construction "support the political struggles of decolonizing and internally colonized Pacific peoples"? As cultural constructionists teach us, discourse is culturally constructed. What, then, is the context in which the cultural construction discourse is constructed? What are the politics of the politics of culture?

A Micropolitics of Culture

Hawai'i provides an especially rich context in which to study the interaction between cultural construction and Native nationalism. Between the East-West Center's Institute of Culture and Communication and the University of Hawai'i's Department of Anthropology, cultural construction dominates the anthropological discourse of Hawai'i. The Institute's Cultural Construction and National Identity project is but one very large example of the prevalence of the cultural construction discourse in Hawai'i. Few, if any, "naïve positivists" are writing about culture in Hawai'i. Native nationalism also thrives in Hawai'i. Calls for sovereignty have grown so strong in recent years that the debate within the Hawaiian community has moved from whether self-determination should be sought to disputes over strategies for

8. Roger Keesing, "Creating the Past: Custom and Identity in the Contemporary Pacific," *Contemporary Pacific* 1 (1989): 37.

achieving it. Groups including ʿOhana O Hawaiʿi, Ka Lahui Hawaiʿi, Na ʿOiwi O Hawaiʿi, Protect Kahoʿolawe ʿOhana, and Nuclear Free and Independent Pacific have grown significantly. Sovereignty has become such a dominant issue within the Hawaiian community that even the Office of Hawaiian Affairs (a state agency) has begun to hedge its bets, publishing its own plan for achieving self-governance. In Hawaiʿi, Natives are just as committed to cultural politics as anthropologists are to the politics of culture.

As might be expected, the conflict between cultural constructionism and Native nationalism is rampant in Hawaiʿi. It is not necessary to imagine how Native nationalists might respond to the cultural construction discourse. In Hawaiʿi, the dialogue that anthropologists have called for is flourishing. At the center are anthropologist Jocelyn Linnekin and Hawaiian nationalist Haunani-Kay Trask. As Linnekin phrases it, there is a "micropolitics" of culture in Hawaiʿi, involving her ongoing dialogue with Trask.[9] Linnekin, who teaches in the Department of Anthropology at the University of Hawaiʿi's Mānoa campus, specializes in the politics of culture in Hawaiʿi and the Pacific. Hers are among the very best analyses of cultural construction, displaying theoretical sophistication and subtlety rarely encountered in the field. Linnekin is also among the anthropologists who are most active in working for Native Hawaiian land rights. Trask, the Director of the University's Center for Hawaiian Studies, is a prominent Hawaiian nationalist. She is an active citizen of Ka Lahui Hawaiʿi, the leader of the Hawaiian community at the University of Hawaiʿi, and has been active in Pacific-wide and global Native nationalist coalitions. Furthermore, Trask stands out among Native nationalists for her analyses of critical discourses, including feminism, Marxism, and cultural constructionism.

Linnekin and Trask have much in common: Each is forty-two years

9. Jocelyn Linnekin, "Text Bites and the R-Word: The Politics of Representing Scholarship," *Contemporary Pacific* 2 (1991): 172–77. If there is a micropolitics of culture in Hawaiʿi involving Linnekin and Trask, there is, for me, then, a molecular politics. I locate myself as a student of both Linnekin and Trask. I have been in the consistently privileged position of learning from each of them, but I have also found myself in the occasionally awkward position between them—for example, being asked to comment on drafts of papers each has written about the other. This essay is the result of such an exchange. It began in the comments I gave to Linnekin on a draft of her response ("Text Bites and the R-Word") to Trask (Haunani-Kay Trask, "Natives and Anthropologists: The Colonial Struggle," *Contemporary Pacific* 2 [1991]: 159–67). At Linnekin's suggestion, I turned those comments into the first draft of this essay. It was finished as part of a directed reading I had with Trask, and, at Trask's suggestion, I submitted it to *Contemporary Pacific*. The board of that journal—of which Linnekin is a member—rejected it.

old, was educated in Marxism, has published a book of feminist investigations,[10] began with a focus on Hawai‘i, and in recent years has branched out into broader, Pacific-wide issues. Yet, Linnekin and Trask consistently oppose one another on political and scholarly issues. At the center of their debate has been the conflict between Linnekin's politics of culture and Trask's cultural politics. The problem is surely not that Linnekin and Trask fail to understand one another; they understand each other all too well. For almost a decade, they have been reading and responding to each other. Linnekin, the cultural constructionist, has repeatedly written about Hawaiian nationalism, and Trask, the Hawaiian nationalist, has written regularly on cultural constructionism.

Culture, Political or Politicized

A recurring issue in Linnekin's and Trask's dispute involves Kaho‘olawe, a relatively small island lying eleven kilometers southwest of Maui. The United States Navy has been using the island for target practice despite repeated and increasing protests from Hawaiians—and others. At the forefront of the efforts to stop the Navy's bombing is the Protect Kaho‘olawe ‘Ohana, a group of Hawaiians dedicated to caring for the island, which they assert is sacred to Hawaiians. Both Linnekin and Trask are opposed to the Navy bombing, but they disagree about the sacredness of Kaho‘olawe.

Linnekin has argued that the sacredness of Kaho‘olawe is probably a recent invention. She cites ethnohistorical evidence that the island was formerly forbidden, or "taboo."[11] Linnekin observes that many Hawaiians, such as those in the Protect Kaho‘olawe ‘Ohana, assert that the island has "historical, cultural, spiritual, and social significance."[12] According to Lin-

10. See Haunani-Kay Trask, *Eros and Power: The Promise of Feminist Theory* (Philadelphia: University of Pennsylvania Press, 1986), and Jocelyn Linnekin, *Sacred Queens and Women of Consequence: Rank, Gender, and Colonialism in the Hawaiian Islands* (Ann Arbor: University of Michigan Press, 1990).

11. Jocelyn Linnekin, "Defining Tradition: Variations on the Hawaiian Identity," *American Ethnologist* 10 (1983): 241–52. Linnekin determines that Kaho‘olawe was *kapu*, or "marked." But she notes that this begs the question: in what sense *kapu*? *Kapu* as in "sacred" or *kapu* as in "forbidden"? She answers that the island was probably *kapu* in the sense of having been forbidden and thus was rarely inhabited.

12. Walter Ritte, Jr., and Richard Sawyer, *Na Mana‘o Aloha o Kaho‘olawe* (Honolulu: Aloha ‘Āina o na Kūpuna, Inc., 1978), quoted in Linnekin, "Defining Tradition," 248.

nekin, "it is not the 'facts' of Kahoʻolawe's not-so-glorious past that have imbued the island with this significance."[13] Rather, she argues, the tradition of the island's sacredness is constructed in response to the Navy bombing:

> Kahoʻolawe has acquired a new meaning for Hawaiians as a political and cultural symbol of protest, which is entirely distinct from its historical significance as a tabooed land. The bombing of the island is a graphic example of disregard manifest by white colonists for native lands and culture; in this sense, Kahoʻolawe is an apt focus for Hawaiian protests.[14]

Linnekin does not deny the significance of Kahoʻolawe as a symbol of protest against American colonialism, but she sees the island's contemporary significance as distinct from its former significance—or lack thereof. Her point is not that the tradition of Kahoʻolawe's sacredness is historically false; rather, Kahoʻolawe serves for Linnekin as an example of how "in nationalist movements, tradition is formulated as it is used for political ends."[15]

Trask's response is that Hawaiians care about the Navy bombing precisely because Kahoʻolawe is sacred, not the other way around. Politics have not made Kahoʻolawe sacred; rather, in the context of American colonization, the sacredness of Kahoʻolawe and all Hawaiian land has been politicized:

> Hawaiians assert a "traditional" relationship to the land *not* for political ends, as Linnekin argues, but because they continue to believe in the cultural value of caring for the land. That land is now contested makes such a belief political. This distinction is crucial because the Hawaiian cultural motivation reveals the persistence of traditional values, the very thing Linnekin claims modern Hawaiians have "invented."[16]

According to Trask, it is not a case of politics producing culture but of culture being politicized. It is because Kahoʻolawe is sacred to Hawaiians that the Navy bombing has become a political issue. In the context of colonialism,

13. Linnekin, "Defining Tradition," 248.
14. Linnekin, "Defining Tradition," 246.
15. Linnekin, "Defining Tradition," 250.
16. Haunani-Kay Trask, "Politics in the Pacific Islands: Imperialism and Native Self-Determination," *Amerasia* 16 (1990): 15–16 n. 3.

being Hawaiian is overwritten with political implications, but, according to Trask, this does not make Hawaiian-ness a political or colonial invention.

Both Trask and Linnekin recognize that Hawaiian culture has been drastically transformed by colonization, and that certain Hawaiian values have survived.[17] Still, Linnekin sees the resulting culture as political, whereas Trask sees Hawaiian culture as incidentally politicized. Linnekin locates culture in a relevant political context, whether that context happens to be pre- or post-"contact." She consistently understands culture as a political process. For Trask, culture *is*. Sometimes culture is surrounded by a colonial context, and *then* culture is politicized. But the politicization is incidental to the culture per se. Linnekin locates Native nationalism in the context of colonialism. She argues that Hawaiian nationalism is largely determined by its opposition to colonialism. Trask, however, argues that her own Native nationalist opposition to colonialism is secondary to her commitment to Hawaiian culture. She sees her Hawaiian-ness as the cause, not the effect, of her nationalism.

Linnekin's and Trask's disagreement echoes the testimony at the 1977 trial of five Protect Kaho'olawe 'Ohana members who were charged with trespassing on the island. At issue was whether the defendants had gone to the island with "criminal intent." Special Prosecuting Attorney Robert Manekin asked the defendant Walter Ritte, "Is it not true that you were politically, as well as spiritually, motivated to go on the Island?" Ritte replied, "I was motivated because I am Hawaiian." Ritte and the other defendants refused the prosecutor's description of their motives as "political." Similarly, their membership in "a political organization"—the Protect Kaho'olawe 'Ohana—was introduced as evidence of their political motives, to which they replied that "the 'Ohana is a family—not a political organization—which has spiritual roots in the concept of *aloha 'aina* [love of the land]." The prosecution responded with an expert witness who "identified

17. Linnekin notes similarities between hers and Trask's concepts of Hawaiian culture ("Text Bites and the R-Word"). For example, Trask writes that "culture is not static. . . . Without doubt, Hawaiians were transformed drastically and irreparably after contact, but remnants of earlier lifeways, including values and symbols, have persisted" (Trask, "Natives and Anthropologists," 165 n. 1). Compare Linnekin's conclusion that "cultural reproduction is never perfect, but neither is cultural transformation entire or complete. . . . What changes and what stays the same is a matter of values—what a society considers important, desirable, and high" (Jocelyn Linnekin, *Children of the Land: Exchange and Status in a Hawaiian Community* [New Brunswick, N.J.: Rutgers University Press, 1985], 247).

aloha ʻaina as a political concept that became popular around the time of Annexation."[18] Kahoʻolawe, he said, has no special significance. The judge ruled that the desire to stop the bombing of Kahoʻolawe was "a political purpose, not a religious one," and so the five were convicted.

The 1977 trial indicates a context in which Linnekin's and Trask's disputes can be understood. Linnekin, like the prosecutor, suggests that Hawaiians are politically, as well as spiritually, motivated to sanctify Kahoʻolawe. In the trial, having a political motive was grounds for being found guilty. No such immediate condemnation is attached to Linnekin's identification of political motivation in contemporary Hawaiian culture. Yet, Trask, like Ritte, resists the representation of her motives as political, and she similarly asserts that she is acting as a Hawaiian. I suggest that for Trask, as for Ritte, being described as politically motivated constitutes a threat. The imputation of political motives is perceived as a challenge because the "political" label carries connotations of "manipulative," "false," and "insincere." The separation of political from spiritual motives is seen as a misrepresentation that lessens the legitimacy of the resulting act. The analysis of motives is perceived to be a misleading and disempowering endeavor. Trask, like Ritte, protects the legitimacy and power of her acts by attributing them to being Hawaiian in a full, holistic sense; she resists analysis. Thus, she resists Linnekin's attempt to identify and isolate political components in Hawaiian culture.

For Linnekin, attributing political motives to Hawaiians does not delegitimate Hawaiian claims. The "political" for Linnekin is not false; it is inevitable. Her argument that Hawaiian efforts to protect Kahoʻolawe have a political context is not intended to undermine those efforts. To the contrary, Linnekin agrees that Kahoʻolawe is an apt location for engaging in anti-imperialist politics.

Culture as Process and as Privilege

Ultimately, Linnekin refrains from ruling on Trask's claims about Hawaiian-ness. Linnekin's contextual approach prevents her from either confirming or denying assertions about Hawaiian culture. Linnekin offers evidence to suggest that Kahoʻolawe was not formerly considered sacred, but she is not actively committed to such a historical argument. Her inten-

18. The preceding quotations from the trial are from Pam Smith, "Kahoolawe: Hawaiians on Trial," *Hawaii Observer*, 28 July 1977, 15.

tion is not to compete with her subjects to define their traditions. Indeed, Linnekin finds fault with Keesing for making just this mistake. Linnekin notes that cultural constructionists "explicitly and repeatedly reject the premise that anthropologists are privileged to define a "real or 'authentic past . . . real ways of life' which people in the present distort." [19]

Linnekin has argued that "there are no unequivocal 'facts' to be discovered in the relationship between past and present" and that "authenticity is always contextualized, always defined in the present." [20] Furthermore, writing with Handler, Linnekin has provided a particularly lucid contribution to the politics of culture discourse:

> Traditions are neither genuine nor spurious, for if genuine refers to the pristine and immutable heritage of the past, then all genuine traditions are spurious. But if, as we have argued, tradition is always defined in the present, then all spurious traditions are genuine. Genuine and spurious—terms that have been used to distinguish objective reality from hocus-pocus—are inappropriate when applied to social phenomena, which never exist apart from our interpretations of them. [21]

They argue that there are no "unauthentic" traditions or cultures, for no standard of the "real" past exists against which other pasts can be found wanting. Linnekin has thus championed a thoroughly contextualized approach to tradition, a position from which she can neither confirm nor deny, for example, the precontact sacredness of Kahoʻolawe.

While Linnekin does not distinguish between genuine and spurious traditions, she still makes a distinction between "real" and "false" cultures. The distinction separates culture-as-process from culture-as-product. Linnekin argues that "the process of cultural transmission . . . is dynamic, creative—and real," whereas "false cultures—static and passively transmitted—are produced by tourist industries, by nationalists, and by scholars, both Western and indigenous." [22] Linnekin thereby classifies Native nation-

---

19. Linnekin, "Text Bites and the R-Word," 172, quoting Keesing, "Creating the Past," 35.
20. Linnekin, *Children of the Land*, 241.
21. Richard Handler and Jocelyn Linnekin, "Tradition, Genuine or Spurious," *Journal of American Folklore* 97 (1984): 288.
22. Jocelyn Linnekin, "The Politics of Culture in the Pacific," in *Culture Identity and Ethnicity in the Pacific*, ed. Jocelyn Linnekin and Lin Poyer (Honolulu: University of Hawaii Press, 1990), 161. Benedict Anderson makes a similar distinction between "a genuine, popular nationalist enthusiasm and a systematic, even Machiavellian, instilling of

alists alongside travel agents and anthropologists—all three reify culture. "Certainly the nationalist and rural models of Hawaiian culture are not the same as the version promoted by the tourist industry," explains Linnekin; "the point is that neither are they isolated from it."[23] Hawaiian nationalists, according to Linnekin, see their own culture as a thing, and instead of unselfconsciously reproducing (and transforming) their culture, they have taken to representing it as something fixed. They "tend to circumscribe and delimit the range of behavior that conforms" to their model of culture: "the definition of 'acting Hawaiian' takes on a new rigidity; it becomes obligatory, rather than customary."[24] According to Linnekin, nationalists constitute their own culture as a product, whereas true culture is a process. To the extent to which Native nationalists objectify their cultures, the resulting representations of culture suffer from the same falseness as those of non-Native reifiers, such as travel agents and anthropologists.

Trask, like Linnekin, makes a distinction between "real" and "false" cultures. For Trask, however, the shibboleth separates Hawaiians from *maha'oi haole* (rude foreigners). Trask agrees with Linnekin that the tourist and anthropology industries construct false cultures. But Trask sees Natives, including Native nationalists, as being engaged in processes of true cultural transmission. Conversely, *maha'oi haole* construct false representations of Hawaiian culture. For Trask, the decisive issue is being Hawaiian. Consistent with her assertion of self-determination, Trask argues that Hawaiian culture is determined by Hawaiians. The truth of a cultural claim is, to a great extent, determined by membership in the Hawaiian community. Thus, Hawaiian nationalists and *haole* anthropologists might each speak deliberately about culture, but the Hawaiians are members of the Hawaiian community, and the *haole* are not. In ethnomethodological terms, Hawaiians have access to "members' resources" that anthropologists do not have.

For Linnekin, culture-as-process is real; culture, whether or not it is colonial, is a political process in which meanings are constructed. But culture-as-product is false; culture that is reified and referred to is divorced from the true processes of cultural construction, reproduction, and transformation. For Trask, culture as practiced by its members is real, whether

---

nationalist ideology" (*Imagined Communities: Reflections on the Origin and Spread of Nationalism* [London: Verso, 1983], 104).

23. Jocelyn Linnekin, "Selling Hawaiian Culture," *Cultural Survival Quarterly* 6 (1982): 29.

24. Linnekin, "Defining Tradition," 248.

or not those members are intellectually aware or politically active, but culture as defined or practiced by foreigners is false.[25] Linnekin sees Trask's definitions of Hawaiian culture as false in that they are references to culture-as-product—a fixed, obligatory thing. Conversely, Trask sees Linnekin's categorization as false, because it involves a non-Hawaiian's determination of "Hawaiian-ness."

The Ivory Tower Defense

A related dispute between Linnekin and Trask concerns whether their dispute is worth having. Linnekin doubts she is worth so much of Trask's attention. Linnekin argues that "anthropologists have very limited power to control public representations or to influence the course of events" and that "scholarship—when it is used at all—is most often used politically to confirm preconceptions and rationalize decisions already made by the powers that be."[26] She also observes that anthropologists tend to oppose development and to support conservation and indigenous land claims. According to Linnekin, the real "bad guys" at the university are not in the Anthropology Department but in Travel Industry Management, Business Administration, and Law. The struggle against colonization would be more worth waging in fields that have more impact than anthropology has on culture, capital, and land.

Trask responds that anthropologists are not her only target but that they are worth attacking because they are "part of the colonizing horde."[27] Her point is not that anthropology is worse than tourism but that anthropology in Hawaiʻi is an integral part of a colonial system that dispossesses Hawaiians of their land as well as their culture—a colonial system that includes tourism, development, and anthropology. Returning to the issue of Kahoʻolawe, Trask calls attention to the fact that an anthropologist employed by the United States Navy "cited fellow anthropologists, including Linnekin, to argue that the Hawaiian assertion of love and sacredness re-

---

25. Thus, Trask adamantly rejects the concept of "Hawaiian at heart." She denies that those who are not born Hawaiian (genealogically) can become Hawaiian (sympathetically). But Linnekin argues that membership in a Hawaiian community can be, and has been, extended to foreigners. For her, culture is a matter of participation, not of birth. See Haunani-Kay Trask, "Review of *Islands of History* by Marshall Sahlins," *American Ethnologist* 12 (1985): 784–87.

26. Linnekin, "Text Bites and the R-Word," 195.

27. Trask, "Natives and Anthropologists," 162.

garding Kahoʻolawe was 'fakery.'"[28] In this instance, at least, Linnekin's writing on cultural construction was used in opposition to Hawaiian interests.

Linnekin acknowledges that her work was used against Hawaiians in the case of Kahoʻolawe, but she adds that Trask fails to note that "at the request of the Protect Kahoʻolawe ʻOhana I wrote a lengthy critique of that report in a letter to the Navy."[29] Linnekin argues that the Navy's archaeologist's misuse of her article does not belie her opposition to the Navy bombing of Kahoʻolawe. Rather, the Navy's appropriation of her cultural construction argument demonstrates how little power she and other anthropologists have.

Trask responds that anthropologists do have power and that *that* is precisely the problem. According to Trask, what anthropologists say should not matter but "what Linnekin or Keesing or any other anthropologist writes about Hawaiians has more potential power than what Hawaiians write about themselves."[30] A case in point is the report Linnekin wrote for the Protect Kahoʻolawe ʻOhana. Trask observes that Hawaiians, just as much as the military, are required to enlist anthropologists to strengthen their case in the American legal and political systems. Hawaiians are not granted the authority to speak for themselves, to define their own culture. Rather, they must depend on the aid of foreign anthropologists and lawyers. Hawaiians and other colonized peoples do not have a voice within the colonial system but are obliged to seek paternalistic spokespeople from within that system who are sympathetic to their plight. Having to depend on outside experts, such as Linnekin, to define Hawaiian culture constitutes for Trask a violation of Hawaiian sovereignty—of Hawaiians' right to define their own past, present, and future.

Logical Rudeness

Anthropologists, including Handler and Keesing, have imagined a dialogue between anthropologists and their subjects. But Linnekin's and Trask's attempts at debate raise questions about whether such a dialogue is possible. Their exchange casts doubt on whether the subjects of anthropological inquiry can retain their subjectivity in relation to anthropologists.

28. Trask, "Politics in the Pacific Islands," 16, referring to Linnekin, "Defining Tradition," 246–49.
29. Linnekin, "Text Bites and the R-Word," 175.
30. Trask, "Natives and Anthropologists," 166 n. 4.

Edward W. Said has observed that Third World critiques of anthropology are inevitably converted into curious behavior worthy of study. "The Western Africanists read African writers as source material for their research, . . . while the direct, even importunate solicitations of debate and intellectual engagement from the formerly colonized are left largely unattended."[31] The "native point of view" is inevitably constituted as an interesting object for study rather than as a legitimate voice to be reckoned with. No matter what Natives say, to anthropologists they remain "natives." Anthropologists' use of the "native point of view" is an example of what Peter Suber calls "logical rudeness." It is "the sort of rudeness that studies critics as specimens to the exclusion of (rather than in addition to) hearing their criticism."[32] Those who would criticize the cultural construction discourse are subsumed by it; they are analyzed rather than listened to. Even Said's impassioned plea will not necessarily—or even very probably—be heard. It is likelier that anthropologists will rudely analyze Said than that they will actually respond to him. In short, Said's voice is doomed to be turned into the "native point of view," and thus to go unheard.

As Trask so colorfully explains, "anthropologists without Natives are like entomologists without insects."[33] What would happen if insects began to speak for themselves, to expound on their own physiology? Would mammalian entomologists defer to the entomic experts? If the scholarly reception of Native intellectuals can be taken as a model, entomologists would not learn from, but rather they would learn about, the talking insects. New specialties would be created in entomological linguistics, and the politically inclined would explain why the insects began to speak in this place at this time. The insects' discourse would be historicized, contextualized, and, not incidentally, ignored. Just so, Native scholars have been received into the academy, and Native nationalists have been received into dialogue with anthropologists.

31. Edward W. Said, "Representing the Colonized: Anthropology's Interlocutors," *Critical Inquiry* 15 (Winter 1989): 219. See also Bronislaw Malinowski, *The Dynamics of Culture Change* (New Haven: Yale University Press, 1945), 59 n. 4: "The literature produced by the educated Africans, some of whom frame their views with grave moderation and considerable perspicacity, constitutes a body of evidence on which scientific work by a White anthropologist must sooner or later be undertaken." For Malinowski, as for contemporary Africanists, Native critiques of anthropology are a "body of evidence," to be safely contained within the anthropological discourse.
32. Peter Suber, "Logical Rudeness," in *Self-Reference: Reflections on Reflexivity*, ed. Steven J. Bartlett and Peter Suber (Dordrecht: Martinus Nijhoff, 1987), 49.
33. Trask, "Natives and Anthropologists," 162.

The dialogue between the cultural constructionist and the Native nationalist is an illusion.[34] In its place is the hierarchical relationship of the analyst and the object of her analysis. The new anthropologist's call to dialogue turns out to be more of the same old totalizing discourse, differing from "old-fashioned" anthropology only in its greater sophistry and sophistication. Genuine dialogue remains impossible so long as anthropologists persist in analyzing, rather than listening to, Natives. So far, Natives have been able to enter the anthropological discourse only as "the native point of view." A Native may even become an anthropologist. But if she dares to claim subjective authority to expound on her own culture, she is instantly re-relegated to the status of informant—a voice to be interpreted. The cultural constructionist's commitment to historicize, contextualize, or otherwise analyze the Native voice invariably serves to shut that voice out.

Putting Cultural Construction in Its Place

Linnekin is well aware of the peculiarity—even the rudeness—of cultural constructionists' contribution to a dialogue with Native nationalists.

Nationalists may wish us to nod our heads uncritically, and silently, at whatever cultural reconstructions they advocate. Instead, maddeningly, we talk about their representations, situating them in time, place and point of view, just as we talk about and situate our own.[35]

It is clear that cultural constructionists contextualize nationalists' discourse. I question, however, whether cultural constructionists are as tenacious about contextualizing their own discourse as they are at contextualizing that of others. To be sure, cultural constructionists have contextualized the discourse of earlier anthropologists. Handler, for example, notes that "it is well known that nationalist ideologies and social-scientific inquiry

34. See Stephen Tyler, *The Unspeakable: Discourse, Dialogue and Rhetoric in the Post-modern World* (Madison: University of Wisconsin Press, 1987). Tyler has made the corollary observation that attempts to include the native voice in a "dialogic" ethnography are illusory. In such texts, "the informant's appearances in the dialogue are at best mediated through the ethnographer's dominant authorial role," (66). And, "in order that the native have a place in the text, they [some ethnographers] exercise total control over her discourse and steal the only thing she has left—her voice" (205). The anthropologist's authorial/authoritative stance relative to the Native precludes genuine dialogue.
35. Jocelyn Linnekin, "Custom/*Kastom*/Tradition: Theory and Politics in Cultural Representation" (Paper presented at the meeting of the Association for Social Anthropology in Oceania, Lihue, Hawai'i, 1990).

developed in the same historical context—that of the post-Renaissance European world—and the two have reacted upon one another from their beginnings."[36] This awareness allows Handler to see connections between Québécois nationalism and traditional anthropology, but Handler's own cultural construction approach, indeed, remains "maddeningly" above it all.

Cultural construction has been located within anthropology, as a contest between generations of anthropologists. Cultural constructionists frequently constitute themselves as a radical movement, writing against old-fashioned anthropology.[37] For example, Allan Hanson has presented the constructedness of Maori culture as a challenge to logocentric anthropological knowledge,[38] and in the New York Times, Hanson's efforts were said to raise "some troubling questions for anthropology."[39] Alternatively—but not contradictorily—P. Steven Sangren has represented the reflexive turning of the anthropological gaze as a play for power by a new generation of tenure-seeking professors.[40] Whether recent currents in the anthropological discourse are seen as subversive, self-serving, or both, the context being taken into account is limited to the discipline of anthropology.

I suggest that the cultural construction discourse is best understood in relation to worldwide Native nationalist insurgency. In this context, the vogue for cultural construction arguments appears as a hegemony-preserving reaction to decolonization movements. Trask notes that "in the Hawaiian case, the 'invention' criticism has been thrown into the public arena precisely at a time when Hawaiian cultural assertion has been both vigorous and strong-willed."[41] The Hawaiian case is typical of the historical relationship between cultural construction and Native nationalism. The cultural construction discourse serves to undermine the authority of the people who are actively engaged in defying European and North American hegemony.

36. Handler, Nationalism and the Politics of Culture in Quebec, 8.
37. Perhaps the first, and still the clearest, example of cultural constructionism located within the context of anthropology is Roy Wagner, The Invention of Culture, rev. and exp. ed. (Chicago: University of Chicago Press, 1981).
38. Allan Hanson, "The Making of the Maori: Culture Invention and Its Logic," American Anthropologist 91 (1989): 890–902.
39. John Noble Wilford, "Anthropology Seen as Father of Maori Lore," New York Times 20 Feb. 1990, sec. C, p. 1, 12.
40. P. Steven Sangren, "Rhetoric and the Authority of Ethnography," Current Anthropology 29 (June 1988): 405–35.
41. Trask, "Natives and Anthropologists," 163.

Joan Peters's *From Time Immemorial* is a particularly striking example of a book in which a specific nation is revealed to be invented. Other cultural constructionists could reject the book because of its sloppy scholarship and overt political bias.[42] It is easy to dismiss a Zionist's argument that the Palestinian people are a recent invention because of the transparency of her motives, but Peters's work makes explicit the overriding politics of the contemporary cultural construction discourse. Here, there is no doubt that a cultural constructionist argument serves to undermine the legitimacy of a nationalist movement.

Cultural constructionists are correct in locating earlier anthropologists in the context of European and North American colonialisms, but they are wrong in presenting their own discourse as somehow outside this same context. Reflecting on colonialism does not make it go away. Anthropologists, including cultural constructionists, continue to be pros of counterinsurgency. As Ranajit Guha observed of Marxist approaches to Indian historiography, the current discourse differs from earlier discourses "only by a declaration of sentiment."[43] Simply having "radical" or "progressive" intentions does not allow cultural constructionists to avoid reproducing anthropology's colonizing role.

For many years, European colonial interests were served by the division of the "primitive world" into administrative units such as cultures, tribes, and kingdoms. During this epoch, anthropologists had little difficulty recognizing and contributing to such a taxonomy. So long as the culture concept served the interests of European and North American colonialisms, few anthropologists noticed (or called attention to) its artificiality. Similarly, during the era in which nationalism served to establish colonizing and colonized identities, historians had little compunction about naturalizing nations and their histories. In more recent years, Natives have begun to find concepts such as "culture," "nation," and indeed "native" to be adaptive to their own decolonizing interests. Precisely in this postcolonial era, anthropologists and historians have come to notice that these concepts are artificial,

---

42. For an exposé of Peters's work, see Norman G. Finkelstein's "Disinformation and the Palestine Question: The Not-so-strange Case of Joan Peters's *From Time Immemorial*," in *Blaming the Victims: Spurious Scholarship and the Palestinian Question*, ed. Edward W. Said and Christopher Hitchens (London: Verso, 1988).
43. Ranajit Guha, "The Prose of Counter-Insurgency," in *Selected Subaltern Studies*, ed. Ranajit Guha and Gayatri Chakravorty Spivak (New York: Oxford University Press, 1988), 84.

even colonial. As Western scholars have lost control of the culture/nation discourse, they have taken to proclaiming "culture" and "nation" to be Western, colonizing inventions. Just as Natives engaged in decolonization have begun to find these concepts useful, anthropologists and historians have begun to feel the urge to demystify them. What seemed so natural in colonial contexts is, in a postcolonial context, perceived to be constructed.

Critique in Context

The cultural construction discourse is not an isolated occurrence of progressive scholarship gone bad. Rather, it is part of a poststructuralist trend in which the tools of radical critique are employed to undermine the authority of counter-hegemonic actors. The Native is but one of the actors who has suffered some form of deconstruction. The Worker, the Woman, and the Black have also been disappeared from poststructuralist discourse,[44] just as the Nation has been wiped off of the poststructuralist map. It is safe to assume that any "group" engaged in resistance activities will be discovered to be no group at all but rather a reproduction of the system that it is resisting. It is tempting to argue that Marxism is the mirror of production, or that female is the Other to the male Self, or that Native nationalism reproduces colonialism. As Raymond Williams observes,

> It can be persuasively argued that all or nearly all initiatives and contributions, even when they take on manifestly alternative or oppositional forms, are in practice tied to the hegemonic: that the dominant culture, so to say, at once produces and limits its own forms of counter-culture.[45]

But whose interests do such arguments serve? What do such arguments explain, and what do they obscure?

Nancy Cott has warned that "in deconstructing categories of mean-

---

44. See Jean Baudrillard, *The Mirror of Production*, trans. Mark Poster (St. Louis: Telos Press, 1975); Jacques Lacan, *Feminine Sexuality: Jacques Lacan and the École Freudienne*, ed. J. Mitchell and J. Rose, trans. J. Rose (New York: W. W. Norton, 1982); and Tzvetan Todorov, " 'Race,' Writing, and Culture," in *"Race," Writing, and Difference*, ed. Henry Louis Gates, Jr. (Chicago: University of Chicago Press, 1986), 370–80. Despite this publisher's normal practice, I have intentionally capitalized these nouns.

45. Excerpted in George Marcus, "Some Quotes and Queries Pertaining to Bourdieu's Own Scholastic Point of View," *Cultural Anthropology* 5, no. 4 (1990): 393.

ing, we deconstruct not only patriarchal definitions of 'womanhood' and 'truth' but also the very categories of our own analysis—'women' and 'feminism' and 'oppression.'"[46] Sandra Lee Bartky cautions that Foucault's writings can be similarly disempowering:

> Foucault often writes as if power constitutes the very individuals upon whom it operates. . . . Nevertheless, if individuals were wholly constituted by the power-knowledge regime Foucault describes, it would make no sense to speak of resistance to discipline at all.[47]

To the extent that Foucault focused on the constructedness of the individual, he denied the possibility for the individual to resist. There remain no actors, only the acted-upon. This is what Ana Margarita Furlong refers to as the "obscene strategy" of postmodernism: "a strategy of domination, a totalizing sermon on behalf of the system, and an abandonment of the potential for struggle."[48] What makes this strategy obscene is that it is politically perverse; it turns all political acts inside out: Decolonization is colonialist, feminism is sexist, Marxism is capitalist, and racial politics are racist.

This poststructuralist trend is an inversion of Marxism. Just as Marx stood Hegel on his head, others have now upturned Marx. For Marx, criticism was a social act aimed at denaturalizing ideology, which he defined as "the ruling ideas":[49]

> Clearly the weapon of criticism cannot replace the criticism of weapons, and material force must be overthrown by material force. But theory also becomes a material force once it has gripped the masses.[50]

46. Quoted by Joanne Frye as quoted by Frances E. Mascia-Lees, Patricia Sharpe, and Colleen Ballerino Cohen, "The Postmodernist Turn in Anthropology: Cautions from a Feminist Perspective," Signs 15, no. 1 (1989): 27.

47. Sandra Lee Bartky, "Foucault, Femininity, and the Modernization of Patriarchal Power," in Feminism and Foucault: Reflections on Resistance, ed. Irene Diamond and Lee Quinby (Boston: Northeastern University Press, 1988), 82.

48. Ana Margarita Furlong, "La Creación de la Postmodernidad: Una Estrategia 'Obscena,'" in Propuestas para Anthropología Argentina, ed. Carlos Enrique Berbeglia (Buenos Aires: Editorial Biblos, 1990), 213–21, my translation.

49. Karl Marx and Friedrich Engels, "The German Ideology: Part I," in The Marx-Engels Reader, trans. S. Ryazanskaya, ed. Robert C. Tucker, 2d ed. (New York: W. W. Norton, 1978), 146–200.

50. Karl Marx, "Critique of Hegel's Doctrine of the State," in Early Writings, trans. Rodney Livingstone (New York: Vintage Books, 1975), 251.

Conversely, for many contemporary social critics, criticism is an intellectual exercise aimed at denaturalizing any group of ideas and any grouping of people. No distinction is made between the ruling ideas and ideas of resistance, no attention is paid to the position of the people producing the ideas in question, and no effort is made to make the criticism available beyond the confines of academia. Thus, Handler finds it appropriate to begin his meditations on Québécoise nationalism with a statement by Ronald Reagan about the importance of borders to a nation. He does not distinguish between the nationalism of an imperialist power and that of a separatist province. To cultural constructionists in general, nationalism is nationalism; critiquing a decolonization movement is part of the same theoretical project as the critique of imperialism.[51] Any group identity, whether it be built on culture, nation, ethnicity, race, gender—whatever—is considered ideological. Even class consciousness, to this way of thinking, can be interpreted as a mystification—a false consciousness that makes the individual's status as a worker "seem like an eternal law."[52] Yet, domination and resistance are not the same thing, an idea's relationship to power does make a difference.

Immanuel Wallerstein observes that there are significant differences between nationalism as domination and nationalism as resistance.

> What I am suggesting is that we begin to distinguish between those rarer but very important moments when nationalism mobilizes significant antisystemic sentiment, and thereby affects the politics of the entire world-economy, and those more frequent moments when nationalism operates, to use another metaphor, as the nervous tic of capitalism as a world-system.[53]

I suggest that a similar distinction can, and should, be made between all discourses of resistance and the dominant discourses they seemingly reproduce. This distinction requires paying attention to context. Native nationalist discourse may have much in common with the colonial discourse with which it contends. For example, Linnekin is able to find correlations between what Hawaiian nationalists say and what *haole* travel agents selling trips to Hawaiʻi say. One discourse, however, is spoken to victims of U.S.

---

51. See Eric Hobsbawm, "The Perils of the New Nationalism," *The Nation*, 4 Nov. 1991, 537, 555–56.
52. Marx and Engels, "The German Ideology," 173.
53. Immanuel Wallerstein, *The Politics of the World-Economy: The States, the Movements, and the Civilizations* (Cambridge: Cambridge University Press, 1984), 130.

colonialism, and in this context the words help mobilize people to resist. The other discourse is spoken to tourists, and in that context it helps motivate them to buy airplane tickets. Both discourses may objectify and even essentialize Hawaiian-ness. But the tourist discourse produces a largely inaccurate image of contemporary Hawaiians as happy Natives, just waiting to serve *haole* visitors, whereas the nationalist discourse emphasizes the glories of pre-*haole* Hawaiian culture.

Anthropologists could argue (and have) that Native nationalist versions of precolonial history are inaccurate. It is more accurate, however, to argue that victims of Western imperialism were happier before Westerners arrived than it is to argue that they presently enjoy being toured. Anthropologists could argue (and have) that Native national, cultural, and ethnic identities are all attempts to essentialize or naturalize historical constructions. It is important, however, to distinguish between discourses that naturalize oppression and discourses that naturalize resistance. To say that Natives are essentially less intelligent than Westerners would be to naturalize the oppression of Natives. To say that a Native culture has an essential existence can help make resistance seem natural. Idealized discourses of nation, race, ethnicity, and gender are relatively effective at mobilizing counter-hegemonic actions. Being idealized does not necessarily make a discourse false. Rather, I suspect that for a resisting discourse to be effective, it must be true to contemporary material conditions. Anthropologists could argue (and will) that Hawaiʻi is a colonial invention, that the unity of the Hawaiian islands came only after the arrival of the *haole*, but even the most vulgar Marxist would find that Hawaiian ethnic/national identity is strongly correlated with material conditions, such as low income and high infant mortality.

It should not come as a surprise that resistance is more effectively rallied around national, ethnic, racial, or gender pride than around having low income or high infant mortality, for example. The role of victim does not tend to inspire people to social action, but Native national identity does. "Victims of the world, unite" is hardly stirring. To the extent that categories of victimization and of pride overlap, a social movement will clearly be counter-hegemonic. What seems to trouble Western critics are cases in which this overlap is less than complete. Keesing, for example, calls attention to the "male- and (in many cases) elite-dominated" indigenous Pacific societies.[54] He warns that "cultural nationalist rhetoric is increasingly deployed

54. Roger Keesing, "Creating the Past," 37.

by Pacific elites to camouflage these issues of power and interest."[55] In this context, Keesing sees intellectual Native nationalists as "invoking bonds of shared essence" as a way to bridge the "wide gulfs of class interest, political power, perception, life experience, and material circumstance" that separate them from their "rural poor cultural cousins." Keesing's solution is to call attention to what "we"—anthropologists and Pacific Islanders—can do together to demystify Pacific history; to which Trask responds, "What do you mean 'we,' white man?"[56] There is an insurmountable contradiction in the notion that Westerners can advise Others on how to decolonize themselves. Sovereignty and self-determination are not reconcilable with intervention by outsiders, even if the outsiders happen to perceive themselves as "radicals."

Many Westerners feel an ethical imperative to protect Third Worlders, to ensure that they are not burdened with sexism, racism, or classism. These good intentions often lead the Western observer to pass judgment on the credentials of Native activists. "Is he poor enough?" "Is she dark enough?" Needless to say, Western intellectual radicals rarely pose such rude questions to one another. Yet, tenured White males feel comfortable critiquing supposed wealth, whiteness, and maleness among Native nationalists, thereby correcting the false consciousness of political activists. Now, as before, the educated White man offers to open the Native's eyes, to expose superstitions to the light of reason. In this, the cultural constructionist critique of Native tyranny is hardly discernible from the missionary critique of Native religion. The message may be to decolonize, but the relationship remains colonial. In the case of Hawaiʻi, the critique from on high is especially audacious, since the Hawaiian sovereignty movement is thoroughly dominated by women.[57]

Here, the critic should reflect on his position relative to a nationalist movement. We are not free to choose the location from which we write. The right declaration of sentiment does not allow an anthropologist to stop being a representative of outside power, much less to become an honorary Native. We must pay attention to the context in which we produce knowl-

55. Roger Keesing, "Reply to Trask," Contemporary Pacific 2 (1991): 168.
56. Here, Trask is borrowing Tonto's response to the Lone Ranger's query: "We're surrounded by Indians. What are we going to do?"
57. See Berna-Lee Lehua Riveira, "Hawaiian Women and the Self-Determination of a People," Voices 4, no. 2 (Winter 1990–1991): 6–20.

edge. We cannot foresee all of the uses to which our argument might be put. It should not surprise us, however, to find critiques of counter-hegemonic movements used to help preserve hegemony. If we acknowledge that criticism can be a weapon, then we must accept responsibility for the weapons we produce.

Hawai'i

Haunani-Kay Trask

I.
The smell of the sea
at Hale'iwa, mixed with
early smoke, a fire
for fish and buttered clams

in a rapturous morning.
Vines of *naupaka*
leafy and stiff over

the puckered sand
and that ruddy face
coming from cold breakers

mesmerized by the sun.

They take our pleasures
thoughtlessly.

'Hawai'i' by Haunani-Kay Trask is reprinted by permission of the publisher from *Light in the Crevice Never Seen* (Calyx Books, 1994).

II.[1]
The *kōlea* stilts its way
through drooping ironwoods
thickened by the fat
of our land. It will eat

ravenous, depart rich,
return magnificent
in blacks and golds.

Haole plover
plundering the archipelagoes
of our world.

And we, gorging ourselves
on lost shells
blowing a tourist conch

into the wounds
of catastrophe.

III.
The dancer's hem catches
a splintered stair. Descending
in a crash of couture

she winces over a broken
toe, hating the glittering
prison of Waikīkī

but smiling stiffly
into the haze of white faces;
a spiteful whiteness

---

1. The *kōlea*, or Pacific golden plover, is a richly colored migratory bird that arrives in Hawai‘i about August and departs for Alaska in May. Usually the *kōlea* arrives as a thin, almost emaciated stilt but leaves fattened and beautiful. According to Mary Kawena Pukui, the expression *haole kī kōlea* refers to the "plover-shooting white man" and was said "in astonishment and horror at the white man's shooting of the plovers, contrasting with the laborious Hawaiian methods of catching plovers, a way of saying that white people are strange and different." Today, *haole* who exploit Hawai‘i, especially developers and tourists, are referred to as *kōlea* by many Hawaiians.

in the reef-ringed island
world of her people

now hawking adverts
in their lilting pidgin;
filthy asphalt feet

unaccustomed to muddy
lo'i, kicking
Cadillac tires

for a living.

IV.[2]
Green-toothed *mo'o* of Kaua'i
raises his *mo'o* tail
peaked in fury.

A rasping tongue hisses
in rivulets to the burning sea.

Near the estuary mouth
heiau stones lie crushed
beneath purple resort

toilets: Civilization's
fecal vision

in the native
heart of darkness.

V.[3]
Glint of life
in the graveyard's ghost
one yellowed eye

2. Along the Wailua River, Kaua'i, are found some of the oldest *heiau*, or sacred temples, in the Hawaiian archipelago. One of these *heiau* rests on the sand at the estuary of the Wailua River. A large hotel complex has been built adjacent to it, with guest restrooms built on it.
3. At Honokāhua, Māui, a large Hawaiian cemetery containing perhaps two thousand or more ancient Hawaiian skeletons was threatened with destruction, including disinterment of the burials, to make way for a Ritz-Carlton mega-resort. The cemetery was on land owned by a missionary-descendant whose hotel was to be funded by a silent Japanese investor. A huge outcry among Hawaiians stopped the disinterment and led the state of

and a swell of heat:
two thousand bodies
exhumed for Japanese

money, developers' dreams,
and the archaeology
of *haole* knowledge.

Māui, our own fierce *akua*
disembowelled
by the golden shovel
of Empire.

VI.[4]

> *E Pele e, fire-eater*
> *from Kahiki.*

Breath of Papa's life
miraculously becomes
Energy, stink with

sulfurous sores. Hi'iaka
wilting in her wild home:
black *lehua*, shrivelled
pūkiawe, unborn *'a'ali'i*.

Far down her eastern flank
the gourd of Lono dries
broken on the temple wall.

Cracked lava stones
fresh with tears, sprout
thorny vines, thick
and foreign.

Hawai'i to purchase the land. While this episode ended well, the disinterment of Hawaiian burials for all manner of resort and residential development continues.

4. Papa—Earth Mother—and Wākea—Sky Father—are progenitors of the Hawaiian people. Geothermal energy development on Hawai'i Island threatens the sanctity of Pele, Hawaiian deity of the volcano, and her sister, Hi'iaka, deity of the forest. Pele and her family were originally from Kahiki in the South Pacific and migrated to the Big Island of Hawai'i after a long and dangerous journey across the Hawaiian archipelago. Today, Pele and her family continue to be worshiped by practitioners of the Hawaiian religion and members of *hula hālau*, or dance academies.

VII.[5]

From the frozen heavens
a dense vapor
colored like the skin

of burnt milk, descending
onto our fields, and
mountains and waters

into the recesses
of our poisoned
na'au.

VIII.[6]
And what do we know
of them, these foreigners
these Americans?

Nothing. We know
nothing.

Except a foul stench
among our children

and a long hollow
of mourning
in our *ma'i.*

---

5. *Na'au* means, literally, intestines. But metaphorically, *na'au* also represents what the heart means to Westerners, that is, the home of emotions, of understanding. *Na'au* can also refer, in a figurative sense, to a child.

6. Our Hawaiian *lāhui*, or nation, is now inundated by a foreign culture and people whose practices are antithetical to the Hawaiian cosmology in which the universe is a creation of familial relations. Therefore, *all* family members (the earth, the people) must be cared for and protected. The *ma'i*, or genitals, are honored by our people (as in *mele ma'i*, or genital chants) as the source of our continuity. Thus the "hollow/of mourning/in our *ma'i*" refers to our dying out as a nation, as a people.

Da Mainland to Me

Joseph P. Balaz

Eh, howzit brah,
I heard you goin mainland, eh?

   No, I goin to da continent.

Wat? I taught you goin San Jose
for visit your bradda?

   Dats right.

Den you goin mainland brah!

   No, I goin to da continent.

Wat you mean continent brah?!
Da mainland is da mainland,
dats where you goin, eh?!

Eh, like I told you,
dats da continent—

Hawaiʻi
is da mainland to me.

Childhood as a Fiction

Subramani

For Anshu

Mother dies on May 4, 1988, in the middle of our troubles in the country. A week earlier: the long empty afternoon is filled with memories. Mother is resting on a mattress in the sunny annex, a covered passage with walls and broad windows, joining the wooden house to the newly con-structed washroom with a flush toilet. The simple wooden house was built on a hillside after the old barrack-type house, lower down by the mud track, was demolished in the late 1960s. Since then, Mother has lived in this house with one of my younger married sisters.

Mother holds me in her arms for a long time, without a sound, with only a dull tension in her body. We both know that the inevitable cannot be held off forever. I feel a rush of love, something long locked-up, ready to erupt. I lower her head gently on the embroidered pillow. Her eyes are peaceful, cleared of memories and dreams. Her voice quavers: Gradually it would recede and she would stop speaking altogether.

She's tired now, on the verge of sleep. My eldest sister hands me a glass of water with *tulsi* leaves in it. I pour a few ritual drops between mother's clenched lips. I notice that her teeth are still white and strong, her hair has more black than gray, and her face is without any deep marks. It is remarkable that in spite of her loneliness and grief, in this drab surrounding, she has achieved so much control over herself. She is almost like someone who could begin life all over again.

For over twenty years I've returned to this village, the village of my childhood, with an image, invented by a neighbor, of a woman working in her yard, staring at the aeroplane and asking news about her only son. She has become a fictional character more than a real person, in the same way I have become for her a fictional son who would return one day and make her life whole.

Mother has given instructions about her funeral. She will be cremated. My sisters had hoped that she'd be buried by her husband's side in the backhills. Instead, she has chosen the quickest way to return to her beginning.

The following day at noon, a young man arrives in working clothes to read from the *Gita*. He has done that since Mother fell ill. He has come to read to an old neighbor, the oldest member of that community, a community that seems as deep-rooted as the hills when the young man prostrates himself before the red bundle. Mother turns her eyes toward the young man and brings the palms of her hands together. The young man raises his head slowly, opens the holy text, and begins to read:

Mṛtyuḥ sarva-haraś cāham udbhavaś ca bhaviṣyatām kīrtih śrīr vāk ca nārīṇāṁ smṛtih medhā dhṛtiḥ kṣamā

I am the all-destroying Death, and I am the origin that are to come too. Among the virtues considered as female I am fame, fortune, speech, memory, intelligence, constancy, and patience.

Childhood is myriad pieces, existing only in fragments. I'm sitting on a wooden chair in the breezy annex, following the traces of memory on faces that have grown unfamiliar. I'm left with many unrelated fragments, fragments that release further memories. Events that had slipped out of memory, experiences that had become suppressed, emerge from the deep unconscious like yellowed photographs or clips of old movies. I'm aware of their altered significance as I try to recover them, clarify their links, frame them; I know there's a child who acted and the adult who must reflect and interpret.

Before me is a boy of three leaning against a thatched hut. I can hear the whistle of a train from another country, see the shuddering shapes of cane trucks, and smell the burning coal.

There's a brief disruption in the life of the family when the parents, two girls, and the three-year-old boy shift from the countryside to a village near the Sugar Mill and Town. The household things are taken off a truck and piled on the side of a gravel road. A little girl comes from the village to carry their things to their new home. She picks up a lantern and starts walking in the narrow path between the sugarcane fields.

The house is situated below a hill, bushy on one side and scantily clad on the other. There are six large mango trees behind the house like six sentinels watching over the house. The house has a detached kitchen and a toilet at the edge of a bush. The galvanized iron roof and walls, painted red, have taken on the color of rust, with attractive red patches where they are rusted. There are two rooms with a mud floor: The floor of the inner room, the bedroom, is raised, and the front room slopes toward a crude mud path. The mud path curves below the backhills on the left of the house, linking the two clusters of barracks—the Old or Big Barracks, a ghetto of charred warehouse-like structures, and the New Lines, a dozen iron and wood buildings with red roofs and cream-colored walls. It peters out in the golf course on the right as a faint trail. On the right also, close to the golf course, is an identical house facing our house. The two identical houses and the New Lines form a small village.

The sloping roof and floor make the front window low enough for a child to peer out. The view from the window is reproduced in a crayon drawing during the boy's third year at school: a proliferation of hills, hillocks, humps; blue hills in the distance with wisps of clouds; green cone-shaped hills with smooth contours; bush-clad hillocks in the back, and in the front on one side, above the golf course, hills leveled to accommodate bungalows that are like castles at night. And sugarcane fields, creeping up to the foot-hills, and traversed by a river that is a wonderful stream in the hills, bending and broadening at the school and shops, and past the Sugar Mill merging into the sea.

In the crayon drawing, there is one bright imagined flower in front of the house, and a dazzling sun is fixed in a dome-shaped sky.

The hills, the barracks, the sugarcane fields, the river lined with man-groves, where the night comes suddenly; the silent, empty golf course; the mysterious bungalows; and midway between the house and the New Lines, an ancient banyan tree with intricate roots and overhanging branches full of ghosts at noonday casting deep shadows at night over the mud path— the landscape of my childhood memories.

The people of the New Lines refer to our village as *vanua* simply to assert our difference from the feud-ridden Old Barracks. The New Line dwellers live in family houses, the Old Barrack dwellers in coolie lines. But we are not rural people. There's no center within and hardly any sense of community. The Sugar Mill is the center of our life. The two brothers who live next door, strong men, as handsome as princes, try to construct a community, awaken a community sense, and illuminate the lives of the people with faith by organizing *mandali* evenings for the *Ramayana* recitals. They invent community projects to bring the people together. On Sunday, when the two brothers are out with their shovels to clean up the ditches, the place seems without inhabitants: No men appear in their hammocks on the verandas, no women are at the wash tap, and the children stop playing chasing games.

The two brothers complain about the unpleasant clannishness of the closed families. I suffer their frustrations.

Our world is closed, and we see it as complete. No one ever leaves the village. There are marriages, of course. The good-looking daughter of the ex-sea captain is married off to a nondescript farmer from a faraway village. The event that causes the most excitement is the departure of the ex-sea captain's son for Suva to be trained as a policeman. At about the same time, a young man from the other side of the backhills leaves on a ship to become a school teacher. These are the only movements.

Years later, when I'm leaving the village to study in Suva, the villagers travel in three buses to see me off at the airport. This is a more spectacular event because I'm leaving on an aeroplane. I'm farewelled with gifts and money. I climb into the tiny plane with two umbrellas in my hands, two bags, and the pockets of my trousers swinging awkwardly with pennies.

And who comes to the village? A Gujarati jeweler who spends an inordinately long time caressing the hands of young women before slipping on them blue, pink, and green bangles. The *satua* woman in her full skirt and kurta selling *satua* and *bhuja*. A Chinese vegetable seller—tall, bent, and toothless—his baskets balanced on a bamboo pole across his shoulders. Muni, the madman, humming like a bee, wobbling from side to side on the mud path, wiping the drool from his snout with the back of his hand and asking for food. George, the photographer, tuning his instrument like a sitar player, giving instructions from under his black cloak to a woman who will be photographed with a sprig of wilting marigold in her hand. And the scavenger with a sweet name—Mithailal. And Shanker, the potter, who comes to the village once a year at *diwali* to sell *diya* and earthen pots.

And finally, Lovely Singh, the movie billboard man, the billboard hanging from his shoulder, ringing a bell, followed by a ragged troop of women and children and unemployed youths. Lovely Singh stops on a patch of grass outside our yard. "*Ram Rajya, Ram Rajya, Lanka Dahan*," cries Lovely Singh like a messenger of god, summoning pilgrims to the Bombay mythologicals at the Majestic Theater. The ragged troop clusters around him, demanding another inspection of the billboard. We gaze at the stills. Each still has a story. We let our imaginations play on the stills. After the inspection of the stills, "Sing a song, Lovely, sing a filmy song." Lovely fixes his eyes on the thin woman of indeterminate age who has made the request, clears his throat, and croons *Babul Mora*, like Saigal on His Masters Voice, his voice overflowing with poignancy, and then, abandoning Saigal and Raga Bhairvi, he croons like Kanan Devi. We ask Lovely, "How does Hunuman fly, and Krishna vanish, and how Ravan's ten heads speak at once, Lovely?" Lovely is ready to move on, "*Agaya, Agaya, Toofani Mail*. Coming once again *Hunterwali*. See fearless Nadia and brave John Cawas, see the antics of Punjab ka Beta (horse) and Moti (dog)!" Now the billboard is hanging on the dream-vendor's side, and the bell starts ringing again. "*Chandraleka*, girls dancing on drums, horsemanship, dazzling sword fights." The scrawny woman of indeterminate age says, "Hai Daiyya, let the shameless sit in the dark with other men, and gaze at the *nautanki* dance." Her good-for-nothing unemployed husband, wearing a silk handkerchief around his neck, obviously a moviegoer, retorts, "Listen to her, listen to Taramati!" The bell is still ringing. "All-star picture, six songs, three dances. . . ."

A flash of memory. The distant years come racing to the fore. Images like faded scenes in an old documentary. Mother and I are in a crowd at the Big Barracks ground. The glare of the early February sun and the excited march in the sticky heat through the dusty gravel road. Some men and women are carrying placards and photographs of Mahatma Gandhi. There's a continuous chanting of the Mahatma's name and singing of *bhajans*. The stones are hurting my feet. A passing train attracts my attention. At the junction near the Sugar Mill, we are joined by more marchers who have come through different routes. We take the shorter route that goes by the Sugar Mill. At the Sugar Mill, the pace of the marchers changes, the singing ceases, and the marching comes to a halt. The mill sirdar comes down the steps of a wooden building, his hands raised. There are angry exchanges. The leaders of the march are in a defiant mood. There's confusion in the crowd. Some are turning back. The disorganized crowd finally accepts the head marcher's instruction to return to the junction. From the junction, we take the longer route. The march ends in front of the Majestic Theater. The theater is full. Mother and I squeeze in on a bench between two perspiring women. A fat man is making a speech on the stage. There are garlanded photographs of the Mahatma in the background. I'm staring at the huge black curtain behind the fat man. After several more speeches, the stage is cleared, the black curtain parts, and two columns of green, red, and blue lights come on. When the lights go off, the screen is filled with moving pictures. The crowd in the hall seems to have expanded into the moving images. In the middle of the crowds of people is the dhoti-clad Mahatma, marching or making speeches or just smiling. When the lights come on again, the crowds from the moving pictures spill into the crowded hall. I'm afraid of being lost. I hold my mother's hand.

Fiction makes childhood happy. In the early evening, through family chatter, the voice of the storyteller drifts toward the corner where I'm sitting. Mother is still resting in the annex, the light shining on her face. Her feet are being washed by my eldest sister. Mother has spoken to everyone she wanted to speak to, and her voice has slowly grown frail: Finally, she is quiet and peaceful.

The storyteller is my nine-year-old nephew. He is perched on the wooden steps of the house, and his audience is huddled on the annex floor at his feet. His exceptionally beautiful five-year-old sister has succeeded in marshaling order in the audience. She wears an elusive smile and lowers her eyes: She is aware I'm gazing at her. The storyteller's voice, more self-conscious after the hush, is starting to crack. My eldest sister, who is crossing the annex with a basin of water, nods encouragement. The storyteller's toothy grin shows again. He starts, more deliberately now, and soon he is in control of the narrative. The blind brother in the story is telling his lame brother, "Our mother is so unfair. She saves the best food for our fair brother, keeping the chaff for us. And our father hardly takes any notice of us." The lame brother replies, "This isn't our home anymore. We have to leave this house, my brother." Driven away by neglect, the two brothers are soon on the open country road. Shortly, they find a shaggy mule. The lame brother, saddled on the mule, describes the countryside to the blind brother, who leads the animal. We are puzzled by the objects that attract their attention, which the blind brother collects in a bag: an elephant's tusk, a bundle of hair, a heap of hardened dung. The gleam in the storyteller's eyes suggests there will be use for these objects in the story.

At nightfall, the two brothers and the mule find shelter in a hut. Late in the night, the owner of the hut returns. The storyteller succeeds in convincing us that the creature outside, without a name or a form, is something dark and mysterious and frightening. "Declare who is inside my hut," roars the monster when he realizes someone is inside his hovel. "Only someone more fearful than you are!" reply the two brothers together. "Prove that you are more fearsome," the monster seems no more than a wolf now. The two brothers, one lame and the other blind, captives inside the monster's hovel, are suddenly transformed into a couple of tricksters. Out goes the coil of hair followed by the heap of dung. The startled monster sends off a long howl, and challenges the creatures inside the hut to produce a roar to match his own. At this point, the storyteller chortles, baring his shell-like front teeth. His pretty sister blushes. She is on the verge of losing her authority, but she quickly asserts control over her restless brood. The storyteller's voice reaches the cracking point, "The blind brother collects the elephant's tusk and sticks it up the mule's arse." The audience roars in unison.

As a child, I heard the mule's painful cry, and wished it was the monster whose rectum was violated.

After the monster episode, the storyteller carries on in a voice that has lost its correct pitch. He is clearly tired of his narrative. But he must go on to the end. He has taken the risk of starting the story; he knows the perils of abandoning it in the middle. So: The two brothers arrive at a far-away town, find employment with a wealthy businessman, and impress the businessman with their resourcefulness so much that, after some years, he lets them marry his two daughters.

The storyteller tries to repossess the archetypal content of this part of the story, but he is defeated. His sister picks up her doll in flustered haste and slips away, avoiding my gaze. But my eyes are fixed on the fair brother of the story who has the power to change the tale into an endless narrative. Suppose after some years the two successful brothers receive news about the bad times into which their parents have fallen, suppose the two brothers send their servants with gifts to take to the parents, suppose the family is united, and suppose after a short time the fair brother, who is already gambling away their future, discovers a scheme to take away everything from the two brothers, one lame and the other blind. . . .

For Mother the story ended happily with the marriage of the two brothers.

Fleetingly, on the face of the young storyteller, I see the face of another storyteller, the old man who shows up periodically at our house at dusk on a Friday. He is *Jahaji*, Shipmate to my father and a fellow Malayalee. Mother doesn't like the man. "He's a liar, a thief," she says to me. Even his stories aren't his own. They are stolen from Ganga, the vagrant storyteller who sleeps with his bundle in shopfronts. Sometimes we see the nomadic teller of nocturnal tales in his black coat trailing behind a farmer. Although Mother doesn't like Jahaji, he is never unwelcomed. She cooks fresh fish in coconut milk with plenty of green chilies specially for him. I serve him *kava*.

The mango trees behind the house casts deep shadows over the old house. Now and then a ripe mango falls on the roof like a pelted stone. The storyteller is settled on a straw mat thrown over a sugar bag. My father lights up a cheroot, stares at the glowing end, and turns his attention to his Shipmate. My sisters, slumped forward on the mud floor, laugh at the Shipmate's habit of wagging his head and sucking his tobacco-stained mustache. He spits out the tobacco juice into the spittoon.

His stories don't come out freely. Talanoa-fashion, the storytelling begins with the ritual importuning of children, the digressions into another language, swapping tales about the old country and other Jahajis in distant villages, always deflecting from the main purpose, and just when I have assumed the customary role of the awe-struck listener, he begins with a mischievous grin, "There was once a skinny boy who liked stories. . . ." My sisters laugh, but for me the spell is almost broken. My father, seeing the frown on my face, makes a sucking noise and taps the storyteller on his knee.

Jahaji knows only a few words of Hindi and has little knowledge of the intricacies of its grammar. Since his audience, except my father, does not understand Malayalam, he works his way with the few words of Hindi until the narrative reaches the tragic moment in the *Nel Tenge* story: the protagonist in rags pausing at the village well with her three children before she will end all humiliations—here the narrative lapses seductively into musical Malayalam. Having set the tragic scene, the narrator, like the *Joruri* chanter in the Japanese Bunraku play, withdraws in the background and invites the audience to reflect on the sad plight of the protagonist.

My sisters are already dropping off to sleep on the mud floor when, in the next tale, Mother's favorite tale, the Big Hearted Hen sings a melancholic song in perfect Malayalam and inquires of the farmers' wives at the village well if they have seen her beautiful yellow-coated babies who have been kidnapped by the dastardly Tirokodu, a man of limitless rascality. Tears squirt into Mother's eyes as the singing Hen approaches Tirokodu's house and her tragic fate.

In the thickening silence of the night, narratives multiply. Little by little, the glass on the lantern blackens, the shadows leave the walls and disappear into the night. The faces before me are blurred. I continue to nod my head at each coda, holding off sleep, until sleep starts to tumble down my head like falling birds.

I wake up with a start under the mosquito net and listen to the disjointed conversation between the two men in the next room. A locomotive halts in my halfsleep, the Pointman jumps off to switch the lines. How does the Pointman's story infiltrate into my dream? In the dim light of the swinging lantern, a woman in white backs away in the night mist. She is the elusive demon-lover the Pointman invents to keep him company on long monotonous nights in the train.

The phantasmagorical figures of the stories are pursuing me on a train. I want to scream, but the scream is stuck in my throat.

The old storyteller is up early in the morning, taking in the sun, crouched in the yard without his posterior ever touching the ground, his body resting on the balls of his feet. He is strangely reticent, almost unhappy. The muddy pools of his eyes show a glint of red. He asks for water and walks behind the house with a bucket. He gurgles and retches fiercely. Like a man who doesn't want to waste time on words, he demands his food, eats his roti soaked in red tea, and drinks a large bowl of tea. He is agitated, wants to leave quickly.

Late in the morning, Mother points him out to me at the market: He is strolling between stalls, no longer in a hurry. At noon, we find him sitting on a sack of rice, gazing in amusement at two old men in dhoties, old shipmates, greeting each other in rustic verses.

There will be a male child. Ganga is famous for telling the Markandeya story. But it comes to us from Jahaji. It is the favorite story of my two elder sisters.

The great sage Mrikandu has no male offspring. He observes great austerity to impress Lord Shiva, who, pleased with Mrikandu's *tapas* appears before the *rishi* and instructs him to choose between a son who will have every virtue but who will die at sixteen, and a son without exceptional gifts who will live a long life. Mrikandu, being the *dharmatma* that he is, naturally chooses the first. Mrikandu has a son who brings great happiness to his parents. As Markandeya approaches his sixteenth birthday, his grief-stricken parents recount to him the story of his origin. Markandeya, who is full of learning and wisdom, consoles his parents, "My dear father and my dear mother, do not grieve for me. Shiva who gave me life is also the conqueror of Death. As a devotee of Shiva, I shall win immortality."

Through his great tapas Markanadeya defeats Yama, the messenger of Death.

Am I dreaming my sisters' voices? I check the time on my watch in the light of a window. It is past midnight. Mother has been carried inside the house. My sisters are keeping vigil. In sober, sleep-free voices they are arguing about a detail in a dredged-up narrative, broken and buried in my own consciousness. I'm drawn to my sisters' narrative in my half-sleep.

The man in my sisters' narrative, like Mrikandu, craves a male child (unlike Mrikandu, the man already has two daughters, but it is a male child that he wants). This craving turns into an obsession, and gradually, through prayers and fasting, it acquires a religious meaning. The woman suffers great humiliation: The failure to give her husband a male child is like the failure to procreate at all. She is convinced that it is indeed a misfortune to be without a son. However, despite the man's prayers, despite his role as Yudhistra in a religious performance, despite the vow to walk on fire (he is dissuaded because of the troublesome corns in his feet), despite all these he is not blessed with a male offspring. Finally, the dazzling Subramanya, the second son of Shiva, appears in the man's dream. There will be a male child, and the child will bear the exalted name of the deity.

It is possible that the man wanted more sons, but the woman defiantly produces three more daughters, and the dream-child continues to be the only son. The family comes to be the reverse of the Pandavas in the *Mahabharta*: Instead of five sons, there are five daughters, and the boy is their beloved Draupadi!

The line between fiction and reality blurs, and for a brief moment, we are all part of a huge mythology: I'm Subramanya, my father is Rama, my mother Lachmi, and my five sisters are daughters of Brahma!

In the expanding light of a Tuesday morning in late September, before the farmers have taken their animals to the fields, a man, a woman holding a baby, and two girls strike out from a small barrack by the railway lines. The man, ashen-faced, gaunt, is carrying a brown paper bag in his hand. Eager to reach his destination before the sun shows up above the hills, he forces the pace, and the woman, small, but not quite squat, trudges behind him with the baby. The girls trip along recklessly on the two sides of the railway lines. A jeep comes down a hill from a red-top bungalow, where the man works as a cook-cum-gardener, whirs dust as it turns into the main road, and speeds away in the opposite direction.

The small procession marches quickly along the railway lines, which run parallel to the gravel road. The gravel road snakes uphill, while the railway lines cut through a pass in the hills. The man's face is raised toward the hills. The sun is still behind the hills when the party reaches the pass. Although the pass is small and narrow, for the girls it is a booming cavern; they loiter in its cool gloom, enjoying the smell of moss and ferns on the slippery sides. On the other side of the pass, the man and woman pause briefly, their clothes stirring and ballooning. Their eyes are screwed on the glinting sea. Now the man is carrying the baby, and presently he starts walking, the women following him, and the two girls trotting ahead despite the nettles on the sides and their aching heels, gulping drafts of salt air. Still on the railway track, they walk between mangroves and bushy hillsides, and after a while, the railway lines and the gravel road start to converge and then fork out at the bend in the hills.

The shrine comes into sight suddenly at the convergence: black stony Snakehead separated from the rock face of the hillside, where the rain trees, guavas, bamboo clumps, and wild brambles fringing the hills fade out. Sesh Nag of a thousand heads, called Anant because he survives the destruction of the world, the one that supports the universe and provides canopy for Lord Vishnu.

Everything is shrouded in shimmering light. The dew is gleaming in the temple precincts. The naked baby is placed on a straw mat under the looming Snakehead. The woman is coaxing a fire under the open sky, and the aromatic smoke rises pleasantly from the mango twigs. On the other side of the shrine, the man, who seems to have made connection with a timeless world, is chanting. The singing recedes as the *dhotied* figure disappears into a hole in the rock face, into the Nag Lok of his imagination (City of Snakes with pleasure gardens and a thousand springs). He reemerges with a *lota* of cool springwater. He washes the Snakehead, daubs its dark face with turmeric paste and vermilion dust, and lights camphor on the four corners of the shrine and around the Snakehead. Assuming a yogic posture, standing on one leg with the lota cupped in his hands, he starts the chant again. The woman is going round and round the Naga Baba, head swaying and palms coming together rhythmically, the two girls following her, miming a prayer.

A brief idyllic moment in the life of that family. The mystical light, the smell of *kheer* and burning camphor, the chanting, and the ritual motion around the awakened god, precipitate a blurred mystical luminescence in the minds of the participants. A perfect moment for a magical happening: A brown and black cobra, three feet long, slithers down the lip of a cavern and crawls toward the baby. The two girls, stupefied and atremble, clutch their mother's long skirt, the woman lurches toward the baby, but she is restrained by the man, now on two feet, still chanting and unmoved by the agitation around him. The snake pauses at the edge of the mat, raises its agile head, and then slides toward the bowl of milk.

Everything happens at a dizzy speed, and, within a second, the magic is over. The satisfied snake disappears into a cave. The baby is safe.

Subramanya, son of Shiva and Parvati, less famous than Ganesha, the Remover of Impediments, is born to destroy Tarakasura. Etymologically, according to Swami Harshananda, the word *Subramanya* means one who attends to the spiritual growth of the aspirants. A heterological deity, Subramanya has six heads, representing the five sense organs and the head, says Swami Harshananda, and there are also six centers of psychic energy and consciousness in the human body. "Before conceiving him," writes the Swami, "even these Parents of the World had to perform severe Tapas or austerities! This teaches the world of the great need for Tapas on the part of the parents desirous of excellence of offspring."

There is an ironic side to the Subramanya story. The Parents of the World, Shiva and Parvati, organize a suitable competition for their children, Ganesha and Subramanya: a race across the universe. The hulking Ganesha makes a round of his parents and rests at their feet, declaring, "I've done the universe." The other son, in the meanwhile, races away in the opposite direction!

My two elder sisters, quick to discern mythic meanings, attach the most extraordinary importance to the apparently trivial events of my childhood. They compete for every activity associated with the child in order to be a part of that larger significance. My eldest sister, the more shrewd of the two, organizes a goo-licking contest to decide once and for all who loves the baby best. My second sister wins, and ever since I have been aware of her as a person, her accusatory voice has suggested to me that somehow I had failed to reciprocate the great love she had shown by tasting the goo from the baby's napkin.

As soon as I begin to walk, I cease to be their archetypal brother. My sisters part my hair one way, I immediately matt it another way. I resist their scrubbing and combing and cleaning my ears, turning me into their prissy Draupadi. I demand my own choice of clothes. Finally, they stop indulging the petulant boy and show their affection from a distance. Mother cries, "How can a gift of Shiva be like this?"

Mother's love for me remains mute and vague.

My sisters' predilection for mythmaking doesn't fail to affect me. In the open van, despondently holding my mother's coffin, and tears flowing freely from eyes, suddenly a fine drizzle of rain falls on us, washing away the tears from my face. I regain my repose, even feel mildly happy.

And again on the morning after the cremation, at the sea, the same fine rain blesses us as I wade into the water with my mother's bones and ashes. Later, I find myself talking about the mystical rain.

Let noble thoughts come to us from every side. At the end of the third year at school, I bring home a golden prize. At night, I waft away from the cramped room plagued by the smell of kerosene and mothballs, from the interminable singing of mosquitoes and feuding termites, into the surreal world of my golden book. Like a privileged child tourist, I wander in its idyllic world, gape at a red and blue cottage with a sculptured butterfly on the front wall by the door. A tall man with a pipe in his mouth is raking gold-speckled leaves into a smoldering heap. I pick up a gold leaf as a souvenir. The man smiles approvingly with his blue eyes. Behind the kitchen window, the happy face of a woman, and farther on the laughter of children playing in the tall grass with their dog, the girl in a red coat and the boy in checked shirt and blue pants. In the star-filled night that is almost blue, I peer through a window: A fire is burning in the living room, the tall man is napping in front of the fire, and the woman is reading a book with a blanket over her feet. The girl is sleeping on a pink bed, the boy in a blue bed.

I have a glimpse inside a hilltop bungalow.

Now on Friday night, Jahaji provides the half-Hindi, half-Malayalam stories, and I read from my golden book in English. My father nods his head with pleasure. I read to them with obvious keenness, until I start to suffer the embarrassment of reading to an audience that doesn't understand the language. Mother is hurt when I stop reading. Gradually, I discover the art of translating, and now I read to my audience from *Vivid History Reader* and interpret to them the adventures of Greek gods and heroes. My father nods his head with pleasure.

Impressed with my reading ambition, my father, a cook-cum-gardener at a hilltop bungalow, becomes a collector of books: He picks up moldy volumes from rubbish heaps, asks for discarded magazines, buys small parcels of books and magazines from the sales at the Mill grounds. The tattered volumes are offered for immediate edification, the more precious and wholesome items are locked up for the future inside a wooden trunk containing my mother's jewelry and other possessions. Offered for immediate consumption is Boccaccio's profane tales, which I read by the lamplight with great curiosity and shame. A badly mildewed hardcover copy of Ruby Ferguson's *The Moment of Truth* provides me with large tracks of English prose, which I explore without fully comprehending the meaning (narratives always come to me in fragments).

One day, out of curiosity, I open up the great wooden trunk: The precious literature my father had selected for me is gold-covered volumes of *The National Geographic*.

At high school, I discover more extensive prose in Thomas Hardy's novels. I stumble through the pages like a drunk without the skills to unlock the knots of complicated prose. Nonetheless, I am enthralled by the sounds of his words, astounded by the structure of his sentences and the contour of the narratives. Hardy's vocabulary remains submerged in the texts; sometimes they float in my school essays like fetish words.

My blundering, indiscriminate reading does not deepen my knowledge of the language, but the leaping, swirling imagination convinces me that the best things in the world are in books.

One Mandali evening, when I'm about eleven, the elder princely brother calls me to the front of the reciters, and thus turns me into a famous reciter. I intone Tulsidas's *shlokas* like the bard himself. The older women in the audience are agog with the solo performance of the child reciter, whose confident voice makes other voices seem repressed. My father's meditative eyes are turbid and glistening, and when Mother is told, tears jump freely from her eyes. I become a regular reciter and, within a short time, a trusted interpreter of Tulsidas's shlokas.

I espouse vegetarianism. The elder princely brother, interpreting it as Hindu zeal, offers his *Ramayana* to me for my spiritual advancement. My objective, however, is to refine my interpreting ability and to search for "secrets" that would enable me to match arcane knowledge with arcane knowledge at the after-recital debates. My effort is thwarted not only by the complexity of the shlokas themselves but also by Valmiki's postmodernist narrative techniques. Who is Kagbhusunda telling the stories to Garuda? What kind of a narrator is Shiva who interprets the narratives for Parvati? And why the endless digressions, stories-within-a-story, and biographies?

My vegetarian phase comes to an end after two years. I'm as thin as a Chinese opium-eater. My mother revives me by ministering enormous quantities of cod-liver oil, and we make another pilgrimage to the shrine of the snake god.

There is another reader of books in the village, materialized in the barracks by some awful violation of history. I know her only as an old woman who is hard on her daughter-in-law. She is referred to as "Mrs. Sukha Sagar" because of her devotion to the mystical *Sukha Sagar*, Ocean of Bliss.

The "vain reciter" is summoned to her lair. She is, indeed, from a different frame of reference. Her hair is a hornet's nest, her eyes like those of a bird. She looks more like a clairvoyant or a palmist than a reader of books. She is reading her book like a bird pecking.

"Do you know Ravana was a reader of books too?" She is obviously challenging me to a debate.

"Ravana was vain, and do you know what happened to Ravana?" Her voice suggests that she has been affronted.

"Ram destroyed his Lanka," I reply reluctantly, in an overmodest voice.

She darts a glance at me and continues reading, not with half-closed eyes but with a trained fingertip that plods across the yellowed pages. The paper smells of eucalyptus oil.

She tells me about *Sukha Sagar*—the purpose of her invitation. *Sukha Sagar* is the end of all reading, she sighs breathing out eucalyptus fumes. After reading it, you are in an Ocean of Peace, her eyelids flicker serenely.

Mrs. Sukha Sagar's reading is not restricted to mystic literature. She is also a regular reader of Hindi romances. She brings out for my inspection several slim volumes, in cheap paper with garish covers, also smelling of eucalyptus: *Gul Sanohar*, *Tota Maina*, *Hatim Tai*, and adolescent romances of Kushwaha Kant. I flip through the pages of the latter's *Akela*, *Basera*, *Churiya*, *Nirmohi*, all dedicated to a mysterious "Turan": the writer's romance, the romance of being a writer! Mrs. Sukha Sagar notices that my eyes are riveted on the pile of books, but she is a collector of books, not a lender of books. Her books have to be read under her strict supervision.

I read her romances under her protective eyes, while the children outside chant "Mrs. Sukha Sagar," "Mrs. Sukha Sagar."

I'm saved from Mrs. Sukha Sagar's romances by stumbling upon Prem Chand's *Go Daan*. Here, finally, is a real book. From the opening line, I'm in a familiar world: *After serving the two bullocks with feed and water Hori Ram said to his wife, Dhania, Send Gobar to hoe the sugar cane. I am going out and may return late. Hand me the staff.* I recognize this as our own world. The knowledge that Prem Chand's rural India, with its feudal order and caste system, isn't our world comes years later, when I start to think seriously about our colonial situation.

My reading companion at the primary school is Simon, the townboy who devours comic books and lives in the moviehouse. He initiates me into another language, but his influence, like the influence of Mrs. Sukha Sagar, is also palpable and short-lived.

On Saturday morning, the old galoot is waiting for me in the one-street town in his cowboy outfit. The grin on his pale blond face is relaxed, his ears and hands, however, are alert, because there are "enemies" behind the old wooden building on the two sides of the street. His walk is like Audie Murphy's in *Duel at Silver Creek*. Together, we ride into the moviehouse and stroll in the darkened aisle, looking for empty seats like a couple of strangers in a gloomy saloon. On the screen, the troubled gunfighter Gregory Peck is waiting in a dreary saloon for the last gunfight of his life.

The transition from the Indian mythologicals, which I'm allowed to see, to the Westerns is simple; the icons are similar, and so is the uncomplicated struggle between good and bad.

Then, at one Saturday matinee, our horizon is subtlely altered: A stranger, Alan Ladd, wearing his beautiful fringed buckskins, rides into a prairie settlement and changes the lives in a family. The de-centered narrative keeps us immersed in complex emotions until our perception is changed. After that, although we are prepared to revisit *Stagecoach* and *High Noon*, we are no longer patient with the endless repetitions in the conventional Western: The form has been beautifully violated in *Shane*.

My father puts on a tragi-comic mask. On a splendid Saturday afternoon at a wedding, after my father has paraded his magical son, after the mock feuding with his old friends, after we have eaten the sweetmeats: "Play the ukulele, Rama," exhorts an old man who has the smile of a rogue and is capable of saying any wicked thing. "Do the Rotuman dance," he persists. Soon, my father is singing an exotic song and dancing. His culinary expertise is required at an open kitchen, but, to my disappointment, he chooses to be an entertainer. The movement of his arms and hips suggests he is impersonating a female dancer of the island. Yudistra has taken off his crown and put on the mask of a fool. Gone is the piousness. He is dancing like an unrestrained child, lost in his revelry, enjoying the applause. He is dancing as if this is the greatest moment in his life. Someone fetches a wedding drum. There is a brief suspension of other wedding activities to watch the clown. I recede into the crowd. Pranksters are mocking him, and I have the image of the children chasing the "fool" to the *mela* grounds.

I have known his deep brown eyes, his gardener's delicate hands, his fussiness about food, as well as his other worldliness, but the extremes of seriousness and comic disposition that I now perceive in him make him a different man. I no longer know him. I do not know the unruly adventurer who wandered in the islands, nor do I know anything about his family line in India, or his reason for being in this country. My father becomes a stranger to me.

Just before he dies in the hospital, a few years later, my father holds my hand and says faintly, "Write it all down." I gaze at Mother's face, but she is too overwhelmed by her own feelings to explain. Afterwards, she says he meant dates for the death certificate. But my father's words have another private meaning for me. There is an event that I want to write about most fervently—the killing of stray dogs at the Big Barracks. I shall certainly write it all down, I promise myself. It will be fiction's vengeance on behalf of the slaughtered canines and the man who dies because of the killing. I turn the details so many times in my mind that eventually they acquire the concreteness of fiction.

On a hot Friday afternoon, the Overseer is wearing an army jacket and boots, and he is driving his own jeep instead of the Mill landrover. My father knows immediately that this is something personal. "We'll catch some dogs," the Overseer grins at my father. My father leaves the flower beds for another day and gets into the green jeep. The jeep stops a couple of chains away from the Big Barracks so that the Overseer can study the movement of the canines—brown and black, flea-ridden and hairless, old dogs and young puppies. Diggers of gardens, creators of turds, barrack defilers! After my father orders the women and children inside the barracks, the jeep moves close to the barracks. The Overseer jumps off the jeep in his army jacket and boots, a gun in one hand. Wiping his ginger beard, he says to my father something about roasting the curs. A couple of faces show at one window and disappear in a hurry. The Overseer is on his knees with his gun, my father behind him.

From the corner of one barrack, an unsuspecting brown mongrel, a juvenile vagabond, loiters into the open, and the next instant it leaps into the air and falls with a thud in the dust, its back broken, the furs turning crimson.

The Overseer gives himself orders, falls on his stomach to aim at the creatures under the barracks, and pulls half a dozen shots. There are cries from inside the barracks. Silence under the barracks. The Overseer is waiting for the animals to start running in all directions, under other barracks, into public toilets. More silence while the pack-leader organizes a gallant escape. The Overseer has only a glimpse of them disappearing under a barrack.

He is running now, swinging his gun like a whip. He is angry because the animals are defending themselves. A complete hunter now, he is stalking them stealthily, breathing as if he himself is struck, growing more vicious as the killing proceeds. The women and children, peering through the half-closed windows, shudder as another shot rings in the air. Hot sticky blood in the concrete gutters clots quickly, inviting clusters of flies.

When the shooting stops, the women and children come out of their hiding places to watch the old man pulling out the bloodied corpses from under the barracks, out of drains and toilets, and throwing them on the back of the jeep. The women, who are sickened by the mess left by the killing, say to each other, "It would have been more merciful to have poisoned the lot."

The Overseer is already in the landrover, wiping the sweat off his face. My father is carrying another animal in his arms, his headcloth firmly over his nose to keep off the smell of blood.

It is my father's last working day.

In another version, the last bleeding animal reclined in my father's arms is a sleek dachshund. The house-dog, sleeping in the back of the jeep, leaps out unnoticed when the first shot is fired.

In the night, my father complains of a squeezing pain in his chest and asks for some ash from his prayer place to rub on his chest. In the morning, he bathes for a long time and goes off to sleep without taking any food. He washes himself obsessively, as if he is trying to wash away a sin, and keeps walking about for the fear that memory will settle in again like dust. The women at the public tap see him walking toward the common bathroom and say to each other, "The fate of the dogs killed the man." His sickness finally takes him out of active work. He becomes a pensioner earning ten shillings per week with the right to live in the old house.

When the memory is appeased, the signs of sickness disappear temporarily. His baggy pants and shirt are hung permanently on a nail; instead, he puts on a simple dhoti befitting a sadhu. His bare chest is daubed with sandalwood paste, and his long flowing hair gives him a saintly appearance. In spite of the untreated corns on his feet, his facility for walking doesn't diminish. He walks for miles into remote villages and doesn't return for several weeks. When he returns, he is no longer a householder but a sadhu come to stay with us. He brings with him rice, dried pulses, and corn. The pain in his chest returns, and gradually it worsens. He has to be taken to the hospital, and within a few days, we are plunged into the deepest grief.

I'm given the news at school. I do not return home immediately but hide in a cleavage in the stem of a mango tree. I fix my attention on objects around me—the dead leaves, rotting twigs—and on useless thoughts and the gathering storm, in order to obliterate from my consciousness the image of the dead man's face and my wailing family. The mango tree has a gash on the stem like a wound, and red gluey liquid is collected at the rim of the wound. I tell myself I will not return home ever; I shall wander aimlessly in the hills and forests for fourteen years. I try to sleep in the cleavage. The rain slides down my back, and I feel the ants biting my toes. The branches of the mango tree above are opening and closing and tossing about. The storm is drawing nearer. The birds are preparing themselves in the trees for the storm.

Clutching my books against my soaking shirt, I fling headlong down the hill under a collapsing sky, a melancholic drum beating in my head, and as I cross the wind-driven rain in the golf course, I hear the ululation, and then a piercing wail, and I fall into several pairs of outstretched hands at the door of our house. We grieve together, my sisters and I and my mother, until grief itself seems superfluous.

I'm taken to a newly erected shed where our neighbors and relatives are sitting with bowed heads. Late in the night, I'm still sitting with my head bowed. A steady rain in the dark night creates a hallucinatory effect inside the open shed. Two men are exchanging comments on the instincts and social relations of dogs. "It's very strange," says one of them, now addressing the gathering, "I heard his cry so far away, and I said to the wedding guests, I have to go home because my mother is dead, but they stared at my face thinking I was imagining the barking. Sure enough he was waiting for me in the yard, yelping softly like he was sobbing. Mother was indeed gone."

My father is buried in the backhills the following day in violent rain.

From the web of memories into forgetting. Mother's grief doesn't diminish after my father's funeral. At the time of the funeral, she suffers terrible convulsions, a violent shaking of the body, as if she is possessed by an evil spirit. In the following weeks, her grief takes on the aspect of a dreadful disease. She is by turns hysterical and depressed. She emits a hellish howl and is ready to fly at me when I approach her to comfort her and show understanding. She makes herself inaccessible. My two married sisters' families, whose views constitute Public Opinion, initially claim that Satan is playing pranks; later, they link her lamentable conditions to my refusal to shave my head as custom requires. Already, I'm finding such rituals oppressive, and the idea of shaving my head to express grief seems ridiculous when I had already mourned for my father. My aggrieved sisters agree with Public Opinion. Our house is sunk in gloom.

Mother's hissing and shrieking and clenching of teeth is now followed by ripples of laughter. She stares into the void for hours, her eyes shining; this is followed by bouts of laughter, as if she has seen the emptiness, and laughter is the only medicine. My sisters argue with her that she shouldn't laugh so much. They are afraid that after the long silence and rounds of laughter, there will be flaring rage.

Then she starts to disappear in the backhills. She is brought down by the neighbors or by some stranger who finds her sitting on a hilltop. My embarrassment is complete: Mother is determined to act out this drama in public. I ask myself, "What is it, the dead man, the helpless girls, or the wayward son that causes her to be angry, depressed, and crazy?" Alone in the night, with the three sleeping girls and Mother sitting up under the mosquito net without a sound, the night's silence resounding in my ears, I feel a great anguish sweep through my entire self.

The tricks that we play with memory! Coming so soon after our grief, the incident of Mother's madness is so overwhelming that I obliterate it completely from my consciousness until, after Mother's funeral, the young widow of the second princely brother says to me, "Remember how we brought her down from the hills?" She mentions this event merely to remind me of a shared experience that connects us to the dead woman. All the feelings associated with the event return to me so powerfully, except the feeling of embarrassment. Instead of embarrassment, there is sadness and regret that I shall never know Mother's grief fully, nor understand her resilience.

The cold dry months keep reminding us of death. The strength to withstand her suffering returns gradually, and Mother prepares herself for more bad times without the support of a man and, within two years, without the support of her only son.

Although poverty and disorder arrive simultaneously, we continue to function as a family. Poverty simplifies our life, but we are not daunted by it. That we are abysmally poor we are never allowed to forget by Public Opinion. Our misfortune gives our relatives their power. They remind us of our situation: the sick woman, three helpless girls, and a wayward son, the leaking house and weakening doors—we are a defeated family, open to oppression and harassment, and on the verge of being a burden on other families. We find cruelty where it is least expected. I also discover the power of those who have material things over those who are without them.

Public Opinion is engaged in assessing the worth of each young man in the family in an open *bure* at our elder sister's house. The head assessor is a middle son—handsome, a man of means, a rising patriarch. He is assisted by an extremely vocal younger brother and an elder brother who has no other advantage except the ambiguous advantage of being born before the other brothers. The first to be assessed is a teenager who has turned away from school and now takes an inordinate interest in his father's newly acquired cane farm. He is easily worth five hundred pounds and is bound to go far. Another youngster who is destined for a job either at the weigh-bridge in the Sugar Mill or the boiler room is worth three hundred pounds. But his cousin's brother, an outcast, who squanders his time on tree tops like a lonely hunter, or in the mangrove swamps chasing after shrimps, is worth no more than twenty pounds. The younger vocal brother points his finger at the thin, reserved boy sitting on the periphery, "What's he worth?" The boy on a dark trail, the "flier" who hasn't learned to walk—how can he be assessed? They shudder at the boy's ambition, "What does he want to be—a District Commissioner?" Their inability to fathom the boy's intentions causes suspicion: What if the boy is right, what if the little Machiavelli does become a District Commissioner?

I take refuge in the secret life of the imagination. I answer my enemies back with an inner discourse in which I outline, quoting Tulsidas, the different kinds of *daridra*, the worst being the poverty of soul and imagination.

Become a wage-earner. At mid high school, shortly after my father's death, I'm employed by a rice farmer who pays me six shillings per day and provides two meals. The seedlings are ready, the rain has come, the joyful family arrives early in the paddy field. More paid workers arrive—women and children whose bodies are undergoing seasonal hardening in the paddy fields. I watch their fingers dancing in the shining mud. The green seedlings are held in one hand, a twist of the wrist of the other hand trims them to their stems and roots, the green tops scattering in the murky water, and with the four fingers of the vacant hand, the soggy soil is parted, the thumb inserts the seedlings into the parted soil, and the fingers come together to build a mound around the planted seedlings. The milky smell of seedlings, whose tops have been shorn, wafts on stench of field mud.

At another end of the paddy field, the farmer's son, Sami, my friend, is ploughing the land with a team of sturdy oxen. The placid white bullock with wide nostrils is an honest worker, and the other, a black and white, narrow-faced steer, snorting and lurching ahead, is still in the breaking stage, but Sami, who understands his temperament perfectly, yanks the drooping rope, shouts obscenities, and keeps him steady under the yoke.

My responsibility is to keep the planters supplied with seedlings and to assist in planting. I stumble in and out of the bog, wade across an overflowing ditch, and collect the seedlings from the seedbed. The seedbed is deep green with a bald patch on one side. A solitary woman is pulling out the seedlings, and tying them up in small bundles.

It's shadowy at noon; black clouds are scudding toward the west. There is a downpour in the afternoon. The raindrops plopping in the muddy water, and the dancing fingers of the planters, create a wonderful music. Extending from my feet are a crisscross of a thousand yellow stalks turning blue in the rain. Late in the afternoon, the sun appears briefly. The stalks are yellow again.

The workers are gone. My friend and I are resting on our backs on the side of a hillock, our feet caked with mud. There is light in the paddy water. The bullocks are feeding on weeds, chewing and ruminating. That farm work comes so effortlessly to me, bringing a small wage, causes a feeling of exhilaration. The euphoria of a working man. At last, I'm free. I say to my friend that I can easily be a farm worker all my life. He laughs because he doesn't believe my words.

The inseparable twins of my being: one playing the role of the only male in the house, the other living his magic life alone. With the savings from my wages, I buy books that I devour till late in the night, suffering the stabbing pain, stomach cramps, developed in the paddy fields.

We gaze into the future. The start of a friendship out of books. Krishna is bright and sensitive, a friend out of a storybook. In the school, the syllabus doesn't satisfy, and the library has nothing for us. Krishna is exploring. That year, we are content to be seduced by his enigmatic hero, the Mad Doctor from Harley Street. We search for his trail through several novels whose very titles are attractive to us: *A Man of Destiny*, *Broken Wings*, *Wind in the Bracken*, *Where Gods Are in Vain*; and the prose is exhilarating: *As we move over the cobbles of life's road we are apt to tarry for a moment, and whilst shielding our eyes from to-morrow's glare, gaze into the future.* The author's credo expresses our own deepest thoughts— . . . *live by what is noble, tolerant, and just.*

And through the fictional anguish of the Mad Doctor, I discover a real anguish. The crate of books with the F. J. Thwaite novels arrives for my friend after his father goes through another bout of insanity and launches on a series of financial misadventures meant to bring about his own ruination. A successful businessman, prominent both in physical stature and status in society, a self-made Hindu scholar and a flawless orator, suddenly he becomes an unusual spectacle in Town: Like an older Hamlet, he stalks the street from one end to the other with his tragic burden; his audience is shopkeepers in doorways and picture-goers in front of the moviehouse. There are allusions to a deep feud, disloyalty, and betrayal by a clansman. Whatever the cause, eventually fact becomes inextricably linked with fiction. His audience is aware that the mad king isn't just promenading. Like a drunken actor, he is staging a subtle play, inviting the townspeople to interpret its meaning. Nothing he does diminishes his authority in the eyes of his die-hard admirers for a long time. In the end, step by step, he accomplishes his overwhelming dream of complete demolition.

We gaze into the future in the composition class. There are future doctors, engineers, and teachers in the class. Krishna is marked for leadership. The leadership will be real, and so will be the betrayal. A perverse sort of continuity from father to son. Krishna is aware that he is tied to the inevitable father.

The teacher is skeptical about breakers of new grounds. In his republic, there will be businessmen, doctors, engineers, lawyers, teachers, but no historians and poets, and no actors. The wayward yearning for what is in books is romantic stupidity, a failure to recognize the limitations of our real world. The would-be businessmen, doctors, engineers, lawyers, teachers chant agreement, their voices ringing with certainty.

Writing is transgression: The young poet who contributes romantic verses to the Hindi paper, under a pseudonym "Madhur" (Mellifluous), is cautioned about poetic excesses that could bring shame to the respected institution. The poet sits at a corner desk in the back, hoping that the chanting of his pseudonym and the derisive laughter would dissipate quickly.

The dream of being an artist is nurtured secretly. Reluctantly, I pull out a slovenly devised novella composed in a flash of inspiration, embellished with decorative Urdu phrases gleaned from Hindi romances and set against Prem Chand's rural life. "It's nothing much," I declare to my readers, hoping to preempt any derisive comments, but secretly enraptured by the romance of having filled the white pages of an entire notebook. The teacher's attention is drawn to it, and discreet praise is given. But there is no future in it.

Suspended between two languages, writing will be a waiting dream, a secret pleasure, the most important of all work, though endlessly postponed, forever causing a nagging dissatisfaction, and in the meanwhile a huge monologue of swirling narratives made up of a multitude of dreams, memories, exiled texts, written and unwritten—Malayalee narratives broken by sleep, half-understood English prose, Hindi romances about feudal relationships; none having any clear definition in my infatuated bookish mind—will be seeking articulateness, a form and an ending, constructing itself in unison and collapsing into fragments.

Mother finds her long-lost relatives. Two years before Mother dies, she is reunited with her brother's wife and daughter. Mother's brother, of course, died years ago in Suva, and his wife remarried and settled in Canada with her children and grandchildren, except one daughter who still lived, during all these years, at the bottom of the blue hills I watched from the window of our old house. My mother was born in a village not far from where she finally lived, but her family disappeared after her marriage. Both her parents died, and her only brother, another adventurer, went away to seek his fortune in the city. My parents went to visit him, before I was born, on the *Adi Rewa*, a legendary voyage in the family annals. Mother sometimes spoke of her brother, his wife, and children, and asked me if I had ever encountered them in the streets of Suva. She spoke about them so distantly that I regarded this story about a lost brother as part of fiction-making.

One Canadian winter, the "Lady from Canada" finds herself overwhelmed by an unexamined feeling. On an impulse, she announces she wants to go "home." Her grandchildren are puzzled, "What's gotten into Grandma?" They are concerned, but they have no time for nostalgia, because they have a different notion of home and identity. Within a few days, she is on board Canadian Airlines bound for Nadi. After years of Church on Sunday, visiting grandchildren, stalking the supermarkets for "specials," slothful habits, drifting toward obesity, rummy meetings, soaps and ice hockey on TV, after years of trying to assimilate, suddenly she has that feeling that home is elsewhere: The immigrant remains an immigrant.

She visits her daughter first. "I've come to see someone who is closely linked to your father. I'm confident she's still living." Her son-in-law takes charge of the search. Discreet inquiries are made, and he himself makes casual visits to several villages. He is elated by his success and surprised that the object of his search is almost in the very next village.

For the recognition scene, he orders the details like an expert director of Bombay Talkies. After all, this is an Indian melodrama, where the disconnected narratives finally come together, and the long-lost relatives are reunited. The protagonists will meet without the mediation of a third party.

The day is a cheerful Sunday. Mother is waiting for an important visitor in her yard. The "Lady from Canada" walks slowly up the incline on the hidden path to Mother's house. She is wearing a blue chiffon sari and expensive jewelry. Her deeply rouged face gives her the appearance of a *Mem saheb*. She greets Mother in foreign Hindi. The two women peer at each other, as in the movies, and at once they are in each other's arms, crying, rejoicing. At this point, their exuberant relatives, as directed, emerge from their hiding places and cluster around the small woman in white and the corpulent woman in blue, who are embracing each other again and again.

Shortly before Mother dies, she takes me to visit her brother's daughter, her husband, and two children. While Mother is turning the pages of an album, smiling to herself, and now and then looking at her newfound relatives, I try to imagine how different her life could have been if the families weren't separated, how less lonely she would have been. She is studying a photograph for kinship signs. She is gazing quizzically at a young man wearing a safety pin in his ear. She already knows the faces in the photographs, knows the brash young men and women, dressed up like the stars in their favorite rock groups and posed against the background of a park or a street that I might have visited during my years in Canada. How different it might have been if I hadn't treated her story about the lost brother as mere fiction! For Mother, it is enough that contact has been made with her lost brother's family. She looks at each of us again with a tiny smile playing on her lips. The photographs have messages; she is reading them like real correspondence, turning the album around to study the photographs from another perspective, and when the sequence is broken, she looks up puzzled, then starts on a new sequence.

For a moment, the photographs integrate the families.

My mother's house is empty. My sister, who lived with my mother, and her husband are in the yard saying farewell to us. Their beautiful daughter is also in the yard. Her overflowing hair is causing her irritation. Her face is inclined sideways like a sunflower, showing us her slender neck, the arc of her cheek, the half-smile on her lips. Her agile fingers are chasing the stray strands of hair on her forehead. Her face turns to offer us a full smile instead of a furtive glance. She is obviously making an impression on us so that we will remember her as a beautiful child-woman. Now her attention shifts to the blue-eyed, blonde-haired doll that she is holding, and her body is moving rhythmically like someone who is about to dance.

Her father says he plans to take his family to another village. There are too many drifters in this village. Disquieting thoughts. If he leaves, we will have no reason to return to this village. He points to the colony of shanties on the other side of the old mud path. The land has been subdivided, and subdivided, and denatured, and young married couples have moved in from nowhere and created their pastiche of box timber, glass, weatherboard, and roofing iron. The shanties have started to crawl uphill like sugarcane. For an instant, an image comes to me of the shanties and sugarcane blown over the hills, and a new relationship emerging between the land and people.

This morning, the shanty dwellers are waiting in their limbo territory for the man from the Native Land Trust Board. He has been promising to pay them a visit for some months. He is bound to come this morning and make things permanent for the shanty dwellers.

When Mother first learned that the piece of land she regarded as her own was on a temporary lease, she wanted me to look up my father's papers immediately, because there was an enormous mistake somewhere; the land belonged to the Colonial Sugar Refining Company, and it was given to my father for his service. We explained the new situation, but Mother continued to believe there was, indeed, something wrong. "No one ever had anything against your father," she said finally, turning away from us.

The shanty men are sitting under an open sky. They are still waiting for the man from the NLTB, for his footfall and familiar laughter. Once they considered themselves lucky because they found a piece of vacant land to put up their shelter, but now they are not at ease; they will not be at ease until the man from the NLTB arrives. They will give account of themselves; he will not turn them out.

The old train driver, after Mother's death the lone survivor from the old village, walks into the yard to say goodbye to us. "They are waiting for the wrong man," he gives a short chuckle. I like the train driver's candid eyes. He is looking at the shanty men and talking about the death of a community. The village died before it had the chance to lay roots, he says to me. And there's an ill-wind blowing, and everyone is for himself. The village has turned into a shanty before it could become a genuine village. I'm assessing his words when a young man drifts in. He is the train driver's self-employed son, a maker of photograph frames and vendor of framed photographs of Hindu deities and film stars. He describes his business, blushing frequently. The business is satisfactory: Saraswati, the goddess of learning, is in decline, the film stars are out of favor, but the shanty women are buying Lachmi, the goddess of fortune.

Lachmi still holds hope!

Three Poems for Kenzaburō Ōe

Albert Wendt

1) In the Barber's Chair

An ancient barber's chair like a throne
in a silent shed in a remote village
snared in the mountains of Japan.
In it is a man
armored with five years of silence.

One day his ten-year-old son
enters the sacred shed
and to his father trapped in
the throne asks: What are you
doing in that chair?

The man swivels his chair round,
not even his favorite son will make
him break his vow of silence.

A year later he hangs himself.
His body is a wombed question mark.

Today the son is a famous writer
who believes that to know
the meaning of his father's protest
he must occupy that barber's chair, soon.

2) Ōe, You

In Samoan your name means "You."
When I tell you this you chuckle
and say, No wonder I have
always considered myself
an alienated man—it is
never "I" but always "You."

3) Your Son

Your eldest son you talk about constantly.
Your books are filled with him:
how he was born with a brain tumor,
the operation that saved him,
his learning to feast on music.

You carry him everywhere with you
even in your sleep and here to Hawaii
like a golden crucifix of hope,
your diviner's rod to the dark springs
of the world's unquenchable pain.

Reading toward the Indigenous Pacific: Patricia Grace's *Potiki*, a Case Study

Miriam Fuchs

The phrase "cultural holism" has been used to characterize recent modes of cross-cultural inquiry. According to Betty Jean Craige, holistic scholars are like ecologists, investigating the diverse parts of ecosystems for patterns of interactivity and reciprocal change. No single organism (or population group) within the environment (or global community) is superior, and each supports the workings of the larger system. Writing in the guest column of the May 1991 *PMLA*, Craige explains holism as an approach that "privileges study of a system over analysis of the system's discrete parts," and she urges literary scholars to view holism as a useful "model of connection" that can draw its constituent parts into a slowly evolving, universal

I thank Joan D. Peters for her astute reading of earlier drafts of this essay and for her extremely helpful suggestions.

Throughout the essay, I have italicized Maori and Hawaiian words. However, when quoting from other essays or from *Potiki*, which do not always use italics, I follow the format of the original text.

community.[1] Catharine R. Stimpson, in her 1990 MLA presidential address, counts herself among the holists, who "cannot think of culture unless we think of many cultures at the same time—whether we define culture broadly as a shared set of values . . . or more narrowly as the most valued aesthetic objects."[2]

As useful a model as holism may seem to many Western academics, it often strikes scholars who come from and write about the indigenous cultures of the Pacific as a critical form of ecocide. Polynesia, Melanesia, and Micronesia are comparatively small in population, separated by vast distances, and geographically remote from metropolitan centers of academic discourse. Among the least visible of holism's "discrete" units, they are also the most likely to be elided by holism's intercultural paradigms. For example, Haunani-Kay Trask, a Native Hawaiian activist and scholar, has criticized the academic community for ignoring indigenous and nationalist sources while establishing a tradition of Pacific scholarship based primarily on the findings of non-Polynesian researchers. Writing in *The Contemporary Pacific: A Journal of Island Affairs*, Trask calls the majority of historians and anthropologists *maha'oi haole*, the Hawaiian term for intrusive outsiders who casually place themselves where they do not belong. Trask also argues implicitly against holism for allowing its practitioners to be complacent toward historical and specific errors while they design broad networks of relationships and common values. Her strongest objections concern *haole* researchers, who use intellectual paradigms in order to criticize the non-

1. Betty Jean Craige, "Literature in a Global Society," *PMLA* 106 (1991): 397 and 396, respectively. By examining, in this essay, the controversy over Salman Rushdie's *The Satanic Verses*, Craige illustrates the fierce disagreements between holists and those who resist holistic ideologies and methods.

2. Catharine R. Stimpson, "On Differences," *PMLA* 106 (1991): 403. In this essay, her 1990 presidential address, Stimpson makes a statement that she means to be all-inclusive. Her word choices, however, would suggest omission and exclusion to many Pacific Islanders. Referring to literatures written in English, she states that "literary English will differ if the writer is from the Pacific Rim, Asia, Africa, the Middle East, the British Isles, the Republic of Ireland, the Caribbean, the United States, Canada" (406). Because Stimpson cites the "Pacific Rim" but omits the "Pacific Basin," her sentence could be interpreted as excluding such areas as French Polynesia, New Caledonia, Western Samoa, American Samoa, Fiji, Tonga, the Cook Islands, Guam, and many other islands and island nations. In other words, not all of the "discrete" units within a multicultural paradigm are equal or equally visible.

holistic politics and land claims of Native nationalists "from Australia and New Zealand through the Solomons and New Caledonia to Hawai‘i."[3]

Applying Trask's argument to studies of Polynesian literature, we can see that critics who use holistic methodologies often articulate cross-cultural judgments and subordinate the work's ethnic differences to Western forms and tropes—even as they attempt to do otherwise.[4] Maori literature, for instance, is often called too candid, not sufficiently complex, or overly sentimental. In an essay on Witi Ihimaera and Patricia Grace, Bill Pearson disapprovingly mentions two critics who express embarrassment at the un-restrained emotions in Ihimaera's early fiction, specifically his 1973 novel *Tangi*, which is about a son grieving over his father's death.[5] Yet, a few pages

3. Haunani-Kay Trask, "Natives and Anthropologists: The Colonial Struggle," *The Contemporary Pacific* 3, no. 1 (Spring 1991): 160, 159. Trask takes issue with Roger M. Keesing and Jocelyn Linnekin on a number of Nativist subjects. Among these are assertions that Nativist genealogical claims are often inaccurate, the politicized nature of contract archaeology in Hawaii today, and conditions that existed in the precontact Pacific. Keesing and Linnekin respond to Trask in the same issue of *The Contemporary Pacific*, 168–71 and 172–77, respectively. See also Jocelyn Linnekin and Lin Poyer, eds., *Cultural Identity and Ethnicity in the Pacific* (Honolulu: University of Hawaii Press, 1990). On the Trask and Linnekin debate over Pacific anthropology, see also Jeff Tobin's essay in this issue of *boundary 2*.

4. Although he focuses on Maori writers in New Zealand, Norman Simms, in *Silence and Invisibility* (Washington, D.C.: Three Continents Press, 1986), draws connecting links to Singapore and Malaysia, while he ignores Hawaii and Micronesia in the Northern Pacific. Paul Sharrad, in "Breaking the Silence: The Problems of Studying New Literatures," *World Literature Written in English* 29 (1989): 152–61, objects to this broad scheme in which Southeast Asia and one Polynesian culture are side by side. According to Sharrad, "the social dynamics of language and literary expression in English in Singapore are not really very similar to those affecting the Maori. Inclusion of such a comparison requires more justification and takes the focus of debate away from a specifically Pacific arena" (153). Sharrad further notes that Simms assesses Albert Wendt as "the major Pacific writer," essentially because he thinks that Wendt is "the most European of Pacific writers, *pakeha* New Zealanders and Australian *gubbas* . . . included" (155).

5. Bill Pearson, "Witi Ihimaera and Patricia Grace," *Critical Essays on the New Zealand Short Story*, ed. Cherry Hankin (Auckland: Heinemann, 1982), 166–84. Pearson cites H. Winston Rhodes for "finding himself embarrassed by the suffocating intensity of the bereft son's feeling for his father in *Tangi*" (167). A few paragraphs later, Pearson describes his own embarrassment over a short story by Ihimaera for its depiction of both the *pakeha* and their Maori neighbors. Sharrad and Reed Way Dasenbrock refer to the tendency of critics to wish that Maori writing were less emotionally expressive. Simms illustrates this tendency in "A Maori Literature in English, Part I: Prose Fiction—Patricia Grace," *Pacific*

later, Pearson describes his own embarrassment at the pervasive, simple goodwill of characters in Ihimaera's "The Other Side of the Fence," and then his own preference for the unsentimental story, "One Summer Morning." In other words, literary discussion begins to take shape as comparative statements about acceptable types and intensities of expressed emotion. Keri Hulme has been similarly questioned for grafting onto her mythic, feminist, labyrinthine *the bone people* an ending that some readers consider conventional and sentimental.[6] Critics have also cited problems of believability in Patricia Grace's first novel, *Mutuwhenua* (1978), although within Maori tradition phenomena such as physical illnesses linked to ancestral spirits, or natural stones with vital, spiritual presences would not need extended analysis.[7]

The breach between holistic and Nativist positions would then seem absolute and insurmountable. What one offers as nonhegemonic inclusion in a universal world order, the other censures as a philosophy that, ac-

---

Moana Quarterly 3 (1978): 186–99. He classifies Grace's stories in *Waiariki* into three groups: "Maori," those written in English but containing some Maori syntax and thought; "Macaronic," those with "a high frequency" of Maori words and thought; and "English," those with "no sense of disturbing English syntax beyond its normal bounds" (189). Despite his schematizing, he still makes Western-based judgments concerning appropriate degrees of emotion. One story is sentimental ("Valley"), while another ("Holiday") that is full of "sentimental details" has "just enough of something more profound to sustain the story" (194). In *Silence and Invisibility*, Simms cites Grace's *Mutuwhenua* as an overly sentimentalized novel, which exemplifies "so many similar weaknesses in Maori writing in English" (74). See Miriama Evans, "Politics and Maori Literature," *Landfall* 31 (1985): 40–45, for her response to Simms, who, she emphasizes, finds Grace's experiments " 'of limited esthetic value' " (41).

6. Aorewa McLeod, "Private Lives and Public Fictions," in *Public and Private Worlds: Women in Contemporary New Zealand*, ed. Shelagh Cox (Wellington: Allen and Unwin, Port Nicholson Press, 1987), 67–81. McLeod calls Hulme's *the bone people* a "radical" and "utopian" text that interrogates traditional black-white and male-female polarities. Nevertheless, she adds that many women find the conclusion "unconvincing and unsatisfactory," as she herself does, because of the "happy-ever-after of the whanau—the final vision of the extended family and the communal vision" (81). Susie O'Brien also faults Hulme's conclusion, because the protagonist, Kerewin, appropriates the otherness of the child, Simon, and offers him her name, as well as her protection. O'Brien wonders if the end "signifies anything more than the fulfillment of Kerewin's desire to 'tie up loose ends' " (91). See O'Brien, "Raising Silent Voices: The Role of the Silent Child in *An Imaginary Life* and *the bone people*," *SPAN: Journal of the South Pacific Association for Commonwealth Literature and Language Studies* 30 (1990): 79–91.

7. Lauri Anderson, "Maoriness and the Clash of Cultures in Patricia Grace's *Mutuwhenua*," *World Literature Written in English* 26 (1986): 188–90.

cording to Trask, will "take away from us the power to define who and what we are" and stifle cultural expression.[8] Critics who advocate holism because they believe it exposes colonial and postcolonial oppression and empowers disenfranchised communities must realize that they themselves, holistically studied, are a late twentieth-century version of other Western scholars and observers who also did not see themselves as an incursive presence; most outsiders historically have considered their causes to be just and their behavior more ethical and justifiable than that of their predecessors. But if outsiders have always been problematic for the indigenous Pacific, which has both welcomed and cannibalized them, to follow Trask's argument to its logical conclusion would require that scholars limit their investigations to the most narrow perimeters of their own affiliated group. Consequently, the Oceanic literatures written in English, at the same time as territories, trusts, former colonies, and indigenous groups across the Pacific Basin attain political representation and develop strong ethnic and nationalist movements, would be purposefully ignored. If Maori and other indigenous literatures are not drawn into a transcultural network, Pacific nomenclature will eventually exclude them.[9] *The Rim* and *the Basin* will signify countries that most profitably engage in Western exchange networks of goods and services and whose emigrants are well dispersed throughout Europe and America. In other words, *Pacific Rim* and *Pacific Basin* will become synonymous (and already have, to some extent) and designate the major commercial trading partners Japan, Korea, Malaysia, China, and Singapore.

Some critics, implicitly recognizing this polarity and attempting to breach it, maneuver between holistic and Nativist extremes. Cautious of the West's ability to sweep across the globe, but skeptical of declarations of forbidden areas of study, they merely introduce the literature to the Western public and thereby reduce literary interpretation to discussions of what appears in the plot.[10] For instance, despite the promise of his title, "Pakeha and Maori behind the Tattooed Face: The Emergence of a Polynesian Voice

8. Trask, "Natives and Anthropologists," 162.

9. Paul Sharrad effectively assesses the problems of nomenclature in "Imagining the Pacific," *Meanjin* 49, no. 4 (1990): 597–606.

10. Examples of "literary description" include John Beston, "Potiki," *Landfall* 40 (1986): 501–2; John B. Beston, "The Fiction of Patricia Grace," *Ariel: A Review of International English Literature* 15 (1984): 41–53; and Shaun F. D. Hughes, "Pakeha and Maori behind the Tattooed Face: The Emergence of a Polynesian Voice in New Zealand Fiction," *Modern Fiction Studies* 27 (1981): 13–29.

in New Zealand Fiction," Shaun F. D. Hughes offers very little about the Polynesian dimensions of Polynesian literature. His essay, which appears in *Modern Fiction Studies*, primarily summarizes works by Heretaunga Pat Baker, Albert Wendt, Witi Ihimaera, and Patricia Grace, and then makes broad judgments regarding degree of accomplishment. Using the problematic qualifying phrase, "to the extent that New Zealand culture is more complex than Samoan," Hughes says that Ihimaera's collection, *Pounamu, Pounamu*, is more complex than Wendt's stories, although some of Grace's writing "lack[s] the conceptual originality of works by Wendt and Ihimaera." [11] The assumption here seems to be that any rigorous examination, any use of Western critical theory, for example, will subsume a work's Polynesian elements and drive whatever remains into inappropriate categories. Critics such as Hughes, who operate from this assumption, may find that their mediating strategy turns in on itself. Left to repeating the plot and asserting its historical relevance, they tend to repeat one another's summarial remarks and violate the work's integrity on two fronts—cursory treatment (or neglect) and unsupported judgments.

Patricia Grace's writing, I have found, is particularly susceptible to this type of analysis. [12] Her apparently straightforward plots, clear diction, and nearly transparent prose make her fiction seem relatively uncomplicated. Because nothing blatant provokes the smooth surface of Grace's plots, critics do not feel compelled to marshal theoretical apparatus but rather assume that attention to the storyline is an adequate approach. In the pages that follow, I will use Grace's 1986 novel, *Potiki*, to illustrate, first, that by assuming it to be no more than its plot, critics reduce this complex novel to the familiar, representative Pacific tale of indigenous people versus *pakeha*. [13] Although this surface story does have historical validity,

11. Hughes, "Pakeha and Maori behind the Tattooed Face," 23, 28.

12. My discussion centers on Grace's *Potiki* (Auckland: Penguin, 1986), hereafter cited parenthetically in my text by page number only. Grace's major publications, excluding her children's books, are *Waiariki* (Auckland: Longman, 1975); *Mutuwhenua* (Auckland: Longman, 1978); *The Dream Sleepers and Other Stories* (Auckland: Longman, 1980); and *Electric City and Other Stories* (Auckland: Penguin, 1987). *Cousins* (Auckland: Penguin, 1992) was published after this essay was prepared for publication.

13. John Beston's emphasis on what appears to be *Potiki*'s plot, in a review in *Landfall*, foregrounds the problems that are caused by an overreliance on plot description. Sharrad, in "Breaking the Silence," comments on the same problem in Simms's full-length study, *Silence and Invisibility*. Sharrad notes that it may be "commendable" to try "to understand Pacific writing in the context of its shifting 'mentalities' (descriptive criticism)" but that the effort is problematic, because description "slides into evaluative distinctions." Sharrad

Potiki supersedes the past two centuries of New Zealand's geopolitics. Second, by applying principles of narrative theory, as they have been refined by Gérard Genette, I will illustrate ways in which Western theory, unlike either description or holistic paradigms, is indeed capable of revealing the indigenous dimensions of a work—with important qualifications and limitations.[14] Through this perspective, Grace's novel emerges as a text about the Maori themselves, their means of orally recording their own histories, genealogies, mythologies, and myth-histories, centuries before the *pakeha* and presumably after the *pakeha*. It is about the Maori, separate, distinct, and, to some extent, sealed off from the country's settler Anglopopulation and, even more, from academic cross-cultural scholars. Suffused with pre-Christian spirituality, *Potiki* is deeply engaged in nearly unrecoverable, exclusive differences, and, paradoxically, this becomes apparent by applying Western narrative methodologies.

If we insist on concentrating solely on plot, as does John Beston, for example, *Potiki* is a fairly simple story that a *maha'oi* reader, as well as a Maori, can readily understand. The novel traces the struggle of a coastal Maori community against *pakeha* insensitivity and capitalist scheming. According to Beston's version, *Potiki* "tells of a misused people who, having through hard work succeeded in making a living from their land, find that the land is coveted. Again and again they withstand pressure upon them to yield."[15] The Maori reject increasingly large sums of money that the developers, intent on purchasing the ancestral land for an ocean resort, offer them. In time, the cemetery (*urupa*) and gardens are suspiciously flooded, their meeting house (*wharenui*) burnt down, and the youngest child (the *potiki*) is killed. Beston continues to summarize the story, but he has dif-

---

notes also that the descriptive approach leads Simms to counterpoise what Simms calls " 'the strategies of the good authors' " with the " 'second-rate or naïve authors' " (Simms, *Silence and Invisibility*, 34, quoted by Sharrad, "Breaking the Silence," 157).

14. Gérard Genette, in *Narrative Discourse: An Essay in Method*, trans. Jane E. Lewin (Ithaca: Cornell University Press, 1980) and *Narrative Discourse Revisited*, trans. Jane E. Lewin (Ithaca: Cornell University Press, 1988), outlines a systematic theory of narrative. Based upon structuralist principles, Genette's narratological classifications foreground alignments and discordances of such elements as voice (point of view, levels of narrative), content (order, duration, frequency) and mood (perspective, distance, focalization). His following comment, from the introduction to *Narrative Discourse*, reads like a gloss of *Potiki*: "Analysis of narrative discourse . . . [is] a study of the relationships between narrative and story, between narrative and narrating, and (to the extent that they are inscribed in the narrative discourse) between story and narrating" (29).

15. Beston, "Potiki," 501.

ficulty maintaining the line between description and judgment: "Under the cover of darkness . . . the Maori . . . dynamite the road, bulldoze the construction work, and then drive the bulldozers into the sea, thereby accomplishing what endurance or legal recourse never would. The moral of this parable is that one should fight back, with appropriate retaliation. Grace has joined the ranks of the Maori who believe that justice can only be obtained by direct action." [16] Fashioning the novel into a parable and designing a moral for it, Beston evinces a contradictory stance that infects his objective account. He writes sentimentally about the Maori as hardworking and misused when they are the constituents of a fictional text. Shifting his view to New Zealand's politicized, and sometimes violent, ethnic tensions, he becomes sarcastic and accusatory toward Grace for joining "the ranks" of Maori who believe "only" in direct action. In the midst of summarizing the plot, Beston projects a holistic ideology that allows him to reproach the "discrete," nonholistic activities of New Zealand's political and cultural minority as it tries to protect its ownership of ancestral lands.

Perhaps the most glaring problem with the descriptive approach, and one that Beston acknowledges, is that by concentrating on the narrative line and the events spun out from it, he cannot account for important, basic elements—the title, the title character, and the title character relative to the apparent story. This leaves him insisting that the youngest child of the Tamihana family, the handicapped *potiki* named Toko, is not the focus of the novel. Nor is he vital to its narrative development. Confined to a wheelchair and unable to participate directly in the actions and reactions that fuel the confrontational plot, he must therefore be a peripheral figure. (Beston does not say that a *toko* is an elaborately decorated wooden figure that served as a material symbol of a Maori god.) [17] Even if the *potiki*'s prescience and oracular and recollective abilities mark him as a spiritual presence with symbolic import, Beston's approach obliges the critic to conclude that the *potiki* story is but "loosely linked to the main plot." What cannot be designated as integral to the plot becomes a problem of the text.

It is this specific focus on plot, with its concomitant categories of main and subordinate and its emphasis on deliberate, concrete action that creates a hegemonic structure within *Potiki*—despite Beston's intent to treat the novel carefully. In addition, the focus on plot skews Grace's work and conceals its deeper layers of significance. The *potiki* is surely not a subor-

16. Beston, "Potiki," 501–2.
17. David Lewis and Werner Forman, The Maori: Heirs of Tane (London: Orbis, 1982), 35.

dinate character, and his "story," by which I mean his rhetorical, dynamic, linguistic production of events and plot, is far from ancillary to *Potiki*'s development. It is, instead, part of its very core, and it spans out across the novel, reaching far into genealogical history and generations of prophetic vision. In fact, the process of dramatic storytelling, and not plot, is nearly all there is to *Potiki*.

If we reject Trask's isolationist stance, we need to recognize that neither the descriptive mode employed by critics such as Beston and Hughes, nor the increasingly popular practice of holism when used *in the service of holistic ideologies*, is an adequate tool of study. I suggest, instead, that the methods upon which holists rely, including narrative and structuralist analyses, be utilized, but without the holistic ideology that promotes ecosystems, commonalities, and hybridity. In other words, we can use holistic methodologies not to universalize Pacific literatures but to discover their deeply embedded elements, which an ideology of goodwill and globalized, reciprocal interdependencies can easily obscure. Willing to look to Western narrative theory, for instance, we find that its emphasis on voice and time is fundamental to indigenous Polynesian literature as well. The gap between the critical system and the indigenous subject remains formidable, but at least the indigenous elements are not ignored. Thus, an additional step in the holistic approach involves our drawing back from our systems and accepting the limits of multicultural theorizing and the inadequacy of our interpretations.

Using modern narratology to examine Grace's *Potiki* may seem to be a form of cultural impositioning, since it is a Western holistic system that adheres to common structures and categories of rhetoric and voice. If, however, the method is used within an ideological context of singularity rather than globality, it has a number of advantages. First, it provides a link to what is traditional to Polynesian culture—formal modes of oral production such as song-poems, proverbs, stories, and action-songs.[18] These,

18. Helen Metge, *The Maoris of New Zealand: Rautahi*, rev. ed. (London: Routledge, 1976). The term *traditional* does not necessarily designate oral literary forms that have gone unchanged through the years. As Metge explains, *traditional* applies to literary forms that may be precontact but that have been "handed down through the generations from Maori ancestors" and, thus, have undergone changes (265). Metge describes the six categories of Maori literature: *whai-kōrero* (speeches), *kōrero* (stories), *whaka-taukī* (proverbs), *mōteatea* (song-poems), *haka* (shouted exhortations with actions), and *waiata-ā-ringa* (action-songs) (266). Of the six, the *whai-kōrero* and *kōrero* are unique each time they are performed.

and other genres, existed long before the missionaries transcribed verbal communication into the Western alphabet and gave Polynesia a form of written discourse. Second, a willingness to examine verbalizing patterns, at the very least, acknowledges the existence of complex rhetorical issues within indigenous works and opens up discussion of orality within these texts.[19] Western narratology can only partially account for the positioning and dynamics of Grace's speakers, but the collision of critical system and subject text presents a single, overwhelming advantage. Ironically and dramatically, it pushes to the surface the spiritual and cosmological qualities of *Potiki* and Maori culture. These elements are more than "discrete parts." They are traces of over half a millennium of precontact Polynesia, which are unassimilable without some degree of violation.

Reading *Potiki*, then, not for its confrontational plot but as a series of predominantly spoken chapters, we find that almost nothing takes place, for almost everything has already occurred. With their dramatic voices enframing nearly all of the events, the *potiki* and his adoptive mother Roimata themselves narrate twenty-two of twenty-eight chapters and make frequent references to their present time and place. Of the remaining eight chapters, most contain events that these speakers allude to or recount within their own narrated sections, and two of the chapters are essentially the free indirect discourse of the *potiki*'s father (his thoughts and diction rendered through the third-person). Thus, all of these narratorial positions acquire a degree of autonomy that draws attention to the generating instances of the spoken or privately uttered text rather than to the events being recalled, anticipated, or lived through. In other words, plot in *Potiki* is controlled and directed by voice.

The correspondence between the enunciating voices and the events they relate, technically called narrative anachronies, indicates the complexity of Grace's discourse levels and the traces of "Maoritanga" that nudge at the surface story. When the *potiki* speaks for the first time, his diction, focus, and tense indicate that he is a young boy living with the Tamihana family, who adopted him at birth. He explains that his "birthing mother" left him in the sea, that he was saved from drowning by the Tami-

---

19. Metge explains that oral literature in Maori has "strong rhythmic patterning" and "concrete imagery to convey abstract meaning" (*The Maoris of New Zealand*, 267). These elements, interestingly, are characteristic of Grace's prose as well, but any adaptation or echoing in written English (to say nothing of actual translation) from oral Maori is extremely complex.

hana daughter, Tangimoana, and named Toko by the grandmother. Using the present tense and childlike diction, he also accounts for his extrasensory abilities: "Perhaps it is the magic from Granny's ear that gives me my special knowing, and which makes up for my crookedness and my almost drowning. But I have been given other gifts from before I was born. I know all of my stories" (43). His mother's speech confirms the specifics of Toko's narrative site and time: "My name is Roimata Kararaina and I'm married to Hemi Tamihana. We have four children. . . . We live by the sea, which hems and stitches the scalloped edges of the land" (15). Roimata's formal introduction, which she follows with descriptions of each child, establishes the enunciating times for both her and her son as prior to the time when the developers threaten the Maori community. Accordingly, Roimata, also in the dramatic present tense, says of her *potiki*: "Toko is a gift that we have been given, and he has gifts. He has a special knowing" (46).

Because the speakers draw attention to their own enunciating time and place, and because these intermittently change, the temporal and spatial dimensions of their articulated chapters slip between the various stages of what critics usually consider to be *Potiki*'s "primary" plot—the antagonism between the developers and the Maori. This means that the dynamics of Roimata's and Toko's speech create all sorts of intercalary figurations. For instance, Roimata's narrating frame moves chronologically forward from her position in chapter 1, in which she is a mother of four young children. In chapter 15, she states that her daughter is fully grown and, with her recent degree in law, is defending the rights of the Maori in disputed land claims. Thus, the primary plot activity—between the developers and the Tamihana family—which chronologically followed Roimata's and Toko's initial speeches, is suddenly earlier than Roimata's new enunciating time, thus exemplifying what Genette would call an analepsis. Then, in chapter 25, Roimata speaks out from the immediate drama, in which the developers have just bulldozed the hillside in order to trigger landslides and pollute the water. She surveys the landscape and, in the present tense, remarks: "The hills are quiet and the machines have been taken away. After a while the trees will begin to grow again and soon the water will be clear. There is comfort in knowing these things, but is there enough comfort?" (159). Her enunciating time has again shifted, and in this instance it has actually converged with plot time, creating a homodiegetic correspondence that does not seem consistent with a simple, linear storyline.

No sooner does this character's plot time and narrating time converge than they again split apart. She continues to speak and, without apparent logic, shifts from the present perfect into the past perfect and goes from being a narrator and a protagonist to just a narrator:

> We *have known* what it is to have had a gift, and have not ever ques-
> tioned from where the gift came, only sometimes wondered. The gift
> has not been taken away because gifts are legacies, that once given
> cannot be taken away. . . . The gift we were given is with us still.
>
> His death *had been* with us a long time but not the manner of it.
> The manner of his death, that is where the pain is—the manner of
> his death, and the brokenness and suffering. (159, my emphasis)

Unfettered to her previous enunciating sites, and now in a posterior narrating position, Roimata here laments her son's violent death, even though
Toko has not yet been murdered within the linear plot, and thus expresses
herself by what narratologists call prolepsis. Moreover, because this second
position is so much later than the previous one, she is able to say that the
potiki's death "had been" with them for an extended period of time. Other
shifts nearly as disjunctive occur elsewhere and can be charted by narrative analysis, but yet the ideology of holism cannot adequately account for
the reasons behind this activity. Each of a work's "analyzable features," according to Genette, leads to "some connection, comparison, or putting into
perspective," and the direction is not "from the general to the particular, but
indeed from the particular to the general" to reach "universal, or at least
transindividual" elements.[20] *Potiki*'s analyzable features do not, however,
approach universals. Nor do they disclose anything precise regarding how
the Maori traditionally view time, tense, and death.

If we continue to apply narrative principles to Grace's work, it becomes clear that the most dramatic maneuvering of voice, time, and place
occurs with Toko himself, whose collocations of these elements suggest
different ways of viewing and experiencing them. Like Roimata's, Toko's
narrating times move about, so that his narrated sections are sometimes
simultaneous to plot time and at other times retrospective or analeptic. In
the middle of the novel, for instance, his narrative stance is sufficiently distant from events to enable him, as a storyteller, to transform the climax of
the *pakeha*-Maori conflict into oral myth. In so doing, he absorbs its catastrophic events into his own, more encompassing version that interprets
the tragedy by mythifying its details; the destruction of the *wharenui* by fire
becomes an account of dancing colors, and the screams of the children

20. Genette, *Narrative Discourse*, 23.

are rhetorically transmuted into a story of sounds (134). Even the incontestability of the ruined building and the shattered ancestral statues is merely one curve of a story that reaches out to another curve of another story, which absorbs the rebuilding of the *wharenui* into oral text. This version affirms that ancient skills such as wood carving and using natural materials such as *pingao* and *kiekie* have not been lost. From this perspective, as long as human beings know, and then articulate, their histories, physical destruction can be reformed into a continuous spiral of cross-generational, ongoing narratives. The past is both unfixed and revocable, capable of being altered into the present, which gradually slips into the future and thus becomes present time.

Toko's narrating position toward the end of the novel shifts back into present-tense plot time and creates a startling dramatization of time becoming unhinged. The meeting house has been rebuilt, and the ancestors have been recarved by Toko's brother, James. The *potiki* comments on the structural changes that allow him to enter the building in his wheelchair:

> There *is* a special door that was made for me and my chair. It *is* a door at the side of the new wharenui specially hinged so that it opens either out or in. There *is* a ramp and a wide pathway from the road to enable me to come and go easily. It *was* not easy by then, for me to be without my chair. (153, my emphasis)

No sooner does Toko, in this passage, embed himself *within* plot time ("There is a special door . . .") and render his narrative simultaneous to it than he reverses himself to be *outside* of it ("It was not easy by then . . ."). Once he is posterior to plot time, he then looks backward at what he has just narrated. Then, on the very same page, he makes a second shift, this one catapulting him back into plot time. He peers at the front of the rebuilt structure and remarks, "It is a beautiful door that opens without noise" (153). Still again, Toko vaults forward only to narrate backward: "Once inside the house someone would help me. . . . I was always given a time to speak even though speaking is mostly done by those who are old" (153–54). Narrative analysis can follow Toko relocating himself at various enunciating times and spaces as it did for Roimata. Still, it does not bring us closer to understanding why, when Toko's purpose is simply to describe the *wharenui*'s new door, his narratorial positions are so complex. And summoning an ideology of connections and Western universals only pulls the work further out of its Oceanic context, which is the only context that could offer an adequate response to these narrative convolutions.

Taken together, these examples of narrative discordances indicate that in contrast to the story that critics prefer to summarize, *Potiki*'s other "story" has no single climax or denouement. Something else is occurring in this work, some other scheme of events. Partially told and partially sensed, it presses at the linear sequence, and it circumscribes simple plot time within its more dynamic structure. This other scheme is located within the work's oral dimensions, which are necessarily textualized into a written genre. It embodies, but is not strictly determined by, the historical collisions of the European and the Maori. The collisions may be described (fires, floods, murder, the village's counteractions of dynamiting the resort's foundation and plunging the bulldozers into the ocean), but *Potiki*'s performative dimensions draw these conflicts into harmonizing voices that penetrate and incorporate any single story.

The *potiki*'s final, spoken chapter, which projects the most inconceivable slippage between narrating and narrated times, also offers the most powerful suggestion that Grace's text supersedes its linear dimensions and literally performs Maori ideas of life and death and the passing of time. Spinning his own myth-narrative, Toko makes it utterly clear, first, that he is dead; second, that he is an ancestor; and, third, that he is enunciating the details of his own death—from a post-death time frame and a post-death location. He speaks directly "from the wall," "from the tree" (181). Toko *is* the wooden figure that was carved in the rebuilt *wharenui* and described previously:

> . . . the tamaiti, the mokopuna, the potiki, with all his stories entwined about him. . . . [T]he head of the tamaiti, alive with fire, had been widened and drawn down on one side. On that side of it was a small, shelled ear that listened to the soft whisperings, the lullabies, the quiet lamentations. . . . [T]he wide mouth . . . had at its corners the magic swirls, and . . . the talking, storytelling tongue whirling out and down to where the heart began. . . . The chest . . . was full of life and breath, and the large heart was patterned over the chest in a spiral that covered it completely. It was a spiral heart that had no breaking—no breaking and no end. (171–72)

What seemed, in this earlier passage, to be a wooden representation is, at the end of the novel, animate and articulate. The stories represented here in whirling patterns are the stories that Toko has been producing and that readers have been reading. The representation of his breath is vitalized and made immediate in Toko's narrated chapters; and the carved "storytelling tongue" has come alive as the force that enunciates *Potiki*'s final chapter.

In effect, the speaker suddenly is, has gradually become, or always was the wooden representation of himself. If this ambiguous shift were described by the other characters, we could contest it as their own misperceptions. However, because we have been receiving parts of Grace's text directly through this voice all along, we have to acknowledge that at some point the child in the wheelchair, who was producing text, died; that he continued to produce text and was buried; and that he now continues to produce text from his material incarnation. This singular shift, which is unaccountable in realistic Western terms, has the effect of setting all the preceding chapters spinning into ontological and epistemological uncertainties. When, in basic plot time, was the *potiki* murdered? When, in enunciating time? For how many chapters has he been narrating from an afterlife that is both spiritual and material? Why has his death been recomposed into, and obscured by, levels of spoken discourse? How do these shifts affect the full span of narrating positions, as well as the prologue and the epilogue? How do we rationalize Grace's strategy for compelling us to conclude that much of *Potiki* has been narrated from the dead and by a wooden statue? Without adequate answers, it is not possible to address with any degree of authority such issues as the speaker's source of knowledge, its accessibility, and the private modes of transmission in anything other than generalizations and rudimentary inferences.

Other narrative discordances additionally point to the overriding problem of holistic inquiry, which is the way that it moves in the direction of broad statements based upon a limited amount of information. This process makes it extremely difficult to analyze a text in all of its "discrete" details. In the case of Grace's work, the performative dimensions seem to offer a link to Maori oral literature, but actually they reveal little of the specific ways, if any, the speakers invoke or adapt Polynesian song (*waiata*), proverbs (*whakataukī*), and other indigenous genres for their own purposes. Judith Binney explains in "Maori Oral Narratives, Pakeha Written Texts" that Maori narratives tend to be restrictive and project boundaries that exclude the Western world.[21] Because they are primarily concerned with their own leaders, their own people, and their own customs, Maori narratives most often consist

21. Judith Binney, "Maori Oral Narratives, Pakeha Written Texts: Two Forms of Telling History," *New Zealand Journal of History* 20 (1987): 16–28.

of family myth-narratives of filiality and social relatedness, not the single ethno-economic story that seems to be *Potiki*. This exclusivity makes the process of incorporating indigenous narrative into contemporary, written texts quite difficult. Presumably, it is even more difficult for holistic readers to disentangle the traditional rhetoric from the writer's own stylistics and imaginative vision. A typical response to this difficulty is to turn away and draw general connections to other Oceanic cultures and then to other bi-cultural communities. But these intercultural diagrams lead head-on to the objections of scholars who characterize non-Nativist study as inaccurate and partial, but an effective means of robbing individual communities of their authentic history. And the problem for readers who choose the other alternative, that of descriptive case study, is that they produce what Rob Wilson has termed "illusions of de-politicized empiricism." [22] These self-conscious, ostensibly objective observations reveal more about the problematics of Western theorizing than about the subject they purport to examine.

A further obstacle for holistic critics is that Grace and other indigenous writers offer selected aspects of their culture for apparent display, but then they withhold as much as they offer. Grace's work may seem transparent, but as a cultural production it is opaque. How can readers begin to recompose her novel's alignments—or disalignments—of past, present, and future when Grace does not explicitly say that the Maori conceptualize time differently from Westerners? If readers knew, for instance, that in Maori, the past (*nga rā o mua*) translates into English as "the days in front," while the future (*kei muri*) means "the time behind," they would sense, to a greater degree than Western schematizing can suggest, the complexity of *Potiki*'s voicing and rhetorics. [23] Keri Hulme, also, who seems to work

22. Rob Wilson, "Theory's Imaginal Other: American Encounters with South Korea and Japan," *boundary 2* 18 (1991): 220–41. Wilson observes that American ethnography in the 1980s began to turn away from modes of "scientist closure and ideal totalization of other cultures" toward a postmodernist tendency to search for a culture's "unnameable" elements (225).

23. See Metge, *The Maoris of New Zealand*, 68–70, on time and tense in Maori language and culture. For a contemporary example of the Hawaiian perspective of time, Trask writes: "In our language, the past (*ka wā mamua*) is the time in front or before; the future (*ka wā mahope*) is the time that comes after. In the words of one of our best living Native historians, Lilikalā Kame'eleihiwa, . . . 'The Hawaiian stands firmly in the present, with his back to the future, and his eyes fixed upon the past, seeking historical answers for present-day dilemmas. Such an orientation is to the Hawaiian an eminently practical one, for the future is always unknown whereas the past is rich in glory and knowledge' " (see Trask, "Natives and Anthropologists," 164, quoted from "Land and the Promise of

toward accessibility by including a lengthy glossary in *the bone people*, actually uses it as a linguistic decoy. The glossary does not translate all of the Maori passages but instead gives partial explanations of only some of them. Using a glossary that blatantly conceals and incompletely exposes, a reader can only guess what Hulme decided to withhold or what her motivation for doing so was. In fact, many readers will experience the glossary as a metatextual device with secret codes of its own.

Potiki's indigenous story, then, is almost "unanalyzable." It consists of phenomena rather than personages, and of sounds rather than formalized speech. It is a percipient existence, not a series of events, and the speaker who most profoundly knows this, the *potiki*, distinctly hears and senses its manifestations. As traces of a nearly untranslatable Maori communality, they emanate through the walls of the building and take shape as a "stirring within," a "murmuring," an overriding sensibility. The *potiki* listens carefully to the whispering and the lamentations that are discernible, and although he knows what is there, he does not reproduce, explicate, or translate the contents, which conceivably are being produced in his indigenous language. The term *there* loses a clear locus, and the notion of *here* loses immediacy, as Toko declares his final enunciating site to be "this place of now, behind, and in, and beyond the tree, from where I have eversight" (183). If readers are uncertain of the epistemological principles that underlie the powers of "eversight," then surely they further recognize the distantiation between the "story" that Toko himself is hearing and the surface story that they are reading.

Like Toko himself, the ancestors—who must also be wooden carvings—inhabit the *wharenui*, and they have been "stirring," "assembling," and vocalizing as long as Toko and Roimata have been narrating their sections of *Potiki*. He has heard them and has occasionally cited their movements within the walls. When the *pakeha* came to speak to the family about plans for "top-level facilities" and "trained whales and seals" on the ancestral land (which the *pakeha* refer to as Block J136 and J480), "[t]here was in the house a drawing in of breath, and a sighing" (96); most readers, though, naturally assume that this response belongs to the immediate Tamihana family members. The movements and vocalizing intensify as Toko articu-

---

Capitalism" (Ph.D. diss., University of Hawaii, 1986). Kameʻeleihiwa's *Native Land and Foreign Desires* (Honolulu: Bishop Museum Press, 1992), which discusses Hawaii's history of land tenure change until the 1848 *Māhele*, was published while this essay was prepared for publication.

lates his final chapter. He comments that his family members are asleep and "do not clearly hear the footfalls." Nor do they see the "shadowless forms, forms of which they themselves may be the shadows," nor the "teko-teko as they come, taking up the bones, moving in silently beside them" (184). Only Toko, himself an ancestor, intuits this activity, and, together, the activity and his rhetoric set *Potiki* resonating with a breathless spirituality that surpasses any specific references to Maori life and custom.

The problem is that while Grace amplifies the profundity of her Poly-nesian "story," she draws it further away from the multicultural reader. Reed Way Dasenbrock calls such barriers to full comprehension strate-gies of "culturally coded defamiliarization."[24] In *Potiki*, the defamiliarization occurs between the reader and Polynesia as it persists behind the folds of *Potiki*'s more obvious confrontational structure. The gap becomes most pronounced in the text's final two pages, where Grace guardedly seals off her deeper, cognitive subject by concluding with a passage written entirely in Maori. Like the comments Toko makes regarding what he hears (from his carved, shelled ear angled toward the ground), the passage reaffirms the private, nearly inviolate, singularity and spirituality of a people. The passage also creates numerous uncertainties, but it does not give enough information for these to be resolved. First, it projects a nonspecific enun-ciating site and time. Although the site and time initially seem identical to Toko's "now, behind, and in" position (with its own uncertainties), the pas-sage is typographically set off from Toko's narration. Thus, it could emanate from the walls, the statues, the ancestral voices, and, in fact, from any time and place, including, presumably, precontact Aotearoa. Second, part of the passage consists of questions and answers, and therefore suggests two speakers. But since the indigenous elements of this novel have perfused Western concepts of individual, cultural, mortal, and immortal identity, indi-vidualized speakers are not necessary. Third, the passage is both strange and familiar. Most of the Maori will be unintelligible to non-Maori readers, but some of it—words such as *tamaiti*, *mokopuna*, and *potiki*—requires no translation, for by the end of the novel, most readers will understand their definitions. Grace has worked to situate non-Maori readers at the edge of her Polynesian narrative, where they can sense its innermost components but are unable to engage fully or even penetrate beyond the borders.

The closing off of the powerful signifiers of *Potiki*'s indigenous ele-

24. Reed Way Dasenbrock, "Intelligibility and Meaningfulness in Multicultural Literature in English," *PMLA* 102 (1987): 10–19.

ments suggests a deliberate statement of forbidden territory. Geographically, most of the Pacific has been colonized, nationalized, declared trusts or territories, or brought into statehood. Only a few countries like Tonga, Nauru, Fiji, Western Samoa, and Papua New Guinea are today independent, and each of these has economic or political affiliations with First World nations. But elements of precontact culture that exist in genealogies, non-Christian mythologies, reverence for, and intimacy with, the natural environment are all part of the psychology of the contemporary Pacific. According to Albert Wendt, the earlier generations coexist for Oceanic populations, because "our dead are woven into our souls like the hypnotic music of bone flutes." [25] If the soul of the Pacific has had little political exigency in the region's colonialist history, its spiritual power has, in some way, been operative and omnipresent.

In view of the enormous ground that lies between Trask's warning against, and Craige's advocacy of, multicultural inquiry (Trask for what it excludes, and Craige for what it includes), there ought to be room for cultural study that neither triggers attack nor absorbs cultural differences into totalizing paradigms. Descriptive approaches obscure the contradictions that underpin their ostensible objectivity. Many anthropologists, for instance, used to describe cultural identity among Pacific Islanders as fixed according to ancestry and biological descent. In the past few decades, based on increased "field work," some of them have reversed this position. Now anthropologists have begun to view cultural identity, especially among groups such as the Hawaiians and the Maori, as more fluid, based upon changing social networks and shifting relationships. [26] Undoubtedly, notions of cultural identity and ethnicity will continue to be theorized, retheorized, and reversed. Descriptive modes, in the case of literature, can relegate a

25. Albert Wendt, "Towards a New Oceania," *A Pacific Islands Collection: Seaweeds and Constructions* 7 (Honolulu: Elepaio Press, 1984), 71–85. Reprinted from *Mana: A South Pacific Journal of Language and Literature* 1 (Jan. 1976).

26. Linnekin and Poyer's introduction to *Cultural Identity and Ethnicity in the Pacific* (Honolulu: University of Hawaii Press, 1990), 1–16, reviews historical and contemporary models for conceptualizing cultural identity, from Western ethnotheories to what anthropologists *believe to be* (my emphasis) strikingly different Oceanic schemes. Linnekin's "The Politics of Culture in the Pacific" (149–73), Michele D. Dominy's "Maori Sovereignty: A Feminist Invention of Tradition" (237–57), and Alan Howard's "Cultural Paradigms, History, and the Search for Identity in Oceania" (259–79) offer a useful variety of viewpoints. Other contributors to the volume write on such islands as Truk, Pohnpei, Vanuatu, and communities in Papua New Guinea.

subject to its most superficial lineaments. As I have illustrated with Patricia Grace, description is capable of denuding a work of crucial levels of signification. Although the *pakeha* lose the land battle in *Potiki*, historically the *pakeha*, the *haole*, and the *papalagi* have most often won, and thus a so-called summary not only misses unique parts of the novel, it also fits right into Western colonialist paradigms of political dominance.

The crucial operative paradox is that by detaching more sophisticated Western modes of study from Western ideologies of connections and globality, there exists an aperture through which indigenous writing becomes visible. Western critical systems may be unable to focus sharply upon it. The subject may elude Western schemes of composition and perspective. The writers themselves may conceal their subject from an outsider's extended gaze. Yet, the opportunity to sense its power, to recognize our utter exclusion from ever knowing the subject, and the provisional nature of our interpretations, is a viable beginning.

The Last Frontier:
Memories of the Postcolonial Future in
Keri Hulme's *the bone people*

Chris Bongie

Joseph Conrad's *Heart of Darkness* (1899) conjoins the self-satisfied racist sensibilities that characterized much Victorian literature and a nascent disgust with the rapidly industrializing and culturally homogenizing mass society that Conrad saw looming on the horizon of the twentieth century. It is this disgust that would come to characterize the dominant strain of twentieth-century literary modernism in ensuing decades and generate a quest for cultural alterity that often bore the name of "primitivism." Conrad's novella is situated on a historical borderline, simultaneously recoiling from and, with an as yet unformulated longing, looking forward to an untouched "wilderness" that it can neither fully repress (as demanded by the Victorian cult of "efficient" Progress) nor desire (in the manner of the full-bodied desire for otherness infusing D. H. Lawrence's mornings in Mexico and the existentialist high noon of Paul Bowles's sheltering sky). *Heart of Darkness*, in the Guyanese novelist and critic Wilson Harris's words, is thus a "frontier novel," marking one of the first points of entry into modernist territory.[1] On

1. Wilson Harris, "The Frontier on Which *Heart of Darkness* Stands," in *Explorations: A Selection of Talks and Articles, 1966–1981* (Mundelstrup: Dangaroo Press, 1981), 134–41.

the other side, on one of modernism's last frontiers, we find a Cuban novel that purposefully echoes both the thematic concerns and narrative trajectories of Conrad's novella: Alejo Carpentier's The Lost Steps (Los pasos perdidos, 1953).[2]

This frontier, which marks the end of primitivism as a viable project, is not, however, immediately visible in Carpentier's novel. In his apparently successful quest for an "authentic primitivism" in the jungles of South America (74), the anonymous narrator of Carpentier's novel seems to be treading exactly the same modernist ground as an enthusiast like Lawrence. Convinced of "the bankruptcy of Western man" (89), he has set off from the Modern City in search of other worlds, and claims to have found them. In the narrator's enthusiastic account of life in this remote part of the globe, the South American interior serves as an originary counterbalance to the "era of the Wasp-Man" that he is fleeing (9). This modern era is characterized by psychic automatism, rampant theatricality, and Spenglerian decline; it is an era which, as the narrator frequently finds occasion to affirm, makes Sisyphuses of us all. By his own account, this part-time organographer's trip up-river in search of musical instruments used by "prehistoric man, our contemporary," permits him to escape the "net" of modernity (200); gradually attuning himself to the "genesial rhythm" of the jungle, he comes upon, at the very heart of this wilderness, "a city born in the dawn of History" and "withdrawn from the horrors of the Epoch" (197, 189). However, his resolve to become a citizen of this quasi-Adamic community proves short-lived: lacking the paper upon which to compose the ambitious threnody inspired by his encounter with the primitive, the narrator allows himself to be rescued by a helicopter team sent out to find him. Although he vows to return as soon as possible, various circumstances prevent him from doing so; by the end of the novel, although continuing to affirm that "the Stone Age is still within our reach" (278), the narrator realizes that he has lost his chance to inhabit the primitive world of his anti-Western desire. For him it can henceforth be no more than a wrenchingly exotic memory.

This novel appears to be a casebook example of modernism's valorization of worlds at antipodes to the West. There can be no doubt of Carpentier's own investment in the primitive: his autobiographical accounts of a trip into the interior of Venezuela, out of which The Lost Steps developed,

2. Alejo Carpentier, The Lost Steps, trans. Harriet de Onís (New York: Farrar, Straus, and Giroux, 1989); references to this novel will be made parenthetically in the text.

feature many of the sentiments voiced in the novel.[3] His earlier published works consistently invoke visions of radical alterity, from his investigations into Afro-Cuban culture in the 1930s through to his influential concept (first voiced in the 1948 preface to his *The Kingdom of This World*) of "marvelous reality" (*lo reel maravilloso*), "that which we encounter in a raw state, latent, omnipresent, in everything Latin American,"[4] and that he argued to be irretrievably absent from a modernized, secularized Europe in which all sense of wonder had been lost. *The Lost Steps* pursues Carpentier's primitivist dreams, then, but also distances itself—though *without comment*—from these dreams; alongside its constant affirmations of Otherness, the novel also lays the groundwork for a self-consuming irony that is never explicitly activated.

The more one reads and re-reads *The Lost Steps*, the less possible it becomes to say whether the narrator's search for the primitive is to be taken seriously, or whether he is being set up as a victim of his own inflated rhetoric and expectations. He is clearly unaware of the extent to which his language and his desires are contaminated by the very world he is attempting to abandon: episodes from Western literature and history, especially the colonial myth of the Conquistadors' search for El Dorado, provide him with his framework for understanding the jungle. The sheer anteriority of this supposedly pre-modern space is everywhere disrupted by the traces of a world that comes after it: the "city withdrawn from the horrors of the Epoch" has, for instance, been founded by a renegade gold miner known as "the Adelantado"—significantly enough, a title applied to governors of frontier provinces in post-Conquest Spanish America. The space of the Other is not the "virgin world" its narrator, echoing Sir Walter Raleigh's portrait of the Guiana as a "country that hath yet its maidenhead," claims it to be (208), but is always-already penetrated. As Roberto González Echevarría puts it in his seminal study of Carpentier, it is a world "littered with texts."[5] This inscribing of the precolonial within colonial terms is only one among many

---

3. In newspaper articles published in the late 1940s, for instance, he identifies the interior of the continent with a "virgin America" and the "world of Genesis," going so far as to anticipate and refute potential critics for whom "speaking about the virginity of America is merely a cliché of some new Americanist rhetoric." See *Letra y solfa* (Caracas: Sintesis Dosmil, 1975), 320, 321, 330.

4. Carpentier, *Tientos, diferencias y otros ensayos* (Barcelona: Plaza & Janés Ed., 1987), 115.

5. Roberto González Echevarría, *Alejo Carpentier: The Pilgrim at Home* (Austin: University of Texas Press, 1990), 174.

possible ironies that the novel offers up to its reader: the narrator, for instance, often conflates the scene of the primitive with the theatrical world of modernity that he is attempting to escape, as when he likens the jungle at several points to a "real and visible stage" (150).

To complicate matters even further, near the end of the novel the narrator himself angrily denounces European modernism-primitivism, viewing it as nothing more than an instantiation of the very Cartesian rationalism that it ostensibly seeks to displace:

> For more than twenty years a weary culture had been seeking rejuvenation and new powers in the cult of the irrational. . . . By labeling such things "barbarous" the labelers were putting themselves in the thinking, the Cartesian, position, the very opposite of the aim they were pursuing.[6]

Is he merely denouncing a flawed version of primitivism here, or is he attacking *all* versions of primitivism, including, unwittingly or not, his own? Is his every gesture no more than an ironic repetition of the very thing he despises and would detach himself from? The issue is, I believe, strictly undecidable—and it is for precisely this reason that Carpentier's novel does not inhabit the central ground of modernism, but one of its frontiers. If his subsequent novels, as González Echevarría points out, explicitly abandon the modernist commitment to the primitive, replacing "the myth of a past utopia . . . by the correlative myth of the future,"[7] *The Lost Steps* inhabits an intermediary space, a way station or crossroads between these two myths, in which it has become impossible to discern exactly what the real status of the primitive is.

But this last frontier of modernism-primitivism does not merely mark the boundary between a past-oriented aesthetics and a revolutionary one that, albeit in a baroque spiral, points forward to the eventual emancipation of history, as in Carpentier's later *Explosion in a Cathedral* (El siglo de las luces, 1962). In crossing over this frontier, we also enter into the territory of postmodernism, in which the myths of both past and future are ironically hollowed out; the postmodern vision puts into question the postulation of spatial and temporal otherness that was at the heart of both the primitivist project (and its earlier nineteenth-century exoticizing avatars) and such teleologically minded projects as Marxism. Lacking the grounds

6. Carpentier, *The Lost Steps*, 254.
7. González Echevarría, *Alejo Carpentier*, 212.

for a belief in radical difference, the postmodern sensibility is unable to ac-
credit either the integral reality of a premodern past, which it knows can
be reached only through the mediation of texts, or the possibility of a truly
revolutionary future. *The Lost Steps* can thus be read as the site of a tense
interchange between a modernism in which the object of primitivist desire
may still be taken as real, and a postmodern excavation of that cultural
alternative, in which its existence can at best only be conjured in the mode
of a s(imul)acralizing nostalgia.

Forty years after the publication of Carpentier's novel, when it has
become even harder to credit the existence of premodern and colonial
ways of life, the status of the primitive—and, by extension, of tradition itself
within the regime of a global modernity—nonetheless remains a pressing
issue for those who feel uneasy with what Marianna Torgovnick, in her
recent book on primitivism, has anxiously referred to as a "postmodern
mélange of us and them" in which cultural differences, historical disjunc-
tions, and political and economic imbalances are erased.[8] She argues that
a word like "primitive," notwithstanding its obvious contentiousness, serves
to mark out an important difference between cultures—as do other, apparently less objectionable, labels like "Third World," or "First Nation Peoples."
A vocabulary of difference would appear to be essential in the formation
of any anti-imperialist identity politics intent on marking itself off from the
West and its hegemony. This act of differentiation is precisely the project
of postcolonial literature—a literature, as Simon During puts it, grounded in
the need of "nations or groups which have been victims of imperialism, to
achieve an identity uncontaminated by universalist or Eurocentric concepts
and images."[9] The postcolonial sensibility is, by this definition, essentially
autarkic: it engages individual writers and entire societies in a struggle to
establish a self-sufficient identity at some point in the future by telling different stories about themselves and their past than the ones foisted upon
them by colonial authorities. It holds forth the prospect of a *post* once and
for all detached from *colonialism*, in which one might speak in one's own
voice and on one's own ground. A primary consequence of this "decontami-
nation" would be to create the conditions for establishing new connections
with the traditions that colonialism has both disrupted and worked to efface:

8. Marianna Torgovnick, *Gone Primitive: Savage Intellects, Modern Lives* (Chicago: University of Chicago Press, 1990), 41.
9. Simon During, "Postmodernism or Post-Colonialism Today," *Textual Practice* 1:1
(1987): 33.

for instance, in the particular case of New Zealand, which will be occupying us for the greater part of this essay, a decolonized future would allow for the restoration of "Maori sovereignty"—a sovereignty that Donna Awatere has argued can only be achieved by ridding her islands of such colonial "illusions" as capitalism and its concomitant concepts of individualism and property, and by replacing "artificial religion with natural spirituality" and the West's "mechanical materialism with spiritual materialism rooted not in man-made artifice, but in land-based dialectic."[10]

Can those modern "illusions" which are the legacy of colonialism, and the "postmodern mélange of us and them" for which it laid the ground, be so easily done away with, though? Two major strains of postcolonial literature have arisen around that question: a revolutionary literature, especially strong during the period immediately following decolonization, which adamantly maintains, in the manner of Awatere, the reality and the desirability of this once and future "uncontaminated" identity; and a reformist literature, now gaining ascendency, in which such an identity is radically put into question. The existence of real alternatives to the regime of modernity no longer seems so obvious in the wake of the now shattered aspirations of Mao, Castro, Nkrumah, and other such architects of decolonization, and the consequent problematization of their progress-oriented "myth of the future," grounded as it was in a "strong" vision of political and cultural liberation.[11] The sort of self-identity that postcolonial societies envision as an ideal, and that precolonial societies *hypothetically* embodied, has become questionable. How can one continue to deploy such differentia as the primitive or the aboriginal, or invoke other such foundational differences (e.g., the biological grounding of Senghor's Négritude) that might allow for a vitalizing return, in an emancipated future, to the autarky supposedly characteristic of the precolonial past? Isn't the idea of a continuum more appropriate than that of a rupture, given the realities of globalizing economies and media? Under these circumstances, doesn't it make more sense—indeed, it has increasingly come to sound like theoretical common sense—for the postcolonial critic to speak in terms of a contaminated and contaminating

10. Quoted in Michele D. Dominy, "Maori Sovereignty: A Feminist Invention of Tradition," in *Cultural Identity and Ethnicity in the Pacific*, ed. Jocelyn Linnekin and Lin Poyer (Honolulu: University of Hawaii Press, 1990), 253.

11. On the distinction between "strong" and "weak" thinking, see Gianni Vattimo, *The End of Modernity: Nihilism and Hermeneutics in Post-Modern Culture*, trans. Jon R. Snyder (Baltimore: Johns Hopkins University Press, 1988).

hybridity compatible with the postmodern sensibility and that is perhaps the very "essence," not only of the West and what Heidegger referred to as its "technologism," but (reversing the hegemonic gesture by which the West gets all the blame, or credit, for "modernity") of what we have hitherto conceptualized as stable, "traditional" cultures.[12]

This reformist position is a very attractive one, and I will be making a case for it here—and for the ethics of hybridization, contamination, and, inevitably, compromise, which it entails. I will, however, also be making a "weak" case for the recuperation of the "strong" differential categories that such a position delegitimizes. My argument is thus double, and some might say duplicitous, acknowledging the ironic admixtures of the postmodern condition, yet nonetheless insisting on those differences which postcolonial writers remain intent on asserting, and which were also basic to the aesthetics of European modernism. The autarkic dreams of both postcolonialism and modernism, it will be argued, can and must be pursued, but with the knowledge that they are groundless, founded upon differences that are essentially unreal, origins that are irrevocably absent, and an emancipated future that is strictly unthinkable. In my examination of the New Zealand writer Keri Hulme's Booker Prize–winning novel *the bone people* (1983),[13] I will be applying this argument to one important differential category: that of tradition, be it the literary tradition of (European) modernism or the cultural tradition of *Maoritanga*. In *the bone people*, Hulme carefully deconstructs and simultaneously reconstructs the ground of tradition, treating it as a disempowered but empowering origin that, she argues, can only be accessed fictively and with a full awareness of its unreality and inadequacy. The steps which would take us back to this origin are forever lost, and yet inescapable; it is both this loss and this inescapability that will shape our future in a postmodern age. Although the international success of an author like Hulme—her ability to cross national boundaries, as it were—may well sully her in the eyes of those critics for whom the idea of cultural and political autarky still holds true, I would argue that it is cosmopolitan writers such as she who, in their insistence on not thinking the local and the global antithetically

12. James Snead argues this point with regard to African culture, pre- and postcolonial; see "European Pedigrees/African Contagions: Nationality, Narrative, and Communality in Tutuola, Achebe, and Reed," in *Nation/Narration*, ed. Homi K. Bhabha (London: Routledge, 1990), 231–49.
13. Keri Hulme, *the bone people* (London: Picador, 1986); references to this novel will be made parenthetically in the body of the text.

but rather as part of a single textual and geopolitical space, best anticipate the challenge of living in a world in which such boundaries are becoming at one and the same time ever more nebulous, and ever more calcified.

The question of ancestral identity is central to Keri Hulme's *the bone people*—indeed, not only to the novel, but to the biographical blurbs that have prefaced it. The descriptions of Hulme in the Picador and the later Penguin edition are the scene of a revealing shift in which her European origins get erased: where, in the former, she is someone who has "Kai Tahu, Orkney Island and English ancestry," in the latter she has become simply a "Maori writer." Regardless of the provenance of these blurbs, Hulme herself seems to endorse the latter monolithic identity at times, as when she speaks in a conference talk of "we, as a people, the Maori people,"[14] although she has also insisted that "you can't section up your Maori side and your Pakeha side because they are intimately intertwined."[15] What are readers to make of this erasure of Europe, and this identification with her "best part"—as Kerewin Holmes, the autobiographical protagonist of *the bone people*, characterizes her one-eighth Maoriness (62)? Is this a repetition of Rimbaud's proto-modernist proclamation of himself as a "nègre"? Is it an exclusionary claim, along the lines of the one that has created the concept of "Afro-American" in the United States, that a single drop of Maori blood erases seven drops of Orkney and English? Is it, by contrast, a radically inclusionary gesture, giving new meaning to an old word, reinventing the identity of *all* residents of New Zealand as Maoris, regardless of their biological origins? Or is it just some callous publisher's idea of how to sell an "exotic" novel? Perhaps the word must be made to encompass each of these possibilities, and more. In any case, the problematic issue of the author's, and the novel's, Maoriness has raised lengthy polemics about who is, and who can write as, the Other.[16] That the novel doesn't fit *comfortably* into traditional categories is, at the very least, clear. As one critic has pointed out, the attempt to claim *the bone people* as a "Maori novel" is seriously compromised "by the admixture of cultural beliefs and values expressed

14. Hulme, "Myth, Omen, Ghost and Dream," in *Poetry of the Pacific Region*, ed. Paul Sharrad (Adelaide: CRNLE, 1984), 33.
15. Elizabeth Alley and Mark Williams, eds., *In the Same Room: Conversations with New Zealand Writers* (Auckland: Auckland University Press, 1992), 149; see also 143–44.
16. See Margery Fee, "Why C. K. Stead Didn't Like Keri Hulme's *the bone people*: Who Can Write As Other?" *Australian and New Zealand Studies in Canada* 1 (1989): 11–32.

and practised" therein.[17] The title itself, to cite but one example, situates us in an ambivalent territory somewhere between the world of Maori myth and the bone-covered landscapes of T. S. Eliot's *The Waste Land*. Any reading that ignores the centrality of this admixture to Hulme's novel is seriously incomplete, and I will be charting the dimensions of this uncomfortable, interstitial space in the remainder of this essay.

Hulme's novel tells the tale of a mixing together, or what might be more forcefully described as a synthesis. Kerewin Holmes, a New Zealand painter and self-styled "octoroon," lives in a six-floored tower that she has constructed for herself from the huge sums of money she won at a lottery; estranged from her family, she lives in what has become an increasingly unhappy and sterile isolation, amid a vast array of esoterica and exotica. This physical and spiritual isolation is disrupted by Simon, an obviously troubled child of indeterminate age who lacks the power of speech, and who proves by turns endearing and infuriating. As Kerewin learns from Simon's surrogate father, Joe Gillayley, the child is the lone survivor of a shipwreck, whom Joe and his late wife Hana had adopted three years before. The three characters, all painfully isolated in their own way, all of mixed or unknown ancestry (Joe is mostly Maori, but had an English father; Simon is clearly "white" but otherwise of undetermined, possibly Irish and French, origins— a point clarified in Hulme's short story "A Drift in Dream"[18]), begin to spend a lot of time with one another. But this promising alliance is eventually shattered. Simon is often uncontrollable, and Joe, who sometimes responds by beating him, finally goes too far and hospitalizes the child, landing himself in jail. Kerewin, feeling a certain amount of complicity in these events, burns down her tower and wanders around South Island in search of death or healing. After he is released from prison, Joe, guided by his instincts, retreats to a remote part of the islands where he comes upon a mysterious old Maori guarding an ancestral site and awaiting its new watcher. In a brief and euphoric epilogue, which few critics have found artistically convincing,[19] the three main characters are united again at the end, on the site of the old tower. The foundations for a new community have apparently been laid.

At the level of allegory, which is an insistent feature of much (if not,

17. Chris Prentice, "Re-Writing Their Stories, Renaming Themselves: Post-Colonialism and Feminism in the Fictions of Keri Hulme and Audrey Thomas," *SPAN* 23 (1986): 71.
18. See Hulme, *Te Kaihau/The Windeater* (New York: George Braziller, 1987), 195–209.
19. See, for instance, Miriam Fuchs's "Reading toward the Indigenous Pacific" in this collection.

pace Fredric Jameson, all) postcolonial literature,[20] Kerewin and Joe can be read as representing, respectively, an imported modernism gone fallow and an indigenous tradition adrift. Hulme's novel is, according to this reading, a story about the obstacles separating the modernist and postcolonial projects that I discussed in the introductory section, their attraction to each other, and the necessity for thinking them together—however paradoxical, or initially unproductive, the results of that union may be. Each project already contains a part of the other within it: Kerewin's bit of Maori and Joe's bit of Pakeha problematize the categorical boundaries that might once have separated them. This creates the condition for a confusion of roles, a postmodern *mélange*, that not only threatens the idea of a single cultural identity—Maori, Pakeha—founded upon sheer difference, but ironizes the projects themselves. The sterility of Kerewin's existence at the beginning of the novel bears witness to the exhaustion of the modernist project; Joe's sense that he is not a "proper Maori" (61) attests to the necessity of an "improper" identity politics incompatible with an autarkic-minded nativism—one, perhaps, "in which mutable diacritics such as language and behavior (rather than the fixed diacritics of race) comprise the essence of identity."[21] And yet, despite the differences that separate these two people/traditions, and their obvious inadequacy to an ambivalent present that has displaced them both, Hulme's novelistic enterprise will be one of bridging the gap between them and piously paying tribute to pasts that have not *truly* survived into the present.

The presence of modernism in *the bone people* is pervasive: as Simon During puts it, the novel's "psychologisation of the characters, its symbolism and most importantly, the overarching narrative frame which tells of voyages through and beyond death to regeneration are exactly modernist."[22] The symbolic play of light and dark, of sun and moon, of fire and tides, structures the novel and gives it an overwhelmingly Yeatsian feel, which is matched by its insistent appeal to the geometrical shapes of the circle (the prologue is entitled "The End at the Beginning") and the spiral. The novel's emphatic use of the stream-of-consciousness technique, which promotes the idea of an inner, and somehow more authentic, voice lurking beneath

20. See Stephen Slemon, "Monuments of Empire: Allegory/Counter-Discourse/Post-Colonial Writing," *Kunapipi* 9:3 (1987): 1–16, and his "Post-Colonial Allegory and the Transformation of History," *Journal of Commonwealth Literature* 23:1 (1988): 157–68.
21. Dominy, "Maori Sovereignty," 249.
22. During, "Postmodernism or Postcolonialism?" *Landfall* 39:3 (1985): 373.

the surface of events, is distinctly modernist, as is the exoticizing use of the Maori language, which is sprinkled throughout the novel and translated in a by-no-means exhaustive glossary at the end of the book. Most importantly for our purposes, the novel puts into play the notion of the individual artist as a repository of values that are absent from the degraded, and increasingly fragmented, world of modernity—an originally Romantic notion that, as I have argued elsewhere, forms one of the cornerstones of modernism.[23]

Kerewin, as a prototypical modernist artist, is "self-fulfilling, delighted with the pre-eminence of her art, and the future of her knowing hands" (7). She inhabits a realm apart, at a distance from the vagaries of history. She is "cyclopaedic" (240), possessed of a "broad general knowledge, encompassing bits of history, psychology, ethology, religious theory and practices of many kinds" (90), much of which gets displayed in the novel. She has collected all this cultural debris with the goal of reworking it into an artistic whole. As the novel begins, however, she has come face to face with the bankruptcy of this project; the pinnacle has become an abyss, and the individual as a result needs to be reintegrated into some sort of community. Of course, this scenario is itself central to the modernist imagination, which incessantly tries to rewrite, as Hulme's novel does, Dante's familiar progression from Limbo—"the private introductory malbowge" (36) of the novel's first two parts—through Hell (Part Three) and on to Purgatory (Part Four) and a Paradise that, as Ezra Pound pointed out in one of his last Cantos, and as the brevity of Hulme's epilogue attests, it has become increasingly hard for our modernity to write. If the novel renders patent the inadequacy of Kerewin's initial position and of the modernist project itself, it is equally clear that Kerewin's "cyclopaedic" language and pretensions are also the author's, and that Hulme is taking a great, at times even embarrassing, pleasure in her protagonist's artistic "pre-eminence." The happy ending allows Kerewin to become again who she once was—an artist, albeit one who is now firmly ensconced within a community, who has found a "home" (the novel's last word); it represents Hulme's own fantasy of redeeming the modernist ideology of the heroic artist—not to mention the dictates of a Promethean feminism.

And yet our experience of the failure of this ideology throughout the novel forces us to view the positive assertions at the end in a somewhat different light. The inadequacies, and even the dangers, of this project are

---

23. See Chris Bongie, *Exotic Memories: Literature, Colonialism, and the Fin de Siècle* (Stanford: Stanford University Press, 1991), 110–18.

manifest, especially as regards her relation to Maori tradition. There is, for instance, something suspiciously *appropriative* about her (Holmes's/ Hulme's) undertaking: Kerewin's "hoard" of Maori jade (33), like the collection of Maori myth with which Hulme lards the novel, signals a proprietary, indeed *colonial*, dimension to this project that Hulme criticizes and yet cannot help engaging in. This ambivalent dimension is emphasized most notably toward the end, during Kerewin's recuperation, when she has a dream about a "wrecked rusting building" that will inspire her to rebuild an old Maori hall:

> She touched the threshold, and the building sprang straight and rebuilt, and other buildings flowed out of it in a bewildering colonisation. They fit onto the land as sweet and natural as though they'd grown there. (428)

Here is the dream of the modernist-primitivist artist, and the dream exposed: she finds herself on the threshold of another world, which she revives, with a Gauguin-esque touch that is inseparable from a "bewildering colonisation" (significantly, this is the only time a variant of the word "colony" appears in the novel) and that necessarily passes off what is artificial as natural ("*as though* they'd grown there"). There is thus something clearly dubious, not to mention aesthetically forced, about Kerewin's restorative project, and in emphasizing this point, Hulme keeps the reader at a distance from the very dream to which she herself so clearly subscribes.

Such modernist heroics, which are likely to entice the feminist reader in search of "strong" women protagonists, must, by contrast, make the postcolonial critic rather uneasy inasmuch as Kerewin's relation to the tradition that she discovers and saves from ruin has such an uncomfortably appropriative dimension. On the surface, Joe's relation to Maori tradition seems rather more straightforward than Kerewin's simultaneous assimilation and critique of European modernism. His initial distance from, and consequent need to rediscover, his non-"Western" roots is a familiar motif in postcolonial literature—although this motif may itself cause uneasiness among some readers because of its potential connection to an exclusionary identity politics. At the beginning of the novel, Joe describes himself as not a "proper Maori" (61): he is not "yer 100% pure" (62), and it is not surprising that Kerewin, with her modernist dreams of sheer alterity, initially wants to be spared the "contamination" that he embodies (12). Joe's violent acts toward Simon, which bring to mind Frantz Fanon's theories about the "absolute violence" that is indissociable from the decolonizing gesture, mark a stage that he may have had to pass through, but that has clearly led nowhere. Like Kerewin, he has reached a dead end—one that, if we are to believe the narrative trajectory of the novel, can only be escaped through a purgatorial return to the fullness of Maori tradition.

In the chapter of Part Four devoted to him, "The Kaumatua and the Broken Man," Joe comes face to face with the cultural past from which he has been estranged. After his release from prison, Joe decides, on the basis of some unexplained intuition, to betake himself to a remote littoral of the islands. No sooner has he arrived there, than he recklessly decides to leap off a bluff in order to reach the beach, "thirty shadowed feet to the bottom" (335). This symbolic leap, this return to the "bottom," leaves Joe injured, but he will be healed by a mysterious Maori elder, who sports an archaic tattoo and knows "the old words." The *kaumatua* has been waiting for many years for the appearance of this "stranger" to whom he can pass on the guardianship of a *mauriora*—a pierced stone, hidden in a deep pool and still inhabited, according to the old man, by "the spirit of the islands," the spirit of Aotearoa, which once allied itself with the Maoris and now rests in this godholder. It is "the heart of this country," the *kaumatua* asserts (364), significantly echoing the title of Conrad's *Heart of Darkness*. Having found his successor, the old man dies, passing on the land to Joe, who guards the stone until an earthquake liberates it from its hiding place. He then gathers the rock—out of which emanates, from "the hole in the centre, light like a glow-worm, aboriginal light" (384)—and takes it back with him to the former site of Kerewin's tower, where it sinks itself "into the hard ground," thus providing the epilogue's newly constituted community with a spiritual foundation.

There is something very forced about this episode, which sticks out from the rest of the novel. Indeed, the influential New Zealand critic C. K. Stead, who has remarked that Hulme's "uses of Maori language and mythology strike me as willed, self-conscious, not inevitable, [and] not entirely authentic," finds this section of the novel to be "almost totally spurious." [24] Stead is right, given that the emphatically modernist dimension of Hulme's work, and of the character of Kerewin, is in some basic ways incompatible with (although envious of) the postcolonial direction that Joe's character takes in this chapter. The affirmation of a biological continuity with Maori tradition can only be the work of postcolonialism, not of modernism. What is

24. C. K. Stead, "Keri Hulme's 'The Bone People,' and the Pegasus Award for Maori Literature," *Ariel* 16:4 (1985): 104, 107.

spurious from one perspective becomes absolutely necessary—even predictable—from another. And yet, as with Kerewin's modernism, Hulme is both playing along with this foundationalism, and its language of "bottoms" and "hearts," and emphasizing the problematic status of the very tradition to which the postcolonial part of her novel appeals. This doubleness is most notable in a dream sequence that, matching Kerewin's vision of a naturalized "colonisation," reflects back ambivalently on the affirmative events surrounding it.

While recovering from his injury, Joe dreams that he is "swimming down a foul mud-coloured river" (351). In fact, he is "not really swimming: the water gets so shallow that he can pull himself along, hands walking on the river bottom," which serves as a foundation for him, amidst a foulness that is "contaminating" and "corrupting" his body. Eventually, he submerges himself in this "stinking stream," and finds to his surprise that it is sweet. He then follows it back to its source, as it becomes increasingly "sparkling and ice-clear": the stream, it turns out, flows from his dead (Maori) wife Hana's vagina, "in a steady pure rivulet." She gives him her breast to suck, while his natural son Timote looks on. Simon then appears, and also begins to suck at her breast, but as he proceeds to suck, Hana turns into a moth and the dream becomes a nightmare. As the *kaumatua* helpfully explains when Joe awakes, with a significantly improbable nod to Western literary terminology, the dream is an "allegory" (354): that is, it refers to something other than itself. It refers, I would venture, to the events of the chapter that have led up to it and that will follow it: the simple resolution of Joe's search for his origins, which the happy ending of the chapter underwrites, is here negated.

This allegory invokes the encounter with the traditional past that Joe is in the process of living, but provides it with another ending—one that acknowledges the absence of the very thing that is so urgently being invoked in the rest of the chapter. The search ends with the loss of the source he seeks and its transformation into an object signifying death (as moths do, according to the *kaumatua*). The dream alerts us to the fact that what is at stake is not simply the salvaging of a culture, but also the repetition of its death in the form of Hana and their child; Joe's encounter with an apparently living tradition is in fact a reinvocation of this tradition from the distance created by mourning—a distance that cannot help registering the dreamlike nature of the primordial source for which it longs. Perhaps Joe himself is already aware of this fact, for after having taken the leap that enables his encounter with the world of his ancestors, he looks back up at the bluff and says in Maori, "I shall remember it as long as I live" (347). What he will remember, and what *the bone people* itself insistently remembers, is not the "bottom," a pure origin from which the foulness of the present has disappeared, but the distance that keeps the two worlds of the contaminated present and a desired past apart—a distance across which the postcolonial subject must *invent* traditions that s/he can no longer directly receive.[25]

As we have seen, the uneasy pairing of Kerewin and Joe, of modernist and native tradition, is central to *the bone people*. In its chronicling of their mutual attraction and opposition to each other, the novel can, as Graham Huggan has pointed out, be seen as one of countless postcolonial rewrites of Shakespeare's *The Tempest*, with Kerewin in the role of Prospero and Joe as Caliban. Stressing the obvious sea changes that both roles have undergone (notably, Kerewin's gender and what we discover to be Joe's bisexuality), Huggan is nonetheless uncomfortable with both characters. Equally suspicious of the modernist and nativist projects, he views Simon as the true hero of the novel, an Ariel figure who "acts as a catalyst for and transmitter of the tensions involved . . . in Prospero and Caliban's increasingly uncertain allegiance with their ancestral past."[26] His stance is exemplary of a recent reformist approach to issues of cultural alterity that is in many ways compatible with the insights of postmodernism: the new postcolonial critics reject the radical oppositions, such as Prospero/ Caliban, that structured revolutionary postcolonialisms and find their ideal protagonists in translation figures who will supposedly lead us out of the ideological impasses that weigh down the likes of Kerewin and Joe. For theoretical support, Huggan cites the Barbadian poet and historian Kamau

25. For an extended analysis of the role that the "invention of tradition" plays in contemporary Pacific Island societies, see the essays collected in Linnekin and Poyer, *Cultural Identity*, especially Linnekin, "The Politics of Culture in the Pacific," 149–73 (n. 10). For a discussion of the stalled dialogue between cultural constructionists and native nationalists, see Jeffrey Tobin's "Cultural Construction and Native Nationalism" in this collection. While there can be little doubt, as Tobin argues, that "the vogue for cultural construction arguments appears a hegemony-preserving reaction to decolonization movements" such as those in Hawaii, there can be even less doubt that taking these arguments seriously into account rather than naively writing them off à la Haunani-Kay Trask makes for a more supple (to say nothing of less narcissistic) politics of identity in our transnational and postmodern age.

26. Graham Huggan, "Opting Out of the (Critical) Common Market: Creolization and the Post-Colonial Text," *Kunapipi* 11:1 (1989): 30. For a relevant extension of his argument, see "Philomela's Retold Story: Silence, Music, and the Post-Colonial Text," *Journal of Commonwealth Literature*, 25:1 (1990): 12–23.

Brathwaite's idea of "creolization," which he glosses as "an intercultura-tive process within which a series of intermediary postures are struck up that elude or actively work against the binary structures (white/black, mas-ter/slave) which inform colonial discourse but which have also survived in modified or transposed forms in the aftermath of the colonial era." [27]

Huggan's reading of Simon in light of Brathwaite's idea of creoliza-tion (an idea to which I will return in the conclusion of this paper) is very convincing up to a certain point. Situated between the two adult protago-nists, Simon, this "magpie child" (322) who first appears in the gap between two tiers of bookshelves (16), and who Kerewin initially views as one of the "contaminating" (17), clearly disturbs their lives and their agendas: he shows up the gaps in each of their worlds, signalling by his very presence the need for these worlds to meet on some middle ground that necessarily transforms and ironizes them. Huggan's reading becomes less persuasive, however, when he argues that this irony is evidence that Hulme is simply distancing herself from the projects of Kerewin and Joe. Unable to credit Hulme's untimely attachment to these projects, Huggan attempts to isolate Simon as the novel's ideological hero, suggesting that through his silence and the "poetics of disturbance" he embodies, Hulme "hints at the potential emergence of an emancipated post-colonial voice containing within it the contradictions of and hybrid elements in post-colonial cultures which per-ceive their creolized status in terms other than those of self-deprecatory as-similation or self-glorifying recuperation"—in terms, that is, other than those of modernist aesthetics and ethnic identity politics.[28] For Huggan, Simon does not really occupy a middle ground, but an avant-garde: he functions as a "dialectical" figure who might break the ground for a future free from the binarisms that confine the "unemancipated" voices of past and present. Sneaking his own "strong" binary structure, emancipated/unemancipated, back into the critical scheme of things, Huggan would privilege only this one figure—and one poetics and politics—in *the bone people*, thus misreading the novel *as a whole*.

To be sure, Simon's silence is a vital part of the novel, and one to which a new breed of postcolonial critics must be particularly respon-sive. However, if Hulme insistently notes his hisses, giggles, screams, and songs, all of which point in the direction of a distinctly new voice, she is equally careful to portray him as *already* possessed of a "voice": not only

27. Huggan, "Opting Out," 31.
28. Huggan, "Opting Out," 35.

are we presented with frequent examples of his writing, but of his stream of consciousness as well, which is, as one might expect, essentially no different from that of the other protagonists. Simon has, in other words, already entered the domain of a language from which his silence appears to exempt him, and his "emancipatory" potential is, as a result, substantially voided. Well aware that "any voice we can hear is by that very fact purged of its uniqueness and alterity,"[29] Hulme at one and the same time preserves Simon's silence, and with it a powerful "myth of the future," and demonstrates the questionableness of this myth by emphasizing the extent to which the unemancipated language of his elders speaks through him. The "emancipation" that Simon's silence anticipates is a lure at which critics cannot help biting, but it is only a part of the story, and a necessarily absent part at that. Because of this absence, Simon is first and foremost a "tragic presence,"[30] the sign of a cross-culturalism that is less a progression toward some Other future than a shuttling back and forth, in the Same old language, between ideological extremes that have outlived themselves but will not disappear. He bears the cross, and bares the crossing, of the now groundless ideologies of modernism and nativism, without offering in and of himself a positive alternative to them.

Hulme has clearly *not* abandoned these extremes that Huggan, in his admirable argument on behalf of a creolized future, feels duty-bound to reject because of their evident lack of foundation in a postmodern age. Huggan's emphasis on one particularly seductive aspect of the novel avoids a full grappling with the whole. Because he finds "the implied essentialism of projects of cultural recuperation" distasteful,[31] and inadequate to the realities of a hybridized present, he cannot admit that such essentialism is germane to the novel's Maori half. Furthermore, the novel does not merely ironize, as he wishfully argues, "the assimilative procedures of High Modernist art"; its other half indulges rather spectacularly in them. The acknowledged presence of gaps in these unilateral, synthesizing projects does not prevent Hulme from continuing to engage in them, with both an inescapable irony and an obvious piety, at the same time as she explores the dimensions of the gap that serves both to hollow them out and bind them together. As we are told at the very beginning of the novel, it is only when Kerewin,

29. Derek Attridge, "Oppressive Silence: J. M. Coetzee's *Foe* and the Politics of the Canon," in *Decolonizing Tradition: New Views of Twentieth-Century "British" Literary Canons*, ed. Karen R. Lawrence (Urbana: University of Illinois Press, 1992), 226.
30. Judith Dale, "*the bone people*: (Not) Having It Both Ways," *Landfall* 39:4 (1985): 421.
31. Huggan, "Opting Out," 35; 37 for following quotation.

Joe, and Simon are considered "together, all together," that they can be "the instruments of change" (4). In *the bone people*, the modernist longing for redemption through an art that might promote the creation of visionary communities, or the "nativist" desire for pure origins and an autarkic identity, stand alongside the spirit of disturbance that Simon embodies, and if the latter undermines the former, the former also undermines the latter. This is one lesson that a great number of contemporary critics, ever intent on asserting the novelty and "subversive" potential of their "strategies of resistance," have a hard time digesting,[32] but it is surely a lesson that is present in Hulme's novel, which argues that in a postmodern world irony is all-encompassing, but also that in a postcolonial world it needs to be turned back on itself, as we ourselves turn back to affirm ideological positions we know to be no longer viable.

Hulme's emphasis on the necessity of thinking several apparently contradictory and patently inadequate ideological positions together, rather than categorically opting for one position, or naively appealing to an "emancipated" future in which these positions no longer hold sway, must strike single-minded critics as an unsatisfactory, perhaps even scandalous, compromise (especially when it is a matter of showing piety toward a "Western" literary tradition such as modernism). One critic, for instance, who wants to valorize the novel's nationalist line, its emphasis on a coherently unified Maori identity, can only view the modernist dimension of *the bone people* as a politically regressive error: she laments the existence of an "ideological contradiction informing, and ultimately compromising, the text's overt politics" and goes on to add, with a Fanonesque insistence on rupture, that "in order to emerge as a subversive political tool, the novel must eventually break with its acquiescent fostering of high and first-world culture."[33] To thus isolate any one of the novel's constituent parts, and to reject all form of compromise in the name of some nationalist or even creolizing agenda, is to miss Hulme's point, and the political realities of a globally hybrid age. If there is an urgent need for thinking the Maoriness of New Zealand/Aotearoa—its *Maoritanga*—there will always also be, as C. K. Stead has recently

32. To cite but one particularly relevant instance of this refusal to think ambivalently about the problem of "resisting" the past, Linda Hutcheon improbably claims that "postmodern historicism is wilfully unencumbered by nostalgia in its critical, dialogical reviewing of the forms, contexts, and values of the past." See *A Poetics of Postmodernism: History, Theory, Fiction* (New York: Routledge, 1988), 89.
33. Anne Maxwell, "Reading *the bone people*: Toward a Literary Postcolonial Nationalist Discourse," *Antithesis* 1:1 (1987): 82, 72.

argued, a need to reaffirm the island's British and European inheritance.[34] If the two positions are in some ways deeply incommensurable and antagonistic, they must nonetheless both be thought, and be thought together. Hulme's emphasis on totality, in what she knows to be a postmodern age wherein the very idea of such totality has become discredited, is itself one final sign of the tragically compromised position that she chooses to occupy as a writer in her quest to assimilate a literary tradition that she can no longer fully credit and to simulate an ethnicity to which she can no longer substantially lay claim. It is this curious allegiance to modernist and precolonial traditions, I have been suggesting, that makes *the bone people* what it is: a postcolonial, and postmodern, classic.

As Simon During has pointed out, "post-colonial identity politics tend towards paradox and irresolution because, with the coming of Europeans, the narratives, signifiers and practices available to Maoris (for instance) to articulate their needs and wants are at once inscribed within Eurocentric modernity—and vice-versa."[35] "Maori identity and distinctiveness," in the words of one anthropologist, "have always been created against a background of European technological superiority and Pakeha political and social institutions."[36] In this paradoxical and irresolute situation, which a reformist postcolonialism rightly takes as its point of departure, the possibility of a definitive resolution to the question of cultural identity lies only in the past and its "strong" ideological distinctions. This possibility is now no more than a dream, but one that still, and again rightly, haunts us: ineradicable and unrealizable, it is an absence that compr(om)ises us. While we must rigorously counter the claims of all those who, in "their distrust of their processual selves, [act] as if they think being Hawaiian or being Tahitian is some positive, unchanging essence that is now lost but is somehow recoverable,"[37] we ought not, and indeed we cannot, abandon our memories

34. Stead, "Pakeha Provincialism, Maori Small-Mindedness," *Times Literary Supplement*, 28 December 1990–3 January 1991, 1398. Taking this argument seriously does not, to be sure, mean supporting Stead's at times contentious presentation of it—a presentation that has led Hulme, along with some of the other best-known writers of the Pacific Rim and Basin (Albert Wendt, Patricia Grace, and Witi Ihimaera) to opt out of his recent edition of *The Faber Book of Contemporary South Pacific Stories*.
35. During, "Waiting for the Post: Some Relations between Modernity, Colonization, and Writing," *Ariel* 20:4 (1989): 41.
36. Karen P. Sinclair, "*Tangi*: Funeral Rituals and the Construction of Maori Identity," in Linnekin and Poyer, 220.
37. Greg Dening, "A Poetic for Histories: Transformations That Present the Past," in *Clio*

of an incessantly deferred future that this absence offers us, as During goes on to argue when he speaks affirmatively of "the impossible preservation of lost auras."[38] It is only in this impossible spirit of "preservation," whereby the present goes back over the falsely auratic and irrecuperable ground of a cultural tradition or a literary heritage that has been essentially dissolved or hollowed out, that the question of identity in postcolonial societies—in this "third" world that has opened up between the old worlds of colonizer and colonized without, however, as one might once have hoped, doing away with or redeeming them—can now (not) resolve itself.

In his study of late-eighteenth- and early-nineteenth-century Jamaica, the poet and historian Kamau Brathwaite defines creolization as "a way of seeing Jamaican society, not in terms of white and black, master and slave, in separate nuclear units, but as contributory parts of a whole." Notwithstanding "the dehumanizing institution of slavery" and the tremendous injustices that were a commonplace of colonial rule in Jamaica, Brathwaite finds a great, if relatively unexplored, potential in the confluence of the two worlds of Europe and Africa, master and slave, white and black: both groups had "to adapt themselves to a new environment and to each other. The friction created by this confrontation was cruel, but it was also creative." At that time, Brathwaite goes on to argue, Jamaican society "did not recognize these elements of its own creativity," and this blindness to its creolized potential resulted in "the failure of Jamaican society" as a whole: the colonial power structure would come to prefer a "bastard metropolitanism—handed down to the society in general after Emancipation— . . . to a complete exposure to creolization and liberation of their slaves." Brathwaite's claims in this work run counter to the manichean politics of colonialism and decolonization, both of which are grounded in essential distinctions between colonizer and colonized. Rather than stressing the pure apartness of cultures, Brathwaite identifies "interculturation" as the central factor in the eventual emergence of a successful Caribbean, and world, order; the creation and the creativity of Caribbean—and by extension postcolonial—literature and culture, will derive from the existence of this intermediate, confluent space.[39] The "unceasing process of transformation" that the

---

in Oceania: Toward a Historical Anthropology, ed. Aletta Biersack (Washington: Smithsonian Institute Press, 1991), 369.

38. During, "Waiting for the Post," 51.

39. Kamau Brathwaite, The Development of Creole Society in Jamaica, 1770–1820 (Oxford: Oxford University Press, 1971), 307.

Martiniquan critic Edouard Glissant has identified with creolization occurs on this middle ground, whereon two or more extremities are conjoined in one textual and geographic space.[40]

However, in Brathwaite's works this apparently de-essentializing emphasis on creolization, which Huggan valorizes in his discussion of *the bone people*, emerges alongside, and perhaps even hinges upon, an affirmation of cultural essence that, Brathwaite argues, survives this process of "interculturation." The creolized space which we, as (post)moderns/ (post)colonials, inhabit is doubled by another, more primordial one, because "no matter how intimate the symbiosis, there remains the residual nam which, at moments of crisis, has the ability to reactivate itself."[41] This residue, "nam," is what Brathwaite describes as "an indestructible culture-core, imparting to each group an identity which in normal times one is proud enough of, but which, at times of crisis, may be fiercely defended by its possessors." The parts which constitute the creolized whole are thus for Brathwaite themselves potentially autonomous wholes; and yet, despite their "indestructibility," they too are fragmentary inasmuch as "nam" is "the reduction of one's *name* to its essentials." In the Caribbean context, this reduction, the loss of an e which once made indigenous cultures truly whole, was the work of colonialism:

> The name that you once had has lost its "e," that fragile part of itself, eaten by Prospero, eaten by the conquistadores, but preserving its essentialness, its alpha, its "a" protected by those two intransigent consonants, "n" and "m." It can return to name. But we are saying

40. See Edouard Glissant, *Caribbean Discourse: Selected Essays*, trans. J. Michael Dash (Charlottesville: University Press of Virginia, 1989). It is, I should add, in the name of this cultural syncretism that Wilson Harris attempts to salvage *Heart of Darkness* from Chinua Achebe's harsh attack on Conrad: if for Harris *Heart of Darkness* is a "frontier novel," as opposed to the "offensive and deplorable book" that Achebe makes it out to be, this is because it stands upon "a threshold of capacity to which Conrad pointed though he never attained that capacity himself"—namely, the text's capacity to consume its own (colonial) biases. This "consumption of bias" enables the premonitory New World vision of "a complex wholeness inhabited by other confessing parts that may have once masqueraded themselves as monolithic absolutes or monolithic codes of behaviour in the Old Worlds from which they emigrated by choice or by force" but that, under conditions of global cross-cultural contact, must abandon the "masquerade" of cultural integrity and acknowledge the "partiality," the incompleteness, of each of the cultures that goes toward making up the creolized whole ("The Frontier on Which *Heart of Darkness* Stands," 135). 41. Brathwaite, "World Order Models—A Caribbean Perspective," *Caribbean Quarterly* 31:1 (1985): 63; 56 for the following quotation.

that this return is already present, and that one must start in the middle.[42]

There is a certain ambiguity to this statement that encourages one to read it against its emphatically essentializing grain: if the "essentials"—the core of one's identity—are nothing more or less than a transformation of some even more original identity to which one can only "return" by taking the middle, rather than the beginning, as one's starting point, then how essential are they? However, notwithstanding this potential for ambiguity—a potential explored in Hulme's novel—there can be little doubt of Brathwaite's commitment to the reality of this original, and still active, identity.

For Brathwaite, this "indestructible" identity will necessarily play a foundational part in any contemporary politics based on that process of creolization which some critics would like to identify as the anti-essentializing path to an "emancipated" future. Even if such things as modern travel and technology have made a global cross-culturalism and "shared style" inevitable, "the essentiality of each culture must also be recognized and employed in the new transcendence," he argues.[43] Brathwaite stresses the artist's special responsibility to this original identity: the Caribbean artist must, for instance, recognize "the primordial nature of [African and Amerindian] cultures and the potent spiritual and artistic connections between them and the present." In claiming an-other past that a colonial education taught him to despise, the artist establishes "an ancestral relationship with the folk or aboriginal culture [that] involves the artist and participant in a journey into the past and hinterland which is at the same time a movement of possession into present and future."[44] Notwithstanding the fragmentation that the ancestral past has undergone in the face of colonialism and a globalizing modernity, it is, he argues, "preserved for us in a most miraculous way within those fragments."[45]

In his emphasis on this "miraculous" preservation—on the continued reality and potency of a past upon which a politics of ancestral identity could be based and serve as the foundation stone for a politics of creolized (non-)-identity—Brathwaite is specifically arguing against his literary alter ego, the

42. Brathwaite, "History, the Caribbean Writer and X/Self," in Crisis and Creativity in the New Literatures in English, ed. G. V. Davis and H. Maes-Jelinek (Amsterdam: Rodopi, 1990), 34.
43. Brathwaite, "World Order Models," 63.
44. Brathwaite, "Timehri," in Is Massa Day Dead? Black Moods in the Caribbean, ed. Orde Coombs (Garden City, N. J.: Doubleday, 1974), 41–42.
45. Brathwaite, "History, the Caribbean Writer and X/Self," 31.

St. Lucian poet and Nobel Laureate Derek Walcott, for whom the starting premise of Caribbean (and by extension New World) literatures and societies is, by contrast, the irretrievable absence of an original, and originary, culture to which one might return from the always-already creolized middle. In the passage from the Old World to the Americas, the former has, according to Walcott, been essentially forgotten: "what has mattered is the loss of history, the amnesia of the races, what has become necessary is imagination, imagination as necessity, as invention."[46] The great poets are those in whom history has been annihilated, and who, "whether they are aligned by heritage to Crusoe and Prospero or to Friday and Caliban," rise to the "Adamic" occasion of this amnesia, rejecting "ethnic ancestry for faith in elemental man."[47] Ironically enough, however, despite its concern with such radically new, and incessantly renewed, beginnings, despite its grounding in an Adamic ideology that bears clear affinities to the primitivism of Carpentier's *Lost Steps* as well as in that "myth of the future" explored in the Cuban writer's later novels, Walcott's poetry is saturated with the past: that which has been obliterated, according to his argument, nonetheless continues obsessively to surface in his verse as an object of interrogation. Indeed, it is perhaps Walcott's attempts at figuring a past he knows to be well and truly lost and forgotten that constitute the most exciting aspect of his creative work.

It has been my argument that one can abandon the extremism of neither Walcott's Adamic aspirations nor Brathwaite's ancestral preoccupations, at the same time that one must, from the perspective of a creolized middle and a reformist postcolonialism, admit to their unfoundedness, and make of this admission the uneasy grounds for a postcolonial poetics and politics. Such differential projects as Walcott's Adamic creationism and Brathwaite's cultural essentialism cannot hold, like Yeats's center, and inevitably call forth the very thing that undermines them—the obliterated past in Walcott, the creolized (loss of) identity in Brathwaite. Yet an awareness of their unfoundedness need not end simply in a debilitating scepticism. We must find ways to re-envision our once-cherished dreams of cultural and literary alterity in the light of epistemological scruples that are endemic to a global modernity. The postmodern world of which Torgovnick warns us, caught up in a process of what one can view negatively as global homolo-

46. Derek Walcott, "The Caribbean: Culture or Mimicry?" *Journal of Interamerican Studies and World Affairs* 16:1 (1974): 6.
47. Walcott, "The Muse of History," in *Is Massa Day Dead?* 5.

gation or positively as intercultural dialogue, is also a postcolonial world that cannot resign itself to not harboring such empty dreams. The need to "put into place rituals of remembrance that commemorate the past and renew our spirits so we can free the future,"[48] to speak out in our own voice and upon our own ground, cannot be denied, but neither must we fail to keep in mind the unfoundedness of those rituals, and of the traditions we commemorate and the future we invoke.

A work like Keri Hulme's *the bone people* meets this double and duplicitous challenge: endowing her modernist/nativist work with a self-consciousness that was only implicit in Carpentier's *Lost Steps*, Hulme maps out a f(r)ictional textual and political space of loss and desire, situated between the ideological certainties of the past and the ungrounded assumptions of that future to which these give rise. Occupying an impure middle ground, she nonetheless continues to interrogate, in a mode that is simultaneously deconstructive and (re)constructive, the purity of traditional beginnings and of revolutionary endings, directing her work back to an absent past and forward to a future that does not lie *beyond* modernity, but on its unendingly last frontiers.

48. bell hooks, *Yearning: Race, Gender, and Cultural Politics* (Toronto: Between the Lines, 1990), 226.

The 747 Poem

Terese Svoboda

From behind the roof, jets shoot at dawn.
To Samoa, I whisper to my son, Tahiti,
Venus—some more imagined isle of love.
Under these sparkling exits, nothing moves,
cars with dust drops suggest the death
of these suburbs, with feral cats
the only mourners. He crows,

my son, at a double take-off.
My mother used trains. She drove
to the tracks and the clacking quieted
we four under three. As the jets rise,
the gods inside see toy cars and toy palms,
the whole, they think, where the effort
of living is only red mud on a thong.
No tourist wants more. But from my vantage,
small as it is, I see their plume
of exhaust fall as a feathered cape,
and the sun rise into it.

The Little Grass Shack

Terese Svoboda

Give, like blood, money—
let it flow or the Hollywood flat
that's Honolulu will fall
and the burrows behind tell.

You're here to buy the beaches
for the natives. See the fish
frenzying over your peas—
no parallels, please. Yet no one

sees you. No wonder you stare
at the water—it's clear, you can
see yourself in it. That's romance.
What about the asphalt that licks

the porches like lava? Say
it's the weather you love,
not the exotic. But do not invoke
with gin any god (you don't believe it,

do you?). Do not use star fruit
to mean subtle or ginger without
the man. Actual travel schools
refine this pact but you're not

the devil, you're "howl-ee"
as a full moon that rises apart
from the condos must be howled at.
What does the tourist earn?

The right to return,
As wave covers wave covers
shark, the animals come,
or pollen.

Flows

The Possibility of Imagination in These Islands

Tsushima Yuko

Translated by Geraldine Harcourt

Introduction by Masao Miyoshi

Introduction

Throughout ages, people have always been on the move from place to place, from continent to continent. Wherever they went, they met earlier settlers or indigenous people. The encounter was at times peaceful but was most likely accompanied with violence and slaughter. An endless series of such conquests and atrocities make up the stuff of human history.

Since the Renaissance, the Europeans were the dominant voyagers and adventurers. They defined the contours of their new settlements, and, modeling after their own homeland format of nation-state, they imposed mirror images on their seized lands. Toward the end of the nineteenth century, Europeans sailed out in a mad dash to discover all the leftover territories, and by 1900, well over 80 percent of the land surface was placed under the rule of or control by the Westerners. As the colonies were reorganized into the shadowy simulacra of nation-states, the status of the indigenous people, the so-called Natives, or Aborigines, had to be renegotiated. In the newly formed colonies, a large number of people witnessed the acts of exclusion and suppression of the Aboriginals. And the memory is vivid. Longer history is apt to diminish the intensity of memory and the weight of guilt. In the five centuries since Christopher Columbus's "discovery" of America, 90 percent of the Native Americans have been exterminated, and the surviving populace has been herded into impoverished reservations miniscule in comparison to the vast continent that was once theirs. In the two centuries since Captain James Cook's landing in Australia, the Aborigines there, too, were brutalized and separated. In other regions of the Pacific, where colonization was a part of the fairly recent mad-dash phase of imperialism, the freshness of recollection is mitigated by the remoteness of the whole region. Thus, few outsiders talk about the fate of the Native populations of Taiwan or Hawaii, Borneo or Alaska.

Migration and colonization were, of course, not limited to Westerners. Few remember the existence today of the mountain people of Taiwan who were there before the Chinese takeover several centuries ago. Even fewer know about the Japanese Aboriginal tribe of Ainu. Before the migration of the now dominant Yamato tribe, the archipelago belonged to the Ainu, whose traces have not been quite eradicated yet, although the survivors are steadily disappearing through assimilation and extinction. Their poetry is remembered among the survivors, and outside efforts have been made from time to time to resuscitate its appreciation. But respect for their "exotic" legacies is not enough: The Ainu obviously must have their own life and their own space. These are the Ainu's natural prerogatives that no one else has a right to deny. Furthermore, Ainu presence and Ainu history are vitally important in the context of warped racial politics of Japan. The country whose leaders often speak of its unique homogeneity and ethnic purity in fact refuse to acknowledge a long history of suppressing its other within. Neither for nostalgia nor for aestheticism, but as a vital part of the social policy concerning racial minority and discrimination, the Ainu's existence and history must be brought back into the consciousness of the Japanese— and everybody else—and be firmly kept there.

Tsushima Yuko, a noted Japanese writer, has long been engaged in Ainu issues. While she taught Japanese literature from 1991 to 1992 at the University of Paris, she chose for her seminar not Japan's canonic writers, such as Lady Murasaki and Basho, Soseki and Kawabata, but selections from Ainu poetry, which Japanese literary historians regularly classify as foreign. This is perhaps not surprising in light of all her stories and novels, which are powerfully marked by an unfading involvement with the ignored and forgotten. Her French and Japanese translations of *yukar*, Ainu poetry, are forthcoming.

• • • •

On the last day of August each year, there is a fire festival in the neighborhood of Tokyo where I live.

The festival is held by Fuji Jinja, a shrine dedicated to the highest and most beautifully formed peak in Japan, Mount Fuji. On the last night of August, a great bonfire is lit in the shrine grounds, while smaller fires are lit every ten meters along the main street, beneath the rows of towering high rises.

On this one night, the incessant noise of traffic and construction work is stilled in this central city neighborhood while the fires burn. The summer season, as it draws to an end, is cleansed in the quiet of the flames.

Five hundred years ago, for the common people, climbing Mount Fuji was the holiest of acts, equivalent to the Muslim pilgrimage to Mecca. It was difficult for the poor to make the journey to the mountain, but they didn't give up easily. That is why, in many parts of Edo (as Tokyo used to be called), people built miniature Mount Fujis out of mounds of earth, with the idea that their prayers would be granted if they worshipped there, just as if they had gone to the real mountain. One of these replicas is still there today in my neighborhood.

On the last day of June and the first of July every year, a festival marks the opening of the mountain to climbers. Most of the people who live in Tokyo are unaware of this obscure shrine and its festivals, and its traditions have been kept alive only by those who live nearby. This local "opening of the mountain" celebrates the start of the short summer season during which ordinary people can climb Mount Fuji. A festive crowd fills the approaches to the shrine, which are lined with all kinds of stalls, sideshows, and shooting galleries. These stalls are also a gathering place for itinerant entertainers who travel all over Japan during the rest of the year.

Praying to the mountain itself as a god: This faith of the common people is a vestige of the religious beliefs of the original inhabitants of Japan, dating from before the coming of agriculture. The most primal of faiths is kept alive even now, in obscurity, right in the center of Tokyo. This surprising fact allows me to hold onto some hope for the culture of the country known as Japan.

In considering a nation's culture, in the end the problem comes down to how close one stands to the official version of history, as presented by those who hold power. This is true of my country, too.

For example, the opening of the Japanese rice market is currently a controversial issue in Japan's relations with the United States. The Japanese government offers the defense that Japan must take special measures to protect its rice growers, because rice is a symbol of Japan's unique culture, but this claim is only a half truth.

. . . .

About two thousand years ago, people from the Korean peninsula began a series of migrations to the chain of islands that would later be called Japan, bringing with them an advanced culture. They formed many clans, gaining the advantage over the islands' original inhabitants with the aid of, first, agriculture, then Buddhism, then iron implements, and later the written word. One of these clans eventually came to rule over the islands and established the *Tenno* (usually translated as emperor) of Japan. The institution of the *Tennoke*, or imperial house, has inevitably undergone change in the sixteen hundred years since then, but its form has survived, and the constitution we have today guarantees its existence as a symbol of the nation's culture. Thus, the statement that rice is a symbol of Japanese culture must always be placed in a political context that has its basis in the Tenno system.

Agriculture as the point of departure of civilization: This relationship is common to humankind all over the Earth. In the island country where I live, the shift from hunting to farming, from a nomadic to a settled way of life, was promoted under the Tennoke.

The indigenous hunter-gatherers of the Japanese archipelago are known as the *emishi*, a word that means "barbarians." A primal society is said to have been formed by people who came to the archipelago ten thousand years ago, possibly from the Eurasian continent, or from mainland Asia, or from the islands of the South Pacific—no one knows for certain where they came from. Resemblances have been noted linking their origins with those of the indigenous peoples of Australia and Argentina, with Native Americans, with the Lapps, and other peoples, but apparently none of these theories is more than conjecture.

Japan's oldest historical chronicle is a record made for the Tennoke. We can guess from it that conquering the emishi was the Tennoke's most important and most difficult project. Tracing the history of Japan through the later chronicles, we may even go so far as to say that the history of

Japan is the history of the subjugation of the emishi. I can only give a very broad outline here, but the records show that a systematic war of invasion against the emishi was already being waged some fifteen hundred years ago. The many emishi who were taken prisoner were held in ghettos and used as forced labor. The prisoners, and those who remained beyond the Tennoke's control, fought for their independence in many rebellions. The last of these took place only two hundred years ago. These facts demonstrate, conversely, just how strongly rooted the emishi's presence was in the Japanese archipelago—yet their existence has been all but erased from the official histories of Japan.

One record of the wars tells how emishi women danced on the stockade of an emishi stronghold and sent a victorious war cry after the army of the Tenno as it temporarily retreated. They, too, are our ancestors. The Tennoke left us the well-known high culture of the court, and those in power have done their best to make this aristocratic culture the sole representative of Japanese culture. Beyond the walls of the court, however, the emishi lived together with nature, found their gods there, and handed down a rich oral literature celebrating their dialogue with those gods. Yet, the people of the court continued to fear them as inhuman monsters or wild beasts. The warrior class, or samurai, had their origins in this need to overcome the emishi.

When the samurai class took over the actual exercise of power from the Tenno, the mentality of conquest over the barbarians remained unchanged. Many of the emishi, meanwhile, were reduced to making their living as entertainers or woodcutters, but most remained as hunters. And since they, too, wanted to eat rice, they began a furtive barter trade with the farmers, bringing products of the mountains, such as bear skins and bear's gall, which was prized as a medicine. For the farmers, it seems, these contacts were as terrifying as bargaining with the devil. At the same time, as feudal society tightened its control over the peasant farmers, they seem to have longed for the freedom of the outcasts' way of life. To a woman who had to give birth to an illegitimate child, for example, the world of the emishi was the only possible place of refuge. This longing gave rise to many folktales that are still told today.

The authorities continued relentlessly to treat the emishi as less than human. So deeply rooted was this discrimination that its legacy is seen in Japanese society to this day, in an attitude of fear and loathing toward other cultures that remind us of the emishi.

The emishi were driven steadily to the north, and today a small number of survivors live in the northern-most region of Japan, still facing discrimination, under the name Ainu, which in their own language means "human being." The history of the Ainu people is one of systematic oppression by the rich merchants and the central authorities of Japan, as they went after the abundant natural resources of the lands where the Ainu lived— the gold dust in the rivers, the forests, the fish. The resulting cruel exploitation, hard labor, and destruction of the environment had already decimated their population 150 years ago. Now, they are on the verge of becoming a legendary people, their identity almost extinguished by the same policies that have destroyed much of the life that once inhabited the islands of Japan.

The Ainu people have a festival known as the Bear Ceremony. In the past, they lived by killing bears, but they also revered the bear's spirit. Because the bear-god gave its precious body for the sake of human beings, of course they must not kill wantonly, and when they did kill they must do so with deep gratitude. In a ceremonial expression of this gratitude, once a year, they dance and offer prayers for the bear-god around the fire. The bear was not the only creature that was a god to the Ainu; all of the natural world around them was made up of spirits that they venerated.

A superb tradition of oral literature, known as *yukar*, has been handed down among the Ainu people. Through the efforts of a very small group of reciters and scholars, many of these epic songs have been recorded in writing and translated. Some are long mythic or heroic narratives, but the most beautiful are stories in which the gods of the natural world speak, one by one, in the first person. I am especially moved by the fact that the yukar are all narrated in the first person. We see the world through the eyes of a bear, the world as described by an owl, the different worlds described by a deer, a snake, a fox, a wolf, a spider. The sea, the rivers, the valleys, each speak with their own voice. Sometimes these gods and goddesses ridicule human beings; sometimes they sympathize with them. They may grow angry, or they may promise human beings their protection. The songs celebrate the pleasures of each god and goddess, freely and easily. We can imagine that the people who sang and listened to the yukar *became* the bear or the owl, the deer, the sea, or the woods. They reaffirmed the beauty of nature and reminded themselves that, foolish human creatures that they were, they had been given life within the natural world and must never harm its beauty.

This lively power of imagining in the first person, as seen in the yukar, must once have been enjoyed by people everywhere in Japan. Now, all of us who live in these times must revive our memory of that kind of imagination. This is what I want to say most urgently here today.

In human history so far, it has been seen as inevitable that the advance of civilization will affect every region of the Earth. In Japan's case, after two centuries of self-imposed isolation, the country was forced to open to the West by an American naval squadron 130 years ago, and it then went through another rapid transition to modern civilization, modeled on the Christian societies of the West. In the process, the traces of so-called "barbarous" folk beliefs and oral literature that remained among the common people were deliberately erased. The Japanese modernizers wanted to forget that side of our cultural makeup completely, in order to propel the society forward as a modern state under the Tenno system.

I should add one thing further on this point. From their earliest contacts with the emishi, the Tennoke paid attention to the people's faith and tried to absorb it into the Tenno system by assuming divine status themselves, declaring the Tenno the greatest god who ruled over the gods of the emishi. This divine status was fully exploited in World War II. The brutal imposition of a divine Tenno on the indigenous Japanese consciousness of nature threw the concepts of Japanese folk belief into a state of confusion, from which it still has not recovered today.

But the memory of ordinary people should not be underestimated, however powerless they may be politically. Of course, we cannot expect to return to the days of the ancient hunters, and it would be meaningless to do so. Yet, I believe that it is possible to regain the imaginative power of that age. When I look back over Japanese literature, it seems to me that the finest works are sustained by a revival of the imaginative power of the emishi. For now, the Ainu cannot be left to become a vanished people; this cannot be allowed to happen. And if, over the long term, the existence of the emishi should be erased from the history of the Japanese islands for political reasons, the very life of Japanese culture itself would be cut off. Japan would surely lose all sense of direction in this nuclear age, in spite of having itself experienced nuclear attack.

In my own work, I have attempted to revive the imagination of the emishi in some small way. I believe that such a revival of imagination has the greatest potential for the future, not only of Japan, but of the Earth—for the imaginative power of the hunter-gatherers is clearly a potential that all human beings on this planet have in common. And that imaginative power is no less than a love of the Earth.

Imaginings in the Empires of the Sun: Japanese Mass Culture in Asia

Leo Ching

Kuo-rei Chen slouches in his chair, absorbed intently by the images emitting from his thirty-inch Sony *Trinitron* television. Kuo-rei does not understand the broadcast coming through the stereo-sound speakers. Yet, he recognizes the contest between two 300-pound wrestlers wearing their customary loincloth trying to push the other out of the ring—a traditional Japanese *sumo* match. Switching to another channel with a tap of his finger, Kuo-rei catches the well-groomed Peter Jennings reporting the world's latest on ABC's "World News Tonight." And if Kuo-rei so desires, he can stay tuned for more news from Britain's BBC, Germany's ZDF, and France's A-2. Recently, this has become a familiar sight in Taiwan. From Japanese historical drama to CNN news, from *Ultraman* sci-fi to Tokyo's latest business report, Japan and the world are immediately accessible by the push of a button. The geographic proximity between the two countries has made the approximately twenty million people on this island free subscribers to Japan's latest technological ingenuity: BS, or Broadcasting Satellite.

Edward Chuang works for one of the most popular and profitable department stores on Orchard Road: the Isetan. Clad in the latest from designers Koshino Junko

I thank the following people for reading an earlier version of this essay and for providing useful suggestions and criticisms: Masao Miyoshi, Fredric Jameson, Wai-lim Yip, Irene Wei, and Mitsuhiro Yoshimoto.

and Miyake Issei, Edward has recently returned home after a year of studying Japanese in Tokyo. When he saw an ad from Isetan for a salesperson position, Edward jumped at the opportunity, even though it meant selling baby carts on the sixth floor. After his lunch break, Edward often ventures upstairs to the Kinokuniya Bookstore, where he browses through books and magazines from Japan, including his favorite, the monthly style magazine *Ryuko Tsushin*.

The music and laughter coming from her daughter's room have always perplexed Mrs. Kwok. She doesn't care much for the popular music that has driven her fifteen-year-old daughter Jenny to spend the bulk of her monthly allowance on the newest CDs and cassettes. What bewilders her, however, is that these days, young people such as her daughter listen not only to Cantonese, Chinese, or English songs but also to popular songs from Japan! In her room, Jenny and her friends are humming and moving with the beat from her latest acquisition—Sonentai's newest single, "Funky Flushing." They gossip about the most recent rumor on Japanese singer-actress Imai Miki and teen-"idol" Miyazawa Rie from tabloids such as the *Ming-Pao Weekly*. "Let's play *sutekina* music, let's dance *asamade* disco, Let's make funky night . . ."—the strange mixture of Japanese and English in the refrain enables Jenny to sing along as she convulses her body more rigorously.

Red-faced and sweating, Myung-sung Lee croons passionately with the background music of his favorite song. With his eyes fixed on the video screen in front of him, he closely follows the lyrics that change color with the melody, leading him along. The video, like that of MTV, is a series of images that attempt to approximate the narrative of the song. This is one of many *karaoke* or *bideoke* bars on Student Avenue in Seoul. A sing-along entertainment device, *karaoke* is a direct transplant from Japan and, in recent years, has gained tremendous popularity among business people and students here. As his performance ends, Myung-sung is cheered and jeered by his very drunk colleagues. Customary claps can be heard from other patrons as the next songster hurriedly grabs the silver microphone.[1]

Throughout Asia, Japan is in vogue.[2] From fashion to food to leisure, Japanese cultural commodities are ubiquitous, casting wooing glances at the Orient's nouveaux riches. This is especially prominent in the region collectively known as the NIEs (Newly Industrialized Economies) of South Korea, Taiwan, Singapore, and Hong Kong. And a similar process can also be observed, although sporadically, in Southeast Asia, extending from Thailand to the Philippines. These signs of regionalization of culture suggest a

1. I have compiled these episodes through my own observations, personal correspondence, and stories related to me by friends.
2. This is not to say that Japanese mass culture constitutes the only influence on the symbolic values of these nations. Western, especially American, popular culture still enjoys a tremendous popularity in the region. Beginning with the early 1980s, however, there is a significant, and substantial, growth of Japanese cultural images and products in the area.

cultural integration process that transcends national boundaries but that is confined, for the moment, to a specific region of the world-system. How are we to assess this cultural dominant? Is this the "cultural logic" of Japanese economic imperialism (*Pax Nipponica*), or is it a regional manifestation of a general globalization process that weakens the cultural coherence of all nation-states? And is the discourse of cultural imperialism still an effective counter-hegemonic response to this emerging cultural formation? Asia is, contrary to the notorious dictum by Okakura Kakuzo at the turn of the century, *not* one, and indigenous dependency and response to the growing Japanese cultural presence vary not only between, but also within, nations. For the present study, I have limited my analysis to Taiwan, an ex-colony of Japan, in which Japanese cultural influence is perhaps most pervasive.

The emergence of Japanese cultural presence in Taiwan since the mid-1980s can be attributed to Japan's ascendancy as the world's prominent economic power and to Taiwan's own politico-economic changes. The point should be made here, however, that economic prowess does not necessarily entail cultural dominance. Despite its waning economic presence, American mass culture is still the dominant and powerful cultural industry in the world today. Meanwhile, Japanese cultural influence is primarily constricted to Asia, and Japanese mass culture itself is still plugged into every trend of Western, especially American, pop culture. Today, Japan has more American food franchises than any country outside of North America, and Japan also serves as the largest market for Hollywood films outside the United States. Japan can buy Hollywood, but it is unable to produce films with global appeal. As the United States continues to play the role of "policeman" in the region, however, Japan has increasingly become the primary source of capital and technology for its Asian neighbors, as well as the major market for their exports of foodstuffs and raw materials. Last year, for the first time since 1945, Japan's trade with Asia exceeded that with the United States. Japanese investment and technology have dominated the economies of Taiwan and South Korea, and Japanese manufacturers have established dominant markets throughout Asia. The growing Japanese direct investments and exports, especially consumer goods, have made Japanese cultural images and commodities readily accessible in Taiwan. Nevertheless, it is also Taiwan's rapid economic growth culminating in the affluent 1980s that has created a consumer society capable of absorbing the influx of Japanese cultural goods.

Taiwan, together with the other three "tigers" of East Asia—South Korea, Singapore, and Hong Kong—has forged the fastest growing industrialization the world has ever seen. This economic "miracle" is intrinsically related to, and dependent on, Japan and, of course, the United States. After the defeat by the Communists and the subsequent relocation to Taiwan in 1949, the Nationalist government became one of the largest beneficiaries of U.S. aid. It is estimated that Taiwan received $5.6 billion in massive economic and military aid from Washington.[3] American influence on postwar Taiwan was pervasive. As Robert Elegant writes,

> Between 1949 and 1965, American grants, commodities, subsidized loans, and technical advice . . . laid the foundation for Taiwan's present economic structure. . . . American technology, channeled through the Joint Commission, altered everything from prenatal care and primary education to fertilizers, pesticides, and plows—and made Taiwan a better place to live.[4]

This is only half the story, however. What Elegant, in his ethnocentric posturing, neglects is the geopolitical self-interest of the United States. As the conflict between the United States and the USSR intensified in the latter half of the 1940s, the United States initiated the Marshall Plan and, later, the North Atlantic Treaty Organization to counter the perceived threat of Soviet expansion. The outbreak of the Korean War further extended American containment policy to Asia. Massive aid to Taiwan and South Korea was accompanied by a revision in policy toward Japan.[5] Japanese economy was revamped and boosted during the Korean and the Vietnam Wars as a result of American military expenditure.

In Taiwan during the 1950s, agricultural reform and productivity were promoted to provide the foundation for industrial growth, and the policy of import substitution, a development strategy that sought to replace imports of nondurable consumer goods by labor-intensive indigenous production, was implemented with sizable American aid. In the 1960s, partly under the pressure of U.S. advisers, Taiwan initiated a period of export industrialization, involving the development of low technology light-industrial and labor-intensive products and the assembly of imported inputs for consumer goods such as textiles and toys to the markets of the developed countries,

---

3. Steve Chan, *East Asian Dynamism* (Boulder, Colo.: Westview Press, 1990), 28.
4. Robert Elegant, *Pacific Destiny* (New York: Crown Publishers, 1990), 31.
5. With the U.S. Occupation Authority's assistance, the conservative Liberal Democratic Party was empowered, the leftist politicians purged, the labor unions tightly regulated, and the *zaibatsu* reinstated.

especially to the United States. Today, as real wages erode Taiwan's comparative advantage in labor-intensive industries, the economy has gradually moved toward technology and capital-intensive industries.

Export-oriented growth strategy, American aid, and the relative open trade regime have launched, and sustained, the economic growth of Taiwan. However, one should not overlook the intermediary role played by Japan in the economic success not only of Taiwan but of the rest of the NIEs. In the "triangle of growth," between the pivotal United States and the peripheral NIEs, Japan acts as an important economic agent. To oversimplify the process, as the United States plays the important role of providing an immense market and basic technology development (hardware), Japan imports the basic know-how and applies it to practical use (software). Subsequently, Japan is able to sell/dispose of previously used "secondhand" technology (machines and equipment) to the peripheral NIEs. The NIEs, in turn, use this "secondhand" technology and equipment to launch their export-oriented industries.[6] Perhaps the continual economic success of the new NIEs and the economic hardship faced by the former NICs (Newly Industrialized Countries) of Latin America and Southern Europe can be explained by the NICs' lack of Japan's intermediary role.

Riding on the "triangle of growth," Taiwan's export-oriented economy has posted an impressive annual average real GDP growth of 8.7 percent since 1952. The per capita income has increased from $215 in 1965 to over $10,000 in 1991. And today, Taiwan boasts the world's largest reserve of foreign currency. Since the 1980s, a consumer society surrounded by "the remarkable conspicuousness of consumption and affluence, established by the multiplication of objects, services, and material goods," has been well established in Taiwan.[7] Concurrently, Japanese cultural goods appear to be exerting a discernible influence on the cultural site of Taiwan.

The most frequent and ingenuous response to an emerging foreign cultural presence by local intellectuals is to see this as a degenerative extension of another nation's economic domination. This is no exception in Taiwan's curiously few and feeble discussions on the matter. I will examine the only two works I was able to locate on the topic. The first is an essay entitled "Speed, Infiltration, and Occupation: The Japanese Invades

6. Twu Jaw-Yann, *Toyo shihonshugi* (Tokyo: Kodansha, 1990), 25–26.
7. Mark Poster, ed., *Jean Baudrillard: Selected Writings* (Stanford: Stanford University Press, 1988), 29.

Taiwanese Economy" by Chuang Shu-yu.[8] Chuang sees the growing presence of Japan in the cultural arena of Taiwan, which she describes with
accuracy, as the direct reflection of Japanese economic dominance. As
the martial terms in the title suggest, the article evokes an abhorrent and
sensitive phase of Sino-Japanese relations: Japan's colonization of Taiwan
after the Sino-Japanese War and its subsequent invasion of China. The
article pointedly draws the analogy between Japan's colonial aggression in
the early twentieth century and its postwar economic expansionism. This
is especially evident in the use of military lexicon and warfare rhetoric in
depicting the Japanese "invasion" of Taiwan. Chuang writes,

> Japanese merchants are quietly *positioning* themselves through-
> out the important cities of Taiwan. With *piercing eyes* and *detailed
> strategy*, they are readying for a *long-standing deployment*. And the
> Taiwanese market has become the *fortress* and *testing ground* for
> the Japanese merchants' eventual *invasion* of other overseas Chi-
> nese communities in the world. (SIO, 14; my emphasis)

To the Japanese imperial eyes, Taiwan is the launching pad to the world's
11.5 billion Chinese market. And this scheme of incorporation, argues
Chuang, follows the same logic as the Japanese army's establishment of
the puppet government in Manchuria in 1932.

The success of the Japanese economic "assailants" today, observes
Chuang, is largely due to their well-coordinated strategies. Long-term planning, foresight in investing (real estate and commercial), information amass-
ing, connection establishing, and Japanese-style customer servicing are all
factors responsible for the infiltration of the Japanese business army. Quoting from an interview with Ezra Vogel, an authority on Japanese economics,
Chuang warns the Taiwanese people of the insatiability of the Japanese
economic animal who "will eat when it can" (SIO, 21). The underlying concern, after all, concludes Chuang, is the dwindling market share of the
domestic industries in the now booming Taiwanese consumer market. The
locals would be impoverished if the foreigners were left unchecked. Overall, Chuang assigns a central role to economic practices and implies that
these are *really* what are at stake and that cultural factors are instrumental
in maintaining Japan's economic dominance.

8. Chuang Shu-yu, "Speed, Infiltration and Occupation" *Common Wealth* 1 (August
1989): 12–21. Subsequent references to this text will be cited parenthetically as SIO.

This line of argument—seeing Japan as conspiring an economic takeover of the world and pitting the indigenous population as helpless victims against such a ploy—is similar to those deployed by the Western critics of Japanese economic hegemony: the Japan bashers.[9] Since the 1960s, Japan's economic prowess and its recent conspicuous consumption of American historical landmarks and entertainment industries, such as the Rockefeller Center, MCA Inc., and Columbia Pictures, have incited public fear and resentment. Whereas Japan's Asian neighbors condemn its economic encroachment as the second-coming of Japanese military imperialism, likewise, but from the victor's vantage point, the Americans warn the Japanese of the repercussion Japan will suffer if history were to repeat itself. As Theodore White writes, "The superlative execution of their trade tactics may provoke an incalculable reaction—as the Japanese might well remember of the course that ran from Pearl Harbor to the deck of the U.S.S. Missouri in Tokyo Bay just 40 years ago." [10]

Obviously, I am not suggesting that the relationship between Japan and the United States is identical to that between Japan and its Asian neighbors. The power imbalance between the two is too great to ignore. The two responses to the growing Japanese economic presence may be similar, but they are embedded in very different historical contexts. Because of Japan's ambivalent status as the only non-Western colonial power that has barely escaped colonization itself, its relation and attitude toward the West and its Asian neighbors have been remarkably different. Like all non-Western imagined communities under the threat of imperialism and colonialism, Japan's encounter with the West was traumatic.[11] Western imperialist expansion throughout the non-Western world (by the 1880s, 80 percent of the earth's surface was under European control), the coming of Commodore Perry and the "black ship" in 1853, and the demise of the Middle Kingdom under Western aggression all aroused a sense of urgency and fear for Japan's

9. Masao Miyoshi provides the most lucid and critical analysis on the topic to date. See his *Off Center: Power and Culture Relations between Japan and the United States*, chap. 3, "Basher and Bashing in the World," 62–94.

10. Theodore White, "The Danger from Japan," *New York Times Magazine*, 28 July 1985. Quoted in Miyoshi, *Off Center*, 63.

11. I would like to underscore here that Western imperial expansion and its consequent colonial rule must be seen in the context of the whole history of capitalism on a world scale. For a general outline of the relation between capitalism and imperialism, see Anthony Brewer's *Marxist Theories of Imperialism: A Critical Survey*, 2d ed. (New York: Routledge, 1990).

own survival, and consequently led to its own imperial expansion into Asia in the involuntary pursuit of "modernity." From this perspective, Japan's aggression toward Asia *is* the direct result of Western infringement. Any criticism against Japanese imperialism and colonialism *necessarily* entails the criticism of Western imperialism and colonialism. This point has often been overlooked, especially today, as Americans accuse Japan of "unfair" trade strategies without reflecting on the United States's own imperialist and economic aggression toward countries in Central and Latin America.

It is this lack of self-reflexivity and self-criticism manifested in the chauvinistic expression of nationalism that not only reduces historical differences but also ignores the economic and political complexity inherent in today's global capitalist system. Today, Japan's economic expansion has brought fear to its Asian neighbors, mainly because of the great suffering Japan has inflicted on other Asian countries during World War II and because of Japan's persisting reluctance to face up to its wartime responsibilities. These concerns are genuine in light of Japan's prevailing prejudice and insensitivity toward its neighbors. Unlike the Germans, the Japanese government has never sincerely or formally acknowledged and apologized for its wartime brutalities and atrocities. Although Japan has not categorically denied its involvement, it has meticulously attempted to gloss over and downplay its colonial past.[12] Although Emperor Akihito has issued an apology and has promised that Japan will not repeat its imperialist endeavor during his recent visit to Southeast Asia, one should not overlook the timing of the apology, which coincides with the Asians' growing disenchantment with, and resentment toward, the overwhelming Japanese investment in that region.[13]

12. What immediately comes to mind is the revision of Japanese history textbooks in the early 1980s, which prompted vehement protests from the Chinese and Korean governments. And recent statements by politicians Ishihara Shintaro and Watanabe Shoichi, who suggested that the "Rape of Nanking" was a Chinese fabrication and that Japanese colonial rule of Asia "did inflict some wrongdoings," but has overall benefited the colonial subjects. Furthermore, although the Japanese government has finally, though reluctantly, admitted its involvement with the dispatching of Korean and Chinese "comfort women" as sex slaves for Japanese soldiers, it has firmly refused to make any reparation or compensation.

13. Furthermore, one should not overlook Japan's blatant racism and discrimination against the growing presence of other Asians *in* Japan. Japan's prejudice against Koreans has been well documented. For an overview of Koreans in Japan, see Lee Changsee and George De Vos, eds., *Koreans in Japan: Ethnic Conflict and Accommodation* (Berkeley: University of California Press, 1981), and Michael Weiner, *The Origin of the Korean Com-*

The contempt for Japan's economic buildup by its Asian neighbors is rooted in Japan's colonial legacy and in Japan's present-day prejudice against other Asians. To that extent, the protest against, and the concern for, Japanese economic aggression in Asia is justifiable. This sentiment, however, is diametrically different from the American response, which inevitably equates its declining hegemony with Japan's unfair, treacherous, and sneaky tactics in the global economy, where the rules were made and dictated by the Americans since World War II. The danger of the Asian reaction, however, as I have suggested earlier, lies in the assumption that exploitation is unidirectional, imposed simply by one nation onto another without taking into account their own ever-growing involvement in the global economy. Historical analogies may be rhetorically powerful, but one must probe into why and how different historical contexts are reduced and produced. Taking sanctuary under the name of victimization and fostering an unexamined nationalism would only obscure the complex process of collaboration and justify the "victimized" nations' victimization of other countries. Relegating her analysis on a crude "Japan dominates Taiwan" formulation, Chuang not only reduces the complexity of today's global capitalism into a simple good and evil but also ignores the various order of power and domination involved.

What Chuang inserts, but fails to mention, in the article is a diagram—categorized into food-producing market, servicing market (department stores, supermarkets, and convenience stores), real estate market, and leisure market—that shows sixteen Japanese service industries that have successfully penetrated the Taiwanese market. Chuang does not explain the fact that of the sixteen Japanese companies, only three are entirely funded by the Japanese, with Japanese money. Most of them are joint ventures between Japanese and Taiwanese companies, with 50 per-

---

munity in Japan, 1910–25 (Oxford: Manchester University Press, 1989). Recent Japanese affluence has resulted in the labor shortage in sectors that the Japanese have pejoratively termed "the Three K's": *kitanai* (dirty), *kitsui* (strenuous), and *kiken* (dangerous). This labor shortage has induced an unprecedented influx of Asians to Japan seeking higher wages in factories, construction sites, and restaurants. These Asian laborers constantly face racist taunting and discrimination, despite their growing importance and necessity to Japan's industries. The media often portray these aliens as inherently dangerous and responsible for the growing crime rate in Japan. See the special report on the growing presence of Asian laborers and refugees in "Totsuzen hikkoshitekita 'Nihon no kokusaika'" (The sudden [or unexpected] moving-in of Japan's internationalization) *Asahi Journal* (20 Dec. 1989): 11–20.

cent or more stock shares held by the Taiwanese collaborators. Obviously, one should not emphasize the financial cooperation between foreign and domestic companies and overlook the unequal transfer of information and technologies. Despite domestic financial investment, the center for control and production often lies in Japan. What needs to be underscored, however, is what Robert Reich has perceptively argued: in the "global web" of present-day multinational capitalism, that the notion of a national economy is tied to the well-being of a population and that products that have national origins are becoming obsolete.[14] Companies and corporations are becoming more intrinsically interdependent globally and less connected to any single nation. The conception that different economies compete nationally with well-defined winners and losers not only oversimplifies the issue at hand but also runs the risk of inciting nationalistic and racist fervor. Late twentieth-century capitalism, in its relentless pursuit of profit, knows no national boundaries and feels no geographic constraints. Therefore, it is not surprising that Taiwan and South Korea, two ex-colonies of Japan that have been most vocal and apprehensive of Japan's economic expansion, are themselves investing rapidly in North America and Southeast Asia. Taiwan, especially, has been making a substantial investment in China.[15] In the global division of labor, the "victim" turns around and becomes the "victimizer." It is not the individual constituent but the system as a whole that requires careful scrutiny and criticism.

Furthermore, what makes the unidirectional domination thesis difficult to accept is the Taiwanese cultural producers' eagerness to imitate and transfer existing cultural products from Japan to generate profits. Eager to satisfy and exploit the vibrant consumer market created by rapid economic growth, proven Japanese cultural goods are imitated and imported to reduce cost and maximize profit. Nowhere is this "postmodern mimicry" more prominent than in the cultural industry of popular music. In recent years, Taiwan has witnessed an unprecedented number of young popular singers. These highly commodified performers are young, good-looking, stylish, and usually possess little or no talent at all. The prime example is Hsiao Hu Tui (Little Tiger Team), three youngsters whose popularity created somewhat

14. Robert Reich, *The Work of Nations* (New York: Alfred A. Knopf, 1991), esp. parts 1 and 2.
15. In 1987, South Korean foreign investment amounted to $332.71 million, an increase of 112 percent. Taiwan's investment amounted to $102.75 million, up 81 percent from the previous year.

of a phenomenon since their debut in 1989. Hsiao Hu Tui is a simulacrum of the successful Japanese trio Shonentai (The Young Team). Their young and energetic outwardness, mechanically choreographed dance steps, together with easy-to-memorize melodies, are well packaged and transmitted through various media for tens of thousands of young potential consumers. These young "idols" (*aidoru* in Japanese, *o hsiang* in Chinese) are usually given a particular character trait—cute, naïve, rebellious, or animated—most of which are completely different from their real personalities. Their individualities are completely suppressed. These performers almost never make or play their own music; their songs are written and produced by professional songwriters. Each *aidoru*'s potential hit song is accompanied by, and synchronized with, mechanically choreographed movements that operate with remarkable precision; specific sets of costumes and hairstyles are created so they can be easily identified with each song. The result is a formidable "*aidoru* system," consisting of record companies, talent production companies, and electronic media that cooperatively ensures the availability and that incessantly disseminates these packaged commodities to the growing consumer market.[16]

A typical talent production company in Taiwan would often produce a Taiwanese version of the *aidoru* singers with a Japanese blueprint. The planning department of the company keeps a close eye on the development of the Japanese music industry. Researchers are dispatched to Japan to purchase videos and records of popular Japanese *aidoru*. Cultural affinity and geographic proximity facilitate this imitating process. An already successful model is brought back, and a Taiwanese version is created, at times

16. For analyses of Japanese *aidoru*, see Inamasu Tatsuo, *Aidoru kogaku* (*Aidoru* engineering) (Tokyo: Chikuma shobo, 1989), and Ogawa Hiroshi, *Ongaku suru shakai* (Music playing society) (Tokyo: Keiso shobo, 1988), esp. chap. 5, "Aidoru gensho no tenkai" (The development of the *aidoru* phenomenon). The closest analogy of the "*aidoru* system" in the West is the Hollywood star system of the 1930s and 1940s. As Inamasu and Ogawa argue, however, the two systems differ in their medium of transmission: television and cinema, and thus their respective receptions. Through the cinematic apparatus, film stars are able to distance themselves from the "masses," creating the necessary "charisma" to construct and further advance the "myths" of the stars. However, as television pervades our daily life, becoming part of our living space, the "mysteriousness" of the stars dissipates, while more "familiarity" is expected from the stars of television. In Japan, the *aidoru* saturate TV for greater exposure. From singing programs to quiz shows, from TV dramas to variety shows, a popular *aidoru* easily can appear in five to ten regular programs a week. Inamasu and Ogawa attribute the popularity and success of the *aidoru* to their extensive exposure and to the "intimacy" between them and their fans.

modified, to accommodate domestic needs. Japanese songs are also borrowed, either in complete or partial (especially the refrain) version, or songs
are "spliced" with different arrangements. This imitation and borrowing of
cultural images from Japan is necessary for the financial survival of the companies. These production companies, mostly small- to medium-sized, do
not have the capital or people power to invest and to create talents without
risking financial loss. Japanese culture industry provides a well-established
model that minimizes the financial risk of these companies. If one project
does not fare well, it can be canceled, and another one can be pursued without major financial loss. In this context, to see Japanese or Japanese-like
cultural commodities as the immediate outgrowth of Japanese economic expansion imposed from Japan is to overlook the profit-seeking manipulation
by Taiwan's cultural producers, or what Leslie Sklair has called the transnational capitalist class,[17] in creating an ersatz commodified culture. I do not
want to make light of Japan's economic influence over Taiwan. Japanese
cultural products are transmitted by the major social-economic institutions
of Japan (often with Taiwanese collaboration). There is a clear *economic*
sense in which this process can be seen as being imposed on Taiwanese culture, since they are bound up directly with Japan's emergence as
an economic power. The booming consumer market represents enormous
potential profits for Japanese multinationals (although I have argued that
this process is not unilateral). Even if the significance of *economic* domination is to be taken for granted, however, in what sense they are *cultural*
imposition is not so clear. What are the *cultural* implications of Japanese
multinational capitalism? More important, what are the meanings people
attach to the practice of consuming Japanese cultural commodities?

The second, and more "culturally" directed, analysis of Japanese
cultural influence in Taiwan is Tsan Hung-chih's *City Watching: New Language, New Contact, and New Culture*.[18] Tsan's book is the only substantial
analysis on the recent proliferation of Japanese mass culture that I was able
to locate. Despite the tentative and apologetic tone—Tsan admits that he

17. Sklair defines the transnational capitalist class as "those people who see their own
interests and/or the interests of their nation, as best served by an identification with the
interests of the capitalist global system, in particular the interests of the countries of the
capitalist core and the transnational corporations domiciled in them." See Leslie Sklair,
Sociology of the Global System (Baltimore: Johns Hopkins University Press, 1991), 8.
18. Tsan Hung-chih, *Ch'en shih kuan ch'a* (City watching: New language, new contact,
and new culture) (Taipei: Yuan-liu, 1989). Subsequent references to this text will be cited
parenthetically as Tsan. All translations are mine.

doesn't know much about Japan and the language—he nonetheless provides a perceptive and meticulous description of Japan's influence on the mass culture of Taiwan.

Tsan describes three types of new cultural "contacts" with Japan: the informational, the quotidian, and the industrial. This recent interaction is *new* because before the mid-1980s, contact with Japanese mass culture was minimal, and Japanese songs and films were officially banned in Taiwan. Books, mostly language texts and technical manuals, were scarcely available and then only in restricted bookstores. The study of the Japanese language was mostly for business purposes, although a large number of the elderly spoke Japanese: a legacy of colonial education. Today, despite official ban, Japanese songs and video programs can be heard and rented in every record and video rental store; Japanese fashion and information magazines (or their Chinese versions) are readily available, even from street vendors. Today, Japanese-language learning has shifted from the technical to the practical, from the pedagogical to the commonplace, suggesting a better knowledge and a stronger affiliation with contemporary Japan. Titles such as *Phrases Used by Young Japanese* and *Young People Making Friends in Japanese* are clearly targeted toward the younger Taiwanese with emphasis on playfulness, casualness, and speediness. One book claims, as one of its distinctive features, that it will enable the learner to understand Japanese on TV, radio, and dialogues on the video tape. These are all indications of the prevalence of "Japaneseness" in Taiwan's mass culture today.

The first "reality" of Japanese cultural presence, writes Tsan, can be seen in the form of informational flow. Tsan points out that in 1985, the sales of publications in Japanese has exceeded that of English. If one notes the strong emphasis on learning English in Taiwan's educational system, and the lack thereof on Japanese, this phenomenon is astounding. Furthermore, the increase in circulation of Japanese magazines and regular subscribers to more specialized journals suggests an established demand. The rising demand for Japanese publications is met by the increasing number of bookstores that sell predominantly Japanese books and magazines. Finally, videotapes of Japanese TV programs and movies accounted for 31 percent of Taiwan's entire video rental business.

The second "contact" with Japan, according to Tsan, can be observed in the activities of everyday life, mainly consumption. Citing the flourishing presence of supermarkets and department stores with Japanese investment, the increasing conformity to the Japanese fashion trend, the heavy imitation of Japanese industrial design, and the growing identification with the Japanese life-style (going to coffee shops, *karaoke* bars) as examples, Tsan calls attention to the noticeable change and effect of Japanese culture on the behavior pattern of the daily lives of Taiwanese consumers.

The third new point of contact with Japan, observes Tsan, is in the industries. Although historically Taiwanese industries have always had a long and intimate relationship with Japan, recently there have been new developments. In the past, technology imported from Japan was predominantly "production" oriented (electronics, manufacturing), but today, the introduction of "service know-how" is gaining importance. And this further intensifies Taiwan's reliance on Japan in all sectors of industry.

Tsan's systematic description accurately points out the all-presence of Japanese cultural influence on Taiwan. What is most striking about Tsan's work, as I have mentioned, is his tentativeness. His aim, as he outlines his objective in the outset, is to "describe," to "categorize," and to "classify" the phenomenon, but not to "criticize." Tsan attributes his inability to derive a satisfying conclusion to an ambiguous and murky "perplexity of advantages and disadvantages." On the striking lack of analysis by Taiwanese cultural critics (himself included) of the increasing Japanese cultural presence despite growing anxiety and concern, Tsan writes: "[Japanese cultural influence], lacking an apparent theory and nationalistic ideology, is unable to incite a counter-ideology. Therefore there are no ways to go about criticizing" (Tsan, 21). Furthermore, Tsan observes that Japanese cultural dominance, which already subsumes China, Taiwan, and Hong Kong, will soon include the Philippines. And it would not be incorrect to say that there exists a "Common Sphere of Japanese Modus Vivendi," an obvious insinuation to the Japanese wartime slogan: the Greater Eastern Co-Prosperity Sphere. "From a certain perspective," Tsan writes, "this is an aspect of 'cultural imperialism.'" He is quick to add, however, that he "has not, or is not yet ready to" employ the term to express a strong criticism; rather, he borrows the term only to "explain the existence of this Common Sphere" (Tsan, 33).

This caution and reluctance to employ the generic concept of cultural imperialism to examine the spread of foreign culture is in stark contrast to the response of other "Third World" media and cultural critics, especially in their analysis of American cultural influence. One of the most celebrated studies on cultural imperialism is Ariel Dorfman and Armand Mattelart's *How to Read Donald Duck: Imperialist Ideology in the Disney Comic*.[19] Unlike Tsan's claim that Japanese cultural goods have no conceivable ideology, therefore making criticism difficult, Dorfman and Mattelart's project attempts to decipher the American capitalist ideology hidden behind the seemingly innocent and harmless world of Walt Disney.

Against the common perception of Disney comics, Dorfman and Mattelart argue that these cultural commodities, which are imbued with a capitalist ideology that once consumed and internalized, can normalize and naturalize the social relations of Western capitalism in the "Third World." Meticulously working their way through the Disney comics and revealing their inherent capitalist ideologies, such as the unquestioned submission to moral and physical repression and economic domination, the stereotypical description and deprecation of the exotic "Third World," the frantic chase of money, the insatiable consumerism in a world of magical abundance, and so on, Dorfman and Mattelart are often compelling and convincing. As pointed out by John Tomlinson, however, in his study on cultural imperialism, Dorfman and Mattelart's work, despite being a politicized reading of the "imperialist text," does not take into account the effect on, or the reception of, the general public, who actually consumes these cultural products on an everyday basis. Tomlinson writes:

> What is finally at stake is not the literary-critical merits of Dorfman and Mattelart's interpretations, nor indeed the correctness of their socioeconomic analysis, but the crucial question of how ordinary readers read the comics: that is, the question of if and how the text has its ideological effects.[20]

While Dorfman and Mattelart are able to advance the *potential* manipulative power of imported cultural products, they significantly ignore the possibility of multiple readings of these cultural texts by the people and underestimate their abilities to negotiate and construct meanings within their own particular cultural contexts.

I do not think that Dorfman and Mattelart's work should be dismissed, however. Despite the lack of analysis on the cultural "effect" of imported cultural goods, their work must be read in light of the historical context

19. Ariel Dorfman and Armand Mattelart, *How to Read Donald Duck: Imperialist Ideology in the Disney Comic*, trans. David Kunzle (New York: I. G. Editions, Inc., 1975).
20. John Tomlinson, *Cultural Imperialism* (Baltimore: Johns Hopkins University Press, 1991), 43.

that motivated their project. It is no coincidence that the term *cultural imperialism* emerged during the 1960s, when decolonization and national independence of what is mostly now called the "Third World" was finally taking place. This marked the first time the hitherto underprivileged and oppressed were given a voice of their own. Albeit nations are "imagined political communities," they are the necessary countermeasures and inescapable consequences of Western imperialism and colonialism. For the intellectuals of these new nations, cultural autonomy meant political independence. Against the disfiguring and distorting of their precolonial histories by the colonial regime, many intellectuals began a passionate search for a national culture that, in retrospect, was besieged with problematics. The concept of cultural imperialism, as deployed by intellectuals in the postindependence, neocolonial "Third World," as a historical process of rehabilitation to construct a meaningful resistance to colonial rule, and to mobilize people in the name of national independence, is inevitable and powerful. Written in 1971, in the midst of the Chilean revolutionary process, *How to Read Donald Duck* was indeed a politicized manifesto against the colonial empire of the United States and its multinational corporations. Despite its shortcomings, Dorfman and Mattelart's work should be read as an emerging voice, located historically, against American dominance (political, economic, and cultural) of Chile. To criticize the book for having a specific political agenda (as if there is a "neutral" text) and to overlook the "real" effect of the objects in analysis is to ignore the great disparity and power imbalance between the imperial "First" World and the defiant "Third" World in the specific historical context.

The question still remains, however, as to why Tsan finds Japanese cultural products lacking a discernible ideology and why the phenomenon is difficult to assess? Tsan rightly observes that the cultural merchandise imported from Japan is gradually and increasingly discarding the shade of traditional Japanese culture and ethnic character. What is perceived as Japanese cultural products can easily be of American or British origins. Japan simply reassembles and packages other cultural commodities and sells them to other countries. Tsan cites Taiwanese punk as an example. Punk style, together with other youth subcultures that emerged in postwar Britain, are defiant expressions of British youth. Punk is a "style in revolt, [a] revolting style."[21] It is offensive, threatening, and antisocial. As punk

21. For an introductory discussion of punk and other British subcultures, see Dick Hebdige, *Subculture: The Meaning of Style* (London: Routledge, 1979), 106.

has reached Japan, however, it has lost most of its strength and effective-ness, although the style has remained similar. The Japanese punk is highly uniform and its defiance is very well regulated. Clothing is ripped in the same way, accessories are bought for the same place, all dance steps are performed in a very controlled and unvarying manner. In Japan, punk has literally become a "style," losing all political implications. There is nothing offensive or threatening about Japanese punksters.

It is this depoliticized, domesticated, highly uniform and trendy Japa-nese punk style that has found its way to Taiwan. Taiwanese styles are imi-tations of the Japanese; all accessories and essentials for the punk look are imported from Japan. What Taiwan has received, argues Tsan, is a repack-aged secondhand cultural commodity that has no specific "national" origin or discernible ideology. A similar observation has been made by Anthony D. Smith, as he contrasts earlier "cultural imperialisms" with today's:

> There is an important difference from earlier cultural imperialisms. Earlier imperialisms were usually extensions of ethnic or national sentiments and ideologies, French, British, Russian, etc. Today's im-perialisms are ostensibly non-national; "capitalism" and "socialism," and in a different sense "Europeanism," are by definition and inten-tion "supranational," if not universal. They are supported by a tech-nological infrastructure which is truly "cosmopolitan," in the sense that the same telecommunications base will eventually erode cul-tural differences and create a genuinely "global culture" based on the properties of the media themselves, to which the "message" will become increasingly incidental.[22]

What both Tsan and Smith seem to imply is that in today's global cultural economy, cultures are becoming decontextualized and dehistoricized as they cross national boundaries with unprecedented ease and speed. In a world of transnational corporations, telecommunication, information net-works, and international division of labor, "national" cultures are in danger of becoming obsolete, resorting only to tourist sites and museums.

This new cultural configuration has two implications for the discourse of cultural imperialism and for Japan's cultural presence in Taiwan. First of all, as communication and information technology advance with blazing speed and as cultural boundaries become more fluid, any attempt to block

22. Anthony D. Smith, "Towards a Global Culture?" in *Global Culture: Nationalism, Glob-alization, and Modernity*, ed. Mike Featherstone (London: Sage Publications, 1990), 176.

or limit incoming and outgoing cultural flows is doomed to failure. Japanese satellite broadcasts can be received in Shanghai, Pusan, and Taipei simply by extending the antenna of the TV. The regulation of the transmission of foreign cultural images is beyond the political apparatus of the nation-states. Second, as intranational economic integration and interdependence intensify, the existing center-periphery model of cultural domination is no longer viable. Not only can the institution of cultural production no longer be isolated to a single "center," but the passive reception of the "periphery" should also be questioned. How is one to specify the "source" of production of a dress designed and labeled by a Japanese designer living in France, and assembled in Hong Kong? What is the effect on the cultural pattern of the society when a Taiwanese youth sings a Chinese song with a *karaoke* machine from Japan?

Tsan's work, by claiming a lack of discernible ideology within the very object of analysis, escapes the deterministic ideological incorporation approach of Dorfman and Mattelart. He also recognizes that *economically*, Japan's cultural invasion of Taiwan has made Taiwan both a victim and a beneficiary. In the final section, entitled "How to Face Japanese Contacts?" he writes,

> All Taiwanese exports and sources of competition today, come from Japan. We imitate the Japanese. Although our products are less in quality, they are also cheaper; therefore, we can be quite competitive. The object of our learning is a very competitive Japan, far more than the United States. As a result, we can be as competitive as the United States by learning just a few things from Japan. (Tsan, 26)

Taiwan becomes a quasi-Japan, expanding its influence to others. Tsan urges Taiwan to refute the role of a collaborator, to "turn around" and "compete with Japan." He challenges his readers to ask themselves if they are willing to be "[members] of the Common Sphere of Japanese Modus Vivendi," if they are willing to "lose all history, culture, and independent national character" (Tsan, 26). Tsan's conclusion is far from satisfying. First, despite his suggestion that transnational corporations are responsible for the growth of cultural production, he still holds onto the notion that national industries represent the well-being of the peoples in a nation. How is this competition possible or viable on a national scale within the system of transnational capitalism? And exactly what should the Taiwanese cultural industry compete with Japan for, to be the next hegemon of Asia, the world? Second, Tsan seems to assume that one can step outside the cultural and ideological formation by simply refusing Japanese cultural products; once Japanese cultural products are cut off, cultural imperialism will stop. Does Tsan intend to stop all flow of foreign cultural practices? Who will decide what is acceptable and what is not? Third, by not concerning himself with the effect of Japanese cultural products on the general public, Tsan falls into the determinist trap of assuming that Japanese cultural influence *necessarily* entails the annihilation of Taiwanese culture in total. What does he mean by culture? And whose history is in danger? What is and who represents the national character of Taiwan—the mainlanders, the Taiwanese, or the Aborigines? Tsan's culturalism and Chuang's economism, by ignoring the complex connection between a particular cultural practice and its actual effect (be it foreign or domestic), assume, a priori, that Japanese cultural commodities have an inherent power intrinsic to them that will alter the cultural formation of Taiwan. There is an intended meaning attached that corresponds to a particular text, and the critic has a transparent and unmediated access to it. In other words, they fetishize Japanese cultural practices. Cultural meanings are predetermined and transparent to the critics. The result is always already guaranteed.

What has been conspicuously missing in both analyses of Japanese cultural influence in Taiwan is how these cultural products are actually experienced by the people who consume them. They also fail to allow for the ambiguous, multilayered, and, at times, irrelevant responses of the consumers. While Chuang underscores the economic strategies of the Japanese producers, Tsan concerns himself with the "ideology-less" nature of the product. Both privilege the production aspect of cultural process over consumption. Both assume an unproblematized ideological effect on "passive" consumers as they shop in a Japanese-style department store, sing in a *karaoke* bar, or watch Japanese TV programs via satellite. What is essential is not a separated analysis of production *or* consumption of a cultural process but an analysis of the relationship and interaction between the cultural products *and* their consumers: how they interpret, translate, articulate, and even transform their experiences and meanings of a foreign cultural practice.

In the era of multinational capitalism, as economic interests and interdependence between nations proliferate on a global scale, cultural convergence seems to be occurring at various levels. Foreign cultural products and their meanings are not only readily available but are also easily transferable. Since no one can escape the continuous exposure to the enormous range of presentation and reference to the ever-differentiating and changing commodified cultural practices, the attempt to locate identifiable and stable presentations and relations has become extremely difficult, if not impossible. Do people who have affectedly taken up Japanese cultural practices actually recognize, or even care about, their "Japaneseness?" What if they are not aware that a popular song is of Japanese origin?; what if they did not know that their favorite variety show is a carbon copy of a Japanese show? This raises the difficult question regarding the relationship between the cultural critic (in this case, me) and the people who actually consume the cultural texts. As an "informed" analyst—I have lived in both countries and am acutely aware of the trends in Japanese mass culture—I was able, with my personal, and privileged, experience, to recognize cultural products that were imitated or imported directly from Japan; whereas, perhaps, a large number of people in Taiwan, who have no knowledge of Japan, are unlikely to see certain commodities as emblematic of Japanese culture at all. In this instance, it becomes almost impossible to assess the ideological effect of an alien cultural influence that both Chuang and Tsan see as detrimental to the economical and cultural well-being of Taiwan.

Furthermore, even if the "Japaneseness" of the cultural commodities is recognized, there is no guarantee that the people would be interpellated in an unyielding or particular way. The connection between cultural texts and their actual effects may be quite unpredictable and complex. The same text can be interpreted differently by various people. Cultural meaning is never singular, and cultural texts are at least potentially multifunctional. Therefore, it is foreseeable that people's interpretation and appropriation of certain cultural products are independent from, and not limited only to, their signifying and representational effects. Some people might prefer Japanese goods for the pragmatic reason that Japanese quality and packaging are superior to that of indigenous or American production. Japanese goods are attractive to these people because of their *functionality* and *presentation*, not because of their *representation*. It is certainly possible that if similar products were made elsewhere, people would still buy them. The cultural or national origin of the commodities alone does not motivate the consumer. Furthermore, how these cultural products are deployed and appropriated by people in their distinctive social contexts becomes invisible to critics who see cultural meanings as exclusively determined by the interpretive content of the products. A person, despite possessing a "touristic" view of Japan, by simulating "Japaneseness" in Taiwan, can see it as a way to differentiate him-/herself from others and other forms of popular culture. This "blind worship" becomes a way to define oneself in a rather homogenous and regulated society.

Obviously, there is a danger in sanctifying a kind of populism that seeks and finds resistance everywhere and that avoids the extradiscursive reality of economic exploitation and social injustice. The notion that people are completely "free" and apparently autonomous agents who make choices without any ideological assumptions is itself an ideology. Individuals may have more choices than ever in the growing market economy of differences, but they do not have the choice to refuse. Furthermore, there are no other choices besides the choices that are offered by the institution of a particular society. This is not to say, however, that people do not actively construct and transform meanings from the cultural commodities (foreign or domestic) they consume. Any notion that suggests cultural productions merely manipulate an excessively malleable audience, even if they attempt to, must be rejected. Constant conflicts, negotiations, and articulations are taking place in the "contact zone"[23] between cultural texts and their audience. It is a site of struggle, an arena of contestation in which conflicting and competing political, economic, and cultural forces collide, and the end result is never guaranteed in advance.

Today's Japanese cultural hegemony in the region is a direct result of its economic prowess *and* the recent blossoming and ever-growing involvement of Asian countries in the global capitalist economy. Criticism directed against a single source of domination (in this case, Japan) is unconvincing and lacks analytical sophistication, because, under the competitive imperative to minimize costs and to accumulate, transnational corporations from countries such as Taiwan and South Korea also seek production in the lowest cost location and exploit the indigenous labor force in China, Southeast Asia, and even the United States. If one is to follow Chuang's and Tsan's arguments, today one can easily speak of Taiwanese cultural imperialism in China, and of Korean cultural imperialism in Indonesia. Furthermore, we must shun the naïve notion that foreign cultural texts are prescribed in advance with a certain intention without examining

23. I borrow the term from Mary Louise Pratt, which she defines as "the space of colonial encounters, the space in which peoples geographically and historically separated come into contact with each other and establish ongoing relations, usually involving conditions of coercion, radical inequality, and intractable conflict." See her *Imperial Eyes, Travel Writing and Transculturation* (London: Routledge, 1992), 6.

the point of contact where people actively choose, use, and interpret them. As the polarization between the rich and the poor becomes more distinct and their gap widens in both developing *and* developed nations, an unexamined chauvinistic expression of cultural nationalism is both repressive and futile. The enunciative position and environment of cultural imperialism must be scrutinized: who speaks, who is speaking for whom, from what particular historical specificity and from what power relation is one speaking? Finally, we must be aware of the enormous *global* destruction and economic exploitation that accompany the present cultural development in which symbolic meanings are increasingly commodified, dehistoricized, and depoliticized as they are transferred across national boundaries, and we must also insist on the contingent *local* articulations in which foreign cultural commodities and their potential multiple meanings are taken up by the people who consume them.

The Hong Kong Immigrant and the Urban Landscape: Shaping the Transnational Cosmopolitan in the Era of Pacific Rim Capital

Katharyne Mitchell

Introduction

Disciplining the Transnational Subject

Unholy alliances are often formed in periods of economic transition. In this case I am concerned with the alliance of state and business during the global restructuring of the 1980s. How are subjects disciplined over a plurality of terrains? How is citizenship constructed within a context of transnational movement? What institutions of governmentality are brought to bear to "regulate the conduct of subjects as a population, and as individuals . . . in the interests of ensuring security and prosperity for the nation-state," yet which, at the same time, are bound neither by the territorially defined nor the rhetorically discursive spaces of the nation-state? [1]

The global restructuring of the past two decades has involved local transformations of both economy and culture, the interconnections of which

---

1. Aihwa Ong, "On the Edge of Empires: Flexible Citizenship among Chinese in Diaspora," *positions* 1:3 (1993): 748. See also Michel Foucault, "Governmentality," in *The Foucault Effect: Studies in Governmentality*, ed. Graham Burchell, Colin Gordon, and Peter Miller (Chicago: University of Chicago Press, 1991), 87–104.

are the subject of numerous theoretical inquiries.[2] As nations become increasingly interdependent, and economies and cultures articulate across formerly regulated and rigid borders, the processes constituting "citizens as 'subjects' (in both of Foucault's senses of 'subjection'—subject of and subjected to the nation)" begin to assume a more global dynamic.[3] Strong as they are, however, these forces of globalization are always mediated by local places and people; they "do not, contrary to popular opinion, lead to simple homogenization; globalization also initiates a myriad of local interpretations and transformations."[4]

In terms of the global integration of people, "simple homogenization" is inconceivable—despite the various state rhetorics of melting pots and cultural mosaics. Although immigrants become legal citizens through a prescribed, state-regulated path,[5] immigrants become cultural citizens through a more mediated and reflexive set of formative processes.[6] In the era of

2. See Rob Wilson and Wimal Dissanayake, eds., *Global/Local: Cultural Production and the Transnational Imaginary* (Durham: Duke University Press, 1995); Arjun Appadurai, "Disjuncture and Difference in the Global Cultural Economy," *Theory, Culture and Society* 7 (1990): 295–310; David Harvey, *The Condition of Postmodernity: An Enquiry into the Origins of Cultural Change* (Oxford: Basil Blackwell, 1989); Anthony King, *Culture, Globalization and the World-System* (London: MacMillan, 1991), and "Identity and Difference: The Internationalization of Capital and the Globalization of Culture," in *The Restless Urban Landscape*, ed. Paul Knox (New Jersey: Prentice Hall, 1993), 83–110; and Michael Featherstone, *Global Culture: Nationalism, Globalization and Modernity* (London: Sage, 1990).

3. Stuart Hall, "Culture, Community, Nation," *Cultural Studies* 7:3 (1993): 355. See also Homi Bhabha, "DissemiNation: Time, Narrative, and the Margins of the Modern Nation," in *Nation and Narration*, ed. Bhabha (London: Routledge, 1990): 291–322; and James Clifford, "Traveling Cultures," in *Cultural Studies*, ed. Lawrence Grossberg, Cary Nelson, and Paula Treichler (New York: Routledge, 1992), 96–112.

4. Kris Olds, "Globalization and the Production of New Urban Spaces: Pacific Rim Mega-Projects in the Late Twentieth Century," *Environment and Planning A* (forthcoming, 1995): 2. See also Allan Pred and Michael Watts, *Reworking Modernity: Capitalisms and Symbolic Discontent* (New Brunswick: Rutgers University Press, 1992).

5. This is not to suggest that this "regulated" path is not rife with the same racist and classist roadblocks that beset more informal channels. I am arguing, rather, that legal citizenship is not the end but the beginning of numerous local mediations over the "terms of the local-global integration"—in this case, the integration of people (see Charles Bright and Michael Geyer, "For a Unified History of the World in the Twentieth Century," *Radical History Review* 39 [1987]).

6. These would include negotiating local racisms as well as local cultures (see Paul Gilroy's critique of Raymond Williams in *"There Ain't No Black in the Union Jack": The*

transnational flows of investment and investors, cultural citizenship involves acculturation to both local traditions and global compacts. In order to function effectively in an interconnected, yet locally mediated global economy, the "global subject" must, at one and the same time, be attuned to the nuances of a particular locale and to the transnational flows characteristic of late capitalism.

As greater and greater numbers of transnationals circulate between the new global cities of the Pacific Rim, why and how these terrestrial astronauts[7] become cultural citizens of particular national and metropolitan locales is increasingly bound up with the cross-Pacific movement of capital and commodities. The "why" relates to the rather straightforward premise that cultural and racial friction hinders capital articulation and global integration. Racism, in this context, is clearly bad for business. The "how" is considerably more intriguing as it involves both business and the state in an unholy alliance of ideological production.

In this paper I am interested in how stereotypes of the normative "Chinese" and the normative "Canadian" citizen are coproduced by both a Hong Kong and Canadian business elite, and by the Canadian state. Elsewhere, I have looked at the ways in which state and business alliances were involved in the production of a rhetoric of multiculturalism in Canada.[8] The ideology of multiculturalism was promoted in order to persuade the "host" society of the evils of racism and the benefits of cultural pluralism. The message of what constituted the "good" Canadian society and the "normative" Canadian citizen—tolerance toward racial and cultural difference— was promulgated by the government at a time of increased immigration and capital investment from Hong Kong. In this paper, I examine instead the shaping of the Chinese investor-immigrant. This production involves the workings of hegemony, but also the refashioning of stereotypes by Chinese subjects themselves, who "selectively participate in Orientalist formations as they negotiate shifting discursive terrains in the world economy."[9]

Cultural Politics of Race and Nation [Chicago: University of Chicago Press, 1991], 49–50).

7. Because of the time spent flying back and forth, the term "astronaut" (*tai hong yan*) is a common label for Hong Kong businessmen who establish residency in Canada but continue to do business in Hong Kong.

8. Katharyne Mitchell, "Multiculturalism, or the United Colors of Capitalism?" *Antipode* 25:4 (1993): 263–294.

9. Ong, "On the Edge of Empires," 746.

I understand hegemony to be a shifting and highly contested process—one that is

Class Distinctions and the Manipulation of Chineseness

The process of shaping cultural citizens is multilayered. It involves the self-fashioning of Chinese subjects, and the efforts of the Canadian and Hong Kong business elite to shape prospective Hong Kong Chinese emigrants to Canada before their departure; it also involves the differentiation of emigrants by class fragments. Overtly, the education of future Hong Kong emigrants involves the acculturation to a more Canadian subjectivity; more subtly, however, it can also be seen as an effort to indoctrinate the Hong Kong *middle class* into a kind of "transnational cosmopolitanism."[10] The distinction between the extremely wealthy, "superstrata" Hong Kong transnationals and the *nouveau riche* or bourgeois middle class not only indicates the plurality of this wealthy immigrant group, but also opens up some of the ways in which class and differences in cultural taste mediate the constitution of cultural citizenship.[11]

Bourdieu has suggested that taste is one aspect of cultural capital that is intricately linked with economic capital. Taste, or the preference for one type of cultural consumption and lifestyle over another, is a visible affirmation of economic (as well as cultural) difference.[12] Cultural frictions in Vancouver in the late 1980s included concerns about the changing urban landscape. Speculation in the housing market, the purchase of extremely large "monster" houses, removal of mature trees, and the open display of material wealth by a number of recent Hong Kong Chinese immigrants were among the many irritants which galvanized Vancouver homeowners into the formation of social groups opposed to environmental change.[13] These urban social movements effectively blocked further redevelopment of a number

---

always a tendency rather than a realization (see Stuart Hall, "The Toad in the Garden: Thatcherism among the Theorists," in *Marxism and the Interpretation of Culture*, ed. Cary Nelson and Lawrence Grossberg [Chicago: University of Illinois Press, 1988]): 35–57. In this essay, my primary focus is on the process of hegemonic production rather than the experience and mediation of that process by Chinese subjects.

10. The cosmopolitan, in the sense employed here, belongs to a new international class of people able to manage meaning strategically in new environments (see Ulf Hannerz, "Cosmopolitans and Locals in World Culture," *Theory, Culture and Society* 7:2–3 [1990]: 246).

11. My focus in this essay is on wealthy immigrants and obviously does not address the constitution of cultural citizenship for the poor and working classes.

12. Pierre Bourdieu, *Distinction: A Social Critique of the Judgement of Taste*, trans. Richard Nice (Cambridge: Harvard University Press, 1984).

13. Racism was also a major factor, which I explore more fully in Mitchell, "Fast Capital, Modernity, 'Race' and the Monster House," *Politics and Culture Series*, forthcoming.

of neighborhoods—hindering the spatial integration of the city and slowing the free circulation of capital.[14]

Many of the worst conflicts over housing occurred in the west-side, upper-middle-class areas of Kerrisdale, Oakridge, Dunbar, Granville-Woodlands, and Second and Third Shaughnessy. In these neighborhoods, hundreds of older houses were demolished, and large, boxy houses were constructed in their place. Based on interviews, surveys, observation, and archival evidence, it appears that many of the buyers of these homes in the late 1980s were middle-class, Hong Kong Chinese immigrants.[15]

In an effort to offset the increasingly effective mobilization of Anglo homeowners of these neighborhoods, the wealthy transnationals of both Hong Kong and Vancouver society attempted to lessen neighborhood friction by educating and disciplining (in the Foucauldian sense[16]) the future Hong Kong middle-class homebuyers of cultural norms for the area. *Meet with Success*, a program hosted by the Canadian Club of Hong Kong, ran a series of twice-weekly seminars on Canadian society for Hong Kong citizens who had already received visas and were planning to emigrate to Canada. A substantial part of the video shown during the seminar focused on neighborhood and housing "norms" in Vancouver, as did the enclosed information packet. This program was funded by wealthy Hong Kong and Canadian patrons, and backed by the Canadian Commission in Hong Kong.

In addition to the message of Canadian acculturation, *Meet with Success* introduced contemporary strategies of cosmopolitanism employed by the Hong Kong Chinese transnational elite. In this process, Orientalist stereotypes are aggressively refashioned. The self-representation of Asian Americans as model minorities and global economic subjects, for example, "is never simply complicit with hegemonic discourses, but seeks in this case to reposition Asian Americans as new authority figures."[17] In the context of increasing business opportunities across the Pacific, many Chinese transnational cosmopolitans represent themselves as Pacific Rim "bridge-

14. See Mitchell, "Multiculturalism."

15. Research in Vancouver and Hong Kong was conducted between 1990 and 1992. My perception is based on a wide variety of sources, but exact figures on the original nationalities of buyers and their relative wealth are impossible to obtain and are widely contested. "Middle class" as I employ it here includes the middle strata of Hong Kong society, including the upper middle class and *nouveau riche*.

16. See Foucault, *The History of Sexuality, Volume I: An Introduction*, trans. Robert Hurley (New York: Vintage, 1978).

17. Ong, "On the Edge of Empires," 769.

builders," aiding and abetting in the production of what Donald Nonini terms the "Asia-Pacific Imaginary." [18]

Clearly, the ultimate flexibility of this self-fashioning process can be useful in the contemporary global economy. As capitalist networks articulate, Chinese businesspeople who speak the language of the global economic subject, but are also imbricated in a Hong Kong Chinese discourse, are able to operate as the quintessential middlemen. With flexible citizenship and deterritorialized systems of credit, but with a durable and elastic business network established on the basis of the extended family, overseas Hong Kong capitalists can manipulate images of both the transnational cosmopolitan and the "ethnic Chinese," enabling them to position themselves at the lucrative center of Pacific Rim business. The strategic balancing that this requires, however, is threatened by the "inappropriate" cultural behavior of middle class emigrants who exacerbate local friction through the overt display of material wealth or expressed desire for large "monster" houses and good *feng shui* in established Vancouver neighborhoods.

Middle class or *nouveau riche* behavior, which was negatively represented as "Hong Kong Chinese" behavior by much of the Vancouver media in 1988, disrupts both capital circulation and the neutral, "transnational" image of Hong Kong investors. *Meet with Success*, and a number of other programs and media events in Hong Kong in the early 1990s, were efforts to counter this type of friction and to keep capital articulations and international business networking in the Asia Pacific fluid and faceless.

Urban Mega-Projects and Overseas Chinese Capital Networks

Capital articulations in the Asia Pacific are also multilayered. In my research I have been interested in the business linkages involved with the growth of urban mega-projects in Pacific Rim cities. Urban mega-projects are "large-scale (re)development projects composed of a mix of commercial, residential, retail, industrial, leisure and infrastructure uses." [19] These projects are being developed around the globe in increasing numbers, and are responsible for the restructuring of large chunks of the downtown cores of cities such as Singapore, Shanghai, Yokohama, and Vancouver.

Urban mega-projects are usually financed through a consortium of international players. This global financing was greatly facilitated by the lib-

18. Donald Nonini, "On the Outs on the Rim: An Ethnographic Grounding of the 'Asia Pacific Imaginary'" in *What Is in a Rim? Critical Perspectives on the Pacific Region Idea*, ed. Arif Dirlik (Boulder: Westview Press, 1993).

19. Olds, "Globalization and the Production of New Urban Spaces," 1.

eralization of finance systems worldwide in the late 1970s and 1980s, when liberalization and deregulation allowed finance and credit to become more available "on a global 'private' scale beyond the bounds of national control."[20] With credit operating globally through private and informal networks, preestablished Chinese business networks became increasingly important systems for the circulation of credit. In the establishment of urban mega-projects around the world, including the development of the Expo lands by the Li family in Vancouver, these overseas Chinese business networks have been absolutely key.[21]

In this essay I begin by examining some of the ways in which Hong Kong Chinese economic practice in the 1980s differs from Canadian business practice. I focus on three areas: extended family networking and business trust, credit manipulation, and the use of the "gift economy." I argue further that the Hong Kong Chinese style of capitalism in which these features are prominent was particularly effective in the 1980s, when financial deregulation, privatization, and the use of subcontracting networks expanded worldwide. Some of these elements of business practice and timing resulted in the large-scale investment and rapid development of Vancouver real estate by Hong Kong businesspeople during the latter part of the decade. In the penultimate part of the essay, I discuss a few of these real estate links and the frictions that they caused, and then examine some of the self-fashioning strategies of Vancouver's foremost property developer, the Chinese Canadian son of Li Ka-shing, Victor Li. In the final section, I look at the *Meet with Success* seminar and discuss how acculturation programs such as this one may be directly linked with the postcolonial strategies of transnational elites concerned with the development of urban mega-projects and the ongoing capitalist integration of the Pacific Rim.

Contextualizing Hong Kong Chinese Capitalism

In the following section I will outline a few of the ways in which contemporary Hong Kong Chinese business practice has been affected by

20. Olds, "Globalization and the Production of New Urban Spaces," 3. See also A. Leyshon and Nigel Thrift, "Liberalisation and Consolidation: The Single European Market and the Remaking of European Financial Capital," *Environment and Planning A* 24 (1992): 49–81.
21. See Mitchell, "Flexible Circulation in the Pacific Rim: Capitalisms in Cultural Context," *Economic Geography* (forthcoming, 1995); and Olds, "Globalization and the Production of New Urban Spaces."

historical and geographical patterns and relations. By examining the on-going importance of familial ties and business trust, as well as the use of credit in the development of merchant and mutual credit associations in late imperial China, it is possible to locate some of the historical precedents for contemporary capital accumulation, credit practices, and the use of money. These practices are inevitably transformed in the context of new market op-portunities, production strategies, and expanding networks. My aim here is not to identify and fix cultural difference, but rather to briefly explore some of the cultural sedimentations that inform the ongoing construction of subject and institution in contemporary Hong Kong Chinese society.

Familial and Regional Ties, Networks, and Business Trust

Many scholars have examined the importance of familial and regional ties in the business organization and economic practice of Chinese soci-eties worldwide.[22] Family ties are defined broadly, stretching to include dis-tant relations and in-laws. Although usually centered on kinship networks, they may extend outward to include co-regional and college associates as well. These ties form a system of contacts that are often characterized as elastic and flexible, yet durable over time. The relationships between the extended family members are based on established norms of reciprocity that are understood and generally accepted by those operating within this network.[23]

Ownership and management of Chinese businesses usually remain in the family. When large-scale operations are extended overseas, a promi-nent pattern is for the spin-off project to be controlled by a son or son-in-law—even though professional managers may be hired to manage various aspects of the business operations.[24] An important element that helps to

22. See Linda Lim and L. A. Peter Gosling, eds., *The Chinese in Southeast Asia* (Singa-pore: Maruzen Asia, 1983); W. Willmott and L. Crissman, eds., *Economic Organization in Chinese Society* (Stanford: Stanford University Press, 1972); Kunio Yoshihara, *The Rise of Ersatz Capitalism in South-East Asia* (Oxford: Oxford University Press, 1988); S. Gordon Redding, *The Spirit of Chinese Capitalism* (New York: Walter de Gruyter, 1990); and Gary Hamilton, ed., *Business Networks and Economic Development in East and Southeast Asia* (Hong Kong: Centre of Asian Studies, 1991).
23. Gary Hamilton and Wang Zheng, Introduction to Fei Xiao-tong, *From the Soil*, trans. Hamilton and Wang (Berkeley: University of California Press, 1992), 13.
24. See Lau Siu-kai, *Society and Politics in Hong Kong* (Hong Kong: The Chinese Uni-versity Press, 1982); Wong Siu-lun, "The Chinese Family Firm: A Model," *British Jour-nal of Sociology* 36:1 (1985): 58–72; Redding, *The Spirit of Chinese Capitalism*; Clifton Barton, "Trust and Credit: Some Observations Regarding Business Strategies of Over-

cement these extended family ties across spatial divides is business trust. The ethic of trust is absolutely central to the business success of Chinese entrepreneurs in Hong Kong, Taiwan, and in many overseas communities.[25] In order for the established norms of reciprocity to operate effectively, businesspeople must trust that the other players will uphold certain expectations. In large-scale, international business ventures, where transactions must take place across great distances, initial personal trust is often won on the basis of reputation. Reputation is thus absolutely crucial for the extension of the enterprise at every level of Chinese capitalist societies, including the willingness of banks and other businesspeople to extend credit and participate in joint ventures.[26]

Credit and Capital Accumulation

In the late Ming and Qing, much of the standardization of currency and institutionalization of credit and acceptable interest rates was implemented by merchant associations. These associations aided in the organization and disciplining of economic behavior in the marketplace, as well as being involved in money-lending. A number of merchant associations (*huiguan*) are still prominent in Hong Kong, Taiwan, and overseas Chinese communities in Southeast Asia, and are still involved in money-lending in large-scale and long-term transactions. The pooling of capital resources is also a common method of coordinating investment monies within the extended family system.

Many contemporary Chinese businesspeople rely on mutual aid associations (*hui*) for venture capital. In these groups, formal laws and ad-

---

seas Chinese Traders in South Vietnam," in *The Chinese in Southeast Asia*, 46–63; and M. Montagu-Pollock, "All the Right Connections," *Asian Business* 27:1 (1991): 20–24.

25. See Robert Silin, "Marketing and Credit in a Hong Kong Wholesale Market," in *Economic Organization in Chinese Society*, 327–52; Kao Cheng-shu, " 'Personal Trust' in the Large Businesses in Taiwan: A Traditional Foundation for Contemporary Economic Activities," in *Business Networks and Economic Development*, 66–93; Wong Siu-lun, "The Applicability of Asian Family Values to Other Sociocultural Settings," in *In Search of an East Asian Development Model*, ed. Peter Berger and Hsin-Huang Michael Hsiao (New Brunswick, N.J.: Transaction Books, 1988): 134–52; *Emigrant Entrepreneurs: Shanghai Industrialists in Hong Kong* (Hong Kong: Oxford University Press, 1988); "Chinese Entrepreneurs and Business Trust," in *Business Networks and Economic Development*, 13–29.

26. Lin Pao-an, "The Social Sources of Capital Investment in Taiwan's Industrialization," in *Business Networks and Economic Development*, 105; and Redding, *The Spirit of Chinese Capitalism*, 98.

ministrative agencies are rarely used to enforce behavior; trust remains an important element in bonding the business transaction. By pooling 'funds and obtaining capital through informal channels, the bulk of the principle necessary for a business venture can often be accumulated long before the business venture is initiated. In terms of the repayment of interest on the principle, the amount of time taken to repay is less crucial than the eventual success of the operation, since success adds another nodal point in an expanding business web. This type of "long-term" debt, in which the obligations of repayment are based on personal relations and are implicit, but are not necessarily regularized in exact measurements of time or money, allows for different strategies of capital utilization by the debtor. The money may or may not be called upon to produce more money within a set amount of time, but this rate of interest is set by the consensus of the family or informal group rather than by an average, standardized rate of interest. Chinese businesses that borrow from savings pools or from within the extended family network, or even from personal connections within the banking system, are in an advantageous position in comparison with other businesses whose loans are constrained by the necessity to return the capital plus interest at an "average" rate of time.

In examining the mobilization of money as capital in western business society, David Harvey writes that money capital is mobilized via the credit system: banks convert the flow of monetary transactions into loan capital, and financial institutions convert money savings into capital. Several constants are assumed in this picture, including the ability of money to "remain constant with respect to both time and space" and to "function as a trusted store of value"; the necessity for credit money to return to its place of origin for redemption; the ability of the financial system to guarantee transactions through legal means; and the ability of the individual both to own property and make contracts, and to belong to fixed and discrete groups or classes.[27]

In this depiction of the credit system, assumptions are made which do not necessarily hold true for the system of credit in Chinese business society. In late Imperial China, trust was not placed in the constancy of money or the financial system, but in various binding yet elastic relationships between people. This type of trust remains critical in contemporary Chinese credit practices, and functions as an assumed constant with re-

27. Harvey, *The Limits to Capital* (Chicago: University of Chicago Press, 1982), 262, 245–47.

spect to time and space. Maintaining long-term relations between creditor and debtor is integral to the success of an expanding, international web of business connections and networks for *all* players involved. These relations require a close, personal tie and an ongoing involvement in the proposed business venture for which money capital was borrowed. Here Harvey's description of the necessary institutionalization of credit trust through the legally founded guarantees of banks (or through a central bank) relies on a western context that is widely divergent from the Hong Kong Chinese model.

Owing to the reliance on business trust and interpersonal relations, the function of money as a constant and reliable "trusted store of value" is less crucial in the context of most Chinese business practices. Other kinds of capital than money capital can be used to augment business transactions over the long term. Mayfair Yang, for example, has examined the importance of gift exchange in China in the 1970s. In the context of a state distributive economy, *guanxi* (social relationships) may be converted into symbolic capital, and that symbolic capital may be converted over time into eventual material profit.[28] I believe that a form of this "gift economy" also operates in juxtaposition with a complex commodity economy in most contemporary overseas Chinese business societies. In gift exchange, things and people are not discrete as they are in a purely money economy, and debts cannot be repaid with exact accuracy. Money, which Simmel and others have claimed reduces everything to quantitative values and infiltrates all aspects of life in modern times,[29] is mediated in its chilling calculability through the indivisibility of people and things within the world of symbolic obligations. The quality of the personal relations integral to the gift economy is also integral to contemporary Chinese business networks and works in perfect symbiosis: obligations cannot be exactly or completely repaid, and thus the binding quality of the relationship continues. At the same time, although different in form from the symbolic capital of a state distributive economy, the potential profitability of symbolic capital conversion for the creditor can be equally lucrative within the context of the contemporary global economy.[30]

28. Mayfair Yang, "The Gift Economy and State Power in China," *Comparative Studies in Society and History* 31 (1989): 45–48.
29. Georg Simmel, *The Philosophy of Money*, ed. David Frisby, trans. Tom Bottomore and David Frisby (London: Routledge, 1990), 444.
30. I have argued elsewhere that the manipulation of information differs in Chinese and Western business practices and, as a form of symbolic capital, is a key component of the "gift economy" in contemporary commodity economies. See Mitchell, "Flexible Circulation in the Pacific Rim."

Overseas Chinese Capitalism and the Contemporary
Global Economy

In this section I will examine why the type of economic practices I have just described are important in the contemporary international articulation of economies across the so-called "Asian Pacific." In the past fifteen years, qualitative shifts have occurred in the international financial system that have had major implications for the use of money and credit worldwide. Perhaps the most important change has been the growing elasticity of national borders, as economic and political sovereignty in the monetary realm have been undermined by the liberalization of international finance.[31] With the rapid and extensive restructuring of the finance system, the nation-state's control over money supply, allocation, and value has declined, the creation and extension of credit and debt have occurred on an unprecedented scale worldwide, and money has become increasingly mobile and unconstrained—moving through time and across space in a manner previously unthinkable.

Through the innovation of new financial instruments, the ability of nation-states to control the production and circulation of money and credit through traditional forms of regulation, including compartmentalization and the restriction of financial institutions to prescribed areas, has been greatly reduced. As financial flows have become unmoored from national economies and increasingly global in focus, there has been an evolution towards a general "deterritorialisation of credit."[32] In the deterritorialized world, money flows unconstrained and unhindered, seeking out investments, exchange rates, and national macroeconomic policies that will bring the securest profit in the least amount of time.

The deterioration of state control, deregulation of the financial systems, reliance on fictitious capital, and quest for short-term profit has led to a risk-prone global economy, where risk has become both systematized and diffused. New innovations in computer and information technology, and the application of these innovations within the institutions of the financial system, have made it difficult if not impossible to track credit risk or even to comprehend exactly where it lies. In the new deterritorialized spaces of the international finance system, with the continued internationalization of accumulation processes via advanced technologies of computerization and communications, all semblance of regulation and control in the banking industry has disappeared.

31. Leyshon and Thrift, "Liberalisation and Consolidation," 50.
32. Leyshon and Thrift, "Liberalisation and Consolidation," 54.

This feral credit system seems completely disconnected from the productive economy. Despite the many disjunctures, however, the productive economy is bound to the wild speculations of the institutions of money capital owing to the likelihood that, through pension funds, insurance companies, and paper money takeovers of various kinds, they own it. In this light, major conflicts between owners and managers are likely to occur with alarming frequency, as those responsible for the creation of profit through the production process clash with those responsible for creating the illusion of profit in the hall of mirrors known as high finance.

This leads to an interesting contrast with the Chinese business firms discussed earlier. In Taiwan, Hong Kong, and most Chinese business societies in Southeast Asia, businesses are owned *and* managed by the extended family. In this scenario, conflicts between owners and managers are unlikely, and conflict between money capital and productive capital will rarely occur. In contrast to Harvey's view of the limits of family enterprise in capitalist practice,[33] in the new fragmented and schizophrenic period of credit creation, the ability of family networks to produce relatively cheap credit for industrial borrowers through internal processes of subsidization is in fact notably efficacious.

During the 1970s global debt crisis, when regulatory authorities attempted to impose measures to increase financial security, numerous western investors became wary of banks as untrustworthy or costly, and chose to lend directly to borrowers without the aid of a banking intermediary.[34] This reliance on informal credit channels and direct, unmediated contact between creditor and debtor resulted in an even greater deterritorialization and deinstitutionalization of the credit system, one that was more akin to the type already familiar to many Chinese businesses. In the practice of seeking informal channels for capital accumulation, Chinese investors and borrowers were far in advance of most western businesspeople, as they were able to rely on previously established social relations that formed the core of their informal credit networks. This gave them a distinct advantage in a number of business situations in Asia and, increasingly, worldwide. Lim writes of the "deregulation and liberalization of financial markets" in many countries in Southeast Asia in the 1980s and 1990s:

> Local Chinese businesses, already the major players in the private sector, were among the first to benefit from these reforms. It was

33. Harvey, The Limits to Capital, 144.
34. Leyshon and Thrift, "Liberalisation and Consolidation," 56.

they who had the capital resources, the technical and managerial expertise, the local and external market contacts, and the local experience and bureaucratic connections, to take advantage of the new business opportunities created by liberalization and privatization. . . . Financial liberalization and the development of local capital markets made it possible for Chinese firms—some of them huge family-owned conglomerates—to raise more capital for expansion.[35]

Hong Kong Real Estate Investments in Vancouver in the 1980s

In the late 1980s Vancouver was the focus of Hong Kong investment in real estate. Many factors were responsible for Vancouver's popularity, including the effort by the Canadian state and municipal politicians to attract "Asian" investors, as well as the diversification of Hong Kong portfolios in anticipation of the changeover to communist control in 1997. Government efforts to attract the Hong Kong Chinese investors included the new and revamped business immigration program. Other draws included financial deregulation and the privatization of land initiated by the British Columbia Premier, William Vander Zalm, in the 1980s. In this part of the essay I examine a few of these policy developments and their implications for land use and land contestation. Some of the friction over land that arose in the late 1980s was clearly exacerbated by the perception of differing economic practices by the Hong Kong Chinese investors in real estate—particularly the channeling of business opportunities along extended family networks. Great friction was also caused by the construction of "monster" houses, speculation in housing, and the removal of trees in west-side communities—actions which many residents felt were undertaken by Hong Kong Chinese buyers.

The Immigrant Investor Program

The primary means of attracting wealthy Hong Kong investments to Canada was to attract the investors themselves via the lure of Canadian citizenship. Since many Hong Kong residents were hoping to establish citizenship in another country prior to 1997, the opportunity to qualify in the Canadian business immigration program and avoid lengthy delays in processing was highly desirable. The business immigration program was

---

35. Linda Lim, "The New Ascendancy of Chinese Business in Southeast Asia: Political, Cultural, Economic, and Business Implications," unpublished paper, 1991.

established in 1978, but enlarged substantially in 1984, the year that the Basic Law treaty was signed in Hong Kong. The "investor" category, added in 1986, was the most important draw for Hong Kong immigrants to Canada in the late 1980s. The investor category required a significant investment in a Canadian enterprise and a personal net worth of at least C$500 thousand.[36]

Owing largely to the success of the business immigration program, immigration from Hong Kong to Canada jumped considerably in the late 1980s. From 1987 to 1989, the composition of applications to the Canadian Commission from wealthy business immigrants in Hong Kong leaped from 1,991, or 12 percent of all Hong Kong applicants to Canada, to 8,001, or 36 percent.[37] The total number of applications from wealthy business immigrants for all three years was nearly a quarter of all Hong Kong applicants. The number of business immigrants who chose British Columbia as their final destination in 1989 and the first six months of 1990 was significantly higher than for any other province in Canada. In 1989, out of a total of 1,121 "entrepreneurs" departing from Hong Kong to Canada, 384 (36 percent) landed in British Columbia. In the same year, out of 406 "investors," 177 (44 percent) chose B.C.[38] As with the general immigrant population from Hong Kong, the vast majority of business immigrants to British Columbia opted to settle and invest in Vancouver.

Real Estate and the Immigrant Investor

Despite government attempts to channel capital into productive sectors, the majority of business immigrant funds, particularly in the early years of the program, went into property investment. Rather than the creation of businesses and employment for Canadians, much of the capital invested in early funds actually served to subsidize developers in pre-planned business ventures. The *Financial Post* estimated that in 1990, foreign investment in privately held real estate in Canada nearly tripled from the 1985 figure of US$1.2 billion. If the debt portion (bank financing) of the real estate trans-

36. For acceptance into British Columbia before 1990, the investor had to commit C$250 thousand for a three-year period to a project approved by the Canadian government. After 1990 this figure increased to C$350 thousand. It was also stipulated that the investor must have a proven track record in business.
37. These numbers assume an average of just under three people per application, which includes family members.
38. These statistics are from the Commission for Canada Immigration Section, Hong Kong.

actions were included, the total investments of 1990 would exceed thirteen billion.[39]

Vancouver was a particular favorite on the global shopping scene. A real estate broker at Goddard and Smith Realty Ltd. said of the real estate market in Vancouver in late 1989: "The saturation point for Hong Kong investment in Vancouver real estate hasn't been reached yet because people now look at this city in a global context, whereas ten years ago only western Canadians were considered potential purchasers."[40] Donald Gutstein, in his 1990 book on Asian investment in Canadian real estate, chronicled numerous individual purchases of property and buildings in Vancouver, demonstrating on a case by case basis the burgeoning investment in Vancouver property from Hong Kong buyers.[41]

Hong Kong immigrants in the "investor" category were responsible for a large portion of real estate development in Vancouver, despite the effort by the provincial government to channel the required C$250 thousand (later C$350 thousand) into manufacturing, trade, and research and development. Investment categories acceptable to the B.C. government under the business immigration program included "developmental real estate," which was defined as real estate to which substantive improvements would be made in order to carry on a business of significant economic benefit. In practice, this meant investment in virtually all commercial buildings, including office buildings, hotels, tourist ventures, and shopping malls.

In addition to the commercial real estate developments, speculative activity affected the residential housing market in Vancouver as well. The "flipping" of houses for profit became common in west-side communities, where some house prices tripled within the space of a single year.[42] In addition to the rapid rise of house prices (and taxes) in these neighborhoods, other changes included the demolition of hundreds of houses and three-story walk-up apartments, and the construction of what became known as "monster" houses and luxury condominiums. In many cases, the large trees

39. Victor Fung, "Hong Kong Investment Funds Pour into Canada," *Financial Post*, 17 June 1991, 18.

40. Lawrence Lim, quoted in Moira Farrow, "Hong Kong Capital Flows Here Ever Faster," *Vancouver Sun*, 21 March 1989.

41. See Donald Gutstein, *The New Landlords: Asian Investment in Canadian Real Estate* (Victoria: Porcépic Books, 1990), chapters 7–10.

42. See, for example, "Flippers Awash in Profits," *Vancouver Sun*, 8 February 1989; and "City Housing Market Flipping Along," *Business*, 9 September 1989.

and natural-looking landscapes of the older homes were demolished along with the buildings, causing a particular angst in a city that long prided itself on its leafy suburban boulevards.

Selling the Spectacle: The Privatization and Sale of the Expo Lands

Nine days after the closing of the world fair, Expo '86, a new Socred government, under the premiership of William Vander Zalm, won the provincial election in British Columbia. Vander Zalm immediately initiated a sweeping land privatization campaign that necessitated the sale of vast quantities of undeveloped and enormously lucrative land in British Columbia—including the Expo site itself. This site comprised nearly one-sixth of Vancouver's entire downtown land area. Under the new privatization strategy of the Vander Zalm government, these lands, which had been acquired at great cost under the previous government, were scheduled for sale back to the private sector.

In 1988, the Expo land was purchased by the Hong Kong property magnate, Li Ka-shing. This sale, and the subsequent development of the land by Li's son, Victor, caused a heated controversy in Vancouver. Part of the local anger stimulated by this massive real estate transaction was the belief that the provincial government had sold the land to Li at a fraction of its worth in order to attract even more investment to the city and the province from other Hong Kong buyers.[43] It was apparent to most Vancouverites that the effort to attract investment from Asia was linked to the desire to make Vancouver a "world class" city, able to integrate and compete effectively with other global cities in the Pacific Rim marketplace. The other source of local anger was the belief that both Li Ka-shing and his son, Victor Li, channeled real estate opportunities and information primarily to other Chinese businesspeople. This perception was fueled by the exclusive and rapid three-hour sale of 216 luxury Vancouver condominiums in The Regatta to Hong Kong buyers in 1988, and by the sale of large chunks of the Expo land to Hong Kong and Singapore Chinese buyers in 1988 and 1989.

43. It was common knowledge that, due to Li's worldwide reputation for savvy real estate deals, many buyers followed his global leads. Indeed, for two years after Li's purchase of the Expo lands, Vancouver was the hottest property market in the world.

Anti–Hong Kong Chinese Racism and the Rise
of Community Organizations

The friction caused by the massive changes in Vancouver's urban environment was expressed in a number of different ways. In 1989, a series of articles in the major local newspaper, the *Vancouver Sun*, focused on the connection between Hong Kong investments in real estate and the rapid rise of house prices. In an article entitled, "The Hong Kong Connection: How Asian Money Fuels Housing Market," reporter Gillian Shaw discussed the large percentage (85 percent) of Asian buyers in offshore purchases, and noted that "the majority of those were from Hong Kong." She also stressed that many of the new buyers were paying for the houses *in cash*.[44] Other article titles in the series included "Computer Shopping for B.C. Property"; "Investment Anger Confuses Hong Kong"; and "Money is King in Hong Kong: Entrepreneurs Find Paradise in the Streets of Hong Kong." In many of these articles there was a strong emphasis on identifying "essential" Hong Kong Chinese characteristics: these were categorized as a tendency to speculate in the housing market for profit, an aggressive drive toward material wealth and its subsequent ostentatious display, and a general disregard for the natural environment.

These essentialized representations had an incendiary effect on local residents, who were becoming increasingly anxious about housing affordability, neighborhood "character," and the loss of local control over urban development. Hong Kong Chinese investors and home buyers were increasingly targeted as the agents responsible for unwanted neighborhood change, and many urban social movements became imbricated in a racial discourse. Much of the growing antagonism against Chinese buyers was greatly exacerbated by the greater wealth of many of the new immigrants, and by the purchase by some of the "monster" houses burgeoning around the city.

Several of the community organizations that were established during this period were expressly concerned with these kinds of neighborhood change. The Kerrisdale Concerned Citizens for Affordable Housing protested the demolition of walk-up apartments and houses, the Kerrisdale-Granville Homeowners' Association battled the destruction of neighborhood trees, and the Shaughnessy Heights Property Owners Association

44. Gillian Shaw, "The Hong Kong Connection: How Asian Money Fuels the Housing Market," *Vancouver Sun*, 18 February 1989. Other stories on Hong Kong were published on 17, 18, 20, and 21 March 1989.

attempted to amend zoning laws to limit the size of new houses that could be built in the neighborhood. Although these movements were publicly concerned with local control over the urban environment, the strong feelings against large-scale Hong Kong investment in commercial and residential real estate was made clear in association meetings and in a number of interviews with me.

Fashioning the Transnational Cosmopolitan

In letters to the editor, to the city council, and to the Vancouver Planning Department, and in media articles in the late 1980s, it was evident that the two main explicit sources of friction involving Hong Kong Chinese investors and older Vancouver residents were the fear of exclusion in business dealings and the anxiety surrounding the transformation of neighborhoods.[45] The barrage of articles in the media concerning both these topics, and the linkage of "Asian" investment in the built environment with the profound changes occurring in the city, spurred a strong local reaction against further investment and immigration from Hong Kong. In addition to the growth of community organizations against urban change (some of which, such as RSVP and The Spokesman, were explicitly anti-Asian), racist incidents against Chinese Canadians increased during this time period.[46] Methods of combatting the increased friction in the 1990s included appropriation of "positive" Orientalist representations of Chinese by wealthy Hong Kong–Canadian businessmen like Victor Li. At the same time, there was a strong effort to acculturate the middle classes to a new "transnational cosmopolitanism" through programs like *Meet with Success* in Hong Kong.

Victor Li: The Good Canadian Businessman

When Li Ka-shing brought three new Chinese partners into the Expo land deal in 1989, his son Victor reassured jittery Vancouver politicians that the Li family would maintain major control of the extensive downtown property. He emphasized that Concord Pacific, the company leading the development, was not a subsidiary of, or related to, the massive Hong Kong

45. As mentioned earlier, racism was also a factor, though rarely "explicit."
46. According to a coordinator at SUCCESS (United Chinese Community Enrichment Services Society), incidents of racism against Chinese Canadians rose markedly in the 1980s.

and Singapore conglomerates owned by the other partners, but a private company "financed mainly by family money."[47] Victor Li's remarks were intended to placate local Vancouver citizens, politicians, and journalists, who were becoming increasingly vocal against the perceived sell-out of the Expo lands.

The strategy of winning acceptance on the local level was bolstered by the hiring of Stanley Kwok, a highly respected Chinese-Canadian architect in Vancouver, to become senior vice-president of the company. At the time of his hiring, Kwok was friends with the former Vancouver planning director, Raymond Spaxman, as well as personally acquainted with three of the major shareholders in Concord Pacific: Li Ka-shing, Cheng Yu-tung, and Lee Shau-kee. Kwok was recruited by Li to "make Pacific Place happen and, not incidentally, to build bridges between Concord and Vancouver's business establishment." Grace McCarthy, Minister of Economic Development, said of Kwok, "Stanley is a terrific bridge between the Chinese and Canadian business communities. He bridges it well and he brings them together, and that's very important."[48]

The necessity of a spokesperson to act as a "bridge" between the Chinese and Canadian communities was apparent as incidents of racism increased in Vancouver in the late 1980s. The perception of a difference in the economic practices of the Hong Kong Chinese capitalists, and the fear of exclusion from family-oriented businesses, was reflected in the vitriolic reaction against the sale of The Regatta luxury condominiums in Hong Kong in 1988. Following the uproar over Li's marketing of the condominiums, he again attempted to smooth local feathers in a press conference. He spoke of his commitment to Canada and of his Canadian citizenship, and emphasized his intention for Concord Pacific to "be a good blue-chip Canadian company."[49]

Li's effort to appear as a "good Canadian businessman" was a position also advocated by British Columbia's Lieutenant Governor, David Lam. Lam, a Hong Kong Chinese immigrant of the late 1960s, who became a millionaire from his investments in the Vancouver property market during

47. *Globe and Mail*, 21 June 1989, A11. Li Ka-shing holds a fifty percent interest in Concord Pacific.
48. Quoted in Robert Williamson, "Kwok's Connections Open Doors to Asia," *Globe and Mail*, 6 April 1992, B1.
49. Quoted in Anne Fletcher, "Younger Li Tries Hard To Be A 'Good Canadian Businessman,'" *Financial Post*, 9 January 1989, 4.

that boom period, often spoke of the need to "keep what you have but be a Canadian."[50] When the Vancouver housing market heated up in 1988 and 1989, Lam worried that Hong Kong speculation in property would contribute to the growing racial discord in the city.[51] He spoke frequently of the need to assimilate to Canadian norms, but at the same time to maintain Chinese traditional values. In his appearance in the *Meet with Success* video, Lam gave advice for new immigrants. He called on the immigrants to "adapt," and added, "very quickly you'll join the mainstream. You can keep your culture, but be a member of your new community. It is possible to maintain your Chinese roots, but also develop the Canadian flower."

The connection between the business practices employed by the Li family and the fear and antagonism expressed by Vancouver residents against the marketing of condominiums in Hong Kong was apparent to many politicians and businessmen. David Lam's and Victor Li's awareness of the problem encouraged them to represent themselves as "good Canadian businessmen and bridge-builders" to the Vancouver public. Public attempts to herald Canadian citizenship functioned also as a method of reducing friction and facilitating the articulation of international economic networks. These efforts were accompanied by reminders of the superior economic power and the ultimate mobility of global capital.[52]

50. Quoted in *Seniors Advocate*, September/October 1989.
51. See "Hong Kong–Born Lieutenant Governor Warns: Grabby Speculators Risk Creating Racial Discord," *Daily Commercial News*, 23 February 1989, 9, 11.
52. At the same time that Li made several moves to calm fears of marketing exclusion and of the future flipping of the Concord Pacific lands, he also made it clear that he would not tolerate racial prejudice. He noted that negative reactions to Hong Kong investments in Vancouver were being perceived in Hong Kong (and elsewhere) as largely motivated by racism. As racism was bad for the "business climate," he warned that economic projects in the city were being adversely affected, and that Vancouver stood to lose millions of dollars in future capital investment. He said of the reaction of Hong Kong businessmen to the uneasy mood toward foreign property investment in Vancouver in 1989: "I think they're taking a cautious attitude. I don't think right now there's a mass pulling away of investments. . . . But I've seen and I've heard from close business associates that they are slowing down on activities and taking a wait-and-see attitude." To further his point, Li discussed the example of Australia, which had already lost foreign business because of its perceived racism: "Australia, we've absolutely pulled out. Most of the Australian investment is in small businesses, retail and those things. But I know a lot of friends, together with our group, that have absolutely pulled out, deliberately pulled out of that country because of the racist or white policy there." Quoted in *Equity*, June 1989, 26.

Meet with Success: Shaping the Middle Class Emigrant

Cross-cultural training programmes have been developed to incul-
cate sensitivity, basic *savoir faire*, and perhaps an appreciation of
those other cultures which are of special strategic importance to
one's goals.[53]

Meet with Success was produced by the Canadian Club of Hong
Kong in the spring of 1990. When a Hong Kong applicant to Canada was
accepted as an immigrant, he or she was invited to attend a *Meet with
Success* program. The invitation to the program was extended by the Commission for Canada in the same packet as the Canadian visa. Although
attendance at *Meet with Success* was voluntary, there was a ninety percent
turnout each week. One person involved in the program confided in an interview: "some think it is required because it comes from the Commission."[54]
The program was offered every week and consisted of a video, a slide
show, and a question and answer session. An informational packet with a
long survey entitled "Meet with Success: Personal Inventory of Values" was
handed to each person upon arrival.

When I attended the program in Hong Kong I realized that I had
already seen the video, which is shown weekly at immigration and investment seminars in Vancouver as well.[55] The video, entitled "Being Canadian,"
depicts a young Hong Kong couple arriving in Vancouver. The film begins
by describing Vancouver as a city "on the edge of the Pacific Rim." The
narrator, who is a recent immigrant to Vancouver from Hong Kong, says in
Cantonese, "Let me tell you about Vancouver." He is filmed in his home, an
average-looking house on the east side of the city. He says reflectively, "I
love this city or else I would not have moved here" and also, "but lifestyles
here are different."[56] The implication is that he chose to move to Vancouver
for *love* rather than for the pursuit of profit. A Chinese woman then appears
who reiterates the phrase, "life here is so different." She adds, "The first
thing to do was to learn English. Then the new culture and lifestyle. . . ."

53. Hannerz, "Cosmopolitans and Locals in World Culture," 245.
54. Interview with a *Meet with Success* volunteer, Hong Kong, July 1991.
55. The immigrant and investment seminars were given at the World Trade Centre in
Vancouver from January through June 1991. The seminar I attended was focused on
the business immigration program. Although these programs were designed to facilitate
business linkages, the "Being Canadian" acculturation video was shown at the beginning
of every meeting.
56. The narration is in Cantonese with English subtitles.

At this point in the film there are a number of images of downtown Vancouver with a running narration that is consistently didactic. Some of the phrases are as follows: "People here are busy but orderly"; "they don't make unnecessary noise"; "in Canada most people are polite"; "people treat you nicely and politely." One scene involves shopping at the vegetable markets in Granville Island (Vancouver). The narrator says, "People don't bargain loudly. They are very polite to each other. I believe every immigrant will come to like this lifestyle." In another image, several cars are shown at an intersection. The narrator says, "They are patient. Each waits his turn so it doesn't become a traffic jam." There is a scene in a garden, where a Vancouver woman educates a Chinese man about gardening and Christmas. The Chinese man says thoughtfully, "You see, this is our neighbor. She not only helps her neighbors, she also makes her garden beautiful." Most interestingly, there are several images of flowers, large trees, and natural landscaping, which are obviously filmed in Vancouver's west-side suburbs. While the camera pans over the gardens and homes, there appears an image of an extremely large, ostentatious house. The narrator says, "This is a Vancouver neighborhood. Residents are very proud of their gardens. Newer, bigger houses are a new trend. Sometimes the new houses look out of place."

According to two of my sources involved with the planning of *Meet with Success* in 1989, the program was formulated as a direct result of the negative international publicity over the "monster" house controversy in Vancouver in 1988 and 1989.[57] One woman said that in addition to problems surrounding the "monster" house issue latched onto by negative media reports, there were other social conflicts, including "the ostentatious flaunting of wealth," and "double parking by Chinese students outside schools who just paid the fines and continued parking there." She noted that it was "not a smooth adaptation" when Hong Kong Chinese immigrants arrived in Vancouver, and that many Canadians greatly resented the "Yacht People." According to her, the Canadian Club organizers in Hong Kong were concerned about this friction, especially because they did not want Canada to be tarred with the same racist image that was being applied to Australia at that time.

Another organizer told me that the attempt to help Hong Kong immigrants learn about Canada was an attempt to avoid confrontation and

---

57. There were television reports on the controversy on CBC Pacific and TVB Hong Kong, and an article series in the *Vancouver Sun* and the *Vancouver Province*.

"make life easier" for all involved. She noted that by showing various visual images of Canadian life it was possible to demonstrate cultural norms and unacceptable violations of those norms (such as removing trees and building large houses), without having to verbalize the problem, which might be interpreted as racist. The images of unacceptable violations was decided on by members of the board; according to a white Canadian member, the Chinese members of the board wanted to be tougher on cultural "problem areas" such as spitting. In the final decision, however, this was rejected as too patronizing.[58]

In addition to the video, a packet was given to each member of the *Meet with Success* audience. The packet contained a personal inventory of values questionnaire, a series of fact sheets, and the list of contributors to the program. The questionnaire, in both English and Chinese, addresses concerns about lifestyle and consumption. It begins:

> The following questions represent a checklist for your reflection before and after you arrive in Canada. They introduce a wide range of issues and decisions that all Canadians face every day. These are personal values; the choices are yours but please make the commitment to understanding the economic, social and political environment within which you will be making them. Detailed information is contained in the accompanying "Fact Sheets" in this kit.[59]

The respondent is then asked to read several statements and circle "Important" or "Not So Important" in the margin to indicate his or her "personal values." Although it is stressed that these are individual, personal decisions, the didactic intent is clear. One of my informants involved with the program said, "It is their choice as to whether or not they want to modify their behavior. We are just alerting them as to possible conflict areas." The questions in the survey range from the work environment, housing, and family life, to multiculturalism, social skills, and the assimilation process.

The "right" answers to the personal inventory of values are located in the "Fact Sheet" section of the packet. For example, in the category "Housing Options," statements such as the following educate the immigrant about the appropriate feelings to have concerning the home:

> Houses have historically been a good investment in Canada but the gains are not all financial. Communities of house owners tend to be

58. Interviews, Hong Kong, July 1991.
59. From the "Personal Inventory of Values" section of the *Meet with Success* packet.

stable and relatively friendly. Relationships with neighbours are important. Houses are a big commitment in time and lifestyle as well as money.

Here, the warning against the disruptions caused by speculation is clear. As in the video, the correct purchase of a house is shown to be for the love of the neighborhood or the house itself, not for financial gain. In the section "Choosing a House and Neighborhood," the concern about frictions caused by the "monster" houses is broached in an even more warning tone. In this case, if the norms of the society are not willingly assumed, the legal system can be brought to bear on the most egregious offenders of good taste:

> The style of the houses and the amount of green space are serious considerations. Conformity to existing standards is a custom that in some cases is prescribed by municipal by-law. Plans to significantly enlarge houses, change the style of the exterior décor or cut down trees may be offensive if it is legal at all.

In the "Multiculturalism Fact Sheet," the immigrants' responsibility to acculturate themselves into Canadian society is underscored at the same time that the advantages of cosmopolitanism are upheld. Immigrant responsibilities include learning the language and history of the host society, participating in community and political life, and tolerating cultural, racial, and religious differences. "Ways of Preserving Your Own Cultural Background" describes the manner in which both the responsibilities of acculturation and the rights of retaining some features of "Chineseness" can be accommodated. Possible ways of preserving Chinese identity are to: "Join Chinese community groups. Teach your children the Chinese language. Participate in multicultural festivals such as Toronto's 'Caravan.' Listen to Chinese radio, watch Chinese TV, and read Chinese newspapers."[60] Like the pragmatic advice from David Lam, the message of assimilating the cultural values of both the host society and Chinese society is fairly straightforward: it is possible to be both "Canadian" and "Chinese" through a strategic manipulation of cultural citizenship.

This fashioning of the middle class Hong Kong immigrant was promoted by the wealthy patrons and sponsors of both Canadian and Hong Kong society.[61] The video "Being Canadian" was filmed in Vancouver and

---

60. From the "Multiculturalism—Fact Sheet" section of the *Meet with Success* packet.
61. The Canadian Club program was ostensibly directed toward all Hong Kong emigrants to Canada. Most of the very wealthy, however, had already received Canadian citizen-

funded by the Asia Pacific Foundation, a major organization involved with fostering Canadian-Pacific Rim connections. Patrons of the *Meet with Success* program (contributing C$25 thousand or more) included David and Dorothy Lam, the Government of British Columbia, Vincent Lee—the president of the Canadian Club and an executive of Canadian City Capital Ltd., Michael Y. L. Kan, Dr. Chan Shiu Chick, Diana Foong Pui Ling, Helen Foong Pui Ming, Chan Wai Lim, Ng Kin Shek, and Ray Man Leung of S. Megga Telecommunications Ltd. The major contributors included, among others, The Canadian Maple Leaf Fund Ltd. (an immigrant investor program), Michael Goldberg—the chairman of the Vancouver International Financial Center, twenty-one people connected with the Canadian government, and three people associated with the Canadian Imperial Bank of Commerce. All of these individuals and organizations were interested in improving and increasing Pacific Rim connections.

Conclusion

Chinese business practices, including the reliance on extended family networks, informal credit relations, and trust, were especially effective for overseas Hong Kong investments during the economic restructuring of the late 1980s. In Vancouver, this effectiveness translated into a number of successful real estate transactions involving the purchase and development of commercial and residential property. The remarkable scale of Hong Kong property investments in Vancouver during this time was made known through widespread media coverage of the sale and development of the urban mega-project planned on the former Expo site, and by the public controversy over "monster" housing and tree removal in west-side neighborhoods.

Owing to a strong public perception that Hong Kong Chinese immigrants were responsible for many of Vancouver's unwelcome urban changes, the public disapproval of foreign investment and immigration policies grew considerably in the latter part of the decade. Anger toward the Hong Kong Chinese investors and immigrants focused on two areas: the exclusive marketing and sale of Vancouver property to other Chinese buyers, and the ostentatious display of wealth. A number of community organiza-

---

ship or visas by the time the program was initiated in 1990. In my two visits to *Meet with Success*, it appeared to me from the apparel of the respondents and the questions they asked that they were not of Hong Kong's superstrata society.

tions contesting urban change were initiated at this time, most with the express purpose of halting demolitions and limiting house size and tree removal, but some that were also clearly racist and xenophobic.

In reaction to burgeoning social and cultural antagonism, the Canadian and Hong Kong capitalist elite, backed by the Canadian state, established the acculturation program, *Meet with Success*, in Hong Kong. This program was primarily targeted at middle class emigrants to Vancouver, who were educated about Canada, but also about the necessity to adopt a cosmopolitan subjectivity. The manipulation of Orientalist codings was employed at the same time by elite businessmen such as Victor Li, who successfully represented himself and his company as good "Canadian" stock, and also as key bridge-builders in the Pacific Rim business community.

In this setting, the ongoing framing of "Chineseness' and "Canadianness" promoted by the Canadian state [62] is simultaneously reframed by wealthy Hong Kong Chinese businesspeople.[63] However, the ability to employ this kind of strategic repositioning is clearly predicated on the material wealth and cosmopolitan savvy of this elite transnational group. In order to reduce the cultural frictions caused by Chinese immigrants of other classes, who may not have the same cosmopolitan "cultural capital," as discussed by Hannerz and Bourdieu, refashioning efforts aimed at these immigrants are coproduced with the Canadian state and the Canadian business elite.[64] In this manner, the "positive" Chinese roles of "bridge-builder" and "*homo economicus*" can be promulgated,[65] while the "negative," disruptive roles of "profiteering speculator" and "*nouveau riche*" are elided. By reducing conflict over the meaning of the urban environment and over differing economic practices, foreign investment in real estate and the spatial integration of the city can proceed more smoothly and efficiently.

62. See Mitchell, "Multiculturalism"; and Kay Anderson, *Vancouver's Chinatown: Racial Discourse in Canada, 1875–1980* (Montreal: McGill-Queen's University Press, 1991).
63. See Ong, "On the Edge of Empires."
64. See Hannerz, "Cosmopolitans and Locals in World Culture"; and Bourdieu, *Distinction.*
65. Ong, "On the Edge of Empires."

Postmodernism and American Cultural Difference:
Dispatches, Mystery Train,
and The Art of Japanese Management

Thomas Carmichael

Postmodern discourse has always been most at home on the margins. Through its cultural practices and the pronouncements of theory, postmodernism has characteristically presented itself as the sign of the eccentric or of the many ways in which difference might be enabled to speak outside of, and in opposition to, the traditional encodings of gender, politics, authority, and ethnicity. Within contemporary American culture, however, postmodernism might also be read as a discourse that is at once liberating and cynically symptomatic; its subversive irony and disruptive gestures can be, and have been, seen as both resistance and "hip" resignation. This is perhaps the inescapable condition of postmodern culture, particularly if the postmodern is read as the cultural correlative of late capitalism, and it is this homely condition that I want to address in what follows.

If postmodernism might be defined in Jean-François Lyotard's terms as an "incredulity toward metanarratives," then the question of postmodernism's ground for the authority of difference might also be put into question.[1] It is one thing to agree with Edward W. Said that "there is no center, no

<hr>

1. Jean-François Lyotard, *The Postmodern Condition: A Report on Knowledge*, trans. Brian Massumi, Theory and History of Literature, vol. 10 (Minneapolis: University of Minnesota Press, 1984), xxiv.

inertly given and accepted authority, no fixed barriers ordering human history, even though authority, order, and distinction exist"; it is quite another to embrace the assumption of Baudrillard, that "depth isn't what it used to be," or, as he puts it elsewhere and at greater length, "when the real is no longer what it used to be, nostalgia assumes its full meaning. There is a proliferation of myths of origin and signs of reality; of second-hand truth, objectivity, and authenticity."[2] For Baudrillard, the decay of depth is, of course, a function of the increasingly frenetic circulation of capital under the laws of equivalence and exchange. While this description is perhaps hampered by his all too emphatic insistence upon the pervasiveness of the hyperreal, it would be foolish to deny Baudrillard's insight, because it is from within this matrix of simulation and reproduction that postmodern American culture begins to confront claims of cultural difference. Fredric Jameson, for example, asks us to conceive of postmodernism much as Baudrillard does, as an explosion of the cultural sphere, but one in which a culture of the same is simply the realm of infinite replication; within this cultural field, difference emerges at the level of commodity or "neo-ethnicity," what Jameson describes as "something of a yuppified phenomenon, and thereby without too many mediations a matter of fashion and market."[3] And Lyotard comes to the same conclusion when he ponders the present notion of cultural "eclecticism," or what he terms "the degree zero of contemporary general culture: one listens to reggae, watches a western, eats McDonald's food for lunch and local cuisine for dinner, wears Paris perfume in Tokyo and 'retro' clothes in Hong Kong."[4] The notion of difference as commodity is easy to mock, but the question of cultural difference at the level of lived human relations and their representations within a culture governed by the image poses a more disturbing and difficult problem. Jameson refers to it as "the embarrassing historical question of whether the tolerance of difference, as a social fact, is not the result of social homogenization and standardization and the obliteration of genuine social difference in the first place" (*PCLLC*, 341). For the purposes of this discussion, I want to redirect this "embar-

2. Edward W. Said, "Opponents, Audiences, Constituencies," in *The Anti-Aesthetic: Essays on Postmodern Culture*, ed. Hal Foster (Port Townsend, Wash.: Bay Press, 1983), 145; Jean Baudrillard, *Cool Memories*, trans. Chris Turner (New York: Verso, 1990), 6; and Jean Baudrillard, *Simulations*, trans. Paul Foss, Paul Patton, and Philip Beitchman (New York: Semiotext(e), 1983), 12.
3. Fredric Jameson, *Postmodernism, or, The Cultural Logic of Late Capitalism* (Durham: Duke University Press, 1991), 341; hereafter cited parenthetically as *PCLLC*.
4. Lyotard, *Postmodern Condition*, 76.

rassing historical question" toward both the more generalized possibility of representing the other and the form that this impossible/possibility takes in the representation and appropriation of Asian difference in postmodern America.

My first consideration leads directly to the question of the other as the scene of the representation of difference, and specifically to Julia Kristeva's recent remarks on the notions of foreignness and the other. In *Strangers to Ourselves*, Kristeva wants us to envision a social possibility, a "paradoxical community": "The multinational society would thus be the consequence of an extreme individualism, but conscious of its discontents and limits, knowing only indomitable people ready-to-help-themselves in their weakness, a weakness whose other name is our radical strangeness."[5] The foreigner, Kristeva argues, confronts us with a projection of our own strangeness, and, in her terms, "this means to imagine and make oneself other for oneself"; feeling foreign with respect to questions of identity and affiliation is, for Kristeva, an emancipatory condition: "Whether a constraint or a choice, a psychological evolution or a political fate, this position as a *difference being* might appear to be the goal of human autonomy" (*STO*, 13, 19, 41). Kristeva's text is, of course, a response to current tensions in France, but it is curious that a meditation on the notion of difference situates its own preoccupation within the disappearance of the ground for differentiation. According to Kristeva, "the issue of foreigners comes up for a people when, having gone through the spirit of religion, it again encounters an ethical concern . . . [ellipsis in text] in order not to die of cynicism of stock market deals" (*STO*, 40). Throughout *Strangers to Ourselves*, Kristeva returns to the uncomfortable proximity of the cosmopolitan and the cynical, and one might well argue that this discomforting association is a direct consequence of her reading of a recognition of the foreign as a sign of absence, of that which, in her words, "comes in the place and stead of the death of God" (*STO*, 60–61). At the same time, Kristeva tells us that the foreign is simply that old familiar friend, the uncanny, or the *unheimlich*, but as in her discussion of the social significance of the foreign, this attempt to make the strangers feel at home in the familiar world of Freudian discourse simply returns us to the psychoanalytic variant of the "embarrassing historical question" with which we began.

5. Julia Kristeva, *Strangers to Ourselves*, trans. Leon S. Roudiez (New York: Columbia University Press, 1991), 195; hereafter cited parenthetically as *STO*.

Speaking of Freud's significance for her own history of the foreign, Kristeva remarks, "Uncanny, foreignness is within us: we are our own foreigners, we are divided" (*STO*, 181). But to be "other for oneself," which is what the *unheimlich* comes to signify in her discussion, recalls two other formulations that complete this preliminary consideration of the possibilities of a postmodern other. The first is Sartre's description of an antagonistic, humiliating other: "The appearance of the Other . . . causes the appearance in the situation of an aspect which I did not wish, of which I am not master, and which on principle escapes me since it is *for the Other*."[6] Unlike Freud's uncanny homebody, or what he calls "that class of the frightening which leads back to what is known of old and long familiar," Sartre's other, and by implication the other who appears in Kristeva's text, is closer to the position elaborated by Lacan when he suggests that "one can speak of code only if it is already the code of the Other," or, as he puts it elsewhere, if the subject can be defined only as an "effect" of the signifier, then "the subject depends on the signifier and . . . the signifier is first of all in the field of the Other."[7] It is here, also, that one can join the discourse that surrounds subjectivity with the problem of representation in a cultural field that ruthlessly homogenizes difference to the "zero degree" of eclecticism.

There are many postmodern texts and many texts from the postmodern period that one might choose to demonstrate this notion. Michael Herr's *Dispatches*, Jim Jarmusch's film *Mystery Train*, and Richard Pascale and Anthony G. Athos's *The Art of Japanese Management* are eccentric choices, but I want to suggest by these choices and their combination two further lines of consideration: first, the pervasiveness of the dilemma of representation and cultural difference in postmodern discourse; second, that it is at the level of the popular that we confront the various levels and forms of this problem most acutely.

Like Jim Jarmusch's earlier work, his 1989 film, *Mystery Train*, is an ironic representation of desire and difference within a cultural matrix per-

---

6. Jean-Paul Sartre, *Being and Nothingness: A Phenomenological Essay on Ontology*, trans. Hazel E. Barnes (New York: Washington Square Press, 1966), 355, Sartre's emphasis.

7. Sigmund Freud, "The Uncanny," in *Art and Literature*, vol. 14 of *The Pelican Freud Library*, trans. James Strachey (London: Penguin, 1985), 340; Jacques Lacan, *Écrits: A Selection*, trans. Alan Sheridan (New York: W. W. Norton, 1977), 305; and Lacan, *The Four Fundamental Concepts of Psychoanalysis*, ed. Jacques-Alain Miller, trans. Alan Sheridan (New York: W. W. Norton, 1981), 207, 205.

vaded by simulation and the manufactured nostalgia of popular culture. The film's three narratives, overlapping and interconnected in real time, are presented sequentially so as to emphasize both the repetition of the same and the endlessly displaced and deferred trajectory of desire in its successive manifestations. *Mystery Train* is set in Memphis, here presented initially as the sign of American cultural authenticity, and the film's title, as well as the Elvis Presley rendition of the Junior Parker song from which the title is taken, and the opening shots of arriving in Memphis by train across the Mississippi are all designed to reinforce that claim. But Memphis is also the site of a nostalgia for the simulacrum par excellence, the deceased icon, Elvis Presley. Characteristically sentimental portraits of Elvis (preferably painted on black velvet) hang in every room of the hotel in which much of the film takes place, and the film's unmotivated signs and empty repetitions everywhere signal an endlessly deferred and ungrounded process of signification. On one level, this return to a perceived origin of the culture of rock and roll is simply the occasion for an exploration of the humorous miscues of naïve cultural difference, and in this respect *Mystery Train* is continuous with the ironic portrayals of difference in Jarmusch's earlier *Stranger than Paradise* (1984) and *Down by Law* (1986).[8] While this might suggest that various forms of European and Asian difference in *Mystery Train* are to be set over against some authentic American cultural discourse, Jarmusch's film emphatically demonstrates the more commonsense postmodern view that America is equally its own simulation. In this respect, it is most obviously to be read together with *Stranger than Paradise* and *Down by Law*.

In the earliest of these films, Eva (Eszter Balint) arrives in America from Hungary to visit her cousin Willie (John Lurie) in New York and her Aunt Lottie (Cecillia Stark) in Cleveland. Each of the film's three American locations resembles nothing more closely than the gray, decrepit industrial landscape associated with a Cold War Eastern Europe. As Jarmusch himself has remarked of *Stranger than Paradise*, the conventional media representations of Eastern Europe as "completely gray and depressing, with people toiling in factories all day and coming home to freeze in their little apartments" is also an American representation of itself: "I'm reversing that stereotype by showing that the same could be said for the United

---

8. Jarmusch's first film, *Permanent Vacation*, was made while the director was a graduate film student at New York University. The films considered here are, in chronological order: Jim Jarmusch, dir., *Stranger than Paradise*, Cinesthesia Productions, Inc., 1984; *Down by Law*, Black Snake Inc., 1986; and *Mystery Train*, Mystery Train Inc., 1989.

States."[9] This is possible, Jarmusch reminds us, not simply because these are ideologically laden representations but rather because the claims to difference in America are themselves specious, or as he puts it, "there's a certain continuous tone in America, especially if you don't have lots of money."[10] This is often hilariously true in the film, particularly when Willie's sidekick Eddie asks him, in a moment of reflective curiosity, whether Cleveland resembles Budapest. The drive toward homogenization, suggested by Eddie's idle query, is also represented in *Stranger than Paradise* at the level of cultural difference. In a phone conversation with his Aunt Lottie, for example, Willie maintains that he doesn't consider himself part of this family of Hungarian immigrants and reinforces this on the linguistic level by insisting that everyone speak English. He also defends himself against Eddie's probing of his Hungarian roots, and he cuts off this conversation by insisting that he is as American as anyone. While Willie seeks to insist upon his personal difference, his place in a homogeneous America that would forget his Hungarian origins, he is ironically led, at the end of the film, to board a plane bound for Hungary in mistaken pursuit of his cousin Eva. In this respect, the ironies of cultural difference and its eradication in America are also the ironies and frustrations of gender relations in *Stranger than Paradise*. Willie acts hostilely and begrudgingly toward Eva but is also attracted to her, and the frustrations of their relationship suggest again an absence of a ground for communicative possibility that is signed in the text by the oppressively depthless cultural sphere provided by the American landscape. The same can be said for Jarmusch's *Down by Law*, in which the urban decay of New Orleans provides the site of a return to the ironic frustrations of cultural and gender encodings. This film also looks forward to *Mystery Train* in its preoccupation with specifically American forms of actualization and fulfillment. Structurally, the film is a succession of escapes and enslavements, in which fantasies of choice and possibility are always haunted by a world of crime and marginality in which these fantasies are repeatedly undermined. But the film repeatedly foregrounds these fantasies as a distinctly American cultural code. Roberto (Roberto Benigni), an Italian immigrant, fondly recites Walt Whitman as well as Frost's "The Road not Taken" to his American companions, Jack (John Lurie) and Zack (Tom Waits); however, these texts are always recalled in prison or in rooms resembling prison cells, and at the

9. Richard Linnett, "As American as You Are: Jim Jarmusch and *Stranger than Paradise*," *Cineaste* 14, no. 1 (1985): 26.
10. Harlan Jacobson, "Interview with Jim Jarmusch," *Film Comment* 21, no. 1 (1985): 62.

end of the film, Jack and Zack are forced to make a decision at a fork in the road of a Louisiana swamp, in which choice and direction make no apparent difference. The sameness that Jarmusch observes at the edge of American material abundance is presented in *Down by Law* as the condition that is obscured by characteristically American projections of liberal self-reliance. The possibility of any contemporary solution to the postmodern dilemma of relentless indifference is only ironically posited here. Roberto discovers Nicoletta (Nicoletta Braschi), also a recent Italian immigrant with a somewhat imperfect command of English, at her isolated Italian restaurant, Luigi's Tin Top, on a deserted road deep in a Louisiana forest, and he decides to remain with Nicoletta. As the film suggests, however, Roberto and Nicoletta are as different as they are impossible, and here the representation of the other signals an unbridgeable gulf between the successful escape of Roberto and his relationship with Nicoletta and the undifferentiated experiences and frustrating relationships of the two Americans with interchangeable names, Jack and Zack.

Jarmusch's preoccupations with the encodings of postmodern culture and gender are consistent: The second of the three narratives in *Mystery Train* essentially recapitulates the fantasy of fulfillment portrayed in the relationship of Roberto and Nicoletta in *Down by Law*, and the third returns to the worlds of deferral and disappointment we find exemplified in the figures of Willie and Eddie in *Stranger than Paradise* and in Jack and Zack in *Down by Law*.[11] But the first of the three narratives in *Mystery Train* is the focus of my considerations here, particularly for its extension of these preoccupations to the representation of a specifically Asian difference. Entitled "Far from Yokohama," it presents the pilgrimage of two adolescent Japanese lovers to Memphis, the site of Graceland and Sun Studios. The young Japanese woman, Mitzuko (Youki Kudoh), possesses an imperfect command of English idioms (her characteristic greeting is "Hi!, goodnight"), and her post-punk attire, like that of her companion, Jun (Masatoshi Nagase), stands in sharp contrast to the declining, provincial Memphis they encounter. The first figure Jun and Mitzuko meet in Memphis is an African American who asks them for a match, and this figure, although apparently local in every respect, curiously enough, speaks some Japanese.

11. That these narratives are essentially repetitions of the thematic preoccupations and narrative configurations of Jarmusch's earlier work is also indicated by Jarmusch's repeated use of a number of actors, particularly John Lurie, Nicoletta Braschi, and Tom Waits, in his films.

This cosmopolitanism is, however, no more than a moment of unexpected confusion that blurs their expectations of difference, and the ironies of this encounter only look forward to the much more prominent role of the night clerk at the hotel, played by the former R & B performer, Screamin' Jay Hawkins.[12] The presence of Hawkins in this film points toward the patterns of narrative self-consciousness in *Mystery Train*: Hawkins's single hit song "I Put a Spell on You" (1956) is played repeatedly in Jarmusch's first film, *Strangers in Paradise*, and signals here an intertextual network that invites us to read all of Jarmusch's work together. At the same time, and more significant for our present purposes, Hawkins's heavily stylized portrayal calls into question any sense that the Memphis Jun and Mitzuko encounter is anything more than a parodic and depthless realm of essentially free-floating images. Similarly, the experiences Jun and Mitzuko share together are themselves not expressions of significant cultural difference but rather are signs of their appropriation to the international culture of the image. Elvis Presley's 1956 rendition of the Rodgers and Hart song "Blue Moon" (recorded in 1954) plays three times in *Mystery Train*, and, in each instance, it is an ironic commentary on what transpires in the film. While the song celebrates the sentimental fulfillment of a dream of the other, *Mystery Train* repeatedly suggests that one's own dream is always either someone else's or a signifying field to which one's responses are already appropriated and encoded. Mitzuko, for example, keeps a scrapbook of pictures of Elvis in several poses together with various look-alikes, including a Middle Eastern relief sculpture, Madonna, the Buddha, and the Statue of Liberty, so that Elvis is interchangeable with almost every other image. In the same way, Jun and Mitzuko live out their own identities and desires, signaled at the obvious level by their Japanese difference in America, according to the logic of simulation in popular culture. Early in the film, Jun tells us that if one removed 60 percent of its buildings, Yokohama would look just like Memphis; later, he reverses his view with the equally astute insight that America is different because it feels "cool" to be eighteen and so far from Yokohama. Jarmusch's point here, of course, is that one is never far from Yokohama, and in a culture in which difference is homogenized to the unmotivated zero degree of eclecticism, one is only far from oneself or from an other who is always a projection and, at the same time, the field out of which the self is articulated.

12. There is an additional irony here in that the first African American figure they meet is, of course, Rufus Thomas, also an R & B performer long associated with Memphis.

But what Jarmusch presents ironically and sympathetically, more authoritative and discursive contemporary popular texts ignore at their peril. It has become a commonplace among those who would seek to align postmodern culture with transformations in the field of social, political, and economic practices that the postmodern period coincides with the demise of a Fordist economy, whether transferred into a more intensive and ruthless form of exploitation or altered in a post-Fordist economy so as to be unrecognizable in the frenetic circulation of capital within the world financial community. David Harvey, for example, suggests that production techniques such as the much heralded "just in time" delivery system is the commercial correlative of corresponding acceleration in circulation and consumption, and this view corresponds to Jameson's insistence that late capitalism marks the advent of "a vertiginous new dynamic in international banking and the stock exchanges."[13] Philip Cooke situates this transformation specifically within the discourse of difference when he suggests, "If evidence were needed of the penetration of the discourse of 'the other' into mainstream western thinking, then the case of the Japanese overturning of the rational, modernist discourse of scientific management is surely the exemplar."[14] Whereas Harvey and Jameson point to the specifically political nature of these transformations, Cooke's descriptions would direct us to an essentialized vision of Asian and specifically Japanese difference that needs to be deconstructed, and this has been done consistently and carefully in the work of Masao Miyoshi. As Miyoshi points out, in one sense, of course, Japan might be read as the quintessential postmodern culture; the absence of a pronounced theory and discourse of subjectivity, the reluctance to address the historical past, and an enthusiastic devotion to the simulacrum would all seem to correspond to the postmodern dispersal of the subject, the depthless cult of the image, and an undermining of the historical sense.[15] The extent to which Japan might be characterized as proleptically postmodern would seem to confirm the typically postmodern notion of the homogenization of cultural practices in the worldwide networks of late capi-

13. David Harvey, *The Condition of Postmodernity: An Enquiry into the Origins of Cultural Change* (Cambridge: Basil Blackwell, 1990), 284; Jameson, *Postmodernism*, xix.
14. Philip Cooke, *Back to the Future* (London: Unwin Hyman, 1990), 147.
15. Masao Miyoshi, *Off Center: Power and Culture Relations between Japan and the United States* (Cambridge: Harvard University Press, 1991), 15–16; hereafter cited parenthetically as *OC*.

talism; however, when the question of relative economic success enters into the discourse of cultural correspondences, there is a return to essentialism in the name of difference that is alternately threatened or championed depending on the speaker's relation to the question. While our emphasis here is on American representations of the Asian, and specifically Japanese, other, it is worth noting that the recourse to essentialism is a popular strategy in both American and Japanese culture. As Miyoshi has persuasively argued, the Japanese "social imaginary" is still a radical other not only to much of the world but also for the Japanese themselves: "Whether motivated by a self-sufficient narcissism, a reactive defensiveness, or an economic strategy, most Japanese, too, regard themselves as unique and therefore unchangeable—albeit with variants" (OC, 171). This assumption, as Tetsuo Najita has argued elsewhere, might reside historically at the heart of the Japanese lived relation to technology, in which culture is understood as antimodern and autonomous, in order, in Tetsuo Najita's terms, "to distinguish internal truthfulness from the otherness within."[16] It is this same essentialized appeal to uniqueness, as Masao Miyoshi demonstrates, that motivates the recent American discourse surrounding the cultural ground for economic relations between the United States and Japan. Miyoshi, for example, points to James Fallows's "Containing Japan" and to his More Like Us: Making America Great Again for Fallows's culturalist urging of his fellow Americans to recover their uniqueness, and to Karl Van Wolferen's The Enigma of Japanese Power as another instance of Western efforts to account for mercantile practices through an essentialized cultural difference.[17] In contrast to these appeals to an irrecoverable Japanese uniqueness and difference, the popular text I want to consider here attempts to confound these suggestions of profound change by insisting that the other, and specifically the Japanese other, is a figure who ultimately must be denied in order to be retrieved to a specifically American context. Richard Tanner Pascale and Anthony G. Athos's The Art of Japanese Management was an immensely popular text for American business in the early Reagan

16. Tetsuo Najita, "On Culture and Technology in Postmodern Japan," in Postmodernism and Japan, ed. Masao Miyoshi and H. D. Harootunian (Durham: Duke University Press, 1989), 15.
17. James Fallows, "Containing Japan," Atlantic Monthly (May 1989): 40–48, 51–54; and his More Like Us: Making America Great Again (Boston: Houghton Mifflin, 1989); Karl Van Wolferen, The Enigma of Japanese Power (New York: Knopf, 1989).

era, and I want to consider it briefly here not merely for its often depressing and finally racist stereotyping nor for its often unintentional hilarity. (They suggest, for example, that McDonald's is very much like a Japanese corporation in that it owes its success to the espousal of spiritual values and its dedication to a "social mission.")[18] Instead, I want to address the attempt to characterize the radical other as the uncanny familiar, but always within a suspicion that the other is to be written under the signs of theft, duplicitous imitation, and subterfuge. It is as though Pascale and Athos have recast the recent experience of American business as a rewriting of Poe's "William Wilson," in which the narcissistic ego is always at the mercy of a punishing ego ideal, and in this Pascale and Athos demonstrate convincingly their own inability to conceive of the very postmodern condition that they seek to define and master.

It does not surprise us, then, to learn that according to Pascale and Athos, a senior Japanese manager from the Matsushita electronics conglomerate actually thinks of himself "as being on one of our professional American football teams" (*AJM*, 53). Nor does it surprise us to learn that "*modern*" management is "largely a Western creation," or that Matsushita owes its financial success to a planning system borrowed from the Phillips corporation (*AJM*, 30, 50). Pascale and Athos, as I have suggested, want to raise Japanese difference in order to suggest that it is no difference at all. Accordingly, Japanese management has simply "been extremely effective in borrowing from us in areas in which we excel," and while the typical Japanese manager might be differently governed by an interdependent relation to the corporate hierarchy, it is Americans who ultimately equally act out this interdependence (*AJM*, 34, 135, 197). Finally, Pascale and Athos want to reassure their compatriots that successful American managers "do things that are surprisingly similar to what the Japanese do" (*AJM*, 25). Japanese management turns out to be American management: "In short, many American managers live in a world that corresponds quite closely to that of the Japanese. The difference, primarily, is that we have a much more negative attitude toward it" (*AJM*, 202). Japanese management is simply the repressed virtues of American managerial practices, and in this respect, *The Art of Japanese Management* is designed to write out the other in order to avoid the recognition that the sign systems of American manage-

18. Richard Tanner Pascale and Anthony G. Athos, *The Art of Japanese Management* (New York: Warner, 1982), 316; hereafter cited parenthetically as *AJM*.

ment in the postmodern era exist irrevocably in the field of the other. In this instance, the other is appropriated to the realm of the familiar in order to deny the fundamental transformations that have undermined the authority of American business practices.

I raise the claims to authority that motivate *The Art of Japanese Management* in order to throw into relief the very different writing of the Asian other within American history that we find in Michael Herr's *Dispatches*. If, as Hayden White has suggested in many places, every history presupposes a full-blown metahistory, then Herr's account of his experiences in Vietnam at the height of the war in 1967–1968 attempts to represent the presence of the other as an image of the collapse of metanarratives in postmodern history. Herr begins his account with a meditation on a map of Vietnam, left over from the European colonial period: "It was late '67 now, even the most detailed maps didn't reveal much anymore; reading them was like trying to read the faces of the Vietnamese, and that was like trying to read the wind." [19] This inability to read functions in two ways in Herr's text: It signals his insistence that the Vietnamese other is always only understood as he or she can be subsumed under the familiar encodings of American popular culture; and it points to Herr's refusal to construct a master narrative of his own experiences of the war. Like Lyotard's *petit récit*, Herr's narrative is always only provisional in the face of a history whose motivations can only be traced in America through an endless and ultimately empty chain of signification. In a characteristically self-reflexive moment, Herr remarks, "A lot of things had to be unlearned before you could learn anything at all, and even after you knew better you couldn't avoid the ways in which things got mixed, the war itself with those parts of the war that were just like the movies, just like *The Quiet American* or *Catch-22*." [20] Fredric Jameson has remarked that Herr's *Dispatches* is postmodern in its use of language, but Jameson curiously rejects Herr's efforts to write history; however, it is precisely Herr's acknowledgment of historiography as the function of a prior emplotment, in Hayden White's terms, or encoding, that makes his account of the American experience in Vietnam most prescient. Herr remarks that "somewhere all the mythic tracks intersected, from the lowest John Wayne wetdream to the most aggravated soldier-poet fantasy," and these intersections are repeated in the persistent efforts to read Vietnam as

19. Michael Herr, *Dispatches* (New York: Avon, 1978), 1.
20. Herr, *Dispatches*, 224.

"some unnatural East-West interface, a California corridor cut and bought and burned deep into Asia."[21] Herr, as journalistic historian, wants us to see his experience of the war in the field of the other as a revelation of the refusal to acknowledge difference. This inability or refusal parallels, in Herr's text, a fundamental confusion of identity in the American experience in Vietnam, and the effort to assert that identity, most frequently through the discourse of popular images, is ultimately to reveal their cultural bankruptcy. In its uncovering of this failure and the attendant refusal to recognize one's position in the field of the other, Herr's postmodern narrative consistently demonstrates that postmodern America is finally to be understood as that paradoxical construction, the true empire of signs, with all their anxious displacements and deferrals.

Difference does not finally escape the chains of signification that are put into play by the discourse from within which it is articulated. The assumptions that motivate cultural discourse also determine its critical possibilities and are revealed in the text as the political unconscious that both enables and constrains its production. Pascale and Athos in their *Art of Japanese Management* demonstrate this all too clearly, but it is ultimately Jim Jarmusch's *Mystery Train* and Michael Herr's *Dispatches*, in their self-conscious acknowledgment of Asian difference, that urge us to recognize the ways in which the American rewritings and appropriations of the sign of the other are also modes of comprehending, in a particularly postmodern sense, one's lived relation to the world.

---

21. Fredric Jameson, "Postmodernism, or, The Cultural Logic of Late Capitalism," *New Left Review* 146 (July–Aug. 1984): 84; Herr, *Dispatches*, 19, 44.

America's Hiroshima, Hiroshima's America

Peter Schwenger

"This is Hiroshima," the TV host announced, to the accompaniment of a crescendo of ticking. On the screen flashed the image of a clock with its hands at 8:15, then a mushroom cloud accompanied by the thunder of kettledrums. It was the May 11, 1955, episode of *This Is Your Life*, and the guest was an ordinary-looking Japanese man introduced as the Reverend Kyoshi Tanimoto. He was asked to tell, step by step, what he had been doing on the morning of August 6, 1945.

At appropriate moments, a procession of people from the minister's past came through the This

John Whittier Treat

What is "Hiroshima"? No longer just the name of a place but of a place in time—August 6, 1945— "Hiroshima" is now the name of a story. That story has belonged to the world for almost half a century. Yet, since what happened at Hiroshima happened to the Japanese, it is, in the first "place," their story— a story that might seem to demand obvious reference, if at times only obliquely, to someone or something American. There is, however, a notable scarcity of such reference in Japanese atomic-bomb literature. To understand this lack, it must be situated in a wider, and less obvi-

Is Your Life Archway, including an utter stranger: "Now you have never met him," Tanimoto was told, "but he's here tonight to clasp your hand in friendship. Ladies and gentlemen, Captain Robert Lewis, United States Air Force, who along with Paul Tibbets piloted the plane from which the first atomic bomb was dropped on Hiroshima." Lewis walked onto the stage and, after an awkward hesitation, the two men shook hands. The captain was then asked to tell about *his* experience of August 6. His delivery was shaky; he had been drinking heavily and had missed the rehearsal the day before. Whether because he had forgotten his lines or for some other reason, Lewis stopped completely at one point, closed his eyes, and rubbed his forehead before a deep breath steadied him, and he went on to say, "At 8:15 promptly the bomb was dropped." After Tanimoto resumed his account of that day, and concluded it, the host summed up the years that followed: "Out of the carnage . . . the Japanese people have built a new city. But ten years later all is not forgotten. There are still very visible reminders of what atomic power can do." These reminders, it turned out, were the so-called Hiroshima Maidens—twenty-five badly scarred young women who had just been brought to the United States to receive state-

ous, context: Japanese depictions of "Hiroshima" pivot awkwardly and uncomfortably upon that fulcrum where issues of textual representation and ethical responsibility coincide.

The Japanese continue to debate whether the historical singularity of Hiroshima and Nagasaki determines their, or any culture's, particular ability or inability to understand and interpret those events. It has often been taken as axiomatic that the survivors, the *hibakusha*, should rightfully think themselves proprietors of an experience wholly beyond the ken of others (and perhaps even themselves) to comprehend within the confines of pre-Hiroshima cultural discourses and practices. If Hiroshima and Nagasaki are indeed unique, and thus without analogy, then the enabling grounds of representation are at best compromised and possibly obviated altogether. When Hashimoto Kunie described August 6 in her testimonial account as "something so ghastly as to make incredible all that has been until now," that incredulity is all that is left as the token of her experience, and finally all that is left to be, or not to be, "represented."[1]

Hibakusha who were, or sub-

1. Hashimoto Kunie, "Wasureenu shin-setsu" (Unforgettable kindnesses), in

of-the-art plastic surgery. Behind a frosted glass door, two silhouettes spoke in Japanese, which was then translated: They were happy to be in America and thanked everyone for what the United States was doing for them. At the show's close, the sponsor, Hazel Bishop Long-Lasting Nail Polish, promised Reverend Tanimoto a 16-mm print of the show and a projector on which to view it. His wife would receive a specially designed gold charm bracelet to commemorate the significant moments of her life—the *New York Herald Tribune* was to wonder the next day whether the charms included a little gold bomb. Then the host turned to the camera and gave the TV audience an address to which they could send donations for the Hiroshima Maidens. He urged them to be generous, "for this," he concluded, "is the American way."

This episode exemplifies a number of the ways in which America comes to terms with Hiroshima, with its responsibility for Hiroshima. The first of these ways is *Disneyfication*, the tendency to view Hiroshima as a dramatic spectacle, an exercise in special effects: the ticking clock, the rolling kettledrums, and the image of the mushroom cloud produce an emotional *frisson*, and little more than that. This tendency is still with us, and it was with America

sequently became, professional writers, and thus might be thought to have more powers at their disposal to make the "incredible" imaginatively available to us, ofttimes similarly professed a skepticism over the potential for representation. Many were apparently in the grip of an emotional surplus that paradoxically paralyzed those emotions and made communication— most of all, self-consciously aesthetic writing—problematic. Even "grief," wrote hibakusha novelist Ōta Yōko, "is something 'prior' to the calamities of this war."[2] But "prior" to grief looms the experience of nuclear war itself: Ōta's colleague, A-bomb poet Hara Tamiki, wondered whether the meaning of the atomic bomb could be grasped by anyone whose own skin had not been seared by it. By asserting that non-hibakusha were forever exterior to his experience, he placed Hiroshima beyond its assimilation by even the heretofore most reliable cultural tools. Writer Takenishi Hiroko speculated on the potential of language itself after August 6 when she asked, "What words can

---

Gembaku taikenki, ed. Hiroshima-shi Gembaku taikenki kankōkai (Tokyo: Asahi Shimbun Sha, 1965), 97.

2. Ōta Yōko, *Shikabane no machi* (City of corpses), in *Ōta Yōko shū* (Tokyo: San'ichi Shobō, 1982), 1:23.

immediately after the event itself. Ten weeks after the end of the war, one hundred thousand people—approximately the number who died on August 6 at Hiroshima—gathered in the Los Angeles Coliseum for a "Tribute to Victory" pageant reenacting the war in the Pacific. The climax was the simulated dropping of an atomic bomb. A B-29 roared over the Coliseum, and, in the words of the *Los Angeles Times*, "a terrific detonation shook the ground, a burst of flame flashed on the field and great billows of smoke mushroomed upward in an almost too-real depiction of devastation."[1] No fear, I think, that it be too real. But the reality of this domesticated recreational spectacle would tend to displace in American minds the vaguer reality of Hiroshima. Some years later, a Texas air show similarly restaged events from the war. At that time, Paul Tibbets, pilot of the B-29 that dropped the real bomb, flew the B-29 that dropped the simulated one. Here, spectacle encroaches yet further on reality, blurring the line between them. This has its psychological uses; for any spectacle implies spectatorship and

we now use, and to what ends? Even: what *are* words?"[3]

But to erect skeptical obstacles to writing provides, oddly, a kind of consolation. Should language stop "failing" us, and somehow succeed in communicating "what" happened, then what? "How is one to approach this universe of darkness," worried and warned Eli Wiesel, "without turning into a peddler of night and agony?"[4] The dilemma is discursive as well as ethical: Suddenly the atrocity of Hiroshima and Nagasaki is no longer original but available to us in infinite retellings undisciplined by firsthand memory. Most dangerously, the horror would continue to "exist" and thus (perhaps more than imaginatively) menace us. When someone argues that a literature of atrocity is a priori impossible because words do not, will not, suffice, that person is also rhetorically insisting that he or she steadfastly refuses to cooperate with any such attempt, refuses to signify with a presence but instead signifies only

3. Takenishi Hiroko, "Hiroshima ga iwaseru kotoba" (Words that Hiroshima makes us speak), in *Nihon no gembaku bungaku* (Atomic-bomb literature in Japan), vol. 1, ed. Kaku-sensō no kiken o uttaeru bungakusha (Tokyo: Horupu Shuppan, 1984), 322–23.

4. Eli Wiesel, *One Generation After*, trans. Marion Wiesel (New York: Pocket Books, 1970), 16.

1. Quoted in Paul Boyer, *By the Bomb's Early Light: American Thought and Culture at the Dawn of the Atomic Age* (New York: Penguin, 1985), 181. Subsequent references to this text are cited parenthetically as Boyer.

therefore distance from what becomes a sublime drama, removed not only from reality but also from responsibility.

"Out of the carnage . . . the Japanese have built a new city," the TV host tells us, exemplifying a common approach in the journalistic coverage of Hiroshima at the time: the emphasis on *rebuilding*, and American aid in that rebuilding. This strategy survives today, for instance in the subtitle of the 1989 made-for-TV film *Hiroshima: Out of the Ashes*. This film, available at your local video store, is driven throughout by an American urge for self-justification most evident in the film's last words:

"The Americans are here," says a young Japanese doctor to a nurse. "What shall I say to them?"

"There is a haiku," the nurse reminds him: "Now that my house is burned down, I have a much better view of the moon."

The thanks rendered to America by the two Hiroshima Maidens have a similarly skewed effect —although I would not want to reduce the phenomenon of the Hiroshima Maidens to this moment. Rodney Barker, author of a remarkable book on the subject, has captured the blend of genuine altruism and manipulative opportunism that swirled around the maidens, and has resisted the temptation to reduce the episode to a single

an absence. To do otherwise, it is feared, would suggest in the renewal of memory a recognition—perhaps even a legitimization—of the experience recalled. Consequently, it is one of the hallmarks of Japanese atomic-bomb literature, like the literature of modern atrocity everywhere, that it depends to an uncommon degree on implication and insinuation. It is, to borrow Lawrence Langer's phrase, "a literature of innuendo, . . . as if the author were conspiring with his readers to recapture an atmosphere of insane misery which they somehow shared, without wishing to name or describe it in detail."[5]

Within the problem of Japanese atomic-bomb literature as a whole, two points can be made about the positioning of "America." The first point is that the representation of "America" in the literature of Hiroshima and Nagasaki is inextricably implicated in the formal and ethical quandary of how anything would, or could, be represented within the cultural and linguistic discontinuity of a nuclear war. The second point is equally daunting: that the representation of "America" within atomic-bomb literature must necessarily differ from the representation of "Hiroshima"

5. Lawrence L. Langer, *The Holocaust and the Literary Imagination* (New Haven: Yale University Press, 1975), 37.

scenario.[2] Which is more than the host of *This Is Your Life* can manage when he asks for charity in rebuilding the women's shattered bodies because "this is the American way." No room here for other ways to see America except the way of rebuilding and charity and compassion.

Compassion is most readily extended to individuals, who can be comprehended (in its sense both of "understood" and "assimilated") more readily than the massive implications of a city's death by atomic power. As is often the case on the evening news, the human interest angle convinces us that political action is simply a matter of people understanding each other on a one-to-one basis. A kind action to one person can be put in the balance with one hundred thousand dead. Consequently, a strategy of *personalizing* Hiroshima arose. Norman Cousins, the *Saturday Review* editor who spearheaded the Hiroshima Maidens project, wanted above all to keep it a personal event. "That, for me," he explained, "is what history consists of. One makes an impact on history in terms of example, not pronunciamentos. I was trying to

2. Rodney Barker, *The Hiroshima Maidens* (New York: Penguin, 1985). A full description of the May 11, 1955, episode of *This Is Your Life* may be found in the prelude of this book.

within American writing because of the markedly different historical and political circumstances of "Hiroshima" as against "America." In a sense, American literature is free to represent Hiroshima however it pleases, even not to represent it at all. Hiroshima does not lie at the center of American national life, though some have suggested that it should. America, on the other hand, has been a constant presence—force—in Japanese life since 1945 and has been constantly "represented," if you will, by the often heavy-handed demonstration of its national power. It follows that whereas in American discourse the word *Hiroshima* is nearly always coterminous with August 6, 1945, to a Japanese the word *America* signals a constellation of positive, negative, but hardly ever indifferent associations that the American hegemony generated, it is fair to say, everywhere in the postwar world. It is important to remind ourselves that speaking of America's "Hiroshima" and Hiroshima's "America" cannot ever mean speaking in compensatorily balanced equivalencies. As the target of nuclear war, and then as client state and proxy, the Japanese have never been as free to construe "America" as vice versa.

A representation is always a social process, which means it always proceeds within history and often with reference to power. If, as

create relationships, and I thought the relationships would spread and endure. If there was anything to this, the power of the example would find its meaning."[3] More than one meaning is possible, though, in personal relationships as in political ones; and without questioning the meaning that Cousins was struggling for, I must repeat that other, more self-serving meanings are apparent in the process of reducing political events to personal ones. The Reverend Tanimoto is an example of this process, singled out to sum up Hiroshima from a larger group of six individuals whose stories are told under John Hersey's inclusive title *Hiroshima*.

Hersey was one of the sponsors of Tanimoto's appearance on *This Is Your Life*. His book is still the first book, and often the only book, that people read about Hiroshima. It continues to define the event for us, and to do so in individual terms. Before beginning *Hiroshima*, Hersey reread Thornton Wilder's *The Bridge of San Luis Rey*, a book which had served him as a model before. It tells of a bridge that gives way while five people are crossing it, sending all of them plummeting to their deaths. Wilder traces the lives of each of the five in such a way that their deaths seem inevitable and appropriate.

C. S. Peirce defined it, the "sign" is "something that stands to somebody for something in some respect or capacity," then the symbol requires a "somebody" outside that "wholeness" to take note of it.[6] A representation is always, then, a communication requiring both an addresser and an addressee; and because representation is a means of communication, it is itself a potential obstacle to representation. Any spectacle requires spectatorship: an audience before whom the representation is made, and who may quite frankly react not only uncomfortably but even punitively toward it. This is especially true, of course, if it is the audience itself who is being represented. To represent "America" in Hiroshima literature was, in fact, an act that during the Allied Occupation of Japan could not occur, since Hiroshima literature itself was not allowed under the regulations of the American-imposed Press Code. Even after the Occupation, linking the United States to Hiroshima or Nagasaki could, and did, lead to effective ostracization from an established community of native Japanese writers and publishers hesitant to raise the "explosive"

3. Barker, *Hiroshima Maidens*, 98.

6. C. S. Peirce, in *Collected Papers*, vol. 2, ed. Charles Hartshorne and Paul Weiss (Cambridge: Belknap Press of Harvard University Press, 1960), 228.

A trace of this comfort remains in Hersey's much less sanguine book. It arises from the fact that these are survivors whose tales are told, and that these *are* tales, shaped as such and thus given meaning. This effect cannot help persisting despite Hersey's own irony about it; he gives the last word of his book to a schoolboy's narrative on his experience of August 6, a narrative that is childishly inadequate. And any reference in Hersey's book to books always underscores their absurdity in this context of devastation (Boyer, 208).[4]

Yet, Hersey's book created a devastation of its own in the American psyche. It first appeared within the covers of the *New Yorker*, which devoted to it the entire issue of 31 August 1946. Coming out a year after the bombing, it struck readers with the force of a delayed revelation, and all the more forcefully for being delayed. What they knew of Hiroshima had been abstract, as depersonalized as the towering atomic cloud in the only photograph to get printed in the newspapers: a cloud amid clouds, with no trace of a city or the human inhabitants of that city. Hersey's book gave Americans a sense of the terrible human

issues of American power and responsibility.

For these, and other, reasons, America is often absent from works of Hiroshima and Nagasaki literature, and while that absence may itself be read as a kind of covert representation, these "other reasons" to which I refer derive not so much from the particular posture that Japan and its writers found itself under the postwar American hegemony as from the specificity of modern mass violence. Hiroshima's representation of "America" is a (non-) representation that cannot proceed without registering the very real, as well as discursive, places of Japan and America. America's penchant for the "Disneyfication" of Hiroshima cannot be Japan's own, if for no other reason than that the requisite spectatorship is wanting. But more important, to say "Hiroshima" in Japan still suggests more memory than imagination: Japanese atomic-bomb literature and its parallel practice of nuclear criticism— quite unlike the "nuclear criticism" recently in vogue in the West— particularizes and references as it historicizes, and that process is conditioned by the unalterable fact that one of those nations was the nuclear target of the other. With few exceptions has that stark relationship seldom been made the theme of any work of Japanese A-bomb writing.

4. John Hersey, *Hiroshima* (New York: A. A. Knopf, 1946); Thornton Wilder, *The Bridge of San Luis Rey* (New York: Time Inc., 1963).

cost, allowed them to see the Japanese *as* human. The impact was widespread. The ABC radio network read the entire work in four award-winning half-hour broadcasts; the Book-of-the-Month Club distributed free copies to all its members; letters poured in to the *New Yorker* and to newspapers and magazines all over America. One veteran of the Manhattan Project found himself weeping as he read the book and was "filled with shame to recall the whoopee spirit" with which he greeted the news of Hiroshima (Boyer, 208). This kind of turn-around was typical of the reactions Hersey's book provoked. Yet, Paul Boyer, who records all these effects and more, concludes that Hersey's book led to very little change, politically and perhaps even psychologically: "Indeed, for many, the very act of reading seems to have provided release from stressful and complex emotions. [It was] like the funeral rituals that provide a socially sanctioned outlet for grief and mourning" (Boyer, 209).

Boyer's reference to funeral rituals and mourning brings us to Derrida's *Memoires: For Paul de Man*, a book whose themes are mourning, memory, grief, and ghosts. All these terms play their part in the American preoccupation with Hiroshima. Even Paul Tibbets's fact-bound and stupendously dull autobiography speaks of "the ques-

Of all the reasons for this, one inseparable from twentieth-century atrocity is the problem of circumscribing the perpetrator. The lines between the victimizer and the victimized can be obscured by the presence of collaborators, both active and passive; or by those who conceive of lethal decisions and by those who execute them; or indeed, they can be obscured by alternate ethics in competition with each other in pursuit of the purported "least evil." The attempt, however imperative, to define *evil* against all else requires a willful, moral (as well as technological and legal) blindness to ambiguity, a bold resolve to approbate some actions while holding others culpable, even if all are equally bound up in a single, seamless continuum toward the same unbelievable, but irrefutable, end. This quandary arises from the fact that no parts of the bureaucratic, technological operation collectively known as contemporary civilization—Weber's "iron cage"—are easily detached, identified, and purged. The victimizer exists only diffusely, distributed in the relationships between the human parts, and systemic processes, that operated death camps in the middle of Europe or built nuclear piles beneath a college football field.

We do not accept this diffuseness without resistance. When it results in works of literature that do

tion of morality that has haunted the United States ever since 1945."[5] And this haunting, this ghost, is what all the strategies mentioned so far are designed to lay to rest. All of these strategies (and there are more) are fictions, are forms of fiction, whose very presence is the manifestation of a restless spirit. "The ghost, *le re-venant*, the survivor," says Derrida, "appears only by means of figure or fiction, but its appearance is not nothing, nor is it a mere semblance."[6] Derrida's phraseology here—the "not nothing" of fiction—recalls a sentence of his elsewhere about the nuclear age, which he says is "constructed by the fable, on the basis of an event that has never happened (except in fantasy, and that is not nothing at all)."[7] The event that has never happened is nuclear holocaust, a total war as distinguished from the localized event of Hiroshima: "The explosion of American bombs in 1945," Derrida asserts, "ended a 'classical,' conventional war; it did not set off a nuclear war."[8] What it

not accuse, we can be disappointed or frustrated. The story we are told seems to lack an appropriate ending. Contrary to the usual expectations of non-hibakusha readers— who perhaps would have wished their feelings of ill-ease and even guilt assuaged through their literary and thus suitably distal indictment—little atomic-bomb literature notes, much less denounces, the human hand that ultimately inflicted the suffering. This hand, despite the difficulty noted in defining it (Is "hand" literal? A metaphor? Or a synecdoche?), is sometimes assumed to be the militarist clique that led Japan into war, or Truman, or Einstein, or alternatively simply human nature in general. But most of the time it is thought of as "America," that corporate entity that conceived, financed, and largely staffed the research, development, production, and delivery of Fat Man and Little Boy. In some literal and important sense, of course, the "cause" of the atrocities can be mechanically traced through a chain of deliberate and identifiably "American" exercises of agency. As one hibakusha put it, "An atomic bomb is quite different from a landslide. One never falls unless someone drops it."[7] Yet, though we all know who dropped the bomb, "America"

5. Paul W. Tibbets, *Flight of the Enola Gay* (Reynoldsburg, Ohio: Buckey Aviation, 1989), 308.
6. Jacques Derrida, *Memoires: For Paul de Man*, trans. Cecile Lindsay, Jonathan Culler, and Eduardo Cadava (New York: Columbia University Press, 1986), 64.
7. Jacques Derrida, "No Apocalypse, Not Now (full speed ahead, seven missiles, seven missives)," *Diacritics* 14 (1984): 23.
8. Derrida, "No Apocalypse," 23.

7. Quoted in Ōe Kenzaburō, *Hiroshima nōto* (Hiroshima notes) (Tokyo: Iwanami Shoten, 1965), 175.

did set off, however, was the *fantasy* of such a war, as the American psyche instantly extrapolated the consequences of the new warfare. And to the word *fantasy* Derrida appends the following note: "Freud said as early as 1897 that there was *no* difference in the unconscious between reality and a fiction loaded with affect." The unconscious here is America's. That unconscious is trying to comprehend (again, in both senses) the terrifying reality of Hiroshima and the even more terrifying fact of its own moral involvement with this event, in its past history and perhaps in its future one. It enacts this process of comprehension through fictions that are themselves signs and symptoms of the ghost. The very fact that they are available to us in infinite retellings indicates that no one of these strategies or fictions is capable of laying the ghost to rest.

This multiplicity perhaps has another effect, which is described by Derrida. He speaks of the necessarily fragmentary quality of fictions in the memory, the fictions that make up memory, which he says are

> only "parts" of the departed other. In turn they are parts of us, included "in us" in a memory which suddenly seems greater and older than us, "greater," beyond any quantitative comparisons: sublimely greater *than* this other

remains relatively absent in the discourse of atomic-bomb literature, almost as if it were too remote, or perhaps too large, an idea to encompass meaningfully in works otherwise occupied with detailing the minutiae of the immediate deaths of Japanese individuals.

Throughout the history of Japanese atomic-bomb literature, this absence has inspired controversy with very much at stake. Novelist Ōe Kenzaburō, a non-hibakusha who published in the mid-sixties a series of influential essays on postwar Hiroshima political culture, collectively entitled *Hiroshima Notes* (Hiroshima nōto), was vociferously criticized for his near total neglect of human responsibility for the bomb. Why, some of his subjects queried, does Ōe seem to equate the bombing of Hiroshima with a "plague" or a "flood"? Where, others suspiciously wondered, is the assailant in Ōe's account of the victims? But such an accusing finger, and all it might imply, might just as well have been pointed at the testimonial and documentary work of such pioneering hibakusha writers as Hara Tamiki and Ōta Yōko, neither of whom felt compelled to advertise, or even determine, culpability. Seeing America as the cause of Hiroshima, noted Ōta, is finally an emotional response, however satisfying: what of Japan, which doggedly pursued a war already over (23)? Indeed, despite the

that the memory harbors and guards within it, but also greater *with* this other, greater than itself, inadequate to itself, pregnant with this other.[9]

The fact that memory affords us only glimpses of the other—a sense of potential fullness that is never fulfilled—creates, I would suggest, a *mythic* effect. It makes the memory seem "greater and older than us," as Derrida puts it. And so it seems with the memory of Hiroshima. William Pollard, who worked on the Manhattan Project, suggests that the destiny of Hiroshima is "to become a universal myth deeply grounded in the sacred time of all the peoples on earth; the symbol of their conviction that nuclear warfare must never be allowed to occur." [10] If this is the case, then the memory of Hiroshima has become greater than its historical fact, greater in the ways that Derrida speaks of that move beyond the past of history and memory into a future.

In its future orientation, the mythic version of Hiroshima is one of the most responsible of its fictions. Yet, we should proceed with caution here. For Derrida's memory of the dead, he says, *seems*

widespread reputation of atomic-bomb literature as anti-American, "America" in fact recedes from view in most examples of the genre, stubbornly irrelevant to the significance of Hiroshima if not its history. A-bomb writers' grief suggests a scale inconsolable through rage and is a grief hardly comprehensible as the work of a "nation," a concept intellectually valid but cathartically worthless. It is as if the victims were so overpowered by the bomb's effects that its origins are rendered hopelessly abstract and even ultimately pointless. Nowhere in Tōge Sankichi's famous 1951 collection, *A-Bomb Poems* (Gembaku shishū), for example, do the words *America* or *United States* occur (nor does *atomic bomb*, despite the collection's title), and perhaps for the reasons powerfully stated in Takenishi Hiroko's 1963 short story, "The Rite" (Gishiki):

> The great anger, the deep hate, come after the event. The thing . . . that made me cower all night in a hollow in the ground—if I could catch the real nature of that thing and fling the fullness of my anger and hate at it, I would not be in torment this day, well over ten years after, tied to this fierce anger that still finds no proper outlet. I would not be tortured by this name-

9. Derrida, *Memoires*, 37.
10. Quoted in Alvin M. Weinberg, "The Sanctification of Hiroshima," *Bulletin of the Atomic Scientists* 41 (Dec. 1985): 34.

greater and older than us. This may be so, or seem so, only because we have assigned those qualities retrospectively. Apprehending Hiroshima in this way, we are in danger of forgetting what Hersey reminded us of: that these are human beings, even though caught in an incomprehensible nuclear sublime—which was conceived, constructed, and exploded by human beings. In memory, in mythic memory, the figures of Hiroshima move, looming in shadowy grandeur; and their larger-than-life size provides a kind of comfort. More than human, they are heroes, perhaps, or archetypes of suffering, of innocence violated, of death's other kingdom.

This archetypal approach is exemplified by Michael Perlman's *Imaginal Memory and the Place of Hiroshima*, which combines a scholarly analysis of concepts and arts of memory with a Jungian practice focusing on Hiroshima. For Perlman "history becomes myth in memory."[11] But the ways in which this is so are often disturbing. The Reverend Tanimoto, for instance, becomes an archetypal figure. Perlman recalls Tanimoto's work of ferrying wounded people across the river to Asano Park where they could receive help. And this be-

less hate that yet finds no clear object.[8]

The absence of a "clear object," American or otherwise, in Japanese atomic-bomb literature was theorized in a dramatically different way in non-hibakusha Oda Makoto's 1980 novel, *Hiroshima* (translated into English as *The Bomb*). It features an American soldier who, rather than flying aboard the *Enola Gay* (the role typically reserved for the enemy), is a POW on the ground and an inadvertent target. In this ironic reversal, "America" becomes absent again as the distinction between victim and victimizer is blurred. In the crucial second part of Oda's novel, "Joe" is stumbling through the fires in Hiroshima on August 6 when he starts to notice that some of the corpses around him—no, surely their ghosts, he reasons—move toward him. They are so horribly disfigured they must come from another world: and then Joe realizes he looks no different himself.

One of the "ghosts" sees that Joe, despite his disfigurement, is not Japanese. Soon word spreads that the enemy is there among

11. Michael Perlman, *Imaginal Memory and the Place of Hiroshima* (Albany: State University of New York Press, 1988), 33.

8. Takenishi Hiroko, "The Rite," trans. Eileen Kato, in *The Crazy Iris and Other Stories of the Atomic Aftermath*, ed. Kenzaburo Oe (New York: Grove Press, 1985), 194–95.

comes his archetypal essence: "In his guise we meet the Ferryman who takes and pilots the vessel of the dead who are about to go 'on their ghostly way.' "[12] A living man, a survivor, here becomes revenant and ghost. To what purpose? It demonstrates, according to Perlman, "a conjunction of 'timeless' reality and unique historical predicament."[13] But the "timeless" part of this may give us pause. Archetypes, though they may be evinced within history, in themselves are beyond the historical. Unchanging essences, they are also beyond choice. And to the degree that choice is involved in morality, the ghost of morality that haunts America is once more laid to rest, by that very meditative exercise whose intention is to wake it.

August 6, 1945, thus becomes less a manifestation of historical forces than of forces that are eternal and supernatural. Above all, the force of the atomic bomb takes its place among such forces. This kind of translation is a common one: Spencer Weart, in *Nuclear Fear: A History of Images*, has documented the persistent tendency to read atomic power in terms of older paradigms—particularly that of alchemy, which plays such a large role in Jungian thinking. On the last

them. Many "ghosts" start to move toward Joe; a voice from Joe's life back in America warns him to run, run as fast as he did back home on the plains of New Mexico. But such advice is useless.

It was too late to do anything. The ghosts were coming to attack a ghost. They were summoning what little strength remained in their bodies to pounce upon him, another ghost. The dying ran over the dead—the dead over the dying—in getting to him. Using all his might he tried to push through them to run away, but the ghosts kept piling atop themselves in wave after wave, and he was unable to move at all underneath the weight of the heap. . . . Only the dead were within the flames. They were the only ones left behind. Both the ones trying to finish one off, and the one trying not to let that happen, were piled up like so much garbage in the dark depths of a hell burning high with crimson flames. Both died excruciating deaths, both lived by struggling against each other with what little strength remained in their moribund state. He had now closed both of his eyes, but he

12. Perlman, *Imaginal Memory*, 118.
13. Perlman, *Imaginal Memory*, 119.

page of his comprehensive study, Weart concludes that "this book has not been about our real problems at all; it has been about what distracts us from them."[14] Of course, distraction may at times be psychologically necessary, so much so that it may be found in the heart of our most sincere attempts to face our problems, and ourselves.

For instance: in a discussion with Edward Teller over the atomic bomb, an American minister expressed faith that his country would never use a weapon so horrible. When Teller reminded him that America had already done this twice, the minister fell silent, "leaving me," says Teller, "with the indelible impression that he wanted to forget Hiroshima" (Boyer, 183). And plainly he *had* forgotten it—one of those significant lapses that Freud makes much of in *The Psychopathology of Everyday Life*. It is necessary to forget Hiroshima to remember America as the minister conceives of it: morally upright, strong yet compassionate, *good*. This myth of America, America as mythical hero, is in danger of being lost through Hiroshima. The mythification of Hiroshima, then, may meet this danger. A myth displaced is excused through myth. If it is the

thought he could see clearly how it all looked. His progressively weak consciousness of himself ("I . . .") and his words that would follow (". . . am here for what . . . ?") changed to take a plural subject. Those were the final words that passed through his mind.[9]

The "plural subject," a "we" forged in the mortal moments of the world's first nuclear war, refers to a Hiroshima victimhood uninflected by national or racial difference. The new subject position, if you will, is that at the bottom of an undifferentiated, formerly human, heap. When Derrida declares "the ghost" "not nothing," nor "a mere semblance," he reiterates amid the ironies of another place and time Joe's own simultaneously fantastic and real first lesson in the nuclear age.

As other scenes in *Hiroshima* make clear, victimization, too, is not the fixed historical property of any one people but rather the complement of how all of us are deployed unwittingly by the modern state, be it Japanese or American. Oda's contention, as he put it in 1968 while leading a protest movement opposing Japan's role in the Vietnam War—a role that was both

---

14. Spencer R. Weart, *Nuclear Fear: A History of Images* (Cambridge, Mass.: Harvard University Press, 1988), 430.

9. Oda Makoto, *Hiroshima* (Tokyo: Kōdansha, 1981), 238.

product of impersonal and eternal forces, Hiroshima is not the product of Yankee ingenuity and Yankee Doodle patriotism.

These apparently innocent virtues result in an act of overwhelming terror, a terrorism that from then on will hold hostage the world, including America itself. If America mourns nothing else, it must mourn, at some level, a loss of innocence. That loss of innocence can be described as traumatic, in a certain sense of that word. Psychologically, trauma is an event that annihilates a subject's sense of self and of the laws that were assumed to govern its world. It has a characteristic temporality, marked in the first instance by deferral and then by repetition. Deferral takes place because the traumatic experience cannot be psychologically processed at the time of its occurrence—if it were capable of being processed it would not be traumatic—and this may be for a number of reasons: the overwhelming nature of the event itself; the psychological state of the subject at the time; social circumstances that hinder a full processing; or inadequate knowledge of the implications of what is happening. This last is the case, for instance, when a child is sexually molested by an adult and feels disturbance but no sexual stimulation. At a later time— during puberty, for instance—the

one as America's "victim" and one as Vietnam's "victimizer"—is that "in time of war, the state compels the individual to fight. As he fires the shot which knocks over the enemy, he stands as victim in relation to the state and victimizer in relation to the enemy."[10] In Oda's novel, "state" is monolithic and hegemonic: "America" disappears as a meaningful representation, because it is only a local name for a universal regimen we all serve as twentieth-century peoples. America may be absent from the writings of hibakusha, because the assailants in a nuclear war are impossibly remote from the perspective of ground zero; it may be absent from the novels of younger intellectuals such as Oda Makoto, because the discursive construction of any nation-state is now ideologically suspect in an age of ubiquitous duplicity. In either case, Japanese atomic-bomb literature has continually and conspicuously declined to fashion its works around a word, *America*, uncannily emptied of the power and even easy reference we typically ascribe to it.

There are compelling reasons, not uniquely Japanese, why

10. Oda Makoto, "The Ethics of Peace," in *Authority and the Individual in Japan: Citizen Protest in Historical Perspective*, ed. J. Victor Koschmann (Tokyo: University of Tokyo Press, 1978), 160.

event is recalled with the accompaniment of sexual feelings that are so at odds with the subject's feelings of guilt and anger that the entire episode must be repressed. The repressed returns, however, in repetitive dreams and symptoms. None of these is sufficient to discharge the force of the episode. The trauma remains unresolved, an agent working deeply in the psyche, manifesting its presence by hints and signals, and continuing to influence the nature of that psyche. A parallel configuration can be detected in America's reaction to Hiroshima.

At the first news of the bombing, there was no mourning in America: rather, jubilation and a "whoopee spirit." Polls at the time showed overwhelming support for the decision to drop the bomb; this included, in one survey, the 23 percent who expressed disappointment that America had not used many more atomic bombs on Japan before it had a chance to surrender.[15] When a negative emotion was expressed at the time, it was almost always fear for America's own safety, as the implications of the new weaponry became evident. What had happened to Hiroshima could happen to us. But this formu-

15. Michael Yavendetti, "John Hersey and the American Conscience," *Pacific Historical Review* 43 (Feb. 1974): 25–26.

the specific nature of modern atrocity renders the traditional antagonist/protagonist model of representation unworkable, and perhaps especially so on the levels of national discourse. These are reasons made salient in the literary efforts of Hiroshima and Nagasaki writers, but they have been surely evolving over time, as "antagonist" and "protagonist" have lost their utility in describing modern warfare around the globe. World War I came as a technological surprise to its participants: Poison gas and the machine gun enabled killing on a massive, and impersonal, scale achieved in no prior European conflict. As a result, literature between the wars increasingly dwelled on the newly problematic relationship between the victim and assailant in subtle terms. Works such as *All Quiet on the Western Front* take place in a world of trenches where the enemy is unseen. Yet, he is still imaginable; our counterparts are there, just over the ridge, in their own trenches. Technology, by Remarque's time, may have already rendered the forces threatening us perceptually remote, but it would not be until World War II that that force became morally overwhelming as well. Critic Matsumoto Hiroshi, for instance, has noted the complexity—indeed, the impossibility—of ever defining the terms *victim* and *victimizer* within the oblation, and this fear, leads back to the question of what happened at Hiroshima; it may thus lead back to another powerful emotion, that of guilt. In 1946, the Dutch psychologist A. M. Merloo noted the fear over atomic war, which he had found everywhere during his American lecture tour, and linked it to "hidden feelings of guilt" (Boyer, 182). A full year elapsed before the "whoopee spirit" changed to weeping with the publication of Hersey's *Hiroshima*; but mourning was accompanied with shame when recalling the first reactions to the bombing. Mourning and memory are here at odds with one another; shame undercuts the very foundations of America's idea of itself; the trauma remains unresolved.

Another theory of trauma is pertinent here, one that preceded Freud's and is being recuperated today: that of Pierre Janet, whose *L'Autonomisme Psychologique* was published in 1889. For Janet, repetitive compulsions are demands for the dissociated traumatic memory to take a satisfying narrative form, one that will substitute for the action not taken in the first place. Janet asserts, "Memory is an action; essentially it is the action of telling a story." [16] So the

scure labyrinths of modern technological civilization. [11]

In Iida Momo's 1964 novel, *An American Hero* (Amerika no eiyū), the narrator, a veteran of the bombing raid over Nagasaki, notes with inadvertent liberality that "the dead aren't only Japanese. Chinese, Koreans, Indonesians, Burmese, Thais, White Russians, and our own guys, white and black." [12] In other words, the spectrum of victims can conceivably mean that any of us are potential victims, too; there is also the implicit suggestion that the victimizer is also ourselves, indistinguishable from "victim." When the prized product of modern civilization's weaponry is pitted against itself, the victimizer might, in fact, be victimizing him- or herself, especially when that person's means— in this case, hostile adaptations of nuclear fission—are seen as suicidal. A kind of ethically closed circle is created: If "America" is the casualty as well as the perpetrator of any act qualified as "evil," then the opposite presumably obtains for anyone seeking redress for that act. The representation of "America" in

---

11. Matsumoto Hiroshi, "Hachi-roku Hiroshima no imi suru mono" (What August 6, Hiroshima, means), in *Hiroshima no imi* (The meaning of Hiroshima), ed. Oguro Kazuo (Tokyo: Nihon Hyōron Sha, 1973), 133–56.

16. Quoted in Bessel A. van der Kolk, Paul Brown, and Onno van der Hart, "Pierre Janet on Post-Traumatic Stress," *Journal of Traumatic Stress* 2 (1989): 368.

12. Iida Momo, *Amerika no eiyū* (An American hero) (Tokyo: Kawade Shobō Shinsha, 1977), 390.

figures and fictions that emerge again and again since 1946 can be seen as failed attempts to tell a story adequate to America's role in Hiroshima: They are revenants, ghosts of a response that never took place at the time.

The complex temporality of these memories of Hiroshima may be summed up in a favorite tense of Derrida's, the future anterior: it *will have been* so. In *Memoires*, Derrida quotes Paul de Man: "The power of memory does not reside in its capacity to resurrect a situation or a feeling that actually existed, but is a constitutive act of the mind bound to its own present and oriented toward the future of its own elaboration."[17] All of memory's fictions and figures, then, work in the future anterior tense. This construction promises us a future rewriting of the past; at the same time, it promises us an end to the fictive revenants, an end as definitive as that end of the war that Hiroshima is said to have provided. But by now it should be apparent that the end of America's Hiroshima is not to be attained; there will be no time when Hiroshima will have been over.

Hiroshima literature, in other words, is both a representation of who represents and a representation of the new moral equation that technology and a bureaucratic state, which so evenly distribute ethical agency, have worked out for us.

The survivors of Hiroshima and Nagasaki often seemed to intuit the radicalness of these weapons for our traditional models of a "crime"; hence the unexpected absence, perhaps, of strident anti-American sentiment in their works. Their concern is with something even more disturbing but less conventionally available. Our "American" desire to experience the brunt of their absent hate is our insistence on seeing them as less damaged than they are; we seek their recuperation so as to excuse ourselves.

In fact, the victimizer is diffuse, unnameable in whole; and the victims are stunned into a silence on the question of blame that prefigures our own recent powerlessness under the nuclear hegemony, the hegemony that Western "nuclear criticism" in the 1980s sought to disarm by undoing its rhetoric and thus the hegemony that now, post-USSR, looks increasingly "postmodern" as the size of the "nuclear club" swells. The Japanese have their own version of deconstruction: For them, and for their atomic-bomb literature, the collapse of a dramatic confrontation of "good" versus "evil" is linked not to a

17. Derrida cites de Man on page 59 of *Memoires*. See Paul de Man, *Blindness and Insight: Essays in the Rhetoric of Contemporary Criticism* (Minneapolis: University of Minnesota Press, 1983), 92–93.

crisis of an exhausted metaphysics but instead to the repercussions of a murderously successful physics. The modern world has ceased to worry greatly about the absolute origins of its actions, and that is an important premise of a Derridean "nuclear criticism" that takes both meaning and nuclear war as philosophical presences continually deferred. Yet, and so demonstrably for the Japanese, the evidence of the consequences of those actions remain unquestionably "present." We might find this unsettling, not only because it leaves us historically undecided and morally empty-handed but because atomic-bomb literature categorically declines to cooperate with any form of sentimental recompense for, which is to say any further licensing of, the violence. An atomic-bomb literature that details a hate for things American would make things "equal" between us; that has not happened.

The complex nature of Japanese atomic-bomb literature ideally places its readers in an apparently exitless maze that interrogates, rather than excuses, those within it. When the sum total of the story is not simply an elaboration of the exchange between victim and victimizer, there is suddenly uncomfortable new room provided for the reader. Without the familiar binaries, memory is not scripted in easy ethical patterns. Rather, what evolves is an ethics beyond summary judgment, an ethical imperative without the closure that comes with the pronouncement of a verdict; and what persists is Paul Tibbets's "question of morality." August 6 is a moment, and Hiroshima a place, in time, whose implications must haunt history past, now, and henceforth: There will be no time when "Hiroshima" is over.

The Pulling of Olap's Canoe

Translated by Theophil Saret Reuney

Part I: Pukueu

Looking for the suitable time, Pukueu
Went to observe the break of day at the other end of the island.[1]
A steering wind blew, it blew from the east,
His canoe would be pulled out from its headrests:
Yet suddenly came his asipwar[2]
To stop Pukueu's voyage.
But he did not change his mind; his eager heart sought the
    satisfaction
To open up those dark seas.[3]
Knowledgeable in the art of navigation, he begged indulgence from
    Nemwes,[4]

1. island: an island, formerly called Unanu, which is now called Onari, in the Weito group of Truk, Federated States of Micronesia.
2. asipwar: this can be a son or a nephew.
3. dark seas: this is a literal translation of the Trukese *matau apunguroch*, which can also mean "dark oceans."
4. Nemwes: according to legend, she was the daughter of Sou Yap (the high chief of Yap).

Repeatedly had he used his Western star,[5]
Kept sailing toward the rising Altair
Where he encountered Likefailenweiset,[6]
Who only crept groaningly on the sea waves.
"I will throw him an offering of due respect[7]
And make him tell me where he, this new-comer navigator, has just
    come from.
Don't you know my name? I am Pukueu,
And now I am sailing to the island of no talk.
The people there are stupid since they only groan."
He came ashore from his canoe
With his fishing nets,
He filled one up, returned to his canoe
For he had since longed for fonu asuluta.[8]
Returning home his canoe appeared as a speck somewhere east
    of Rachik.[9]

Part II: The New Navigator (Rongechik)

Under preparation was the voyage
Of a new navigator, Rongechik, at the lagoon of Unanu:
He would undertake the offering of our lives.
To begin with, Rongechik counted and named his crew:
A skillful and wise one, a thief, a tame-hearted person,
A good diver, and a knot diviner.
They would go and fetch their un kechau[10] at Tawairek[11]
And then return.

5. Western star: a star used repeatedly as a guide on the same course of sailing.
6. Likefailenweiset: a combination of strong current and wind.
7. due respect: any object, such as a coconut, thrown at another floating object on the sea, or thrown at any other natural phenomena signifying some kind of supernatural power. Pukueu, in paying respect to Likefailenweiset, throws (perhaps) a coconut at it.
8. fonu asuluta: in reference to Unanu (Onari).
9. Rachik: a submerged reef of Unanu.
10. un kechau: a small fish trap usually carried on a sailing canoe.
11. Tawairek: this is comprised of two words: *taw* means "passage," and *rek* means "plenty." Together, these two words give the idea of "passage of plenty."

Part III: The Second Voyage of Paluelap

Getting ready was Paluelap's voyage to depart from Tawaruk [12]
He would sail the sea of Fayeu. [13]
"Rub your mast, and tap it with reverence,
Tie it with young yellow palm shoots for those sea-openers, [14]
They will blow the conch shell
To shorten the ocean
So that the difficulties of navigation will not overwhelm us."
We sailed toward the rising Aldebaran
To meet the white-arm shark
Which usually drank the flow of those over-flowing passes.
"Using the rising Corvus, we will unpluck
From Atinmwar [15] its seashells.
But there is Weito [16] situated against the front of the outrigger,
Fonuuen soma [17] is then located at the setting of Corvus
And the constellation Crux was hidden between the booms."
We were afraid for we had seen
The inhabitants of the land of anu fa [18]
As they swam with their hair buns pointed upward, at Karueleng. [19]
"Let us use the rising of Vega, and we will meet
The whale whose names are Urasa and Pwourasa [20]
They guard those pompano fish which belong to wasofo. [21]
But Manina [22] is there, and Sorota [23] is here.
Let us stop at Tawanior [24]

12. Tawaruk: sea pass of Unanu.
13. Fayeu: East Fayu in Truk.
14. sea-openers: those journeying navigators.
15. Atinmwar: a rock on the reef of East Fayu.
16. Weito: a group of islands in the northwest of Truk.
17. Fonuuen soma: reference is not clear, but it probably refers to one of the western islands in Truk, or to all of them as a group.
18. anu fa: perhaps a legendary land.
19. Karueleng: also known as "lon anufa," referring to a place in the ocean, perhaps for the ghosts' dwelling only.
20. Urasa and Pwourasa: it is not clear whether these two names are given to just one whale or to two different whales.
21. wasofo: literally means "new canoe," but here it means "new navigator."
22. Manina: it is not clear whether this refers to Manila or to the Mariana Islands.
23. Sorota: some say this refers to Rota in the southern Mariana Islands.
24. Tawanior: the sea pass of West Fayu.

To drink from the water at
Chanilemwosor[25] under Polaris,
The goal is reached."

Part IV: Continuation of Paluelap's Voyage

We were amazed for we had seen
The great Pup[26] which belonged to re uon[27]
Its head, Mokur[28]—its tail, Fais[29]—its belly, Wenimerou[30]—this fish
    of Fayeu.
"Steering by the rising of Up,[31] we would encounter Wenimong.[32]
But Vega (the star) is there tying his adze
On the beach of Ikera,[33]
He will use it to cut the front of his outrigger.
He faces the outrigger north to place Pisia and Otong[34] on it.
His (Pukueu's) breaking rock for coconut rubbing oil was Chuetan
    Fanechik."[35]
Using the rising Orion we will sight Ochopwot[36]
And then use Corvus to reach Kapitau.[37]
Mesarew[38] and Antares sleep in a lagoon west of Anpout.[39]
We passed by west of Sau,[40]

---

25. Chanilemwosor: a small underground stream hidden somewhere on West Fayu.
26. Pup: a fish that resembles (in shape) the constellation Crux, thus the name of the Southern Cross (star) in Trukese.
27. re uon: literally means "males from above," but it has been interpreted as "European national of the ruling colonial power."
28. Mokur: an island (Mogur) in the Weito group in Truk.
29. Fais: an outer island of Yap.
30. Wenimerou: a reef northeast of Ifaluk.
31. Up: the name given to the constellation Crux when it is just rising from the sea level.
32. Wenimong: the eastern part of Nometrek Island.
33. Ikera: a beach at the northern part of Pikelot Island.
34. Pisia and Otong: some submerged reefs west of Ulul Island.
35. Chuetan Fanechik: an islet west of Pulap Island.
36. Ochopwot: a submerged reef west of Pulap Island.
37. Kapitau: a sea pass of Tamatam Island.
38. Mesarew: the constellation of two stars.
39. Anpout: an islet of Puluwat Island.
40. Sau: an islet of Puluwat Island.

And by using the Southern star[41] we will arrive at the reef of
  Urouran.[42]
We sighted Uk,[43] and then will pick up the very old hen
That has lived east of Souk,[44] Rasaimo is her name,
We will pluck her feathers for the revelation of our names' fame
While standing to pull our mainsheet at the pass of Naurer.[45]
We drifted, we had lost course west of Namoluk.
We encountered a group of lipwokupwok[46] belonging to Aliar.[47]
You delve deeply into the fish of mataw anu,[48]
Uapwonmwar[49] it is that wears the chicken's wattles,
That wants to wear bracelets[50] at Umun Kouos[51]
And wants to feed on the seafood of Ingachik[52]
That all lie flat on the reef at Le Uou Pwechepwech.[53]
The open sea has made the passage of Ulipi[54] rough.
Let us dive up lemai sar[55]
To sail westward to le Kiliau,[56]
We will remember such sailing under Aldebaran mokuchun ikailo.[57]
He[58] will put coconut oil on his body at esan fai,[59]
And will bathe at fani fai,[60]
And then, finally, will dry up behind Ononat.[61]

---

41. Southern star: this is a translation from *wenewen*, which is another Trukese name for
the constellation Crux when it reaches the halfway point of its path.
42. Urouran: a reef between Puluwat and Pulusuk.
43. Uk: a reef north of Pulusuk.
44. Souk: former name of Pulusuk Island.
45. Naurer: a sea pass of Pulusuk.
46. lipwokupwok: an insect similar to a small grasshopper.
47. Aliar: the sea channel of Satawan Island.
48. mataw anu: meaning is ambiguous, especially since the type of fish is unknown.
49. Uapwonmwar: a sea bird similar to the booby bird.
50. bracelets: translated from the Trukese word *pwoch*, meaning "turtle shells."
51. Umun Kouos: somewhere in the Oroluk Atoll.
52. Ingachik: Ngatik Atoll.
53. Le Uou Pwechepwech: Ngatik Atoll.
54. Ulipi: the sea channel of Nomwin Island.
55. lemai sar: sea shells.
56. le Kiliau: some part of the Oroluk Atoll.
57. mokuchun ikailo: those fish that usually stay in the sandy area in the sea.
58. He: Paluelap (Pukueu).
59. esan fai: between East Fayu and Nomwin.
60. fani fai: between East Fayu and Unanu.
61. Ononat: a place on Unanu (Onari).

Contributors

Joseph P. Balaz is editor of *Ho'omanoa: An Anthology of Contemporary Hawaiian Literature* (1989), which is composed entirely of ethnic Hawaiian writers creating works predominantly in the English language. He was also a contributing editor on the advisory board to *Hawaii Review: Aloha Aina*, a collection with a similar theme (1989), and editor of the Hawaiian journal *Ramrod*. His poetry has appeared in *Hawaii Review*, *Wisconsin Review*, and *Chaminade Literary Review*.

Chris Bongie is assistant professor of English and comparative literature at the College of William and Mary. He is author of *Exotic Memories: Literature, Colonialism, and the Fin de Siècle* and is currently working on a study of Francophone Caribbean writers entitled *Islands and Exiles: The Creole Identities of Post/Colonial Literature*.

William A. Callahan is director of the Philosophy, Politics, and Economics Program at Rangsit University in Putumtani, Thailand, and editor of *Asian Review*. He is now working on two books: *Imagining Democracy: Reading the Events of May 1992 in Thailand* and *Confucian Ideology in Transnational Space*.

Thomas Carmichael is assistant professor of English at the University of Western Ontario. He writes on postmodern American fiction and postmodern theory and culture. His articles have appeared in various journals, including *University of Toronto Quarterly*, *Canadian Review of American Studies*, and *Contemporary Literature*.

Leo Ching is an assistant professor in Chinese Studies at Duke University. He completed a dissertation on Japanese colonial discourse at the University of California, San Diego.

Chiu Yen Liang (Fred) is lecturer at Hong Kong Baptist College. Trained as an anthropologist, he has taught courses on ideologies and social movements, the sociology of work and industry, and organization and management analysis. He is founding editor of *Taiwan: A Radical Quarterly in Social Studies* (Taipei, Taiwan) and *Tiananmen Review* (Hong Kong). He is currently working on a book that theorizes the historicities and moral politics involved in industrial conflicts in multinational corporations in Hong Kong.

Christopher L. Connery teaches literature and cultural studies at the University of California, Santa Cruz. He received his Ph.D. in East Asian studies and has written on early medieval China, modern China, and the Pacific.

Arif Dirlik is professor of history at Duke University, where he specializes in Chinese history. His most recent publications include *The Origins of Chinese Communism* (1989), *Anarchism in the Chinese Revolution* (1991), and an edited volume, *What Is in a Rim? Critical Perspectives on the Pacific Region Idea* (1993). A new study, *After the Revolution: Waking to Global Capitalism*, was published by Wesleyan University Press (1994).

John Fielder teaches communication and cultural theory at Curtin University of Technology in Perth, Western Australia. He is currently working on a research project, *Postcolonial Ambivalence: White Reading Formations and Aboriginality*, at Murdoch University, also in Perth.

Miriam Fuchs is professor of English at the University of Hawaii, where she teaches American, women's, and Pacific literatures. She edited, with Ellen G. Friedman, *Breaking the Sequence: Women's Experimental Fiction* (1989), and the Fall 1989 *Review of Contemporary Fiction*, which featured Kathy Acker, Christine Brooke-Rose, and Marguerite Young. She has published articles on modern and contemporary writers, and her most recent essay, on the Djuna Barnes–T. S. Eliot association, appeared in the Fall 1993 issue of *Tulsa Studies in Women's Literature*. An edited collection of essays on Marguerite Young has recently been published. Fuchs's current full-length project is on women's autobiographies.

Epeli Hau'ofa was born in Papua New Guinea in 1939 to Tongan missionary parents. He went to school in Papua New Guinea, Tonga, Fiji, and Australia and attended the University of New England, Armidale, New South Wales; McGill University; and Australian National University, Canberra, where he gained a Ph.D. in social anthropology. He taught briefly at the University of Papua New Guinea and was a research fellow at the University of the South Pacific in Suva, Fiji. From 1978 to 1981 he was deputy private secretary to His Majesty the King of Tonga, and in early 1981 he rejoined the University of the South Pacific as first director of the newly created Rural Development Centre in Tonga. From 1983 to 1989 he served as head of the Department of Sociology at the university. Epeli Hau'ofa is author of *Kisses in the Nederends*, a novel, and three works of nonfiction: *Mekeo, Corned Beef and Tapioca*, and *Our Crowded Islands*. He lives in Suva with his family, and two desexed pets, Gipsy and Tigger, who think that they are smarter than he.

Lawson Fusao Inada is professor of English at Southern Oregon State College. He is author of *Legends from Camp*, a collection of poems (1993). He is currently writing the script for a video documentary for the Japanese American National Museum.

M. Consuelo León W. is assistant professor of contemporary history at the University of Playa Ancha and former director of the Pacific Basin Research Institute, Chile. She received an M.A. in international studies from the University of Chile and an M.A. in history from Southern Illinois University. She was a Fulbright scholar and has also won a doctoral fellowship at Southern Illinois University, where she is writing her dissertation, "Mutual Misperceptions in the Chilean-American Military Relationship of the 1950s." She is author of many articles, including "Soviet Foreign Policy toward the Third World and the Latin Southern Cone" (1993).

Katharyne Mitchell is assistant professor of geography at the University of Washington. She is an urban economic and cultural geographer who writes and teaches about contemporary global restructuring and its impacts on the built environment. Her essays have appeared in several journals, including *Antipode*, *Economic Geography*, and *Comparative Studies in Society and History*.

Masao Miyoshi teaches literature at the University of California, San Diego. Among his recent publications are *Off Center: Power and Culture Relations between Japan and the United States* (1991) and *Japan in the World* (1993). He is coeditor, with Rey Chow and Harry Harootunian, of a series in Asia-Pacific studies for Duke University Press.

Steve Olive is a Ph.D. candidate in the Political Science Department of the University of Hawaii at Manoa. He is a degree associate in the Environment and Policy Institute of the East-West Center.

Theophil Saret Reuney teaches English at Chuuk High School, Chuuk State, Federated States of Micronesia. He is presently a fellow at the East-West Center in Honolulu and is finishing a master's degree in English at the University of Hawaii.

Peter Schwenger is professor of English at Mount St. Vincent University. He is author of *Phallic Critiques: Masculinity and Twentieth-Century Literature* (1984) and *Letter Bomb: Nuclear Holocaust and the Exploding Word* (1991). He is currently working on *The Translucency of the Page*, a study of visualization in the act of reading.

Subramani has a personal chair in literature at the University of the South Pacific in Suva, Fiji. He is the author of *South Pacific Literature: From Myth to Fabulation*, *The Fantasy Eaters*, and *Reconciliations: Essays and Speeches*. He has edited *The Indo-Fijian Experience* and *After Narrative: The Pursuit of Reality and Fiction*.

Terese Svoboda teaches poetry at Sarah Lawrence College and was distinguished visiting professor at the University of Hawaii. Her most recent book, *Laughing Africa*, won the Iowa Prize for poetry. Also a videomaker, she recently curated a video show for the Museum of Modern Art called "Between Word and Image."

Jeffrey Tobin is a graduate student in anthropology at Rice University and an occasional professor at Argentina's Instituto Nacional de Antropologia. He is writing a dissertation on cooking and sexuality.

Haunani-Kay Trask is professor of Hawaiian studies and director of the Center for Hawaiian Studies at the University of Hawaii. She is descended of the Pi'ilani line of Maui and the Kahakumakaliua line of Kaua'i. She is a member of the Ka Lahui Hawai'i, a native Hawaiian initiative for self-government. She has published *Eros and Power: The Promise of Feminist Theory*; *From a Native Daughter: Colonialism and Sovereignty in Hawai'i*; and a collection of poetry called *Light in the Crevice Never Seen*. She coproduced the 1993 award-winning film *Act of War: The Overthrow of the Hawaiian Nation*.

John Whittier Treat is associate professor of Japanese at the University of Washington. His books include *Pools of Water, Pillars of Fire: The Literature of Ibuse Masuji* (1988) and *Writing Ground Zero: Japanese Literature and the Atomic Bomb* (1994). He is currently writing a cultural history of modern Japan entitled *Governing Metaphors: The Imagination of Modern Japan*.

Tsushima Yuko is a noted Japanese author whose works have been translated into English and include a collection of short stories entitled *The Shooting Gallery* (1988) and the novels *Requiem* (1985) and *Woman Running in the Mountains* (1991).

Albert Wendt, a Samoan, is professor of English at the University of Auckland, New Zealand. He is author of five novels, two collections of short stories, and two collections of poetry. He has also edited and compiled anthologies of writing by Pacific Islands writers. His work has been translated into many different languages. One of his novels, *Sons for the Return Home*, and a novella, *Flying Fox in a Freedom Tree*, have been made into full-length feature films. His collection of Pacific literature, called *Nuanua*, is forthcoming.

Rob Wilson is professor of English at the University of Hawaii at Honolulu. A member of the *boundary 2* and *Bamboo Ridge* collectives and advisory editor to *Pacific Island Voices*, he is author of two books: *Waking in Seoul*, a collection of poetry and prose anecdotes about the American presence in South Korea (1988); *American Sublime: The Genealogy of a Poetic Genre*, a study of American cultural poetics (1991); and a study entitled *Reimagining the American Pacific: From "South Pacific" to Bamboo Ridge* and a collection of essays coedited with Wimal Dissanayake, *Global/Local: Cultural Production in the Transnational Imaginary*, both forthcoming from Duke University Press.

Index